£4

TNA

18/19

NAMES
WITH
WINGS

'Some talk of Alexander and some of HERCULES
Of HECTOR and LYSANDER
And such great names as these.'

NAMES WITH WINGS

The Names & Naming Systems of
Aircraft & Engines Flown by the
British Armed Forces
1878-1994

Gordon Wansbrough-White

Airlife
England

TO THE MANY
who designed, manufactured, flew
and maintained the aircraft and
engines used by British Military
aviation over the past 115 years.

First published in the UK in 1995 by
Airlife Publishing Ltd

British Library Cataloguing in Publication Data
A catalogue record for this book is available from the British Library

ISBN 1 85310 491 4

Typeset by Litho Link Ltd, Welshpool, Powys
Printed by WBC Book Manufacturers, Bridgend, Glamorgan

Airlife Publishing Ltd

101 Longden Road, Shrewsbury SY3 9EB

CONTENTS

FOREWORD

I HAVE FLOWN some forty different aircraft types from the *Tiger Moth* to the *Lightning*, but until meeting Gordon Wansbrough-White I never gave any thought as to why and how our aircraft and engines were named. I certainly was never aware that there were naming systems with which people in the Air Ministry and Admiralty were striving to find appropriate names. One good point made in this book is how inappropriate some of those names were and how much worse were some of the names which were suggested but not chosen! This unawareness of naming would suggest that this book is of no consequential importance, even if one admitted a passing interest. This is a contradiction that has puzzled me since I first became aware a few years ago that the author was preparing a book on British military aircraft and engines, and I was somewhat astonished to learn that the story was to begin in 1878 . . .

It seemed an immense task to little purpose except for that minority of 'train spotter' and 'aircraft registration' enthusiasts, and the avid aviation historian — certainly not a book for the average aviator. However, it so happened that I was preparing a lecture on the Bristol *Blenheim*, and I sought advice from the Author (who once worked at the Bristol Aeroplane Company) over some point or other. He offered the somewhat surprising information as to the origin of its name — a battle at a very small and obscure village in Bavaria in 1742. This proved to be of interest to the audience, and thus I reflected further on the subject.

I surmised that whilst a name was, in essence, a military code (a point well made in the book), it had a psychological importance far beyond that. Our aircraft were not just machines, but had personalities to which we, and particularly aircrew, could relate; one had an abiding affection and perhaps a respect for what, on the face of it, were only complicated bits of airborne machinery.

So a name is important, and I now also appreciate that the meanings and origins of aircraft and engine names can be of considerable interest. This was evident in my case when I was able to see the book in its entirety, and I can now hold forth with complete confidence on the difference between a *Bobolink* and a *Merlin*. The diversity of names is an education in itself. It is certainly a book for 'browsing' but I found — and I guess it will be the same for the reader — that it then became difficult to put down. Initially, I turned to check on some of the classic aircraft and engines which I had flown over the years, and I then became 'hooked' and read the book more systematically. I must say that it is an unusual book in the sense that it is several books in one: it is historical, factual and technical, a unique and comprehensive index produced on a complex computer database, and then in total contradiction it is both romantic and nostalgic. It is said that one should not mix one's metaphors, which I shall promptly do by saying that this book must be the exception that proves the rule.

Tremendous research over some fifty years is behind this book and in recent years I have followed its preparation with much interest. It would have been tragic if the information which the author has acquired over many years had not been preserved for posterity. Aviation folk owe a debt of gratitude to Gordon Wansbrough-White for collating in this book the results of his many years of research into this fascinating and unknown subject.

Air Marshal Sir Ivor Broom, KCB CBE DSO DFC AFC

ACKNOWLEDGEMENTS

MY THANKS ARE due to:

Air Marshal Sir Ivor Broom KCB CBE DSO DFC AFC, for his interest and encouragement, and for which my request of him to write the Preface is a poor reward.

Arnold Naylor, D.Inst.M. MAIAA, MRAeS and Brian Riddle, B.Lib of the Royal Aeronautical Society Library

The Staff of the RAF Air Historical Branch, Ministry of Defence and of the Public Records Office at Kew.

Richard Riding, aviation historian and Editor of *Aeroplane* magazine, and particularly for his great help in providing the photographs.

Staff of the Library of the Royal Air Force Museum

Captain Eric Brown, CBE DFC AFC MA FRAeS RN, for advice on captured German aircraft.

Bill Gunston, FRAeS, aviation historian, for advice on engines.

Jack Bruce, ISO MA FRHistS, FRAeS, aviation historian, for advice on World War One aircraft.

Philip Jarrett, AMRAeS, aviation historian, for general advice.

John Blake, aviation historian, for particular searches.

John W.R. Taylor, OBE FRAeS FRHistS AFAIAA, Emeritus Editor of Jane's Information Group's *All the World's Aircraft*.

To *Flight* magazine, for permission to reproduce letters.

To the many who have written in response for information on nicknames.

Freddy Nicholls and Derrick Rowe for creating calm and order out of computer chaos.

Ann, my wife, for her help and encouragement, and above all for her forbearance.

CHAPTER 1 — INTRODUCTION

'Niceness in words was always counted the next step
to trifling, and so was to be curious about names'
— Miles Smith, Bishop of Gloucester, 1611.

THIS BOOK, THE first on the subject, sets out to record both the names and the naming systems of British military aircraft and engines from 1878 to 1994, 116 years which have seen more change in the circumstances of Man than in his entire recorded history and much of it due to aviation and the stimulus associated with it. The ability to fly was long a dream, even if the 116 years are now history. In its way this book is a history, but seen in terms of names. Military aircraft, yes, but we come to the first of many 'ifs and buts', for many were civil aircraft adapted to or pressed into military service, and these you will find. Of the 'military names', many are wholly pacific in nature, and overall it is surprising how many military aircraft had gentle names, many of them birds that were not even fierce or predatory. As will be seen, these were 'codes' and the psychological implications or public relations image of a name was not recognised in the Royal Air Force until 1932. There has been a wide diversity of names and these are reflected in the 'classification' chapters, for which the research has been a rewarding pleasure. There are some strange names, often of strange subjects, but my own favourite chapter must be that on birds, and therein lies the beginning. . .

As with much of life, my involvement in all this was accidental. I was on RAF leave, and betook myself to the small Cornish village of Mousehole, where I had lived for a short while before World War Two. Two sisters, Dorothy and Phyllis Yglesias with whom I had been friendly and who enjoyed local, and some national, fame with their Bird Hospital, also lived there. Their questioning as to my occupation led to the subject of aircraft, which they promptly condemned as noisy, nasty and dangerous. Hotly springing to its defence, I pointed out that many RAF aircraft had been named after their beloved birds — a remark on my part which I have often regretted for I was immediately asked to produce a list of the same. And so began the long quest; the subject turned out to be bigger than I had ever imagined.

In the short time available in the War years, I was able to do some limited research and built up a fairly comprehensive listing (or so I then thought). This was in part due to being stationed in the United Kingdom, and being able to correspond with aircraft and engine manufacturers who forwarded a wonderful cache of facts which, put together, made a unique library on the subject. Some of the facts I later found not to be strictly factual, but it was generally an unknown history and even then the earlier names — or at least their meaning and naming system — were lost to antiquity. But I was delighted with the response, whilst realising that for many of those who wrote to me it was 'a long time ago'. That also applies in 1994, and it is with the same thought that I recall those fateful words of mine in Mousehole, now over fifty years ago.

After VE Day in 1945, life was somewhat quieter, and I was afforded the wonderful opportunity to search Air Ministry files on 'aircraft nomenclature' and there learned for the first time the official RAF naming systems since the inception of the RAF in 1918. This still left some gaps, filled in during later years. Anyhow, by the end of 1945 I (rashly in retrospect) felt confident enough to offer a book entitled *Fair Names & Famous* to a London publisher and it was accepted, all the papers being handed over. Come 1946, I was 'demobbed' and taken back to my home in Kenya by troop carrier, where in due time the first proofs of the book arrived. Then followed a long silence, and enquiries through friends established that the publishers had gone into liquidation. Only a small part of the photographs and the many original drawings were recovered — and nothing much could be done about it whilst some 5,000 miles away.

In 1952 I emigrated to England, and joined the technical staff of the Bristol Aeroplane Company on the *Britannia* project. A colleague and later good friend was one C.H.

Barnes, who had an encyclopaedic knowledge of British aviation history, and wrote under the name of 'Senrab' (Barnes backwards). The shelves of any self-respecting aviation library will carry his authoritative books on several companies and their aircraft, and to which I often refer. My thanks are due to him (now sadly gone) for rekindling my interest, and for much help over the years, including *Fifty Bristol Years* which I wrote for *Flight* magazine. Later I published articles on the name theme in *Aeroplane*, and two in *Air BP*, and this was the first time that the RAF systems of naming had been made public.

For some time I was Personal Assistant to the Chief Engineer, Dr (later Sir) Archibald Russell, also a Director of BAC and again had an exceptional privilege, that of open access to all the archives of the company. At this time I asked Dr Russell why he was not interested in aviation history, to which he gave the unanswerable reply that he was far too busy making it. The Bristol archives revealed a wealth of information, filling most of the gaps resulting from the Air Ministry search, and gave a special insight into the history of Bristol aircraft and engines. But there was still much aircraft and engine data to be found, although such a book as I had envisaged had of necessity to be limited in this respect. It was to be a book of names and naming, and whilst technical and historical information were a part of it, this was secondary, or else it would become an *Encyclopaedia Aeronautica*.

Publishers seemed uninterested, whilst magazines would publish just parts of the story. But I considered it now unwise just to publish parts and probably spoil the chance of a book. For another twenty years the project lay almost fallow, until *Fair Names & Famous* was accepted by a London publisher of world renown and the adrenalin again flowed through my hardening veins. But it was not to be: they had wanted to change *Fair Names & Famous* to a book on funny old aeroplanes, to which my answer may now be politely (and untruthfully) recorded as 'no'.

So two disappointments to date, but a third had already taken place in 1966. In 1964 I had moved to London, where my home was to be an old Thames sailing barge. *Favorite* was her name, and a little research revealed that she was indeed old. As confirmed by the Maritime Museum at Greenwich, *Favorite* was launched in 1803 and in 1964 was the second oldest floating vessel in the world. One dark night and whilst moored on the river, she was (so far as we knew) struck by a passing ship, and her unequalled 163 years came to a sad end. *Favorite* was salvaged after ten days below the water, but to little avail, even less so in regard to this book. Those cherished records, with few exceptions, were muddy pulp, and together with the loss of a large aeronautical library and almost all personal papers, *Fair Names & Famous* now had little appeal and the project was abandoned.

But some had not forgotten, and from time to time there were enquiries and requests for the published articles, and against my better judgment I again became interested. I seemed to have acquired some little reputation as the 'names' man, and whilst a Member of Council of the Royal Aeronautical Society I was asked to suggest a name for the *Comet* about to enter RAF service. *Nimrod* was my suggestion (probably that of many others) and the spark of interest on my part was later to turn into a raging fire.

Fair Names & Famous became *Names With Wings* after varying vicissitudes with two more Publishers, and finally came to rest happily with Airlife.

But with all the trials and tribulations, why bother, and to what purpose? Some talk of Alexander, and some of HERCULES of HECTOR and LYSANDER, and such great names as these. These words, which form the frontispiece of this book, were written to extol the name of the British Grenadiers, and therein lies the answer to my own question. Apart from a personal aviation interest (and I am still an active pilot), it is a matter of pride in British history. In our victories (and even in some of our defeats) and particularly in our aviation history and in the part that the Royal Navy, Army and Royal Air Force (originally the Royal Flying Corps) have played over those 116 years. The names of the aircraft and engines, some American and French, reflect the times — grim, great and sometimes absurd. To me and I hope to others, it is also a romantic story.

It is a technical book up to a point, much more a record that reflects inspiration and recaptures the aircraft, engines and the events of our aviation history. It started as a 'code', but changed over time and today many of the names belong to our national mythology. Did not tens of thousands converge on central London to see the Battle of Britain fly-past [15 September 1990] with millions the world over watching on television? How come that the *Spitfire* is the most widely known aircraft of all aircraft names? What if it had just been the Supermarine F37/34? And there was surely a psychological advantage in going to war in a *Spitfire* than in a Me 109 F.

> 'Strong Towers decay,
> But a great name shall
> never pass away'
> — Park Benjamin.

A great aeroplane deserved a great name, and whilst there were several great aeroplanes in our 1300 and with inappropriate names, and poor aeroplanes with good names, it's a part of history now told for the first time.

CHAPTER 2 — THE BOOK AS A REFERENCE

'For it is not names which give confidence in things,
But things which give confidence in names'
— Chrysostom

THE 'IFS AND BUTS' were hinted at in the Introduction, and this section is to enlarge somewhat on the limitations of information and its usage in the following chapters.

The first observation is that the primary interest is in names and naming systems, and whilst historical and technical information is given this is limited per aircraft and engine listed, and in no way presumes to be a definitive record of any one item. That is the stuff of the many fine books already published, and a list of some of these is given in the bibliography in Chapter 8.

As also hinted at in the Introduction, there may well be missing or inadequate information on some subjects, which arises from a number of causes:

- the loss of my own notes and accompanying company literature and illustrations
- the destruction of files no longer needed in the Air Historical Branch (RAF) and thus not passed on to the Public Records Office
- destruction of many company records, especially when amalgamated into bigger industrial units
- with such a long time-span, the personal sources of information are in many cases no longer available, and where some are still happily with us, memories are no longer what they were. There are some splendid exceptions!
- the 'Thirty Year Rule' which precludes the sight of such 'closed' files until the due time, even if the papers are listed in the Public Records Office. One surprise was to find that the operative opening date of a Thirty Year Rule file is the last date and not the first. So twenty years, say, of a file covering thirty-five years is not available, even if the twenty years is after the operative opening date. This affects the RAF naming systems from 1960, which are not 'open' and if part of a file over thirty years, then an even longer period would be affected. This is the law and there is no complaint, and both the Air Historical branch and the Public Records Office have been courteous and helpful way beyond the call of duty, and to whom my grateful thanks.

As it happens, there have been comparatively few new aircraft and engine types over this period, and the naming systems are (hopefully) self-evident. But there could be some surprises!

Then we come to the nature of the beast itself, which precludes any absolute accuracy concerning any one particular aircraft or engine. Truth, as a wise man once said, is a house with many windows; it depends through which window you are looking and at what particular time. Aircraft often had more than one engine, sometimes several, and aircraft often changed their roles or were multi-role. They even changed names, and reversion to the original is not unknown. The manufacturers also changed their names: the British & Colonial Aeroplane Company became the Bristol Aeroplane Company; then the aircraft side became British Aircraft, all to be amalgamated into the British Aircraft Corporation which in turn became British Aerospace. The engine side went through similar evolution (to some, devolution) first with Siddeley and Hawker-Siddeley, finally becoming a part of Rolls-Royce.

So what is a poor chap to do? He just gives the name at that particular time, and so far as he has got the right time, that is what you will find. But without going into further detail, even this could be an over-simplification! One problem is that 'authoritative' records are not always in accord: as an example the date of a first flight can differ by as much as eight years, and I began to suspect that the date listed just happened to come from the last book to which I referred. Histories can also be odd. One book referred to a particular flying boat (which shall remain unnamed) as being a decade ahead of its time, whilst another recorded, quite correctly, that it never got off the water, was beached and scrapped. Perhaps the first was correct in one sense – another ten years work and it would then have got off the water.

A problem which confronted me, and seemingly also other researches, was when is a name not a name, or a nickname not a nickname, or indeed both? The 'nickname' was severely disavowed by the Establishment of the RFC — which only produced more of them — and whilst reluctantly recording some of them in 1918 when it became the RAF even the naming systems insisted they were 'nicknames' for quite a few years thereafter. The USA still does!

Many aircraft started as civil, with half an eye on being military. Sometimes the RAF accepted the original name, even if it cut across their own current naming system, and sometimes it had a new name within the system. Without trying to confuse you further, some were outside the system and, oddly, some served in the RAF with no name (and the better known of these break my own rule of 'no name, no mention' and are to be found in Chapter 5 Part 17 'The Great Unnamed'.)

Apart from the manufacturers, government departments are not above some nomenclatural restlessness. The Army Balloon Factory became the Royal Aircraft Factory, in 1918 became the RAE (Royal Aircraft Establishment) and is now the Royal Aerospace Establishment, and more recently the Defence Research Agency. All very sensible, but it complicates the setting up of a data base. So I hope you will bear in mind through which window you are looking, and when.

To pursue the suspected inexactitudes further, and presuming you are steeped in the subject, you may be somewhat surprised at the engines listed in the Contents for a particular aircraft. Does one list the prototype engine, the production engine or later ones? Space allows but one engine name, and generally it is the first one — but there are exceptions. As an example of the list problem of only one engine name, the *Halifax* Bomber will be remembered as having *Hercules* engines, but it began operational life with *Merlin* engines.

Whilst the RAF naming systems (Chapters 4 and 7) are self-evident and straightforward, many exceptions are listed. These exceptions are puzzling, because the Air Ministry and the RAF took names very seriously, and not only did the matter go to the Air Council, but sometimes to the Secretary of State, and once to Sir Winston Churchill. Alliteration, such as Bristol *Badger* or Vickers *Vimy* came about partly through company tradition which was not strong and partly because the February 1918 RAF system said so, and a list of alliterative code letters was allocated to the manufacturers as of 1918, all of which are detailed in Chapter 4. But there are many exceptions, and in later years both the ruling and the practice passed from the scene — but not always. The meaning of some names is an apparent mystery. Note that the RAF were adamant that aircraft should never have the name of an RAF airfield or station, and wisely so, for signals could become very confusing. You will find (Handley Page) *Hinaidi* in no current Atlas or book of reference as a name, nor (Supermarine) *Sarafand;* they were, in fact, RAF airfields — *Hinaidi* near Baghdad (in Mesopotamia as was) and *Sarafand* near Tel Aviv (in Palestine as was). Towns and ports were supposed to be in the British Empire, which included Britain, but supposedly these British Protectorates were near enough to the ruling.

All this is impinging on the book proper, but hopefully it will be appreciated that whilst every effort has been made to produce a book and a reference as factual and accurate as possible, there can be no such thing as complete accuracy in all cases. But there is such a thing as limited accuracy, if such a term is acceptable; I seek not to be economical with the truth, but within the constraints of the book to list what is practicable within the vagaries of the subject.

As to the Database Listings (Chapter 7), a few explanations are in order:-

MAKER	— see the comments above. See also 'Maker' under SYSTEM below.
NAME	— may occasionally be a 'nickname', and where there is a known 'nickname' which gives entry to the book, the type number is given under 'Name'.
TYPE	— these are listed only as 'main' types in the case of aircraft, so as to cut down the complexity of the computer 'Database'. So 'Transport' covers everything from *Puss Moth* to *York* but if these are indistinguishable to you, then reference to Engine Type and the number of engines will give some clue.
NICKNAME	— to some it may have been the name, but not officially, and vice versa. See the comments above.
SYSTEM OF NAMING	— where a date is given, it is the RAF System of that date. Where 1911 is given, that is the RAF (Factory) System of BE, FE, SE etc., for which see Chapter 4.
MAKER	— is self-evident, but with some aircraft it is not clear whether it was a Maker or RAF name. Generally, 'Maker' means just that, for many aircraft were tested by the RAF as possible RAF types or for evaluation, perhaps of some innovation. 'Maker' has one ambiguity. It could be the designer or designer/part manufacturer, for many thousands of aircraft were manufactured in the works of other companies. In some cases, the entire production was by another company, which often was government policy to even the total production load, or to increase overall production such as in wartime.
CLASSIFICATION	— these are Name classifications, such as 'Birds', 'People', 'Animals' and so on. 'Miscellaneous' embraces those names which do not fit into a particular classification. These classifications are the chapter headings as given in the Contents at the beginning. 'Geography — Land' and 'Geography — Water' are titled so as to cut down the otherwise large number of sections if detailed as town, mountain, river or port etc: 'Land' and 'Water' are all-embracing titles, but if given as such could be misleading; thus the 'Geography' prefix.
SERVICE	— self-explanatory. Where a Service appears in ( ), this indicates that it was for evaluation or was purchased but not put to effective use, although in some cases the ( ) is open to debate, and with or without an ( ) could be wrong. This, however, would be in the more obscure cases.

ENGINE — see the comments above. Where it is an engine without a name (or known name) that given is of the manufacturer, and is printed in the lower case. All names are in italics. P = Piston PR = Piston, Rotary or Radial. PL = Piston, In Line. JT = Jet. TP = Turbo-prop, and includes helicopter engines where the blades are, in effect a prop.

NOTES — these are self-explanatory.

Where an aircraft or engine has had extensive use and a particular history (and is not included in Chapter 6) then the computer system presents a problem of only limited text. Which may in some cases not do justice to the subject.

Where there is a duplication of a name, its explanation is given in alphabetical order eg; Felixstowe *Fury* would come before the Hawker *Fury*. To avoid repeating the name explanation this is given only once where a name is used two or more times.

The title and the tenor of this book concern themselves with British military aircraft and engines, but life is not that simple. There have been many foreign aircraft and engines in British military service, and had it not been for the French rotary engines the Royal Flying Corps could have hardly operated in the early days of World War One. These engines are detailed against the aircraft which they powered, but their nationality need not be noted as such in the 'Notes'. *Gnôme*, *Le Rhône*, Caudron and Monosoupape could not be anything else but French! American engines played a big part in World War Two, but as these were mostly powering American aircraft in RAF or FAA service, there is no problem of recognition. The aircraft itself would be noted as 'USA' in the Index 'notes' as would those of other nationalities. Chapter 5 Part 18 covers US aircraft in general, but not in particular, that being the task of the Total Index.

As to the computer-based Index, this in itself is the subject of Chapter 7.

One last point; engine names as power plants of aircraft are given in the Total Index, but not all engines are included by name as a prime reference. Thus all engines will be found under 'Engines', but only the better known under 'Name'.

A CAUTIONARY TALE

To give some relative importance to the aircraft in this book, the numbers built (where available) are listed.

However, these should be viewed as 'of the order of' as discrepancies are found in the many sources of data used for the preparation of this book.

Similarly, the dates of first flights can also differ, but to a lesser extent. One of greater extent was a difference of eight years between two references!

The main references are given in the bibliography in Chapter 8, but data has also been obtained from other sources unlisted such as correspondence and magazines. Some aircraft histories have differences, even among the more authoritative books.

None of which is to complain, for so much has happened in so short a time. The early records are not even accurately known by some of the manufacturers, and far better historians than the author are still puzzling over some machines, and disagreeing. . .

As late as the 1960s the author unearthed a number of aeroplanes and one engine either lost to history or then just the subject of speculation.

It is a rich field, but can be a minefield when you try to set down on paper even the basic data of some 1300 plus aircraft and engines over 116 years in the form of *Names With Wings*.

Sopwith Triplane

CHAPTER 3 — THE SERVICE, MILITARY & MANUFACTURING HIERARCHY 1878-1990

'Indeed there is a woundy luck in names, Sir,
And a main mystery, an' a man knew where to find it.'
— Ben Johnson

OVER THE PERIOD of 116 years covered by this book, there have inevitably been many changes of function and of name in both the government departments serving aviation and the Armed Forces. This is also the case with the aircraft and engine industries. An appreciation of these changes is also a matter of names, in the light of which there is a better understanding of the origin of the aircraft and engine names listed in the index, and noted in various chapters. As an example, the Royal Aircraft Factory, or RAF, was set up in 1912 and the Royal Flying Corps (RFC) and Royal Naval Air Service (RNAS) combined in 1918 to form the Royal Air Force. Two RAFs would further complicate the matter, and so the Factory became the Establishment, and has now been long known as the RAE. But the 'Aircraft' has now become 'Aerospace'!

Consider also the changes on the industry side of British aviation. It is a long and complex story, but to the rescue come the following hierarchical diagrams which if long-winded by name, are simple to follow and admirably sum up the essentials. They are borrowed from Bruce Robertson's *Aviation Enthusiasts' Reference Book* and we are indebted to the publishers, Patrick Stephens Ltd, for their permission to reproduce from their book. The relationship between the Royal Navy and the Air Force has some bearing on the subsequent aircraft naming systems, and is not given in the diagrams. Prior to 1912 the RN carried out its own experiments, but with the setting up of the Royal Flying Corps in 1912, the RN aeroplane side was a part of the RFC as the 'Naval Wing'.

With the advent of war in 1914, the RN became its own aviation entity with the formation of the Royal Naval Air Service (RNAS), and at about this time the RN also took over all responsibility for airships which would include the non-dirigible blimps.

During 1918, the Royal Air Force was formed as an amalgam of the RFC and RNAS, and all naval aviation affairs devolved to the RAF. Thus aircraft procurement, naming (with a courtesy link to the Admiralty), crewing and operating was an RAF responsibility. At the advent of World War Two, control reverted to the RN in the form of the FAA or Fleet Air Arm, the name also used by the RAF from 1918 to 1939. Thus naval aircraft names have been, during various periods, RN, RNAS, FAA (RAF) and FAA (RN). All of which, hopefully, explains that which might otherwise appear to be somewhat inexplicable.

The fortunes and the names of the engine manufacturers also changed from time to time, and the story (from both a civil and military viewpoint — and they are inseparable) is outlined in the 'family tree'. A system of naming engines was set up by the newly-formed RAF in 1918, and this may be found in Part 3 of Chapter 4.

Reorganisations of British aircraft & engine manufacturers since 1935. (See also page 47)

Airspeed	Purchased by de Havilland, 1940. Became Airspeed Division of de Havilland, 1951.
Armstrong Whitworth	Part of Hawker Siddeley from 1935, became part of Hawker Siddeley Aviation on its formation in 1963.
Auster	Became Beagle Aircraft, 1962; closed, 1970.
Avro	Part of Hawker Siddeley from 1935, became part of Hawker Siddeley Aviation on its formation in 1963.
Blackburn	Merged with General Aircraft, 1949. Taken over by Hawker Siddeley, 1960. Became part of Hawker Siddeley Aviation, 1963.
Boulton Paul	Leased out designs and became part of Dowty Group, 1961.
Bristol	Became part of BAC on formation in 1960.
Cierva	Taken over by Saunders-Roe, becoming part of Helicopter Division, 1951.
Cunliffe-Owen	Ceased business, 1948.
de Havilland	Taken over by Hawker Siddeley, 1960. Became part of Hawker Siddeley Aviation, 1963.
English Electric	English Electric Aviation Ltd formed 1959. became part of BAC, 1960.

Fairey	Became part of Westland Aircraft, 1960.	Miles	Miles Aircraft liquidated, 1947. F.G. Miles Ltd formed 1951. Became part of Beagle Aircraft, closed 1970.
Folland	Taken over by Hawker Siddeley, 1960. Became part of Hawker Siddeley Aviation, 1963.	Percival	Became part of Hunting Group, 1944. Name changed to Hunting Percival Aircraft Ltd in 1946, and to Hunting Aircraft Ltd in 1957. Became part of BAC, 1960.
General Aircraft	Merged with Blackburn Aircraft, 1949		
Gloster	Part of Hawker Siddeley from 1935, became part of Hawker Siddeley Aviation on its formation in 1963.	Portsmouth Aviation	Closed, 1949
Handley Page	Liquidated, 1970.		
Hawker	Part of Hawker Siddeley from 1935, became part of Hawker Siddeley Aviation on its formation in 1963.	Saunders-Roe	Became part of Westland Aircraft, 1960.
		Scottish Aviation	Continued as independent unit until nationalised into British Aerospace, 1977.
Martin-Baker	Dropped aircraft side to concentrate on ejector seats.		

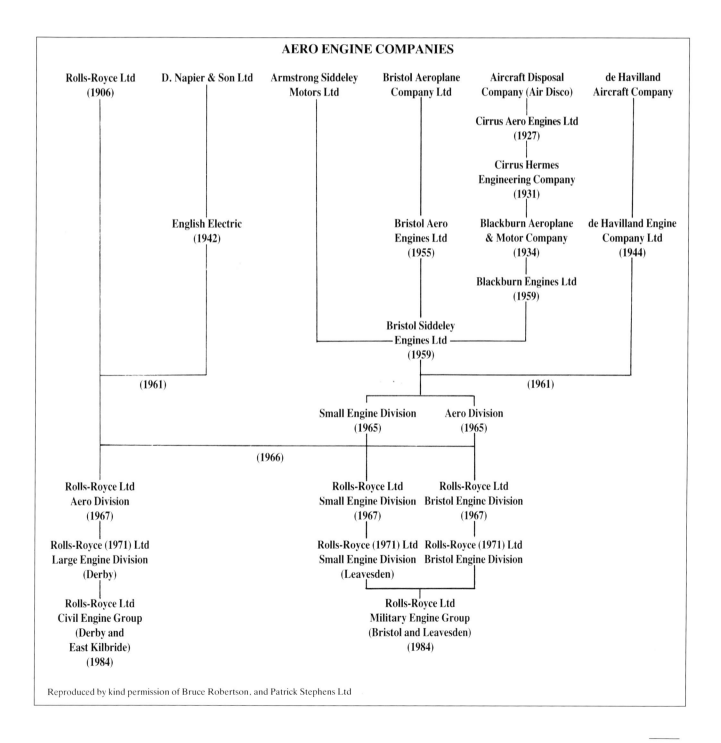

AERO ENGINE COMPANIES

Reproduced by kind permission of Bruce Robertson, and Patrick Stephens Ltd

Short Bros.	Has continued as independent unit.
Vickers	Vickers-Armstrongs (Aircraft) Ltd formed 1954 to acquire aircraft business carried on at Weybridge, Supermarine etc. became part of BAC, 1960.
Westland	Became specialist helicopter manufacturer and has continued as independent group, taking over Saunders-Roe, Bristol and Fairey helicopter interests, 1960.

Aero-engine manufacturers

Alvis	Ceased aero-engine development, late 1950s
Armstrong Siddeley	Acquired Metropolitan-Vickers, 1949. Merged with Bristol Aero-Engines to form Bristol Siddeley Engines Ltd, 1958. Bristol Siddeley taken over by Rolls-Royce, 1966.
Blackburn	Became part of Bristol Siddeley, 1961.
Bristol	Became Bristol Aero-Engines Ltd, 1955. Merged with Armstrong-Siddeley Motors to form Bristol Siddeley Engines Ltd, 1958. Bristol Siddeley taken over by Rolls-Royce, 1966.
de Havilland	Became part of Bristol Siddeley Engines, 1961.
Metropolitan-Vickers	Acquired by Armstrong-Siddeley Motors, 1949 (see above).
Napier	Joined Rolls-Royce, 1961.
Rolls-Royce	Became sole British aero-engine manufacturer through acquisition of Bristol Siddeley Engines, 1966. Liquidated, 1971. Company re-formed as Rolls-Royce (1971) Ltd and now known as Rolls-Royce Ltd.

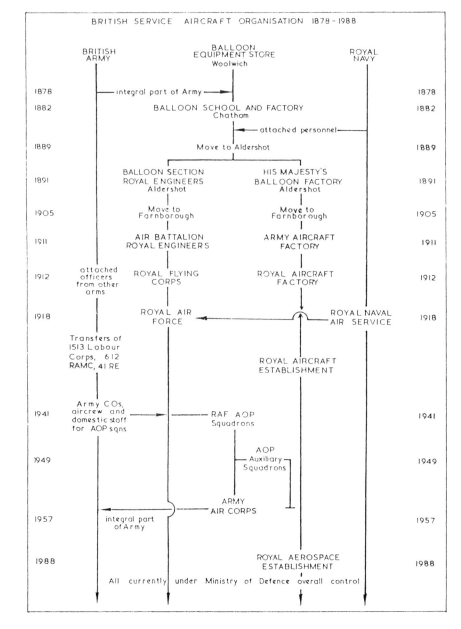

Reproduced by kind permission of Bruce Robertson, and Patrick Stephens Ltd

CHAPTER 4 — NAMING SYSTEMS

Part 1 — Coding

'A little learning is a dangerous thing;
Drink deep, or taste not the Pierian spring:
There shallow draughts intoxicate the brain,
And drinking largely sobers us again.
— Alexander Pope

HISTORY DOES NOT record whether the 1916 Front Line Army Unit received its reinforcements for an advance, but Brigade HQ were somewhat surprised to receive a signal. . . 'request three and fourpence, going to a dance'. In the Crimean War, the famous charge of the Light Brigade was the result of a muddled signal, which occasioned the remark of a French general *c'est magnifique mais ce n'est pas la guerre*. In my own RAF experience, at some point about 1943, a signal was received from a Sunderland Flying Boat Squadron at Takoradi, in West Africa, urgently requesting three aircrews. They were immediately detailed, given tropical jabs, and duly flown out. There followed a plaintive signal that what was really required were three *airscrews*. An AMO (Air Ministry Order) immediately went out that in future all airscrews would be known as 'propellers' — which they are to this day. In 1914, some RFC squadrons were posted to France, where they were neither expected nor accepted, and they duly flew home again — no doubt to be then sent back to their correct destinations.

These instances state the obvious: coding must be simple, clear, unambiguous, and in no way open to misinterpretation. Whilst this book is primarily concerned with *names*, to the military — and certainly in those early days — they were *codes*, a matter of identification by way of word or signal. A good example would be the naval tradition of classes of warship: HMS *Chrysanthemum* does not look, feel, or even smell like its namesake, but it clearly identifies a ship of the 'Flower' class, and which particular ship. Incidentally, the RAF in 1918 included 'Flowers', 'Shrubs' and 'Trees' in their first naming system for aircraft, but the RAF did not take to the idea as kindly as had the Royal Navy. Each and every RN ship is named, even the shore stations, as HMS   , but with few exceptions RAF aircraft have not been individually named. With production orders there would have been just too many; just imagine trying to find names for 21,000 *Spitfires*. There has been enough trouble with just a class name! But, of course, individual aircraft have an identity in the form of a serial number and during World War Two there were individual squadron letters, with two letters indicating the unit. But such considerations were not really part of this book.

Identifying a class of aircraft is achieved either by name or by an alphabetical numerical system, or both. From 1911 to 1918 the choice was a/n, but this had its problems, and certainly had little effect on the many nicknames. Some of the airships had class and/or individual names but in 1914 the Royal Navy took the airships over from the Army and the RFC, at least at top level, frowned on unofficial nicknames which, of course, only furthered their usage. With the formation of the RAF (from the RFC and RNAS) in 1918, names became official; these were somewhat grudgingly known as 'nicknames' but in essence, were codes, so that the relevance of a 'nickname' to a particular type of aircraft was not a matter of great importance. But this attitude did change at a later date.

Additional to the name was the type specification, such as F7/30 (the 7th Fighter Specification of 1930), and to which the first *Spitfire* was built (1932). There would also be a 'mark' or series number, as well as alphabetical 'task' designations, but again, these are not detailed in this book (the bibliography in Chapter 27 includes references to this subject.) The code-names for Fighters posed a problem in 1918, for Rolls-Royce had already established a precedent with 'birds of prey', and were thus excluded as Fighter names. This 'problem' was solved in 1932, as may be seen in Part Four of this chapter.

It has not been an easy task for the RAF to produce workable naming systems, nor even suitable names, and the records show many changes, some in a matter of months due to unforeseen complications or vociferous objections; there was inevitably some conflict between the ministry and the manufacturers over which of them should have the naming responsibility. The initiative changed from time to time for the manufacturers had to look beyond RAF orders in times of peace and seek foreign orders; in the period between the years 1918 and 1939 a civil aircraft could well become military, and vice versa. Whilst an alpha/numerical system, with prefixes and suffixes, is an administrative necessity, the RAF produced some splendid (and some odd) names, and also gave names to the many US aircraft that served with the RAF and FAA, and indeed with the Empire Air Forces. The name of an aircraft begins as an official 'code', which explains why some names, particularly in the earlier days, have had little relevance to the purpose of the aircraft. There were some inspiring names, now part of our national mythology and certainly part of our history. As with great ships, time has added a lustre of affection to what began as a mere code-name. The class of name assumes a unique entity, so that its name is no longer just a code, but at once the focus of its qualities and history. And from a psychological aspect, is there not some advantage in going in to battle in a *Spitfire* rather than in a Bf 109F?

Part 2 — 1878–1911

'A good name endureth forever.
— Apocrypha

THIS MUST OF necessity be a short and truncated history of the early years, but the book being a history of names, it is sufficient to introduce the first 'systems', such as they were.

The very first British military aircraft was a 1878 balloon, the *Pioneer*, aptly named and which set a precedent for the Army Balloons and Airships to follow over the years. The War Office allotted the princely sum of £150 for this experimental venture, little supposing that after the *Pioneer* there would be 1300 others, including some other 'Pioneers'. Even less did they suppose that aircraft would play a significant part in two world wars, or that the world would witness more change in the next century than it had known in its entire existence. Today, that early *Pioneer* is hardly remembered, and certainly wasn't mentioned when the *Pioneer* of 1938 (and the *Twin Pioneer* of 1955) was announced. It achieved little, but it meant much. The £150 seems to have been too much for the War Office and the tax payer for it/they could not afford the second, which was the *Crusader*. This was funded by Captain L.J.B. Templer, of the Royal Engineers. It was 'posted' to the Air Battalion, Royal Engineers, whose immediate authority was no less than the Director of Fortifications & Works at the War Office!

Balloon construction was now at the Balloon Store at Woolwich Arsenal (cruelly referred to by some as the 'Gas Company'), which then moved to Chatham as the 'Factory' producing the *Sapper* (of course) and the *Heron*. In 1884 the War Office pronounced this naming business unmilitary and too prolific; some standardisation was needed, and thus began a balloon class designed 'F', 'S' and 'T', in ascending order of gas cubic capacity. Such were *Fly*, *Spy* and *Swallow*, but it seems that no 'T' was built.

1905 saw great activity in balloon design, but sadly, the names of *Beedle*, *Spencer*, *Barton* and *Welford* were not accepted, and they certainly had no relevance to 'F', 'S' and 'T'. The obvious design step was the elongated balloon, which ultimately led to the airship, and a similar pattern was being pursued in Germany with the Zeppelins. Manned kite balloons were also being developed, and some of the (individual) names were *Manica*, *Hector*, *Menelaus* and *Canning*. The Army airships from 1907 to 1913 were *Nulli Secondus I* and *II*, *Baby*, *Clement-Bayard* (French), *Lebaudy* (French), *Mayfly*, *Willows*, *Astra Torres*, *Parseval* (German), *Beta I* and *II*, *Gamma I* and *II*, *Delta*, *Eta* and *Epsilon I* and *II*. In 1913 the Royal Navy took over responsibility for the former Army airships and balloons, and in particular transferred *Beta*, *Gamma*, *Delta*, *Eta*, *Astra Torres*, and *Parseval* (which was to become Naval Airship No. 4). Also transferred was *Mayfly*, of some significance as it was to be Naval Airship No.1!

It might here be pointed out that whilst balloons and airships were considered potential weapons for war, the aeroplane was not accepted in British military circles, a fact to which these letters of 1907 bear witness:

'12 April, 1907. I have nothing to add to my last letter to you [the Wright brothers]. The War Office is not disposed to enter into relations at present with any manufacturer of aeroplanes'
— Viscount Haldane, Minister of War.

'March 6, 1907. I have consulted my expert advisers with regard to your suggestions as to the employment of aeroplanes, and I regret to have to tell you, after careful consideration of the matter, the Board of the Admiralty, whilst thanking you for so kindly bringing the proposals to their notice, are not of the opinion that they would be of any practical value for the purposes of the Naval Services.'
— Lord Tweedsmouth, First Lord of the Admiralty.

'In view of the somewhat bewildering system used in naming and numbering airships, the following may be of value. The numbers following in succession. These were allocated regardless of the type as each one was ordered, with the result that some of them — for example those of the Forlannini type — were never commissioned. After the transfer from the Military to the Naval Wing, the *Beta*, *Gamma* and *Delta* were given numbers. With the rigid airships, the letter 'R' was placed before the number. The *Mayfly* was called 'No.1 Rigid Airship', but the second built was the 'R9' and the third 'R23'!'
— *The Air Weapon* Gamble.

The RN 'blimp' played a considerable part in the coastal patrols between 1915 and 1919, and various types were developed. Whilst out of chronological order so far as this Chapter is concerned, it is convenient here to name them as:

AP — airship plane, submarine scout, coastal, experimental, improved coastal — C star, submarine scout twin, North Sea, patrol and zero.

The early Army aircraft were prefixed as 'B' or 'F' with a number. There were not many under this system, and those that existed were named after their manufacturers:

B1 Voisin	B7 Bristol Boxkite
B2 Blériot	F1 Henri Farman
B3 Breguet	F2 Paulhan
B4 Nieuport	F3 Howard Wright
B5 Deperdussin	F4 — 8 Bristol Boxkites
B6 Bristol Prier	

No less than eight of these were French, a measure of the predominance of France at this time, a fact which was to have a certain consequence in a naming system shortly to follow.

Whilst this book is military orientated, mention must be given here to the Englishman Percy Sinclair Pilcher (1866-99) who built a series of gliders by the names of *Bat* and *Beetle* in 1895, and *Gull* and *Hawk* in 1896. Later he fitted an engine to one of his gliders, but a broken strut led to his death. Fate then passed the fame that had been lost by Pilcher to the Wright brothers in the USA. Pilcher's was the first *Hawk*, and there have since been four military *Hawks* in the RAF.

In the immediate pre-World War One period, an American, 'Colonel' F.S. Cody (with a resemblance to Buffalo Bill) was to play a great part in early British aviation, and much of his work was done at Farnborough where the 'tree' commemorates his work there. Cody is credited with the first British flight, and he designed and built the following:

Type Number	Name
I	British Army Aeroplane
1A	ditto
1B	Cody Biplane
1C	Cody (Cathedral) Biplane
IIA	Cody (Michelin Cup) Biplane
IIB	Cody (Michelin Cup) Biplane
IIC	Cody (Michelin Cup) Biplane
IID	Cody (Michelin Cup) Biplane
IIE	Cody (Omnibus) Biplane
III	Cody (Circuit of Britain)
IV	Monoplane
VA	Military Trials
VB	Military Trials
VC	Michelin Biplane
VIA	Waterplane (Land Version)
VIB	Waterplane.

The *'Cathedral'* is an interesting name. One explanation for it was that the top wing had an anhedral (opposite of dihedral) inclination — that is, down instead of up — and this was also known as *'cathedral'*. The other explanation is that the shed used during trials was large and cavernous and it was this that was known as the *'cathedral'*, and not the aeroplane!

An Englishman of these times who was later to produce many aircraft for the RAF was Frederick Handley Page, or 'HP'. He came on the civil aeronautical scene in 1909 with *Bluebird* and *Antiseptic*, and the *Yellow Peril* in 1911. Names were now getting interesting . . . In view of the many bird names to be later used by RAF Fighters and Rolls-Royce engines, it is interesting to note that the first British subject to fly was in Canada. He was Mr J.A.D. McCurdy, youngest of a syndicate of five headed by Dr Alexander Graham Bell, the inventor of the telephone. The syndicate was formed in 1907 to build an 'aerodrome' (aircraft). The first flight was in the aerodrome *Red Wing*, followed by the *White Wing, June Bug, Loon, Cygnet* and the *Silver Dart*. And lest the date of the first controlled powered flight be forgotten, this is credited to the Wright brothers at Kittyhawk in December 1903. It, too, had a name — the *Flyer* — but now back to matters entirely military.

The Army, having started it all with the Balloon Equipment Store at Woolwich in 1878, then progressed in 1882 to the Balloon School and Factory at Chatham, in turn moving to Aldershot in 1891. This now became HM Balloon Factory, to become the Royal Aircraft Factory in 1911 at Farnborough, to which we will again refer in due course. The British public viewed all these aeronautical antics with interest, some with enthusiasm and not a few with disbelief. The enthusiastic, as at all times, were wont to put pen to paper with practical suggestions, and here is a letter to the *Aero* from October, 1910:

'Sir — It has occurred to me on many occasions when reading the description of new machines that the lengthy sentences or paragraphs referring to the general arrangement of the surfaces would be unnecessary, if some sort of type classification were adopted. In locomotive engineering there has during the last decade or so been brought into use a most excellent method of classifying railway engines, which so far as I can see might be equally well adapted to aerial locomotives.

The classification consists in the use of numerals arranged in a certain order to represent the wheels (such as 4-4-2 engine or a 2-4-0 type). Now what I want to

suggest is that the same method should be applied to aeroplanes. I have thought over all the existing types, and I find they can all be expressed by the use of three figures with a hyphen between them.

The numerals are, of course, to represent the planes. The first one is to indicate the elevator, the second the main planes and the third the tail. In application to aeroplanes we can go a step further than is possible in locomotive practice, for by the insertion of the letter P we can indicate the position of the propeller.

I have made a few sketches to illustrate the application. . . . .the new *Valkyrie* is a 2-P-1-0 machine. *A.V. Roe* 0-P-3-3 and my own type is like the *Curtiss*, a 2-2-P-1.

I trust that I have not written to an unnecessary length on a matter which may not be deemed of any importance, but it seems to me, Mr Editor, that you might save a little valuable space by adopting the above suggestion.'

E.W. Twining.

And in December 1910 there appeared the following letters:

'Sir — In my system the dash is of much importance, and represents the connecting framework of the aeroplane. Will you, therefore, correct a printer's error in the only two type formulae I troubled you with? They should be — Blériot. . .PS-T. H. Farman. . . .E-2P-T.

I think it advisable to add B for Balancer and to use F for Flaps, as fuselage is already represented by the dash. Perhaps you can find room for a few other formulae, which readers can easily shorten for 'type':

Valkyrie ....$H\ V_2\ E\text{-}C\ M\ P\ S\ A_2\text{-}R_2$
Paulhan ....$E\text{-}C\ 2\ M\ P\text{-}R\ H$
Neale VII......................$E\ C_2\ R_2\ 2\ A_2\ M\ P\text{-}H\ A$
Cody............................$B_2\text{-}C_2\ 2B_2\ M\ P\text{-}H\ R$
Goupy..........................$P\ 2\ F_4\ C\text{-}H_2\ F_4\ R$
M. Farman ....$C\ 2\ A_4\ M\ P\text{-}H_2\ A_4\ R_2$.'

Burton-on-Trent.   C.J. Robinson.

'Sir — I feel I must write to express my admiration for the excellent scheme of describing aeroplanes by formulae. Cannot the idea be taken a step further? The machine which I have personally been flying is a $\nearrow \rightarrow ?\ ?$ *OH!* $\downarrow\ \therefore$ fitted with an engine to which I have given the symbol

$$ZIZ + POP_2 + . + DN_2 + B_3.$$

The essence of this engine formula is in the full stop, which always occurs in the middle. The second half of it is due to the engine being more of an expletive than an explosive one. If an aviator A pilots this machine he will probably find that his own formulae will speedily become

$$\frac{A}{2} + \frac{A}{2}.$$

Some experts declare that this formula could be improved by bringing in MD, but it is a very doubtful point. Of course, the above result can be more quickly obtained by partaking, previous to flying, of large quantities of XXX+*** but this never occurs unless the aviator's intelligence can be expressed by the formula 000000.00000.'

Bulford Camp.   J.D.B. Fulton, Capt. R.F.A.

After the failure of formulae and a dignified period of mourning, *Flight*, in July 1913, offered up a comment and a suggestion:

'Why is a matter of conjecture, and one can only hazard the opinion that although we may copy foreign machines and methods we have a John Bullish hatred of having their names thrust upon us. In conclusion, it is admitted that the matter is a small one, and that 'a rose, etc.': yet if the technology of aviation is not to be left to the invention of a few irresponsible journalists, it behoves the scientific press to educate the public up to a more correct standard instead of allowing them to be imposed upon by fanciful and entirely inapplicable slang-words.'

Cosmopolitan.

'May I be permitted a small space in your valuable paper for the purpose of making a few suggestions in regard to the nomenclature employed to distinguish flying craft?. . . I beg, therefore, to submit the following;

Taking the French word 'Avion' as the basis of all flying machines intended for war purposes, and the English word 'aeroplane, as the basis for all machines intended for commercial or pleasure purposes we get:

(a) For a 'War Flying Machine' intended to alight only on land: TERAVION.

(b) For a ditto, on water: AQUAVION›

(c) For a ditto, on land and water: TERAQUAVION.

(d) For a commercial or pleasure machine, intended to alight only on land: TERAPLANE or TERAERO-PLANE.

(e) For a ditto, on water: AQUAPLANE or AQUAEROPLANE.

(f) For a ditto, on land and water: TERAQUAPLANE or TERAQUAEROPLANE with, of course, the necessary prefixes of BI and MONO to signify the class of machine. Thus — BI-TERAVION, MONO-TERAVION, BI-TERAQUAEROPLANE and MONO-TERAQUAVION.

Trusting these suggestions are not too scientific for general use'

Ealing.   C.F. Webb, BA

If Shakespeare is to be trusted, King Henry V summed the suggestions up very sympathetically by declaring: '. . .Then shall our names/familiar in his mouth as household words. . .'

But, alas, it was not to be, for what the official world had in mind leads us to Part Three of this chapter.

Part 3 — 1911–1918

'Victorious Names, who made the World obey;
Who, while they lived, in Deeds of Arms excelled.'
— John Dryden

THE BACKGROUND TO this section must be the Army Estimates, presented to the House of Commons on 7 March 1910, by Viscount Haldane, Secretary of State for War:

'I want now to say a word about dirigibles and aeronautics. The aeronautical department at the National Physical Laboratory got to work almost at once after it was set up last year, and since then it has been found necessary to increase its staff, and the work at Teddington is in full swing. We have also reorganised the construction department at Aldershot, which used to be under the care of Colonel Capper, who did remarkably good work. We want Colonel Capper's great abilities, however, for the training of officers at the balloon school, and for the work which he has hitherto done we have got hold of a man of great capacity and high eminence, Mr O'Gorman, who is very well known in connection with the construction not only of motor engines, but other subjects connected with motoring.

Mr O'Gorman has now organised a construction department at Aldershot. The next step we propose to take — and we have already decided on its lines — is to substitute for the present corps a regular aeronautical corps. . .'

Thus was formed the Royal Aircraft Factory, known as the RAF until 1918. On 8 March 1911, Mr Mervyn O'Gorman, superintendent of the RAF, announced a 'Factory' naming system to the Society of Automobile Engineers. This seems an odd venue, but O'Gorman's working life had been spent in the automobile industry: the question, however, remains: why did he not address the Aeronautical Society which had been founded in 1866? The system, then published in R & M (Reports & Memoranda) No. 59, outlined three basic types:

BE   Blériot Type — tractor
FE   Farman Type — pusher
SE   Santos–Dumont Type — tail first or canard.

In the *Flight* issue of 11 March, O'Gorman expanded on the them:

'Aeroplanes and Stability — There is a certain similarity in the devices used at present by most makers to get some degree of lateral stability when flying, turning and gliding, but there is apparently greater diversity in their ideas as to longitudinal stability, and the best position of propellers. These two features therefore are used as a basis for a suggestion for a classification — although I admit that there ought to be as many classes as there are designers; these, however, would be useless for memorising, and accordingly I suggest that we take three.

1. Class S. — Those of which the main wings are preceded by a small plane which is more intensely loaded and succeeded by the propeller (Fig. 1).

2. Class B. — These of which the main wings are preceded by the propeller and followed by a smaller plane (or planes), which is more lightly loaded, if at all (Fig. 2).

3. Class F. — Those which have the main wings followed by a smaller plane more lightly loaded, if at all, as in 2, but the propellers of which are placed between the main wings and the tail plane (Fig. 3).

Those familiar with the machines of today will include in Class S the latest Voisin, Valkyrie, Cody, Clarke and Santos-Dumont very early machines &c.; in Class B the Antoinette, R.E.P., Blériot and Avro &c.; in Class F the Voisin, Farman, British and Colonial, &c.'

This, in turn, needs some further amplification, and there were some later changes:

At a later date 'SE' was taken to stand for 'scouting experimental' — the tail-first type having become obsolete — and the 'RE' type standing for 'reconnaissance experimental' was introduced. The former represented high-speed machines, otherwise known as 'Tabloids' or 'Bullets' first introduced to the world by the Sopwith Company, and soon after by the Bristol Company. The 'RE' type was a heavy two-seater, and bigger than the 'BE' type.

In addition to the list given by Mr O'Gorman was the BS1, designed by de Havilland, and which crashed in March 1913. This was probably the first single-seater 'Scout', the BS meaning Blériot Scout type. It has also been stated, however, that it was a combination of research of the Blériot (BE) and Santos (SE) types. It now lost its identity, being rebuilt to become the SE2. Another official designation was TE to represent the tail pusher or Tatin type, but this was not used.

Further information, and reference to R & M 59 was given in Report No. Aero 2150 (Royal Aircraft Factory):

BE Blériot Experimental Tractor biplanes for general purposes.

SE Santos Experimental, after Santos-Dumont, the originator of the 'Canard' or tail-first type of aeroplane. The SE1 was the only one of this category, the subsequent designs being the single-seat tractor scout formula. For this reason the designation was subsequently modified to 'Scout Experimental'

FE Farman Experimental of pusher biplane formula.

RE Reconnaissance Experimental of two-seat tractor biplane formula.

TE Tatin Experimental monoplane formula with pusher propeller behind tail. (This was never actually used and later came to mean 'Two-seater experimental' e.g. TE1 of 1916)

BS Blériot Scout — a combination of Blériot and Santos formulae in single-seat scout form. (BS1 — designed and flown by Geoffrey de Havilland. After a crash, was rebuilt to become the SE2.)

H was a prefix for all sea-aeroplanes, denoting 'Hydro', as HRE2.

Other designations were CE — coastal experimental — and AE — armoured experimental.

The dominance of French design at this time again shows in this British official naming system, and whilst BE was later 'Fighter Experimental' and so on, many did not realise the true origin of the initials which have since become so well-known, and were a way of life in between 1914 and 1918.

Jumping forward a little in time, *Aeroplane* had not forgotten, and in the 19 April 1916 issue wrote:

'It will be noted that no credit was given to any British constructor, although Mr A.V. Roe could claim to have already done well with a tractor bi-plane, and Mr S.F. Cody with a pusher.

This note seems to have dominated the Aircraft Factory Staff ever since, for no credit has ever been given by any member of the staff to any British constructor. Where it has been absolutely impossible for the Factory itself to claim credit, whether for engines, aeroplanes or accessories, the credit has been given to foreign firms.'

The year 1912 saw the formation of the Royal Flying Corps, with a Military (Army) and a Naval (RN) Wing. With the beginning of the war in 1914, the two wings in one corps became somewhat of a myth, and the Naval Wing then formally became the Royal Naval Air Service, or RNAS, as a wholly RN service. The Military Wing

then remained as the Royal Flying Corps, or RFC until 1918.

As already noted, the RN had taken over balloons and airships from the Army in 1913, so the Royal Navy was deeply involved in aviation and were to play a great part in the four years of World War One. One wonders what Lord Tweedsmouth though of it all. . .[see Part Two].

When the RFC came into being in 1912, the basic trainer was the Maurice Farman biplane, which was so docile as to become known as the 'mechanical cow'; the version with the front elevator was naturally the 'Longhorn', and that without, 'Shorthorn'.

Non-'Factory' names of fame were the Sopwith *Camel*, because of the humped cockpit cover, and officially the Sopwith *Scout* F1, and sometimes *Camisole*; Sopwith 1½ *Strutter*, as may be seen from the illustration; the famous Bristol Fighter (flying in service until 1932!) was the F2b, but universally the 'Brisfit', although some World War One pilots consider this was a post-1918 name.

Service nicknames were inevitable and irrepressible. . . the original Army Blériot of 1910 was the *Man-Killer* later to be rebuilt into the SE1 *Canard*. The FE2b was also (semi-officially) nicknamed the *Bloater*, and the BE2 as *Fokker Fodder*, *Stability Jane* or *Querk*.

All Martinsyde products were known as *Tinsides*, although the name is most closely associated with the *Elephant* (G.102). Perhaps less well known is that Captain Albert Ball, VC, designed his own fighter, which was built by the Austin Motor Company, and known as the Austin *Ball*, but it is believed that Austins also built the *Greyhound* and a triplane (Osprey) on the lines of the famous Sopwith Triplane, or *Tripe*. Another Sopwith fighter of note was the gallant little *Pup*. Of *Kittens* there were the Isle of Grain and Eastchurch versions. These, and other famous names of World War One are now legend, and almost part of English folklore.

The industry's system was individual to the manufacturer, but usually consisted of one or all of the following parts: (a) a constructor's type number; (b) a general description; (c) a type name such as Fighter, Scout, Seaplane, and almost inevitably (d) a nickname. The last of these, of course, was not by design, and often led to trouble — but Ministry directives, makers' memoranda and threatened lawsuits (e.g. Sopwith *Tabloid*) only made the nickname the most lasting.

Naval and military design and development was complementary, both for aircraft and airships, so that systems of coding and nomenclature had something in common up to the outbreak of war in 1914.

But from then on, the Admiralty were their own masters. Jack Bruce, an eminent aviation historian, and up to his retirement Deputy Director of the RAF museum, wrote in *The Aeroplanes of the RFC, Military Wing*:

'In the pre-1914 period very few aircraft manufacturers anywhere in the world employed any standard system of designation for their products. This inevitably led to the use of long and windy titles in identifying aeroplane types, and the War Office felt the need for a simple, concise and uniform system for the various aircraft then in service. An initial proposal had been for a very complicated system of letters and numbers, but this was not adopted because it was recognised as no workable improvement on the haphazard and often cumbersome names then in use. Evidently further thought was applied to the matter, for in June 1914 the War Office sent a letter to the OC RFC:

'With reference to previous correspondence on the subject of the adoption of a simple and uniform definitive system of nomenclature for aeroplanes which have passed the experimental stage, please note that it has now been decided to adopt for service machines the following nomenclature, which should be brought into use forthwith for all purposes:

ARMY AEROPLANES

BE2 — 70(hp) Renault to become RA
BE8 — 80 Gnôme to become RB
Avro — 50 Gnôme to become RC
Avro — 80 Gnôme to become RD
RE1 — 70 Renault to become RE
RE5 — 120 Austro-Daimler to become RF
Sopwith two-seater — 80 Gnôme to become RG
Blériot — 80 Gnôme RI
M Farman — 1913 type
　　　　　 70 Renault RK
Sopwith Scout — 80 Gnôme SA
H Farman — 80 Gnôme MA
M Farman, 1914 Type
　　　　 — 70 Renault MB.

New designs of machines will be allotted new letters as they pass the experimental stage and are finally adopted for service.'

This instruction was promulgated in Orders in June 1914, while the RFC was in 'concentration camp' at Netheravon, and these designations were employed to contemporary documentation.

But it seems that in operational service the system led to confusion, and the dangers that lay in possible misinterpretation had to be recognised. The squadrons had not been quite two weeks in France when Lt-Col W. Sefton-Brancker wrote on 26 August 1914:

"Referring to the circular letter issued 10 June 1914, on the subject of nomenclature of aeroplanes, it has been decided, owing to the liability of the letters laid down for designs of types of aeroplanes to be confused in telegraphic transmissions, the use of that nomenclature shall be abandoned, and that types of aeroplanes shall be referred to by their vernacular description as follows:
BE2, BE2b, BE2c, BE8, BEa, Avro 50, Avro 80, RE1, RE5, Blériot 50, Blériot 80, M Farman, old pattern M. Farman *Shorthorn* * H. Farman Sopwith *Scout*."

A long quotation, but is shows the problems, and now the RFC was back to the Farnborough 1911 system for their machines — designed by them, but later built by many manufacturers. * is interesting, a nickname now officially recognised, but yet at the same time nicknames were still not approved! The nicknames of aircraft are listed in the Total Index, and as an easy reference, Chapter 5, Part 16 gives an extended list of nicknames. There must be many more, but time and memory have taken their toll.

By 1916 both the RAF and the RFC were under scrutiny, following serious reverses in the air in France. In November 1916, the 'Bailache' report was issued to

Parliament as the 'Final Report of the Committee on the Administration and Command of the Royal Flying Corps'. That part of the report on nomenclature is reproduced here:

'I cannot (Mr Bright — Addendum Report) help thinking that steps might suitably be taken to adopt a system of nomenclature that would indicate the engine and horsepower that is combined with the machine itself, so that when, say, the BE2c is referred to it is not necessary to investigate with what engine she is fitted at that particular instance. Certainly, so far as it concerns RAF designs, the present more or less haphazard and confusing system of nomenclature ought to be capable of improvement in the way of a consistent plan.

Again, some general agreement should, in my opinion, be arrived at as to the description of different machines relative to their purpose. The most striking need for attention here is the so-called 'Scout'. The term is only at all applied now to a single-seater, comparatively small, agile machine, yet no single-seater is suitable for 'scouting' if that term is taken to mean reconnaissance as involves the services of two officers. On the contrary, machines that are going by the names 'Scout' are mainly Fighters — offensive and defensive — and machines used as guards.

I urge this point — as well as those immediately preceding — whilst the development of military aviation is still in its infancy; for, in my opinion, anything like haphazard nomenclature or standardisation should not proceed further lest at some day it should lead to serious misapprehension of one kind or another.' It already had!

If we revert ⊦ 1914, the Admiralty faced similar problems, but did not have a commission of enquiry into its affairs as did the RAF and RFC. In that year they issued the following designations:

a Seaplanes	Type A1
b Aeroplanes	B
c Seaplanes	C
d Seaplanes	A II
e Aeroplanes	D

These gave plenty of scope for 'serious misapprehension'... Names and nicknames were generally those of the manufacturer, and this accounts for 'maker' in the (name) system column in the indices, together with the fact that many a military aeroplane began in a civilian guise.

Large flying-boats were originally based on the Curtiss boat, brought from America by Commander J.C. Porte. Two versions were known as *Small Americas* and *Large Americas*. A new hull fitted to the latter led to the first 'F' or 'Felixstowe' type, there being F1 to F5. Other notable types of sea aircraft were the Hamble and Sopwith *Baby*, the *Wight*, the Fairey *Campania*, and the Felixstowe *Fury* (1919).

The use of the names 'Scout', 'Bullet' and 'Fighter' (as Mr Bright suggested) became quite confusing (and still is except for the wholly dedicated historian of the period), and I again quote from Bruce's *Aircraft of the Royal Flying Corps*: 'As if to make a confusing system of aircraft nomenclature even more confusing, the Short seaplane (Type 320) was known by the numerical horsepower of its engine!' The Parliamentary Air Committee then suggested the use of sea- and land-birds for naming military aircraft, a proposal which was not received with widespread enthusiasm.

The *Spectator* commented:
'They propose that the present and ugly system of

designating aircraft by numbers and letters should be replaced by the names of birds. The machines would be grouped in classes, and each class would have a distinctive name. The names of seabirds would be given to seaplanes, and the names of land-birds to Army aeroplanes. Just as ships of war are grouped in the 'county' class, the 'river' class, and so on, the aeroplanes would be 'thrushes', 'blackbirds', 'tits', 'swallows' or 'sparrows', and the seaplanes 'redshanks', 'cormorants', 'herring-gulls' or 'guillemots'. The idea has something quite pretty in it, possibly for privately owned aircraft. But for service machines? Well, in this case *we* will wait and see how it strikes others.'

The *Pall Mall Gazette* suggested:

'. . .they should be called "flys" and he was backed in his opinion by others, and it should be remembered that in a way it has pioneer justification, as the Wright brothers pinned their faith in "fliers". It sounds a bit funny at first, but when one thinks about it a bit, one sees how sensible it is. Well, maybe, but why think about it? Would sea-fly and land-fly be the result? I can suppose entomological names also for the various machines. A report from the front that a "bluebottle escorted by gnats gave battle to a swarm of sea-flies" would read like zig-zags from the zoo. From quite an outside source comes, as noted last week, the horror of "birds" as an alternative — land-birds and seabirds. In this direction there ought to be nothing doing. Nicknames always run riot in the Services and I shiver to think of some of the appellations that would be dug up by our light-hearted boys if either "birds" or "flies" gains the day. We have already had the *June Bug* and the *Infuriated Grasshopper*. . .'

But the seed had been shown, and as we shall see, came to fruition in 1918.

The basic need was for a simple and foolproof code, which gave as much information as possible with the shortest possible message or word/number system. Up to a point, the nickname served the point admirably, but it remained unofficial and did not generally appear in (official) signals and correspondence, but as with all rules in life they were proved by the exceptions. As the RFC and the RNAS required new types, these were supplied as requirements to the industry by 'specifications' with an invitation to tender. And some, such as the second *Spitfire*, were specifications catching up on the fact and legalising the position. As noted, every aircraft had its serial number, and there is (with some exceptions) a record of every aircraft, its history and movements. From the beginning, blocks of serial numbers were issued as necessary. Specifications were issued in 1917 for the following types:

Ala — Single-seat Fighter
Alc — Single-seat Night Fighter
A2a — Two-seat Fighter
A2b — Light Bomber
A2d — Elementary Trainer
A3b — Heavy Bomber

Before passing on to 1918, it must be recorded that the Progress & Allocation Committee held its 88th meeting on 6 June 1917, so there was obviously much activity on that front including, presumably, the systems of nomenclature.

On 1 April 1918, the Royal Air Force was formed from the RFC and the RNAS, so that at this juncture both the Army and the Navy handed over their command, aircraft, personnel and all hardware to the new Flying Service. This led to much inter-service rivalry during the inter-War years, with Trenchard, once head of the RFC and now of the RAF, fighting many governmental battle for the future of the RAF. As

Major 'Boom' Trenchard he was the first to command the Military Wing of the RFC, and the man who oversaw its vast expansion in the war years and its contraction after 1918. But this is a subject for other books, and so back to names — not immediately those of aircraft, but of organisation. There could not be two RAFs, so the RAF was now the Royal Air Force, and the Factory was dropped to become the Establishment, the Royal Aircraft Establishment or RAE.

Before the official formation of the RAF (and the war was not yet won) the responsibility for the naming of aircraft had been that of the Ministry of Aircraft Production and the Ministry of Munitions of War, who in February 1918, issued a TDI 506 (Technical Department Instruction) laying out a system of nomenclature for aircraft. Whilst this scheme was amended a month later (by TDI 506A) it was the beginning of the official naming of military aircraft, and from this stems the basic system of all later RAF names. TDI 506, which is known as the 'February 1918 system', was an introductory sheet and a systems table, together with an allocation of initial letters to the 'designing firms' which were required to be the prefix of the class name. These documents later became AP (Air Publication) 547 with the formation of the Royal Air Force, then two months away.

STANDARD NOMENCLATURE OF AIRCRAFT

'It has been decided that from the above date, each new design of aircraft approved for building shall be given a name, and that this name shall be the only name officially recognised for use in respect of such new design.

The following notes are intended to make clear the general system of nomenclature, and more especially to make clear the steps which it is requested will be taken by designing firms in dealing with the matter.

(1) As a result of careful consideration of the various points of view involved, it has been decided to adopt a 'nickname' system.

(2) The 'nickname' system chosen for use is such that the class word employed shall denote the class of aircraft to which it relates, and the initial letters of the word shall denote the firm responsible for design.

(3) No attempt will be made to use the system retrospectively; machines in production, or in use, will therefore retain their present customary names, or designation numbers.

(4) Table A shows the proposed classes of words and the types they denote; table B shows the proposed allocation of initial letters to designing firms.

(5) At the time when a firm is notified that it is proposed to approve a design, and to recommend that it be built, even for experimental purposes [later deleted], a letter will be sent advising the firm of the class of word and initial letter allocated together with a tentative list of possible names. The firm should then select a suitable name (not necessarily from the above list) and forward it for registration to the controller, Technical Department.

(6) If this suggested name is approved as being suitable, and *novel*, it will be allotted as the official name of the design and thereafter shall be quoted as the design reference in all correspondence etc., dealing with the design.

(7) Radical changes of a design which are not considered of sufficient magnitude to warrant a change of name will be denoted by 'mark' numbers. These numbers will be allocated, as and when necessary, by the Controller, Technical Department, from and after the date when the design is passed for

	FIGHTER Spec.A.1.A.,A.1.C.,A.2.A., A.2.D.,A.4.A.		TDI 506 14 February 1918 MACHINES OPERATION BY LAND BOMBER Spec.A.2.B.,A.3.B.		Heavy Armoured Machines.	
Military Duty						
Class Word	Zoological, Vegetable, and Mineral (Terrestrial)		Geographical (Inland)		Proper Names (Male)	
	Size of Machine.	Sub-class word	Size of Machine.	Sub-class word	Size of Machine.	Sub-class word
ZOOLOGICAL						
	Single-seater...	Insects, birds and reptiles.	Single-seater... Two-seater...	Italian towns Gt. Britain towns	Under 2 tons...	Mythological Greek
	Two-seater...	Mammals	Three-seater...	French towns.	2 to 5 tons...	Mythological Roman.
BOTANICAL						
			Crew exceeding 3; Wt, under 5 tons...		5 to 10 tons...	Mythological Eastern & Egyptian
	Three-seater...	Flowers		Towns in Colonies		
	Four-seater...	Shrubs		and Dependencies	10 to 20 tons...	Mythological Northern Europe Europe
	Five-seater...	Trees				
MINERALS						
	Over 5 seats...	Metals & Rocks	5 to 10 tons... 10 to 15 tons...	Towns in Asia Towns in Africa		
MACHINES OPERATING BY SEA						
Military Duty Class Word	FIGHTER Spec. N.1.A.,N.1.B.,N.2.A ZOOLOGICAL (Marine)		BOMBER Spec. N.2.B GEOGRAPHICAL (Seaboard)		PATROL & ANTI-SUBMARINE Spec. N.3.A.,N.3.B PROPER NAMES	
	Size of Machine. Single-seater... Two-seater... Three-seater...	Sub-class word. River Fish Saltwater Fish Shell Fish	As for land machines, but coast towns in place of inland.		As for land machines, but females.	

production. Prior to that date, the allocation of 'mark' numbers will rest at the discretion of the designing firm, subject to the approval of the Controller, Technical Department.

(8) This scheme does not necessarily delete any other scheme of nomenclature used by a firm for internal purposes (e.g. for drawing office or stores indexing), though it is thought probable that modification of such internal systems, so that they may most easily conform with the official system, will be advisable.

(9) In cases where it is necessary to refer to an individual machine, the official 'allocation' number (as stencilled on the machine) should be quoted in addition to the design name.

(10) This system of nomenclature in no way affects the A.I.D. systems of marking detail parts for identification and of denoting the actual manufacturer.'

PROVISIONAL LIST OF INITIAL LETTERS
TO INDICATE DESIGNS

Aircraft Manufacturing Co. ....AM or AB
Armstrong-Whitworth & Co, Ltd. ....AR or AW
Austin Motor Co., Ltd. ....AU
Beardmore & Co., Ltd. ....BE
Blackburn Aeroplane Co. ....BL or BU
Blériot ....BI
Boulton & Paul ....BO
British Aerial Transport ....BA
British & Colonial ....BR or CO
Caudron, Ltd. ....CA
Fairey Aviation Co. ....FA
Felixstowe R.N.A.S. ....FE
Grahame-White Aviation Co. ....GA
Grain, R.N.A.S. ....GR or GI
Handley Page, Ltd. ....H
Kingsbury Aviation Co. ....KI
Mann, Egerton & Co. ....ME
Martinsyde, Ltd. ....MA
Nieuport ....NI

Norman Thompson Flight Co. ....NO
Parnall & Sons ....PA
Phoenix Dynamo Manufacturing Co. ....PH or PO
Robey & Co., Ltd. ....RE
A.V. Roe & Co., Ltd. ....RO
Royal Aircraft Factory ....RA
Short Brothers, Ltd. ....SH
Siddeley-Deasy Motor Co. ....SI
Sopwith Aviation Co., Ltd. ....SO or SA or SN
Spad ....SP or SE
Supermarine Aviation Works ....SU or SW
Vickers Ltd. ....U or V
Westland Aircraft Co. ....WE
Whitehead Aircraft Co. ....WI or WH

An example of the working of the new system, with its amendments in April and July, BOULTON PAUL designed and built a single-seat night fighter and a name was required. This must be a bird, whose name must begin with 'BO', the allocated prefix initials. A search through a bird encyclopaedia would produce little more than a 'bobwhite' or a 'bobolink', and the latter, a North American songbird, was approved by the Ministry. Some seventy years later, few will remember the name, and few even knew it at the time for the system allowed *all* prototypes to have a name, even if not later given a production order for RAF service. Hence names abounded at this time, and this created a problem that remained unsolved until the introduction of the 1927 naming system. A North American songbird would seem to have little relevance to a British fighting aircraft, but remember it was only a code, and beyond that Rolls-Royce had already laid claim to the 'Birds of Prey'.

The February 1918 system lasted but one month, and there must have been some pungent criticism from both the manufacturers and the RFC, and this would have focused on the Fighter section. Flowers, shrubs and trees hardly reflected the aggressive power of a Fighter, and perhaps there were dark imaginings of a de Havilland *Delphinium*, a Parnall

TDI506A 13 March 1918								
		APPENDIX A(a) NOMENCLATURE OF EXPERIMENTAL DESIGNS SINGLE-ENGINED MACHINES						
TYPE OF DESIGN	CLASS OF NAME	SUB-DIVISION						
		AIRCRAFT FOR USE ON LAND OR FROM SHIP'S DECKS					SEAPLANES & FLYING BOATS	
1. Single Seater	Zoological	Insects, reptiles & land birds.					—	
2. More than one seat	Zoological	Mammals					Waterfowl & Fishes	
MULTI-ENGINED MACHINES								
TYPE OF DESIGN	GROSS WEIGHT LADEN		TWIN ENGINES		THREE ENGINES		FOUR ENGINES	
	Over Tons	Up to Tons	Class	Sub-Division	Class	Sub-Division	Class	Sub-Division
4. Machines for use on land or from Ship's decks	—	5		France.		France.		France.
5. Do.	5	10	A	Europe (Except France)	B	Europe (Except France)	C	Europe (Except France)
6. Do.	10	20		Gt. Britain.		Gt. Britain.		Gt. Britain.
7. Do.	20	—		—		Asia or Africa.		Asia or Africa.
Seaplanes & Flying Boats	Type as above.			As above, but Seaboard Towns.		As above, but Female Proper Names.		As above, but Female Proper Names.

A) Geographical Inland Towns

B) Male Historical or Mythological Proper Names connected with:

C) Geographical Names other than towns, rivers, lakes and islands; e.g. counties, mountains, tribes etc.

Pansy or maybe a Fairey *Fir*, or a Grain RNAS *Granite?* And were three-four-five and five-plus seater Fighters in the offing? Whatever the plans were, TDI 506 became TDI 506a, the March 1918 System.

MINISTRY OF MUNITIONS
DEPARTMENT OF AIRCRAFT PRODUCTION
Technical Department

TDI. 506a.   Victoria Embankment
WC2
13 March 1918

Amendment to TDI 506 on Standard Nomenclature of Aircraft.

With reference to TDI 506 dated 14 February 1918, it is requested that the following amendments be noted:

(1) Deletion of the words "even for experimental purposes" in paragraph five.

(2) Substitution of the attached appendices A(a) and B(a) for Appendices A and B.

              J.G.Weir
              Lieut-Col.
              Controller, Technical Department.

TDI 506A did somewhat better than 506, and lasted about three and a half months.

The Society of British Aircraft Constructors, SBAC, was the main channel of suggestion and criticism on behalf of its members, and whilst some of the correspondence was viewed in Air Ministry files in 1944, these letters now seem to have been destroyed or were not found in the Public Records Office. It also seems that the SBAC have not preserved records of this or of some later periods.

February and March 1918 had now gone, and the Royal Air Force came into being on 1 April. TDI 506a would have been reviewed and the RAF's views would have been made known to the Ministry of Munitions who remained responsible for aircraft production and naming. There were still five months

before the end of the war, and it is generally forgotten that it was, at least in title, the RAF and not the RFC who fought in those final months before victory. And so TDI 538 came about on 8 July 1918, and this was to be the 'bible' with which the then and future RAF aircraft were to be named. As with the Bible, there were various versions which we will see, but in essence the system lasted until the 1970s.

Before passing to TDI 538, it is interesting to refer back to 506 of February 1918, where the A1a, A1c etc. specifications were part of the document. Orders under these specifications had been placed in 1917, and the contenders for these 'invitations to tender' are noted in 1918:

A1a — Single-seat fighter (*Armadillo, Bantam, Nighthawk, Osprey, Siskin, Snail, Snipe, Vampire, Wagtail*).

A1c — Single-seat night fighter (*Bobolink*).

A2a — Two-seat fighter (Avro 530, *Bulldog, Hippo*).

A2b — Light bomber (DH10, *Rhino*).

A2d — Elementary training machine (*Baboon*).

A3b — Heavy bomber (*Vimy*).

There was no retrospective renumbering or renaming, so those aircraft that transferred to the RAF from the RFC remained as they were.

MINISTRY OF MUNITIONS —
TECHNICAL DEPARTMENT —
AIRCRAFT PRODUCTION

TDI 538 (later AP 547)   Central House, Kingsway WC2
                                        8 July 1918

Notice: This TDI is issued for information only, and does not in any way affect any contracts with the Ministry of Munitions. Should it be desired to make it applicable to any production contract, instructions will be given by the Supply Dept., the usual notification sheet being used to cover the embodiment of the details of this circular in the official drawings of the machines concerned.

STANDARD NOMENCLATURE OF AIRCRAFT

(1) The standard nomenclature set out in TDI No. 506 amended by TDI No. 506a, is cancelled, and that shown herein is substituted.

(2) This revision has been undertaken at the request of the SBAC, as the Society did not consider the former scheme sufficiently safeguarded the goodwill of the firm originating the design.

(3) The standard nomenclature now consists of two words — the first a name selected by the designing firm to indicate the origin of the design as set out in Table A; the second a nickname falling within the appropriate class of names to indicate the type of design as set out in Table B.

(4) Both names should always be used in referring to any particular design.

(5) The name adopted by the designing firm will in future be prefixed to nicknames registered up to date, but this amended scheme of nomenclature will not otherwise be retrospective.

(6) The procedure for registration of the nickname will continue as before, namely on a recommendation being made that a machine to an experimental design should be constructed, the designing firm will be advised as to the class of name from which the nickname should be selected. The name indicating the origin of the design, followed by the nickname selected, will be registered as the standard names, provided the latter is suitable and novel.

(7) Radical changes in a design which are not considered of sufficient magnitude to warrant a change of name will be denoted by mark numbers. These numbers will be allocated as and when necessary by the Controller, Technical Department.

(8) This scheme does not necessarily delete any other scheme of nomenclature used by a firm for internal purposes (e.g. for drawing office or stores indexing), though it is thought probable that modification of such internal systems, so that they may most easily conform with the official system, will be advisable.

(9) In cases where it is necessary to refer to an individual machine, the official allocation number— (as stencilled on the machine) should be quoted in addition to the design names.

(10) This system of nomenclature in no way affects the AID systems or marking detail parts for identification and of denoting the actual manufacturers.

J.G. Weir
Lieut-Col.
Controller, Technical Department

TABLE A

List of names adopted by designing firms to indicate the origin of their designs

Designing Firm	Name Adopted
Aircraft Manufacturing Co. Ltd.	AIRCRAFT
Sir W.G. Armstrong, Whitworth, & Co.,Ltd.	ARMSTRONG
Austin Motor Co., Ltd.	AUSTIN
William Beardmore and Co., Ltd.	BEARDMORE
Blackburn Aeroplane Co., Ltd.	BLACKBURN
Boulton and Paul Ltd.	BOULTON
British Aerial Transport Co., Ltd.	BAT
British and Colonial Aeroplane Co., Ltd.	BRISTOL
Fairey Aviation Co., Ltd.	FAIREY
Grahame-White Aviation Co., Ltd.	G.W.
Handley Page Ltd.	HANDLEY PAGE
Mann, Egerton and Co., Ltd.	MANN EGERTON
Martinsyde, Ltd.	MARTINSYDE
Nieuport and General Aviation Co., Ltd.	NIEUPORT
Norman Thompson Flight Co., Ltd.	..
Parnall and Sons Ltd.	PARNALL
Phoenix Dynamo Manufacturing Co., Ltd.	PHOENIX
A.V. Roe and Co., Ltd.	AVRO
Frederick Sage and Co., Ltd.	SAGE
Short Bros.	SHORT
Siddeley Deasy Motor Car Co., Ltd.	SIDDELEY
Sopwith Aviation Co., Ltd.	SOPWITH
Supermarine Aviation Works Ltd.	SUPERMARINE
Vickers, Ltd.	VICKERS
Westland Aircraft Works (Petters Ltd.)	WESTLAND
Whitehead Aircraft Co., Ltd.	WHITEHEAD

The names adopted to denote designs by RAF designing establishments are as under:

Experimental Seaplane Station, Felixstowe	FELIXSTOWE
Royal Aircraft Establishment, Farnborough	FARNBOROUGH

It will be noticed that TDI 538 had now done away with the firm's letter prefix as part of the name, and that the firm was now to become the first of a two-part name, a point on which the SBAC had fought hard as the firms were very concerned about losing their trading identity.

July 1918

TABLE B
CLASS OF NICKNAME TO DENOTE TYPE OF DESIGN

TYPE OF DESIGN	CLASS OF NAMES	AIRCRAFT FOR USE ON LAND OR FROM SHIPS' DECKS	SEAPLANES
		AIRCRAFT WITH ONE ENGINE ONLY	
1. Single-seater	Zoological	Reptiles (except snakes)	—
		Land birds (except birds of prey)	—
2. More than one seat	Zoological	Mammals (except felidae)	Waterfowl Fishes

AIRCRAFT WITH MORE THAN ONE ENGINE				
Gross weight, laden over lbs. up to lbs.				
3.	— 11,000	Geographical	Inland towns in England or Wales.	Seaboard towns in England or Wales.
4.	11,000 20,000	Geographical	Inland towns in Scotland or Ireland.	Seaboard towns in Scotland or Ireland.
AIRCRAFT WITH MORE THAN ONE ENGINE				
Gross weight, laden over lbs. up to lbs.				
5.	20,000 45,000	Proper names	Male historical or mythological proper names (excluding names of stars and planets)	Female historical or mythological proper names (excluding names of stars and planets)
6.	45,000 —	Attributes	Terminating in 'ous', 'ant' or 'ent'.	Terminating in 'ic', 'al' or 'er'.
NOTE: The names excluded from the above are reserved for denoting engine designs				

Another point of far-reaching consequence was the 'note' at the end of Table B: 'The names excluded from the above are reserved for denoting engine designs.' As already noted, some engine manufacturers had 'established' their own naming systems before the RAF ones appeared in 1918, and the RAF categories would have opened out their cherished traditions to the aircraft manufacturers. As an example, and again as already noted, Rolls-Royce had started in 1915 and up to 1918 already had the *Hawk, Eagle* and *Falcon*, so making a claim for 'Birds of Prey'.

The engine allocation was as follows:

Rolls-Royce	— Birds of Prey
Napier	— Arms & Weapons
Armstrong-Siddeley	— Felidae (Cats)
Wolseley	— Snakes
Bristol	— Stars & Planets

With 'Bristol' there is an apparent mystery, for the Aero Engine Division of the British Aeroplane Company was not formed until 1921, and this list appeared in 1918! The explanation is that 'Bristol' referred to Cosmos Engineering (previously Brasil-Straker) of Fishponds, Bristol. In 1916 they were sub-contracted to build Rolls-Royce engines with the strict proviso that they did not engage in the design of water-cooled engines. So Roy Fedden, the chief engineer, set about designing air-cooled engines with a *Lucifer, Jupiter* and drawing-board *Hercules*, all later BAC names (see *Jupiter* in the 'Classics' chapter). At a later date Wolseley Motors were allotted 'Signs of the Zodiac, except Planets and Constellations' which must have slightly surprised Bristol. This class of name appears not to have been used except for the *Aries* which is not thought to have had any RAF connotation.

There was another connection, or coincidence, between BAC and Cosmos (from which the cosmic names sprang), and this was a proposal from the British & Colonial Aeroplane Company, as it then was, to the Ministry. This was in December 1917 and was to give distinguishing names to the following 'types'.

Bristol Fighter *Mercury* type ....Series I Rolls-Royce.Series I
(originally Type F2A)
Bristol Fighter *Mars* type ....Series II Rolls-Royce.Series II
(originally F2B)

    Series III. Rolls-Royce.Series III
    Series IV Hispano-Suiza (French)
    Series V Hispano-Suiza (English)
    Series VI Sunbeam

Bristol Monoplane *Orion* type ....Series I 110 hp. Le Rhône
(originally M1B or M1C)

    Series II 110 hp. Le Clerget
Bristol Fighter *Comet* type ....Series I Sunbeam Arab
Bristol All-metal *Saturn* type ......Series I Hispano-Suiza (French)
    Series II Hispano-Suiza (English)

This was a quite remarkable coincidence, for all that Cosmos and BAC had in common at that time was a Bristol address. The proposal was turned down by the Ministry as the new name system was already being finalised but BAC must have viewed the situation in 1921 as somewhat ironic when they took over the Cosmos hardware and the names, later to become world famous.

In May of 1918, AP 424 was issued and was concerned with 'confusion in the designation of engines and the names that have been allotted to them', listing the following:

ABC	*Gnat*
	Mosquito
	Wasp
	BR1 & 2
GALLOWAY	*Adriatic*
	Atlantic
WOLSELEY	*Python*
	Viper
	Adder
NAPIER	*Lion*
	Puma

SIDDELEY	*Tiger*
ROLLS-ROYCE	*Hawk*
	Falcon
	Eagle
	Condor
SUNBEAM COATELEN	*Arab*
	Maori
	Cossack
	Manitou

It will be noted that these names were already in being before the publication of TDI 538.

The following correspondence between Bristol, and the Ministry gives some flavour of the times as regards naming:

A.B. 725/1005/6 TIB   Air Board Technical Department
Embankment WC2
17 January 1918

Messrs The British & Colonial Aeroplane Co. Ltd,
Fitton House, Bristol.

Gentlemen,

With reference to your letter of 29 December on the question of naming Bristol Bomber. I understand that you will shortly receive a circular letter informing you of a general scheme for naming machines, and the steps you will require to take.

In the meantime, it would be wise if you did not go on with the idea of naming your machines by star names, as this will not fit in with the scheme now awaiting approval.

I am, Gentlemen,
Your obedient Servant.
Tunswick (??)
Captain RFC
TIB

TW/MIG

286/163/D   Air Board Technical Department
Embankment
WC2
14 February 1918

Messrs The British & Colonial Aeroplane Co. Ltd,
Filton House, Bristol

Gentlemen,

I am directed to inform you that it is proposed immediately to allot distinctive names to experimental designs of aircraft on a system, particulars of which will reach you shortly.

As regards your experimental design for a triplane bomber, Type B1 with four 220 hp BHP engines now being constructed under contract, the name selected should fall in the class of inland towns in Asia (excluding British Colonies or Protectorates) and should commence with the letters BR, CO, or KO to indicate that the design emanates from yourselves.

It is requested that you will select a name conforming with the above requirements and inform me of it in order that, provided it is novel, it may be registered as the official name for the above design.

The following names are suggested for your consideration: *Brusa*, *Korat*, *Cok*.
Yours faithfully,
Alec Ogilvie
Wing Commander, D. Branch
For Controller, Technical Department.

286/163/D   Air Board Technical Department
Embankment, WC2
14 February 1918

Messrs The British & Colonial Aeroplane Co. Ltd
Filton House, Bristol
Gentlemen,

I am directed to inform you that it is proposed immediately to allot distinctive names to experimental designs of aircraft on a system, particulars of which will reach your shortly.

As regards your experimental design for a single-seater fighter with 200 hp Sunbeam engine now being constructed under contract, the name selected should fall in the class of 'Insects', 'Reptiles', or 'Terrestial Birds' and should commence with the letters 'BR', 'CO' or 'KO' to indicate that the design emanates from yourselves.

It is requested that you will select a name conforming with the above requirements and inform us of it in order that, provided it is novel, it may be registered as the official name for the above design.

The following names are suggested for your consideration: *Cockchafer, Cock, Cockatoo, Cockatrice, Cobra*.
Yours faithfully,
Alec Ogilvie.
Wing Commander, D. Branch
For Controller, Technical Department

With the formation of the Royal Air Force, the Admiralty handed over its command of naval aviation, and this was to have some effect on naming systems and names. All fleet aircraft were to be named under the current RAF system, but Admiralty were consulted before a name was finally decided, and as will be seen later the Admiralty requested a 'reserve' on names that had a particular association with the Royal Navy.

But the RN was not wholly a 'loser' in 1918, it having been decided that the officer class of the new RAF would be based on the Navy, and other ranks on the Army. Some RN officers transferred to the RAF, and several reached Air Rank — Air Commodore and above — and gave most distinguished service to the 'Junior Service'.

The Great War, as it was then known, came to an end on 11 November 1918, and the guns were silent after four and a bit years of the greatest conflict ever known to man. From that terrible battleground military aviation came of age, and together with its legacy of civil aviation, the world would never be the same again. The 1918 Armistice is a natural and convenient point at which to close this chapter, and pass on to the hoped-for period of peace which only lasted for the twenty-one years to 1939. But 'peace' is a comparative term, for the RAF were 'at war' somewhere for almost all that time. It was a big Empire, and for the most part controlled and defended with comparatively small forces.

Part 4 — 1918–1939

'Time takes them home that we loved
Fair Names & Famous. . .'
— A.G. Swinburne

WITH THE GREAT War but recently finished, there remained a vast surplus of war material to be sorted, stored, kept or scrapped. At the same time the very young RAF was also occupied with its own future plans and requirements and also fighting for its own future as the 'Junior' Service.

As noted in Part Three, the command of naval aviation now passed to the RAF, but with such far-reaching changes in all aspects of service life, this could not be other than a somewhat untidy process. The Naval squadrons (RAF) were disbanded in 1923 to form 'Service Flights', to be styled the Fleet Air Arm or FAA in 1924 and RN uniforms were still being worn in the RAF in 1920. All this would appear to have little relevance to the subject of this book, but is mentioned nevertheless as a matter of historical accuracy; so as not to further confuse our computer all naval aircraft from 1918 are given in the indices as FAA.

As suggested, this was a time of extensive stocktaking, and names and naming was no exception. So in January 1919, there appeared TDI 538a (or AP 547a):

MINISTRY OF MUNITIONS
TECHNICAL DEPARTMENT —
AIRCRAFT PRODUCTION

Central House
Kingsway WC2

TDI 538a   January 1919

Notice: This TDI is issued for information only, and does not in any way affect any contracts with the Ministry of Munitions. Should it be desired to make it applicable to any production contract, instructions will be given by the supply department, the usual notification sheet being used to cover the embodiment of the details of this circular in the official drawings of the machines concerned.

STANDARD NOMENCLATURE OF AIRCRAFT

This TDI is a supplement to TDI 538 of July 1918, and comprises a list of names of aircraft registered under the standard scheme of nomenclature (TDI 538) up to 1 January 1919.

J.G. Weir,
Brigadier-General,
Controller, Technical Department.

(A) Designs in Production
    Registered Names

Firm	Nickname	Mark	Engine	RAF Type	Remarks
Airco	Amiens	I	2 BHP		Wash-out.
		II	2 Eagle VIII		Wash-out.
		III	2 Liberty	8	Production.
		IIIA	2 Liberty	8	Modified: dropped engines. Production.
Martinsyde	Buzzard	I	300 Hispano	I	Production.
		IA	300 Hispano	IA	Long-distance fighter. Production.
Sopwith	Cuckoo	I	Arab		Formerly Sopwith
		II	Viper		Torpedo aeroplane. Production.
Sopwith	Dragon		Dragonfly	I	Formerly Snipe, with Dragonfly engine. Production.
Nieuport	Nighthawk		Dragonfly	I	Production.
Parnall	Panther		BR2	21	Production
Sopwith	Snipe	I	BR2	I	Production.
		IA	BR2	IA	Long-distance fighter stopgap. Production.
Sopwith	Salamander		BR2	2	Production
Vickers	Vimy		2,200 Hispano		Wash-out.
		I	2 Maori		Wash-out
		II	2 Fiat		Production + anti-submarine patrol.
		III	2 BHP		Wash-out.
		IV	2 Eagle VIII		Production.

(B) Experimental Designs
    Registered Names

Firm	Nickname	Mark	Engine	RAF Type	Remarks
Armstrong	Armadillo		BR2	I	Wash-out
Armstrong	Ara		Dragonfly	I	For competition.
Fairey	Atalanta		4 Condor	33	For competition.
Boulton Paul	Bobolink		BR2	I	Wash-out.
BAT	Bantam	I	Wasp	I	Wash-out.
		II	100 Mono	I	Wash-out.
BAT	Baboon		Wasp	Training	Wash-out.

	Registered Names				
Firm	Nickname	Mark	Engine	RAF Type	Remarks
Boulton Paul	Bourges	I	2 Dragonfly	4,6 & 8	Suffix A to Mark
		II	2 BR2	4,6 & 8	No. denotes
		III	2 Puma	4,6 & 8	straight thro: centre section. Suffix B — dropped centre section.
BAT	Basilisk		Dragonfly	I	For competition
Blackburn	Blackbird		Eagle VIII	22	For competition.
Bristol	Badger	I	Dragonfly	3	For competition.
		II	Jupiter	3	For engine trials
Bristol	Braemar	I	4 Puma	8	For flying trials. Wash-out.
		II	4 Liberty	8	For performance trials.
Sopwith	Buffalo		BR2	B	Armoured contact patrol.
Sopwith	Cobham	I	2 Dragonfly	4,6 & 8	For competition.
		II	2 Puma	4, 6 & 8	for flying trials.
Short	Cromarty		2 Condor	30	For competition.
Phoenix	Cork		2 Eagle VIII	B	F5 type boat (P5)
Felixstowe	Fury		5 Eagle VIII	B	Formerly PSB
GW	Ganymede	I	3 Maori	8	For trials
			3 Liberty	8	For trials.
Grain	Griffin		Arab	21	Wash-out
Austin	Greyhound		Dragonfly	3	For competition.
Airco	Gazelle		Atlantic	B	For trials.
Nieuport	London	I	2 Dragonfly	7	For trials.
		II	2 Puma	7	For flying trials.
Avro	Manchester	I	2 Dragonfly	4, 6 & 8	For competition.
		II	2 Puma	4, 6 & 8	For flying trials.
Austin	Osprey		BR2	I	Wash-out.
Airco	Oxford	I	2 Dragonfly	4, 6 & 8	For competition
		II	2 Puma	4, 6 & 8	For flying trials.
Airco	Okapi		Condor	B	Single-engine day bomber.
Farnborough	Ram	I	Arab	B	Wash-out.
		II	BR2	B	Wash-out.
Sopwith	Snail		Wasp	I	Wash-out.
Siddeley	Sinai	I	2 Tiger	II	For trials.
		II	2 Condor	II	For trials.
		III	2 Atlantic	II	Wash-out.
Short	Shirl		Eagle VIII	22	For competition.
Sopwith	Snark		Dragonfly	I	Triplane — for competition.
Sopwith	Snapper		Dragonfly	I	Biplane — for competition.
Sopwith	Swallow		110 Le Rhône	C	Monoplane
Siddeley	Siskin		Dragonfly	I	For competition.
Tarrant	Tabor		6 Lion	C	Night bomber.
Fairey	Titania		4 Condor	33	Flap wings. For competition.
Vickers	Vampire	I	200 Hispano	I	Wash-out.
		II	BR2	2	Wash-out.
Vickers	Valentia		2 Condor	30	For competition.
Vickers	Vigilant		8 Condor	B	Sea patrol.
Westland	Wagtail		Wasp	I	Wash-out.
Westland	Weasel		Dragonfly	3	For competition.

2. List of names of aircraft that had been adopted before the scheme of nomenclature came into force:

Sopwith *Bulldog*	Mk.I	220 Clerget	Wash-out
	Mk.II	Dragonfly	Wash-out
Sopwith *Camel*		110 Le Rhône	production.
		180 Clerget	Wash-out
		BR2	Production.
Sopwith *Dolphin*		200 Hispano	Production.
Martinsyde *Elephant*		160 Beardmore	Obsolete.
Sopwith *Hippo*		200 Clerget	Wash-out.
Blackburn *Kangaroo*		2 Falcon	In production.
Grain and Felixstowe *Kitten*		Gnat	Wash-out.
Sopwith *Pup*		80 Gnôme	Obsolete.
Sopwith *Rhino*		BHP	Wash-out.

The 'wash-outs' are interesting as is one aspect of this last list, the fact that all the names are animals, of whom the first-mentioned were for two-seat fighters in the February 1918 system (that is, the 'first' system). Before that there was no animal or other system that might include animals, so one can only conclude that the manufacturers were given advance notice of the system to be, although the correspondence with Bristol given in the previous part of this chapter would seem to rule that out (or the above comment by the Ministry was incorrect). *Camel*, *Kitten* and *Pup* were all nicknames before this time, but after the fuss of the war years are now recognised as names.

'Production & Experimental Lists' were regularly published by the RAF (secretly, of course, in their time) and these have now furnished us with a great deal of information that would otherwise probably have never come to light. Civil aircraft — UK and foreign, borrowed or bought for evaluation — were included in these lists; most, but not all, were given RAF colours and a serial number. So there is some authentic reason for some otherwise surprising names to be included, but the thirty year rule may well have excluded some aircraft with a claim to have names with wings.

The February 1918 system listed a two-letter prefix allocated to all manufacturers, but as mentioned already, was soon dropped so that both the name of the manufacturer and the aircraft was now the official name. Alliteration (e.g. Hawker *Hart* and Bristol *Bulldog*) therefore became very much a tradition, although not officially called for. There were exceptions — there are many in all aspects of the naming game over the years — but the alliteration is still with us, for example with the modern Hawker *Harrier*.

As regards the *Bobolink*, *Ara* and *Vireo* (all birds) some names were obscure as to their meaning, and all these three are American birds and known to none in Europe but the dedicated ornithologist but they were codes within the system, and the requirement was satisfied, however improbable the name.

A reflection of the times was not only the great progress made in aviation, of which the recent war had been the prime mover, but also the great activity that was taking place in the automobile industry. It is interesting to compare the names used for automobiles in 1920 with those for aeroplanes, some of which bear a remarkable similarity to those used or to be used in the RAF:

CARS
Ace, Atlanta, Autocrat, Baby, Berkeley, Buckingham, Cyclone, Delta, Eagle, Ensign, Gladiator, Gordon, Hudson, Iris, Marathon, Meteor, Oryx, Phoenix, Schneider, Stag, Swift, Universal, Victor, Vulcan, Wolf, Zephyr.

MOTORCYCLES
Atlas, Bat, Beaumont, Bulldog, Clyde, New Comet, Princess, Victoria, Viper, Warwick, Wolf.

STEAM WAGONS
Oxford, Tiger, Wallis.

MARINE MOTORS
Ace, Atlantic, Bantam, Britannia, Buffalo, Hercules, Neptune, Wasp.

COMMERCIAL & AGRICULTURAL MOTORS
Atlas, British Ensign, Denby, Eagle, Mohawk, Phoenix, Scout, Victor, Vulcan, Wallace, Warwick.

AGRICULTURAL MOTORS
Beaver, Eagle, Titan, Victoria, Warwick.

There was once a splendid book on the names of every ship that had ever served in the Royal Navy from its inception in the days of Henry VIII, but which now, sadly is out of print. Again, there is a remarkable similarity in RAF and RN names, and in both services names are repeated. With the Navy, this is wholly an Admiralty affair, but with the RAF the manufacturer was usually the instigator.

In 1921, the responsibility for naming aircraft likely to be used in the RAF became that of the Directorate of Research,

Air Ministry. AP 547 was declared redundant, and a new system introduced:

| TYPE | CLASS OF NICKNAME | | |
	LAND AEROPLANE	SEA AEROPLANE	AMPHIBIAN
Single-Seat	Land-birds (except of prey)	Shell Fish	Reptiles (except snakes)
Multi-seat (up to 6,000lb)	Mammals (except Felidae)	Fresh and Salt water fish	Water fowl. (deleted about 1925)
6,000 — 12,000lb	Inland towns in the British Isles.	Seaboard towns in the British Isles.	Islands in the British Isles
12,000 — 20,000lb	Inland towns in the British Empire	Seaboard towns in the British Empire	Islands in the British Empire
20,000 — 40,000lb	Male mythological names.	Female mythological names	Ancient geographical names
40,000lb and over	Attributes ending in 'ous', 'ant' and 'ent'	Attributes ending in 'al', 'es' and 'ic'	Attributes with other endings.
Civil Aircraft	Historical names (other than those of people)	Names of famous historical persons	Astronomical names

As with the 1918 systems, this was entirely code orientated, and the only class likely to have a warlike appropriateness was 'Names of famous historical persons', and even that was not necessarily military, the names destined as ordered for civil aircraft (civil aircraft were an Air Ministry responsibility until after World War Two).

'Snakes', 'Felidae' and 'Bird of Prey' were definitely of the right stuff, but they were reserved for engines. Perhaps it was the engine companies that were the 'Hawks' and the aircraft companies the 'Doves'. . . but no, it was just the system. Up to October 1924 the Air Ministry had a record of the following official names: *Airedale, Ape, Ava, Armadillo, Amiens, Ara, Atalanta, Aldershot, Ayr, Awana, Andover; Bobolink, Bantam, Baboon, Bourges, Basilisk, Bulldog, Blackbird, Badger, Braemar, Buffalo, Buzzard, Bolton, Bodmin, Blackburn, Bison, Bullfinch, Bugle, Bloodhound, Brandon, Berkeley; Camel, Cobham, Cromarty, Cork, Cuckoo, Cubaroo; Dolphin, Dragon, Dart, Derby, Doncaster, Duiker, Denbigh, Dingo, Dormouse, Elephant, Fury, Fawn, Flycatcher, Ferret; Ganymede, Griffin, Greyhound, Gazelle, Grebe, Gloster, Gloster II, Gorcock; Hanley, Hippo, Hyderabad, Handcross, Hendon, Hamilton, Hedgehog, Horsley; Kangaroo, Kitten, Kingston; London; Manchester; Nighthawk, Nightjar; Osprey, Oxford, Okapi; Panther, Pup, Possum, Plover; Ram, Rhino; Snipe, Snail, Salamander, Sinai, Shirl, Snark, Snapper, Swallow, Siskin, Snipe, Seagull, Scylla, Springbok, Swan, Sea Urchin, Southampton; Tabor, Titania, Tramp; Vampire, Vimy, Valentia, Vigilant, Vernon, Virginia, Victoria, Vanellus, Venture; Wagtail, Weasel, Walrus, Wolf, Woodcock; Yeovil.*

This, and the later (1927) system was administered by an Aircraft Nomenclature Committee which continued until 1930.

In general, the constructors suggested their own names within the scheme and if approved by the Air Ministry, the name was 'registered'. Names were sometimes turned down by either side. Bristol suggested the *Bludgeon* but it became the *Bagshot*. Handley Page jibbed at the *Chitral* and it became the *Clive*. The Short *Singapore* was originally suggested as the *Saturn*, and the Westland *Whelp* became the *Witch*. The Hawker *Kingston* became the *Horsley* (so named after Horsley Towers, the former residence of Sir Thomas Sopwith).

What happened when an aircraft was, in fact, two? Such a problem was set by specification no. 2/21, which called — those being the days of economy — for a single-seat fighter monoplane which could be quickly converted to a two-seater biplane. As the former it was required to be named as a land-bird, and otherwise as a mammal. Bristol at first suggested *Platypus* and *Pegasus*, and then neatly solved the problem by adopting **Bull***finch* and *Bull***finch**.

Names under certain classes often ran short and an added difficulty was that the constructors always preferred to have a name alliterating with their own — Bristol *Bulldog*, Gloster *Gorcock* and Vickers *Venom* are good examples. Alliteration is general throughout all naming but there have been many exceptions. Exceptions to the system itself were sometimes allowed, especially if there had been a despairing, and unsuccessful, appeal to the Zoological Society for another name. One result of this was that the 'wildfowl' section was abandoned circa 1925. Some aircraft, particularly Fighters, have had absurd names such as *Armadillo*, *Elephant*, *Kitten*, *Hippo* and *Snark*, and amongst the 'unofficial' names of this time were 'Crow', 'Dove', 'Firefly', 'Goshawk', 'Gnu', 'Grasshopper', 'Rainbow', 'Seal', 'Sparrowhawk', 'Sealion', 'Swift', 'Viking' and 'Vulcan'.

The three letters that follow are from the Ministry to the Bristol Aeroplane Company, and are entirely self-explanatory:

S99315/25/RDI   Air Ministry
London WC2
11 July 1925

Messrs Bristol Aeroplane Co. Ltd.
Filton House
Bristol

Twin-Engined Fighting Landplane. Spec. 4/24
Gentlemen,

With reference to your letter (Ref: EHM/DEL) dated 30 June 1925, submitting the name *Bludgeon* for the above, I am directed to state that the name chosen for this type of aircraft should be that of an inland town in the British Isles. Will you therefore please submit a name within that category for approval by this Department.

    I am,
        Gentlemen,
            Your obedient Servant
                J.S. Buchanan
                   RDI
       for Director of Technical Development.

599315/25/RDI   27 July 1925
EHM/KEA
The Secretary
Air Ministry
Adastral House
Kingsway WC2

Sir,

Replying to your letter of the 11th inst., in place of the name *Bludgeon* which we had applied to this machine, we desire to apply for the registration of the name *Bagshot* which name comes within the definition contained in your letter.

    We are, Sir,
        Your obedient Servants.

———————

                        Air Ministry
                        London WC2
                        30 July 1925

Messrs Bristol Aeroplane Co. Ltd.
Filton House
Bristol

           Twin-Engined Fighting Landplane
                Specification 4/24
Gentlemen,

In reply to your letter (ref EHM/KEA), dated 27 July 1925, I am directed to inform you that the name *Bagshot* is approved and has been registered for the above type of aircraft.

Will you please refer to this aircraft by the approved name in future correspondence.

    I am, gentlemen,
        Your obedient Servant
            J.S. Buchanan
            RDI
      for Director of Technical Development

In May 1925, some dissatisfaction was expressed in the RAF that whilst the 1921 system might, but seldom did produce some splendid names, in themselves they gave very little indication of the operation function of an aircraft. And many did clearly carry out several functions. However, there were divided views in the Air Council, and it was decided to pass on the problem to the RAF Staff College as a student exercise. The commandant was Air Vice-Marshal R. Brooke-Popham, and he forwarded the students' recommendations to the Air Ministry in October. Having duly considered them they reported to the Air Council that whilst a naming prefix was acceptable, it was otherwise not thought to be a satisfactory solution. However, the Chief of Air Staff did thank the commandant for the students' paper, noting that 'the matter contained had been of considerable value in dealing with the problem'.

There followed a period of considerable activity, and a small committee was set up under the Deputy Director of Operations to study the recommendations of the students' report, which were:

— that RAF aircraft will henceforth be named by the Air Ministry and not by the makers.
— that each distinctive type, as before, would be given a name.
— that each name will follow a prefix letter to indicate the function of the aircraft.
— that the type name will not aim at distinguishing the service

to which the type is allocated (RAF, RN or Army).
— that the type name will not aim at distinguishing the construction — land-plane, float plane, amphibian etc.

With the proposed prefix letter, the committee also concerned itself with some suggested names:

FIGHTER — LAND	(F)	*Ferret, Faggot, Fairy, Falcon, Fawn, Fiend, Finch, Firefly, Fledgling, Fox.*
— SEA		*Felucca, Flamingo, Ferox, Flounder, Frigate.*
BOMBERS	(B)	*Bear, Boar, Bee, Buck, Bass, Bat, Bream, Bull, Baboon, Badger, Ballister, Bandof, Bandit, Banshee, Beaver, Beetle, Buffalo, Bison, Bustard.*
TORPEDO BOMBER	(M)	*Macao, Macaw, Mandrill, Marbon, Mackerel, Magpie, Marmot, Mark, Mallard, Mammal, Mongoose.*
ARMY CO-OP	(A)	*Arcadia, Accomplice, Aerobat, Adder, Argali, Alligator, Alaston, Aut, Ape, Apostle, Antelope.*
SPOTTER & REC.	(S)	*Stork, Salamander, Swallow, Sapajon, Squirrel, Starling, Sardine, Seal, Scoter, Sempal, Springbok, Shoveller, Skunk, Sloth, Spartan, Steenbok.*
COASTAL REC.	(R)	*Rabbit, Rook, Ram, Raven, Reindeer, Rocket, Rhino, Roineck.*
TRAINING	(T)	*Tadpole, Tarantula, Tarpon, Trainer, Turtle, Tutor, Tortaine, Trapper, Terrier, Turkey, Thunder, Tumbler, Tirwit, Typhoon.*
TROOP CARRIER	(C)	*Camelot, Camel, Camay, Chameleon, Chieftain, Comet, Crane, Cobra, Condor, Crow, Cannibal, Caracal, Chariot, Cockchafer, Crab, Cariban, Cassowary, Caterpillar.*

In June 1926, Air Ministry reported to the Air Council: 'The proposals of the committee have been carefully considered. . . great difficulty has been experienced, and in some cases it has been impossible to find suitable names. It is regretted, therefore, that no very hopeful list of proposed names can be recommended under this system.' This was not surprising, and it is indeed odd how many impossible names were put forward by various committees over the years (whilst at the same time submitting some good ones; and in the above some will be recognised as future RAF names). But somehow the Committee seems to have forgotten the rulings of 'except' for the Engine Companies (p.85). One can imagine the unsuitability of a company of soldiers about to be transported to some end of the Empire in a Handley Page *Cannibal*, and assuredly a de Havilland *Tirwit* would soon be the 'Twit', even if the student had just graduated from a *Tumbler!* So back to the drawing-board.

In October 1926 the committee was again charged to draw up a list of names, and this was duly done but it seems to have been no more successful than the first. Under 'Fighter —

Land' and 'Pursuit' were the suggested names of *Poltergeist* and *Phlogiston* (no 'Anti-'), which prompted many exclamation marks in the file minutes sheet. As 'Fighter — Land' was to have an 'F' prefix, presumably 'P' accounted for *Phlogiston* and *Poltergeist* if nothing more, they would have alliterated splendidly with Parnall. . . In June the Nomenclature Committee wisely decided to make no further list of suggested names, and now not surprisingly recommended that naming should be left to the manufacturers (back to 1918); but on this issue the Air Council did not agree.

By November the 1927 system was approved by the Air Council and forwarded to the SBAC for their consideration. With some reluctance they agreed, with the proviso that the makers' names should be included (back again to 1918). So, finally, the recommendations of the students of the RAF Staff College became the new system:

NOMENCLATURE

No.	AIRCRAFT TYPES	CLASS	LETTER SYSTEM
1.	Fighters — Land	F	(a) all names to
2.	Fighters — Fleet	N	commence with
3.	Bombers Single-engined	P	appropriate 'class'
4.	Bombers Multiple	B	letter.
5.	Bombers Torpedo	M	(b) the names of 2, 5
6.	Army Co-operation	A	& 12 to have
7.	Spotter & Reconnaissance (FAA)	S	maritime significanc
8.	Coastal Reconnaissance	R	(c) the names of
9.	Troop Carriers	C	remainder to have
10.	Training Aircraft	T	non-maritime
11.	General Purpose Aircraft	G	significance.
12.	Fighter Reconnaissance	O	(d) names already in use not to be used.

A very important ruling was that experimental aircraft were only to be given a maker's name and specification, in contrast to the previous 'loophole' whereby all experimental models required names. The practical implication of this was that aircraft would not be given a name until there was an RAF production order, thus lessening the burden on the Nomenclature Committee. The days of splendid and romantic confusion were over.

In spite of the dangers of the game, naming was still an addictive occupation and at this time some suggested Fighter names were: *Firebrand, Foil, Fencer, Flail, Freebooter, Fock, Foray, Fairfax, Ferox, Fiend* and *Fusilier.* In 1930 the name of the famous Hawker *Fury* was chosen from the three Air Ministry suggestions of *Firebrand, Foil* and *Fury.* It appears that there was indeed some fury, as Hawkers under the 1921 system (and excepting the fact that it was not a bird!), in order to alliterate with their name, had chosen *Hornet.* But the Air Ministry won the day and *Hornet* was only used for the prototype. The author had hoped to locate the correspondence between Sir Sydney Camm, chief designer of Hawker's, and the Air Ministry over the *Hornet/Fury* affair, but this was not to be. It is a pity, because from the author's own acquaintance with Sir Sydney arose a healthy respect for that great man's invective when adversely aroused.

Emphasis has lately been on aircraft and engines, but the airship was still endeavouring to establish some aeronautical respectability, and the RAF were engaged in design and structural considerations over these years (it will be recalled that airships started with the Army, were transferred to the

Royal Navy during World War One and then the RAF took over in 1918). Our attention now turns to the R100 and R101 ('R' for 'Rigid') and, although these were civil aircraft, they came under the jurisdiction of the Air Ministry (civil). Other than the 'R' and the number there was no naming system, but in view of their national importance and the public interest, suggested names were being discussed, particularly for the R101. As to the R100 the only suggestion seems to have been that it should be called the *Canada*, but then only when actually in Canada.

To give the public a chance to offer suggestions, the London daily papers were asked, in 1929, to advise them of the opportunity and to write in with names. The response was very positive, and the heavy load of mail rests to this day in the Public Records Office. From these suggestions is listed some of the more interesting names: *Indomitable, Intrepid, Invicta, Indefatigable, Rex, Imperator, Concord, Pax Concordia, Empire Link, Empire Bond, Captain James Cook, St George* (note this, for it will occur again), *Silver Whale, Silver Fish, Goliathan, Dolphin, Fast Clipper* (this from Dennis Martin Finny, aged eleven). Other suggestions included *Heavenly Bodies* and the rivers *Ganges, Tigris* and *Euphrates*. King George V became very interested in all this, and with both the R100 and the 101 in mind, he let his preference be known for the heavenly twins, *Caster* and *Pollux*.

The R101 had come in for some technical criticism, and apprehension was voiced by many in the RAF and Air Ministry that it was unwise to embark on a long trip to India without modifications and further trials; one wise Air Marshal declared that there should be no name until the R101 had successfully flown to India and back. While still a civil aircraft, the R101 flew the RAF ensign, but this was because Lord Thompson, the Secretary of State for Air, was a passenger as was Sir Sefton Brancker. The tragic history of this Titan of the air is well-known and with the burned and tangled remains of R101 lying in Northern France came the end of the rigid airship in Britain. The German *Graf Zeppelin* was a success without mishap, but the larger *Hindenburg* tragically burst into flames whilst attempting a landing in the United States. And it was thus that the R101 had no name to take to its grave.

The search for aircraft names continued, and the following were suggested by the Air Ministry in 1930:

Coastal Reconnaissance (R) (Fancy names indicating travel) *Roamer, Ranger, Raider, Rambler, Raleigh, Richards, Rhodes.*

General Purposes (G) (British and Imperial place names) *Golspie, Guildford, Grantham, Gath, Gaza, Glossop, Goodwood, Garton, Gilgit, Gordon, Graystoke, Garth, Grange, Grantown, Guisborough, Gainsborough.*

Training (T) (Rivers in the British Isles)
Thames, Trent, Tweed, Test, Tay, Tyne, Tees, Tamar, Tor, Tavy, Torridge, Taw.

Whilst 'T' (1927 system) was used for 'Trainers' (as Avro *Tutor* and Hawker *Tomtit*) the 'River' class as suggested by this list was not used, but was adopted much later by Rolls-Royce for gas-turbines — but not, of course, limited to 'T'. The above suggestions were part of a reassessment of the 1927 system, following on from an Air Ministry minute of June 1930: 'Arising out of the objection received. . . to the names selected by the Nomenclature Committee for the Fairey III F with the *Panther* engine, and the Hawker Interceptor, the committee were of the opinion that some change to its methods of selecting names was necessary.' The

changes proposed were not about the structure of the system itself, but the suggestions as to the type of suitable name. In the case of Fighter Fleet, ('N'), they recorded that 'the committee has, so far, been unable to produce a suitable name'. What about a suggestion of sixty years later — *Nimrod*?

A small mystery surrounds the Fairey III F, which on floats and wheels served the RAF long and well. Oddly, it never had a name and, even odder, it never seems to have even had a nickname. The objections previously referred to presumably came from Faireys, but could have arisen in the Ministry. This was in 1930, but back in October 1927 it was minuted that 'Faireys had not submitted a name, and in the absence of a reply, it was proposed to name the aircraft *Griffin*, or as an alternative *Salmon*.' As one is a fabulous beast of Assyrian mythology, with the head and wings of an eagle and the body of a lion (and was the name of a 1917 torpedo bomber), and the other a fish, the dissimilarity belies the cogency of the system. Why Faireys never did submit a name, and why the Air Ministry did not carry out its threat is not known. Fairey III F never had a name, but nevertheless will be found listed in Chapter 5, Part 17 ('The Great Unnamed').

The early signs of a worldwide upheaval were now evident to those who chose to look and had the courage to see, and far-sighted men in industry, Government and the RAF were endeavouring, often with little encouragement, to improve the quality and quantity of aircraft and engines. The 'doldrum days' were coming to an end, and the 'roaring forties' were not far away, and with this sense of change came about a significant change of thought as to the naming of aircraft, particularly as regards Fighters. A new naming system was needed, with a growing awareness of the fearsome years that were to be. The many 'bird' and 'animal' names were 'pretty' and well-loved (much like the Englishman and his dog), but in no way were they *fighting* names.

On 10 July 1930 Air Vice-Marshal Hugh Dowding fired the first shots: 'I am beginning to regret the assent that I have given to the recent proposals by Nomenclature Committee. I have come to the conclusion that our experiment of naming aircraft by the committee is causing waste of time, and is liable to involve us in a system that is not too successful in practice, and also involves us in a system not congenial to the industry which has given us some good names in the past.' By odd coincidence, 1930 was the year that the Nomenclature Committee, as the official language would have it, was 'terminated'; and from an Air Ministry paper of April 1931 came this:

'For many years the naming of aircraft was carried out by agreement between the Ministry and the manufacturers. To each class of name was assigned a general category — the name of a bird, an animal, a place and so on — and as examples, *Grebe, Siskin, Fox, Hyderabad,* and *Southampton* were named under this procedure. In 1926 the Air Staff decided that Service aircraft names did not give sufficient indication of their operational purpose, and a new scheme was drawn up by which the initial letter of the name indicated the purpose of the aircraft. The scheme was adopted as a compromise between the old system and the present method used in America by naming machines using a mixture of letters and figures.

The (1927) scheme was gradually brought into operation, although it was never received with favour by the SBAC. The first machine named under the system was the *Clive*. It is now considered that sufficient names have been produced for the RAF to be generally informed of the procedure.

When the procedure was first introduced, names were chosen by a Nomenclature Committee, but this was found unwieldy, and names are now selected by the AMSR [Air Member for Supply & Research] and applied by him after consultations.

The manufacturer was always consulted in the early selection of names, and we have agreed to consult the Admiralty in the case of names chosen for aircraft for the Fleet type.

The industry has always opposed the (1927) scheme. Under the earlier systems a tradition grew up whereby the names of machines of any particular maker began with the initial letter of the name of the firm, e.g. HP *Hyderabad*, Fairey *Fox*, Hawker *Hart*, Westland *Wapiti*. These names acquired a considerable general publicity and were an asset to the company. This asset is one which the firms are very loath to relinquish, and it must be admitted that the present system of naming RAF aircraft does considerably diminish it.

There are other objections to the scheme. It has often been difficult to find a suitable name within the confines of the initial letter required. For example, the letter 'N' yielded only one possible name — the *Nimrod* — which, in itself, was not an inspired selection. Under the old system (1921) the manufacturers were well pleased, and the Services were not on the whole let down by either appropriateness or bad taste.

It is conceivable that an inspiration is most likely to occur at the firm's works where interest in the new aircraft is most intense. We are also bound to remember that the name of the machine has considerable value for its subsequent sale to other countries.

I am personally convinced that the old system (1921) was better, as it gave more latitude for finding really good names. If the Air Staff would agree that it is unnecessary to have a mnemonic system, I think everyone would be well pleased.'

         — C.D. Galpin

To the Chief of Air Staff, 25 November 1931:
'On thinking this over, I have come to the conclusion that names are, on the whole, better than the system of letters proposed by DCAS [Deputy Chief of Air Staff]. They are less formal and mechanical, and more alive.

Furthermore, I would prefer to return to a system that does not lead to trouble with the industry. After seeing some of the names that the committee have put up, I am compelled to think that the best person to be inspired with a good name is the manufacturer. The best result, in my opinion, does not emanate from a committee sitting in cold blood, but from the enthusiasm accompanying what, after all, is to the manufacturer a new venture in every case; we hardly need be anxious that the makers will choose absurdly. They have no reason to do so and in point of fact no ridiculous name has got into the lists under the old system.'

Under an undertaking of 1918 to consult with the Admiralty in the matter of 'Fleet' names, on 6 January 1932 the Air Council wrote to the Admiralty in order 'to acquaint you with the fact that the system of nomenclature whereby the initial letter of the name indicated the purpose of the aircraft has

proved in practice to be inelastic. For this reason, the Air Council have evolved a new system' and there followed the details of what was to be the 1932 naming system. 18 March 1932. A letter from the Admiralty advising that their Lordships preferred the present (1927) system

8 April 1932 Air Council to Admiralty: 'Air Council fully appreciate the advantages of the mnemonic system, and have in fact endeavoured to put such a system into operation over the past four years. In practice, however, they have found that good and suitable names are extremely difficult to discover under such a limitation. Their Lordships will recollect, for instance, the difficulty after which the last Fleet Fighter was eventually called the *Nimrod*, and that name could not be considered altogether appropriate to maritime use.

In these circumstances they trust their Lordships will not press their view, and the Air Council is fully prepared to consult the Admiralty before finally approving the name for a Fleet Air Arm type.'

27 April 1932, Admiralty to Air Council: '. . . in deference to the views of the Air Council, my Lords will not press their preference for the retention of a nomenclature by initial letter. But in the system that the Air Council propose to adopt it is essential, in their Lordships' view, that four groups of names, each with a definite maritime significant or association, should be assigned to aircraft for the FAA, and their Lordships suggest the following:

FIGHTERS — mythological name — *Icarus, Triton*
FIGHTER REC. — names of seabirds — *Skua*
TORPEDO BOMBERS — names of oceans, seas & estuaries — *Atlantic, Forth*
SPOTTER REC. — names of marine animals — *Grampus, Seal*'

On 22 June 1932, the proposals were referred to the SBAC, and they replied on the same day: 'I would inform you that members of the society have no comments to make thereon' which, in effect, was a reply in the affirmative, albeit unenthusiastic. But it was to produce a list of names many of which are now household names, not only in Britain but in many other countries. Thus was launched the 1932 system, which except for Fighter names went back in essence to the 1918 and 1921 systems. Clearly, the 1927 system was not popular with either the RAF or the manufacturers. The new system was promulgated as:

Class	Category of nomenclature
1. Fighters	General words indicating speed, activity or aggressiveness.
2. Bombers:	Animals (except felidae).
(a) Day	
(b) Army co-operation	Classical names.
(c) Night	Inland towns of the British Empire or towns associated with the RAF.
(d) General purpose	British historical names.
(e) Transport	General towns and seaports of the British Empire.
3. Flying Boats	Coastal towns and seaports of the British Empire.
4. Fleet Air Arm:	
(a) Fighters	Mythological names.
(b) Fighter Reconnaissance	Names of sea birds.
(c) Torpedo Bombers	Names of oceans, seas and estuaries.
(d) Spotter Reconnaissance	Names of marine animals.
5. Training	Words indicating tuition, and places of education.

An addendum to this concerned engines:

Rolls-Royce	Land-birds e.g. Kestrel, Buzzard
Armstrong-Siddeley	Felidae (Cats) e.g. Jaguar, Panther
Bristol	Planets & Constellations e.g. Jupiter, Pegasus
Napier	Arms & Weapons e.g. Rapier

This is all but the same as the 1918 system, but now Rolls-Royce was 'land-birds' and not 'birds of prey'. This should have been 'land-birds of prey', for there had been the 1930 Hawker *Osprey*, but this name was presumably accepted as it was a *sea*-bird of prey to which Rolls-Royce presumably did not object, or were overruled if they did! Another item of note was that 'aircraft in classes 1-4 adapted as training machines will be named according to their classification with the addition of the symbol "T".'

Compared to the traumas of the previous systems, the 1932 system seemed to have required a minimum of paperwork and few meetings; indeed, there probably was not enough time for anything else. And there was also some determination on the part of the Air Ministry, as may be seen from this memo: 'The Assistant Director of Research & Development is responsible for dealing with manufacturers in regard to nomenclature, and any attempts to introduce unauthorised names are to be immediately reported to him.' There followed two amendments to the 1932 system:

a. Spotter Reconnaissance Aircraft
   Names of fishes have been added to those of marine animals as the choice amongst the latter is being rapidly exhausted.

b. Names of dog tribes (Canes) have been added to the Felidae (cats) previously allotted to Messrs Armstrong-Siddeley for their engines, for similar reasons.

There was a major change to the (1932) system in March 1937 with the Air Ministry deciding that 'for purposes of naming these three classes of bomber aircraft (light, medium and heavy) in future there shall be one category of nomenclature, viz. 'place-names' — either inland towns of the British Empire or associated with British history — and that the class letter for specification shall be 'B'. Now there were to be neither bird nor animal names for RAF aircraft, apart from the Fleet Air Arm with seabirds and sea animals. The present (1966) *Harrier* takes the story right back to 1918 (except that should have been a Rolls-Royce engine) so the birds have not yet been consigned to history, and the tradition did indeed continue in the Fleet Air Arm (*Fulmar*, *Skua*, *Gannet* etc.).

With regard to the Bombers with 'B', *Bombay* already existed under the 1932 system and *Blenheim* was an Austrian village (Blindheim), where the Duke of Marlborough won his famous battle (see 'The Classics'). In the event, the bomber with the 'B' was shortlived, as witness *Wellington*, *Hampden* and so on. The initial letter rule had already been ignored, and it is surprising that it was revived, if only for bombers.

Another interesting case-history concerns the name *Valentia* which was first used by Vickers for the 1918 flying boat, but which did not go into RAF service. The name was originally *Valencia*, presumably an error somewhere along the line for that was a Spanish port and province and in no way part of the RAF 1918 naming system. There is a *Valencia* in Trinidad & Tobago which is British, but as a fishing village it hardly seems to qualify. As to *Valentia*, this was a British province established by Rome in 368 AD, and no other explanation for the name has been found.

The second *Valentia* was a transport of 1934, and the name was again a source of some controversy. The Air Ministry wanted *Victory* (but what about the Royal Navy and HMS *Victory*?) to which Vickers did not agree. The Air Ministry then suggested *Vancouver*, but Vickers pointed out the possible confusion with a Canadian Vickers flying boat of this name. Vickers suggested *Vindhya*, an Indian mountain range, but the Air Ministry then proposed *Valentia*, arguing that the previous flying boat of that name had not seen RAF service (which was a strange argument, as duplicated names have not been uncommon). It was then finally agreed, and *Valentia* it was.

With war all but inevitable, the expansion of the Armed Forces convulsed the industries concerned, and now the RAF fighters would be coming forward with names indicating speed, aggression and activity, and the bombers with British or Empire place-names (not entirely new, as may be seen from earlier systems). Names now better reflected their purpose, especially those of the fighters. Perhaps this period of 1918 to 1939, and certainly up to 1932, was for the Empire and the Armed Forces a time of unreal calm. These were the fighter days of *Ara*, *Bobolink*, *Blackbird*, *Snipe*, *Siskin*, *Nightjar* and *Wagtail*. The rise of the European dictators saw the change to *Bulldog*, *Gladiator*, *Fury* and *Gauntlet*, all indicative of the looming shadows of another war. It may have been but a subconscious awareness for a more dangerous world to come, but that tumult was to be reflected in the new names that would now know the new, harsh reality. The halcyon days were over.

And so came 1939, with a system that made one great change to that of 1932, as may be seen:

Fighters	General words indicating speed, activity or aggressiveness.
Bombers	Place-names — an inland town of the British Empire or associated with British history.
Army Co-operation	Classical words.
General Purpose Torpedo	British historical names (including general reconnaissance land planes).
Transport	Counties or districts of the British Empire.
Flying Boats	Coastal towns and seaports of the British Empire.
Trainers and Target Tugs	Words indicating tuition and places of education (but not Air Force training establishments).
Gliders	Historic military leaders.
Naval Aircraft	As proposed by the Admiralty.

The great change lies in the last line — 'Naval Aircraft — as proposed by the Admiralty' — for in May the Fleet Air Arm (which was the Royal Naval Air Service 1914–1918) came under Admiralty control. On 27 June 1939 'it was agreed that in future FAA names should be the responsibility of Admiralty, but within the categories already agreed'. There followed a lengthy correspondence with their Lordships, who were anxious that the RAF should not use names of particular RN interest or precedent; in their own words: 'lists of names with naval histories which the Admiralty desire should not be used by the Royal Air Force'. There followed a list, which reads like a potted history of the Royal Navy:

ADMIRAL NAMES *Anson**, *Barham*, *Benbow*, *Boscawen*, *Collingwood*, *Drake*, *Hawke*, *Hawkins*, *Hood*, *Howe*,

Nelson, Raleigh, St Vincent, Vernon. (*too late; it first flew in 1933)

NAVY BATTLE NAMES *Aboukir, Barfleur, Camperdown, Nile, Trafalgar.*

CLASSICAL NAMES *Agamemnon*(T), *Ajax*(T), *Aphrodite, Apollo, Bellerophon*(T), *Charybdis, Endymion, Galatea, Hercules, Hermione, Jason, Mars*(T), *Neptune*(T), *Niobe, Naiad, Pegasus, Proserpine, Scylla, Venus, Vulcan, Minator.*

QUALITIES *Arrogant, Defiance, Excellent, Formidable, Glorious, Illustrious, Impregnable, Indefatigable, Indomitable, Inflexible, Intrepid, Invincible, Implacable*(T), *Magnificent, Majestic, Powerful, Renown, Repulse, Resolution, Retribution, Revenge, Sanspareil, Superb, Swiftsure*(T), *Terrible, Terror, Triumph, Undaunted, Vengeance, Victorious, Victory*(T), *Vindictive.*

ELIZABETHAN NAMES *Bonaventure, Dreadnought*(T), *Warspite.*

NAMES OF STARS *Canopus, Sirius*(T), *Orion.*

MISCELLANEOUS *Enchantress*(T), *Leviathan, Royal Oak, Temeraire*(T).

WARRIOR TYPE *Centurion, Colossus*(T), *Conqueror, Devastation, Gladiator, Thunderer, Warrior.*

(T) denotes ships that fought at the Battle of Trafalgar.

The Air Council assured the Board of Admiralty that such maritime names would not be used, but politely pointed out that *Anson* would have to be an exception. However, the RAF did use: *Hercules* (was already a Bristol engine, as was *Pegasus*); *Vulcan* (first flew in 1952, when presumably the agreement was no longer in being?); *Defiant* (had first flown in 1937, and was named under the 1932 system); *Orion* (was a 1928 and 1941 Bristol engine); *Gladiator* first flown in 1934, and named under the 1932 system. The 'as proposed by Admiralty' introduced in the 1939 system was, one suspects, something to do with a former naval person who was to come back as First Lord of the Admiralty and then become Prime Minister for the war years. The index makes reference to him in 1913, with a Sopwith *Tabloid* nicknamed the 'Churchill', in which he received his pilot training.

So, World War One now led to World War Two with only twenty-one years of peace between. The *Snipe* had given way to the *Spitfire* and the *Hart* to the *Hurricane*.

Part 5 — 1939–1946

'The time will come when thou shalt lift thine eyes
To watch a long drawn battle in the skies,
While aged peasants, too amazed for words
Stare at the Flying Fleets of wond'rous birds.
England, so long Mistress of the Sea,
Where wind and wave confess her sovereignty,
Her ancient triumphs shall yet on high, shall bear,
And reign, the Sovereign of the conquered air.'
— Gray's *Luna Habitabilis, 1737*

AS FROM THE commencement of World War Two in 1939, the naming of aircraft became the responsibility of the Ministry of Aircraft Production, as in the previous war it had been that of the Ministry of Munitions. In general, the 1932 scheme was

followed, but some difficulties caused detail changes. One of these was a slight confusion as to what was exactly 'mythological' and what 'classical'. Another — unforeseen — complication was the use of American aircraft by the RAF. (An aircraft might have an American experimental number, a US Army name and a US Navy name passed to the British to have an RAF name — and then have it passed to Russia, to be claimed as an original aircraft. . .) American aircraft were originally supposed to abide by the rules, but preference was allowed to American districts and States, and sometimes the original name was retained.

The details are noted below, and are extracts of an MAP memorandum sent to the SBAC for member firms.

NOTES ON PROCEDURE FOR SELECTING NAMES
(AND MARK NUMBERS)
1. Experimental aircraft, unless derived from an existing type, will be designated by a title composed of the designer's name and the specification number (e.g. Handley Page B5/36).
2. A name will be allotted to aircraft of a new basic type as soon as it is evident that a production order will be placed. The name will be selected from the categories of nomenclature set out below:

Fighters	General words indicating speed, activity or aggressiveness.
Bombers	Place names — an inland town of the British Empire or associated with British history.
Army Co-operation	Classical words.
General Purpose Torpedo	British historical names (including general reconnaissance land planes).
Transport	Counties or districts of the British Empire.
Flying Boats	Coastal towns and seaports of the British Empire.
Trainers and Target Tugs	Words indicating tuition and places of education (but not Air Force training establishments).
Gliders	Historic military leaders.
Naval Aircraft	As proposed by the Admiralty.

3. In the case of American aircraft allotted to Britain, and Canadian aircraft built for MAP, fullest consideration will be given to the wishes of the relevant authorities should they press for the adoption of names not within these categories. Endeavours should be made, however, to follow as closely as possible the basic rules, but names with an American or Canadian flavour will be very appropriate. For instance, American-built transports should not necessarily be named after a county or district of the British Empire, but would preferably be named after a district or State of the United States of America. The US Army Air Corps advised that there was no need to inform the US manufacturers of this ruling, but the British Air Commis-

sion in Washington suggested that it may perhaps be politic!

That names and naming system were no trivial pursuit will now be evident, and the following document is typical of the issues and topics of the day to be discussed and decided:

Agenda of a Meeting to be held on 27 November 1941 to recommended for CRD's approval a revised system of designation of types of aircraft

1. To consider whether any re-grouping of the present basic categories for naming aircraft as regards the name proper is necessary (these several categories are listed in Appendix A overleaf).

2. To consider:

   (a) DAD/RDA's approval for amplifying the name proper by reference to its operation role, e.g. *Spitfire* PR, *Mosquito* B, *Mosquito* F, *Wellingtons* and *Beaufighters* used by coastal command, *Lysander* TT.

   (b) Alternative proposals for denoting the operational role.

   (c) Whether the distinguishing letters should invariably be associated with the name proper.

3. To consider whether mark numbers should continue to be allocated by reference to the principles set out in AMDP Notice to Branches No.188, i.e. a single definite change of material significance from the operational or airworthiness points of view or any change in performance, interchangeability or utility as to make it necessary to segregate the different types in service.

4. To consider DAD/RDA's proposal that suffixes should be reserved for non-inherent differences which it is necessary to discriminate for DGO or DGE purposes, or for the purposes of 41 Group, and if so, whether the suffix thus allotted should invariably be used.

5. To consider whether the reservation of mark numbers for preliminary investigations should be more widely adopted, mark number being officially allocated only when there is clear evidence that the type will go into production.

6. To confirm that all requests for new mark numbers should be initiated through Local Technical Committees.

7. To consider DAD/RDA's proposal that conversion DIS's and conversion appendices to publications should be freely accepted for new mark numbers and whether this should extend to changes in name to designate the operation role.

8. To consider DAD/RDA's proposed use of the term 'nonstandard' to designate small quantities of aircraft of a transitional design.

9. To consider the necessity for notifying the Service of aircraft on the Secret List and if necessary, whether this should be done through Air Ministry Confidential Orders. (Note: Aircraft are normally transferred from the Secret to the Official Use Only List two months prior to their delivery to the Service, in order to enable relevant publications to be issued in sufficient time.)

With this agenda was Appendix A, which was the 1939 naming system, but with another change under 'Fleet Air Arm':

(a) Fighters   Names having the prefix 'Fire'

(b) Reconnaissance   Names of seabirds
    and Fighter
    Dive Bombers

(c) Torpedo   Names of oceans, seas and estuaries.
    Bombers

(d) Torpedo Spotter   Names of Marine Animals and Fishes.
    Reconnaissance
    and Light
    Reconnaissance
    seaplanes

What's in a name? In military hardware more than the name itself, for 'mark numbers' 'prefix' and 'suffix' become an inevitable part, and some little space must be given to this less romantic but important aspect of the naming game. Beyond the following it is not intended to go further into this large subject.

Mark numbers were, in fact, used as early as about 1911 and introduced by the Royal Aircraft Factory at Farnborough, who borrowed the convention from the Army and Navy. In addition to the name or designation, a number such as 'BE2' meant that it was the second of the BE series, and then an added letter such as 'BE2c' indicated a modification of that series. About 1917 the true 'mark no.' in the form of Roman numerals was used to show the variations of the basic type, and the letter was as before. The manufacturers had their own systems, which basically continue to present times, all aircraft (including projects) having a consecutive numeral.

In 1939, the modification letters were dropped except to indicate a change of armament — such as *Hurricane* II a, b, c and d. The war saw aircraft being used for quite unexpected purposes — a de Havilland *Tiger Moth* might have been accurately described as a 'patrol bomber', and fighters were used for every conceivable purpose. This led to a prefix being used before the mark number.

RAF and Naval Types

C	Freighter (Communications)	GA	Ground Attacker
F	Fighter	GR	General Reconnaissance
HF	High Altitude Fighter	BR	Bomber Reconnaissance*
LF	Low Altitude Fighter	FR	Fighter Reconnaissance*
NF	Night Fighter	PR	Photographic Reconnaissar
B	Bomber	T	Trainer
FB	Fighter Bomber	TT	Target Tug
TB	Torpedo Bomber	DB	Dive Bomber
TF	Torpedo Fighter	ASR	Air Sea Rescue

* Army Co-operation types only

Naval Types only

2F	Two-seat Fighter
TR	Torpedo Reconnaissance
TD	Torpedo Dive Bomber
SR	Seaplane Reconnaissance
AR	Amphibian Reconnaissance

AOP Air Observation Post

AS Anti-submarine strike/search

Bound up with 'mark' numbers are the serial numbers of individual aircraft, but this also is a subject very adequately covered in other books, and for which please see Chapter 8 (Bibliography).

Reverting to the 1939 system, to last until 1949, there were two categories which required some ruling: General Purpose Torpedo — British historical names and Gliders — Historic military leaders.

2 August 1939: 'This file deals with the name to be allotted to the Armstrong-Whitworth Composite (which was to become the *Albemarle*). It comes within the category of General Reconnaissance and it should have a name of importance in British history, as for example *Botha* or *Beaufort*.

A principle now arises, and I would like you to obtain CAS's ruling on the following point: Are we to branch out into the names of distinguished RAF officers? If the answer is 'yes', should they be only those who are deceased? Hitherto we have only selected names of deceased people. Such a ruling would, of course, confine lists to a very small number of names, whereas firms like a large selection in that we have in the past agreed to some degree of alliteration.

It seems to me that as a general rule we should avoid the names of famous Army officers if they are only recently deceased, e.g. Allenby. On the other hand I am not willing to accept the name *Albemarle*. He had not, so far as I know, a very distinguished record either as a general at Waterloo or as a Member of Parliament!

However, I won't worry you with details provided you can obtain for me some ruling as regards the use of names of distinguished RAF officers, or recently distinguished and deceased Army officers, both of whom I should like to see ruled out.'

The required answer was soon forthcoming: 'I have discussed your minute with CAS (Air Chief Marshal Sir Charles Portal). He is not at all in favour of using the names of RAF or Army deceased officers.' Yet *Albemarle* (General Monk who became the 1st Duke in 1660) it was, and alliterating with Armstrong-Whitworth was probably in his favour, despite the query as to his distinguished service; and although it was before Portal became CAS, there was the precedent of General Wellesley who became the Duke of Wellington, and whose distinguished career both as a general and as a parliamentarian, including being Prime Minister, could not be queried. But then Wellington was also a New Zealand and [Empire] town! In these Air Ministry Minutes, only the Army and RAF were mentioned, but why not a Royal Navy officer (and there was the precedent of Admiral Anson)?

With 'lease-lend' and the United States's later official entry into the war after the 1941 Japanese raid on Pearl Harbor, US aircraft were to arrive in Europe and North Africa in large numbers, and those consigned to or bought for the RAF then posed the question of naming, although this had been touched upon in the 1939 naming system. US practice had been for letters (P=Pursuit, B=Bomber) and numbers, but there were some names, although not always the same for Navy and Army Air Force, and some of these saw service with the RAF and FAA under original and/or new –British'

names, but sometimes of American place-names! As we shall see, it can become fairly confusing.

A British Air Commission had been set up in Washington, and they wished to advise American Manufacturers and the US government of the RAF naming system. A letter was duly despatched on 29 July and was basically the 1932 (as amended in 1939) system, but with examples of type names as 'samples'. Nothing is to be learned by repeating the system, but the 'sample' names chosen have some interest:

FIGHTER — *Spitfire*; BOMBER — *Blenheim*; ARMY CO-OP — *Lysander*; GENERAL PURPOSE — *Beaufort*; TRANSPORT — *Bombay*; FLYING BOAT — *Sunderland*; FLEET AIR ARM FIGHTER *Firefly, Firebrand, Seafire* (reserve names — *Firecrest, Fireflame*); FIGHTER REC. & DIVE BOMBER — *Skua*; TORPEDO BOMBER — *Baffin*; TORPEDO SPOTTER REC. – *Swordfish*; TRAINING — *Magister*; GLIDER — *Hengist*; ENGINES — *Kestrel* & *Merlin*, *Cheetah* & *Panther*, *Hercules* & *Pegasus*, and *Sabre*.

On 26 December 1942, Sir Charles Portal wrote to the Prime Minister: 'I have been considering the implications of the ruling given in your Minute D 214/2 of 12 December. I agree that types of aircraft are much easier to remember by name, but I do not think that names can ever entirely supersede numbers. Moreover, to apply your ruling to all British correspondence could present difficulties. There are, unfortunately, very often very considerable differences between American and British versions of the same basic type of aircraft. Furthermore, in some cases a particular American aircraft has two British names, and conversely two different American types may have the same British name. Thus a P-40 can either be a *Tomahawk* or a *Kittyhawk* according to the particular modifications, whilst both the A-28 and A-29 are called by us the *Hudson*. In general correspondence it would, of course, be possible in most cases to give the equivalent British name to American aircraft, but in any correspondence of a technical nature it would, I fear, lead only to confusion. I would suggest therefore that your ruling might be modified in the following way: in all British operating reports emanating from the UK, names of American aircraft are to be used with the American code and number in brackets after the name. The Prime Minister took the point, and summarily issued an amendment: 'American designations of US aircraft are much more difficult to remember than names. In all British correspondence emanating from the UK the names of American aircraft (in UK service) are to be used, with the American code and number in brackets after the name, thus — *Kittyhawk* (P-40).

An Air Ministry memo has already been quoted on the use of names for American aircraft to be used by the British forces.

American aircraft in the RAF and FAA made a significant contribution to the total war strength and capability of Britain. Whilst the many types of aircraft and engine and their names are historically part of this Chapter covering 1939 to 1949, the subject deserves a section of its own, which will be found as Chapter 5 Part 18. This will also account for this present chapter being somewhat slimmer than might have been expected; and indeed, there is little else to tell about the 1939 system as such. There was, of course, a mass of minutes, memoranda and meetings, together with correspondence on naming, as would be expected from so large a variety of aircraft, covering seven years of war. The 1939 system worked well, needed little amendment, and with the co-operation of the USA was happily incorporated.

The Total Index details the names and nicknames (if any) of all aircraft and engines. The date of the first flight will indicate the historical period, and the thirty 'Classic' aircraft and six engines will be given a fuller account in Chapter 6.

The naming of two RAF aircraft would be a fitting end to this World War Two story, the first being that of the Avro *Lincoln*, a scaled-up *Lancaster* intended for the Pacific War against the Japanese. In 1944, a shortlist of three names was considered:

Sandringham — 'a great and dignified name indicative of the Home Counties, and the heart of the home country, of the British Empire, and its Sovereign' (It will be noted that even war-hardened Air Marshals can wax lyrical when a name has to be considered. . .)

Stafford — 'A courteous gesture to the Minister of Aircraft production [Sir Stafford Cripps], during whose term of office the aircraft was born.'

Lincoln — 'so be it, a good-sounding name. At the same time, when another new type comes along we ought not to forget that England is not the only country in these islands. The Admiralty never forget Scotland, Wales and Ireland when they're naming ships. It would be a courteous gesture to the chief executive (Sir Archibald Sinclair) to name the next bomber after a Scottish, and if possible, an Aberdonian town.'

Having ruled that distinguished and deceased RAF and Army officers should not be the subject of aircraft names, presumably the same reasoning was applied to politicians; which, entirely out of chronological sequence, recalls a naming anomaly with the old rule that RAF stations should never be used as aircraft names, a possible source of coding error in correspondence and signals. How, then, was the *Hinaidi* so named — an RAF airfield near Baghdad in Iraq? or *Sarafand* — an RAF airfield near Tel Aviv in Israel? Or *Heyford* — near Upper and Lower Heyford?

Undoubtedly the most memorable name of World War Two, and also thereafter, was that of *Spitfire*, and so the most appropriate one with which to end this Chapter.

On 8 June 1936 a short but historic memo was sent to the Chief of Air Staff: 'You will wish to be aware that AMRD has approved the name *Spitfire* for the single-seater aeroplane under manufacture by Messrs Supermarine Works (Vickers) Ltd to specification F7/30 (F37/34 modified).' (On 7 July 1936 a similar memo was sent to CAS regarding the Hawker *Hurricane:* 'A name, and also an omen')

In 1943 there appeared the *Spitfire* 21, the fighter now re-engineered and with the Rolls-Royce 'Griffon' — but not the first mark to have the engine. Several senior RAF officers pressed the Air Ministry to consider a new name for the Mk 21 or *Super Spitfire*, suggesting that *Spitfire* was now an outmoded name for what was now an outmoded fighter; furthermore, morale in Fighter Command would be improved by a new name. The persuasion was sufficient for the Air Ministry to study the matter, and the outcome was to propose two alternatives – a 'V' (Vickers) and an 'S' (Supermarine) set of names. The 'V' shortlist was: *Victor, Valiant, Vampire, Venom, Viper,* and *Vitesse;* the 'S' shortlist was: *Superfire, Super Spitfire, Speedfire, Skyfire, Sapphire, Scorpion, Scimitar, Stormcock, Spiteful* and *St George* (shades of the fated R 101 which was so nearly named St George). Although Supermarine was a wholly-owned subsidiary of Vickers, they took strong objection to the 'V' proposal, and on this matter wished to be considered as entirely separate

from Vickers. The view prevailed, and this left the 'S' alternative and the final shortlist was down to *Spiteful* and *St George*.

On 24 March 1944, the Secretary of State for Air opted for *Spiteful*, but Sir Charles Portal as Chief of Air Staff roundly declared: 'We intend this aircraft to rule the skies. The name *Spitfire* has won world renown, it is a dignified name and one of good omen.' And so it was.

Whilst thus praising the *Spitfire*, and rightly so, it may be recorded that there was never a call for a new name for the *Hurricane*, and so far as the Battle of Britain was concerned, it would not have been won unless both these immortals had not fought together. The one name cannot imagined without the other.

'The gratitude of every home in our island, in our Empire, and indeed throughout the world, except in the abodes of the guilty, goes out to the British airmen who, undaunted by odds, unwearied in their constant challenge and mortal danger, are turning the tide of the world war by their prowess and by their devotion.

Never in the field of human conflict was so much owed by so many to so few.'

— Winston Churchill, in the House of Commons.

Part 6 — 1946–1990

'There be them that have left a name behind them, and were honoured in their generation.'
— Old Testament

THE GREATER PART of this period was the Cold War, and the *Harrier*, illustrated above, recalls the Falklands War and the fact that a bird is again an RAF name — and in particular a bird of prey! And as the engine is a *Pegasus* — the flying horse of Greek mythology — Bristol/Rolls-Royce may share a feeling of pride with Hawker/British Aerospace.

World War Two saw names aplenty, but with the ever-increasing cost of technology and that technology so dramatically enhancing the destructive capability of a single aircraft, there have inevitably been fewer aircraft types and fewer names.

With the exception of the 'V' bombers in the 1950, and the later aircraft such as *Tornado, Jaguar* and *Harrier*, the well-established 1932/39 system (somewhat amended in 1949) remained basically the same. This can only be substantiated as a statement by consequence rather than cause, on account of the 'thirty year' rule which precludes sight of government papers back to 1960. Such files remain in the Ministry of Defence or with the Public Records Office as 'closed', or have been destroyed, and where a particular file spans overlapping years, such as a file marked '1955–1962', then that will also be closed, the closing date being the latter. However, the thirty year rule does not disallow some inspired (?) guesswork — and there have not been too many names at which to guess.

An amended 1939 system was promulgated in 1949; it was substantially the same, but with two subtle changes:
BOMBERS — no longer British Empire; now British Commonwealth
HELICOPTERS — Trees, which takes us right back to the February 1918 nomenclature system. And thus *Sycamore*, its rotating seeds being Nature's nearest approach to the helicopter or autogiro principle.

The Bristol *Sycamore* was a one-off name. Even the most

comprehensive arboreal encyclopaedia does not list *Belvedere*, or even *Puma* as a 'tree'. But the Ministry of Munitions (1918) had to be satisfied that there was a 'tree' name even if it took about sixty years. . . they are still waiting for a 'shrub' or a 'rock'.

There was a further Ministry document of March 1953 dealing with naming and mark (not Mach) numbers, prefixes and suffixes, but nothing was substantially added or subtracted so far as actual names were concerned. And that is the last 'naming system' known, and as noted, any later are 'closed'.

The series of naming systems given in this chapter are assembled as a set and printed at the beginning of the Total Index. This will make for quick cross reference when looking up an aircraft or engine. As an example, *Lysander* was named under the 1932 system, and what that infers can be seen by reference to that system. In this case, the 'notes' inform that he was a Spartan general, but such information may not be given in all cases.

Whilst this book sets out to deal with military aircraft, many were civil in origin, some only for a short while and generally in RAF colours and with a serial number. This qualification, however, ensures their inclusion, at least in the indices. But it is interesting to note that the Ministry also keeps a watch on the purely civil, as in January 1949: 'the de Havilland Company have allocated the name *Comet* to the DH.106 civil aircraft', and which in due course was to have a military application. This was the second DH *Comet*, the first being the 1930s Racer which won, in its class, the McRobertson Race from the UK to Australia, and which still exists. In that first *Comet*, with the later DH *Albatross*, can be seen the beginnings of the *Mosquito*.

The 'military application' was, of course, the *Nimrod* (still serving) and the author takes a modest pride in having suggested the name (despite the Air Marshal's disparagement of the name for the 1931 Hawker FAA Fighter). Being a mixture of *Comet* and *Nimrod*, it could only be known as *Conrod*, and now with the bulbous forward radar housing it certainly has a 'big end'. Before the name *Nimrod* was accepted, an original suggestion had been the *Maritime Comet*, but this was then thought too cumbersome, and it was decided to compile a shortlist consisting of *Plymouth, Osprey, Cormorant, Slessor, Trenchard, Bideford, Calshot, Albatross* and *Drake. Trenchard* and *Slessor* were disallowed by the Chief of Air Staff, with the reminder of the wartime ruling. *Osprey* was thought not to be maritime (an error as this bird of prey feeds on fish found in rivers and usually close to the sea, and the 1930 Hawker *Osprey* was allowed as it did not clash with the 1918 Rolls-Royce ruling in that this was a *sea*bird of Prey. As for *Cormorant*, one member of the Air Board (it was no longer the Air Council) remarked that if his knowledge of ornithology was correct it is a bird which has a habit of diving into the sea.

Albatross was unlucky to shoot at (which might have been no bad thing), and *Drake* was an admiral, or at least a sea dog, and there was an RN barracks named HMS *Drake*. Furthermore, it would undoubtedly end up by being called the 'Duck', and *Drake* was on the 'please don't' list sent by their Lordships to the Air Council in 1939. *Plymouth, Bideford* and *Calshot* were 'seaside towns', sometimes known as 'ports', and the 'Maritime Comet' had neither floats nor hull — which disposed of the entire shortlist.

At about this time, the author met Lord Shackleton at a Council dinner at the Royal Aeronautical Society, and likes to think that the rest is history. *Nimrod*, of course, is the 'mighty hunter' of the Bible (to be more precise, he was also a King and may be found in Genesis 10:8-9). And 'nimrod', with a little 'n' means 'a skilled hunter'.

The old ruling that Trainers were to be named after educational places or people continued, and in 1948 the Percival T16/48 was being considered for a suitable name. The final shortlist was: *Cambridge, Pembroke* (College), *Trinity, Claire, Keble, Chancellor, Warden, Principal, Preceptor, Dean* and *Graduate*. To this was later added *Provost*, to form the final shortlist with *Pembroke*.

Provost it became, and later *Jet Provost*.

When the *Meteor* II followed the I which had first flown in 1944, the subject of a new name was considered at some length, and many names were suggested, but, as with the *Spitfire* 21 (see Part five), the new name was challenged and this time it was the Commander-in-Chief, Fighter Command, who urged that *Meteor* was an historic name and the RAF's first operation jet, to which the Chief of Air Staff quite agreed.

The Hawker F/3 and the Percival C18/49 came up for nomenclatural scrutiny in 1951. The Hawker Fighter was suggested as *Harasser, Hatchet, Hero, Hydra, Halberd, Hammer, Harpoon, Hasty, Havoc, Hound, Hawk* and *Hunter*, the last two being on the final shortlist.

The Secretary of State had his own preference for *Falcon*, but the final choice was *Hunter*, a matter of satisfaction to Hawkers as this was their own preference. So *Hunters*, mighty and otherwise, were in the ascendant. The Percival Transport, formerly the civil *Prince* was suggested as *Prospect, Peebles, Northumbria, Pennine, Portland* and *Plymouth* (someone with a vested interest here), with a final list of *Bedford* and *Pembroke*, which would have pleased the College, the Welsh seaport in Pembrokeshire (now a part of Dyfed), towns in Canada and New Zealand, and not least those who have Welsh Corgi dogs, known as 'Pembrokes'.

In 1954 the Supermarine *Scimitar* was chosen from a list including *Aggressor, Agile, Nightrider* and *Nightspear; Scimitar* was a previous Short Brothers Fighter of 1933. Clearly, the subject of naming systems and names still engaged the higher echelons of the Ministry of Defence (RAF), and these extracts from the minutes (1951) show up the reasoning of the times: 'It is accepted that the Air Council must make the final decision on the name to be given to a new aircraft. It is also most desirable that the name should be given at the earliest stage in the aircraft's life and it would therefore be convenient administratively if the Air Council staff had the responsibility of seeking an Air Council decision on the name to be adopted.' A point that should, perhaps, have been made before. It was not just a name that was being decided, for from that decision stemmed a great mass of necessary, even essential, paperwork: pilot's notes, maintenance and spares schedules, technical manuals, and so on, and all this takes time. So, the earlier the decision, the more time to complete the papers.

The minutes continue: 'Naming of new aircraft . . . it has become a tradition, particularly of Fighter types, to choose an alliterative name to match that of the manufacturer. Although past practice has contributed to building up that tradition, it has the drawback of being unnecessarily restrictive and, in the case of Fighter names in particular, has ruled out a number of outstandingly suitable names. I suggest that the time has come to break away, and to select names on their merits.'

Fifty Years, Fifty Types,

of RNAS, RFC, and RAF Aircraft and Weapons

1 Delta Airship
2 Bleriot Monoplane
3 BE2
4 FE2b
5 Avro 504
6 Sopwith Camel
7 Short Seaplane
8 Bristol Fighter
9 DH4
10 Handley Page 0/400
11 Fairey Flycatcher
12 SE5A
13 Vickers Virginia
14 Hawker Hurricane
15 Boulton Paul Defiant
16 Armstrong Whitworth Siskin
17 Boulton & Paul Sidestrand
18 Hawker Furies
19 Avro Rota
20 DH Tiger Moth
21 Avro Anson
22 Bristol 138A, Height Record, 193 53,937 ft

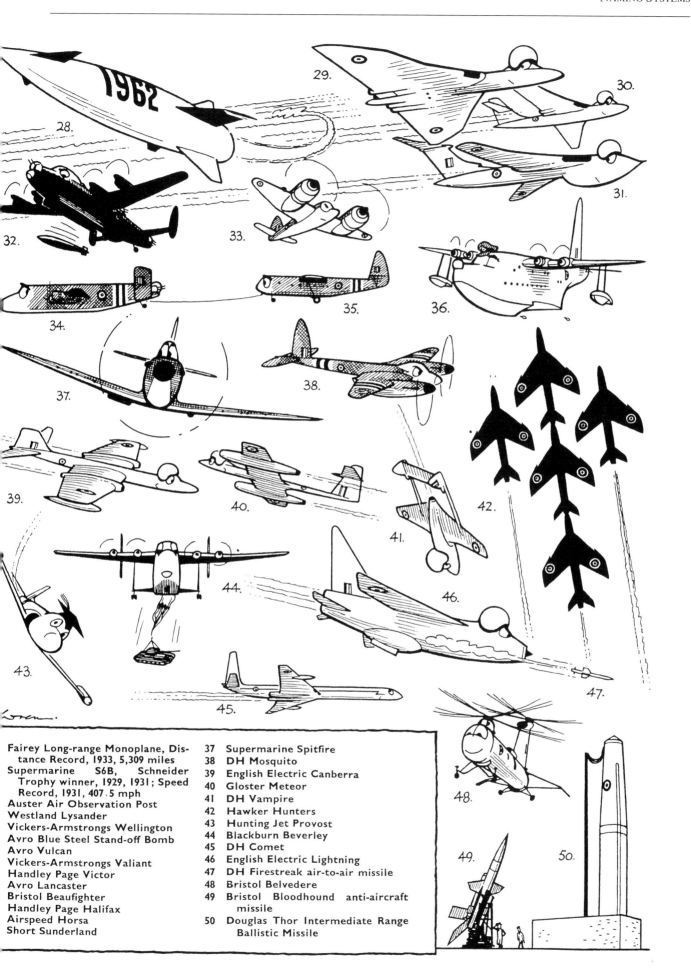

Fairey Long-range Monoplane, Distance Record, 1933, 5,309 miles
Supermarine S6B, Schneider Trophy winner, 1929, 1931; Speed Record, 1931, 407.5 mph
Auster Air Observation Post
Westland Lysander
Vickers-Armstrongs Wellington
Avro Blue Steel Stand-off Bomb
Avro Vulcan
Vickers-Armstrongs Valiant
Handley Page Victor
Avro Lancaster
Bristol Beaufighter
Handley Page Halifax
Airspeed Horsa
Short Sunderland

37 Supermarine Spitfire
38 DH Mosquito
39 English Electric Canberra
40 Gloster Meteor
41 DH Vampire
42 Hawker Hunters
43 Hunting Jet Provost
44 Blackburn Beverley
45 DH Comet
46 English Electric Lightning
47 DH Firestreak air-to-air missile
48 Bristol Belvedere
49 Bristol Bloodhound anti-aircraft missile
50 Douglas Thor Intermediate Range Ballistic Missile

The Gloster F4/48 was considered for a name in 1952, suggestions being *Gallant, Guardian, Squall, Gladiator, Gauntlet, Glory, Gamecock, Gnat, Gadfly, Dart, Hart* and *Wizard*, most of which were names already in use. The Admiralty had asked that *Gladiator* (before Gloster used the name in 1934) and *Glory* be reserved for RN ships. A secondary set of suggestions were *Gannet, Goshawk, Arrow* and *Spearhead*, so they decided to call it *Javelin*. One member of the Air Council wrote in the file memo sheet: 'Squall, a phenomenon that comes upon one quickly, is extremely painful for anything that lies in its path, and is of limited duration before it runs out of motive power.' Whether this was a reflection on internal politics, or an oblique and implied criticism, or perhaps a doubt on the *Javelin*'s range or adequacy of ammunition, shall never be known. It became known as the 'Harmonious Dragmaster'

As for Bomber names, 1952 saw the beginning of some new thinking: 'I strongly oppose the suggestion that we should continue to call our bombers after towns. Most of our bomber aircraft have dull and stodgy names. With the advent of Delta Wing aircraft which are fast and nimble weapons of war, I suggest we strike out into new fields. The Vickers *Valiant*, although it is not a Delta Wing is, I suggest, well named. For the Avro B35 I propose such names as *Adamant, Adventure, Aggressor, Harasser, Harrier* and *Huskey*. The use of these and similar names would do must to remove the idea that still persists in the mind of the ignorant and the uninitiated that bombers are dull and heavy to handle.' Shorter, and right to the point, wrote another: 'I doubt that Bury St Edmunds, or Ashby de la Zouch will ever get into a pilot's log book.'

Which leads us to the big change, the naming of the Avro B35/46 bomber, of which the first was the Vickers *Valiant*, as already mentioned. In 1952, the Vice-Chief of Air Staff wrote to the Air Council:

'(1) Members of Council are aware that production orders have been placed for the Handley Page and Avro B35/46 aircraft, and it is therefore appropriate to consider what names should be given to these two aircraft on their adoption by the service.

(2) The manufacturers strong recommend: Avro — *Ottawa*: Handley Page — *London* or *Hostile*.

(3) From the views expressed by the C-in-C, Bomber Command, it appears that there are two schools of thought: those who favour continuing with, and those who consider we should break from the present tradition of naming bomber aircraft after inland towns in the British Commonwealth, or towns associated with British industry.

(4) In the latter school, it is proposed that we should adopt the names of well-known bomber airfields (e.g. Hanswell, Coningsby), use the names of people famous in the RAF (e.g. Trenchard), and follow the tone set by the *Valiant* so that the new family of bombers has a uniform group of names all beginning with 'V' (suggestions are: *Victor, Vulcan, Vanquisher* and *Vehement*.

The CAS noted that Avro were anxious for various reasons for their version of the B35 to be named *Ottawa*. This would be in line with *Wellington* and *Canberra*, but would not be in line with *Valiant*, and his own inclination was to establish a 'V' class of jet bomber. In that case his preference would be for *Vulcan*, followed by *Victor*. The Under-Secretary said Council ought to have a plan and stick to it. His own preference was for descriptive names, and whilst he disliked being tied down to one initial letter he liked the name *Vulcan*,

and saw no strong objection to adopting the letter 'V' for a class that in the nature of things would not be very extensive.'

The Council agreed that the Avro B35 should be named *Vulcan*, and took note that the name *Victor* was a possibility for the Handley Page version. One would have thought that the 'V for Victory' slogan of World War Two, and its consequent adoption by resistance groups in Europe would have been a consideration. It is also strange that names of airfields and of famous RAF officers should yet again be proposed, but presumably these long-standing rulings were forgotten, or were never known. Precedent being a cardinal rule of government, the civil servants must surely have known of the previous naming systems, their exceptions and rulings, and must have advised their respective departments before the shortlists went to the Air Council.

Thus it came about that there was a *Valiant*, a *Vulcan* and *Victor*, yet this does not tell the full story of the background to these decisions. As has been seen, the *Valiant* was named before there was any notion of a 'V' class, and for what was to become the *Vulcan* there were the following suggestions: *Ottawa* (as noted, Avro's choice), *Andover, Argus, Arcturus, Atalanta, Aries, Artemis, Arthur, Agravaine, Ardent, Adamant* and *Attila*, all of them alliterating with Avro. *Sidney, Raleigh, Drake* and *Grenville* were also proposed naval names which would have upset the Admiralty and contravened the gentleman's agreement of 1939 when the FAA reverted to the Royal Navy. Again, this surely should have been known. For the Handley Page *Victor* there were the following suggestions: *London* (which was HP's choice), *Edinburgh, Hamilton, Hertford, Harwell* and *Hostile*. Oddly, there was a third list of suggestions put forward as suitable for either aircraft, consisting of *Vancouver, Trenton, Toronto, Norwich, Ely, Ipswich, Grimsby, Newark, Peterborough, Grantham, Cambridge* and *Coventry*. But, as the Air Marshal said, such names were unlikely to find themselves in any pilot's logbook. Maybe in an earlier day, but not in an age with nuclear bombers (the *Bloody Paralyser* of 1918 was perhaps more appropriate). And the 'Coventry' suggestion was hardly tactful. The 'V' system applied only to the three nuclear bombers, but was then taken over by the RAF for air cadet gliders. These were *Valiant, Vanguard* and *Viking* — and the gliders were all of German origin.

At about this time there were strange rumours of an apparently large aircraft which had been given the improbable name of *Gheleapandy*, and which, perhaps, has remained a puzzle over the years. It seems that those who take a keen interest in this sort of thing, one day saw a large low loader leave Radlett and slowly and finally arrive at Boscombe Down — and no more was learned. It was obviously a large load or object, and covered with a sheet of canvas to which this odd name had been stencilled. The simple explanation is that the Radlett runway was thought too short for the first take off of the *Victor*, and so it was decided to transport the aircraft, dismantled, to Boscombe Down; but why the stencilled *Gheleapandy?* Some Handley Page workers knew, and some guessed.

The Blackburn C3/46 had a number of competitive suggestions, some from the C-in-C, Transport Command (*Bison, Bullock, Holdall* and *Boxcar*). The Air Staff suggested *Bahamas, Bermuda, Bison, Boscombe, Brisbane, Buffalo, Bulawayo, Bulford, Leviathan, Mammoth* and *Yak*, and Blackburn — but this is not certain — suggested *Hercules* and *Mammoth*. A fourth set of suggestions comprised the names *Birmingham, Brough* (home of Blackburn Aircraft),

Arnhem, Aldershot and Netheravon. So they called it Beverley after a small Yorkshire town. The prototype was known as the 'Universal Freighter'.

Even small aircraft received considerable nomenclatural attention, such as the Slingsby Primary Sailplane purchased by the RAF for the Air training Corps glider courses. The suggestions were: Feather, Fledgling, Cygnet, Airgull, Icarus, Condor, Dabchick, Spinnaker, Tern, Probationer, Kingfisher, Mentor, Aviator, Astra, Zephyr, Kangaroo, Novice and Freshman. After all that it was named the Grasshopper, and that was in December 1952. As an Air Marshal noted, 'both the aircraft's silhouette and its antics on take-off and landing to a certain extent bear out the analogy'. Perhaps it should have been the Kangaroo, thus remembering the name of the 1917 Kangaroo Bomber by Blackburn. Its antics are not recorded, but it was certainly an ungainly creature.

And now to a somewhat larger aircraft, the English Electric F23 Fighter, for which the company put forward its own suggestions: Flash, Defender, Rapier, Scimitar, Scorpion, Harrier, Arrow, Eagle, Challenger, Lightning and Astra. To these the Ministry added (and this was another 'V' class, but it was certainly not a bomber: Vigorous, Vixen, Vizier, Valkyrie, Vandal, Venture, Venom, Vindictive, Virago, Vortex, Van Dyke, Vehement, Vindex and Victory (was there a Royal Navy Ship of this name?), all suggesting that this was a Vickers aircraft and there were more: Excaliber, Dagger, Conquest, Conqueror, Whiplash, Eclipse, Lucifer, Artemis, Atalanta, Alecto, Achilles, Halcyon, Aquilo, Aerial, Defender, Arrow, Mercury, Astra, Bullet, Dart, Electra, Electron, Eagle and Superflash.

From this wide choice, the final shortlist comprised Harrier and Lightning, the maker's choice in the first place (see The Classics, Chapter 12). The name was finally agreed in October 1956, but with instructions that it was not to be made public until production had been authorised. This policy decision was reversed in March 1957, and Lightning was announced at the SBAC 1958 show at Farnborough.

The Armstrong Whitworth 660 was the civil Argosy used by British European Airways (before it was amalgamated with BOAC to become British Airways), and, being adopted into and adapted for the RAF, a new name was sought. The suggestions are recorded as: Abingdon, Achates, Achilles, Aeolus, Aldershot, Andover, Apollo, Arethusa, Argo, Arnhem, Arundel, Atalanta, Atlas, Antomedon, Aylesbury, Ayrshire and then the non-alliterative Coventry and Conventrian. Another military freighter for which names were sought was the Avro 780. The suggestions were: Abingdon, Aldershot, Aden, Arab, Tramp and Andover. A VIP version was suggested as: Adelaide, Auckland, Alberta, Aberdeen, Ayr, Ascot and Ashford. From either list it was decided to have the one name, the final two being Arnhem and Andover.

It will be noted how often the same names were suggested in the later lists. Also very apparent is the reliance on Greek and Roman classical names, which perhaps surprising for us in an age when there is no widespread interest in a classical education, and Latin and Greek are no longer taught at school. The Nomenclature Committees and their like presumably had a well-stocked reference library — the Greek Ilyiad, The Times World Atlas, and, especially in the earlier days, some excellent volumes on natural history, and one would imagine that these were equally matched by the manufacturer's reference libraries. But this may not be so, for Blackburn put it about that the Roc was a Yorkshire seabird, whereas a copy of the Arabian Nights would advise

that it was a mythical bird of Madagascar that had some dealings with Sinbad the sailor (perhaps that's the clue, for the Roc served with the Navy). How the name Roc was chosen has not yet come to light.

The name most used by the Services would be Fury, with three British aircraft and one American serving with the RAF. On the subject of duplication, the following letter appeared in Flight at about this time:

'Although, when compared with other aspects of aviation the naming of aircraft is a matter of minor importance, one cannot help being struck by the present practice of duplication by some firms.

Surely the sole object of giving a name to anything is that it may then be identified and referred to without any doubt whatsoever? Why, then, nullify the purpose of nomenclature by employing the same name again, especially within a few years? One cannot believe that there is any shortage of words, apt or otherwise, so what is the reason?

The position is not so bad when the same name is given to machines made by different companies. When, however, one company — such as Westland — proceeds to repeat its past names, as in the case of the Whirlwind (after far too short a period), the Widgeon (the original Parasol still flying) and now the Wessex, the only result is confusion. Westminster was chosen, so why was it not possible to find alternatives to the last three?

Other examples that come to mind at once are two Furys by Hawker, two Comets by de Havilland, Hornet by both de Havilland and Hawker, in addition to possible confusion between DH's Hornet and the Hornet Moth, owing to abbreviation of the latter. DH's choice of Venom is passable in view of the obscurity of the 1936 Vickers fighter.

Numerous other aircraft constructors seem to find, without difficulty, appropriate names for their products, without having to resort to using the same ones again.

There must be many enthusiasts among the staffs of our companies who would welcome the opportunity of suggesting names for new machines and it would be gratifying to see a little more imagination used in this respect.'

The Fury story has already been mentioned, and reference should be made to an excellent magazine published during World War Two, the Aeroplane Spotter, which was edited by (Sir) Peter Masefield. In this was a series of duplicated aircraft names, quite a long list even in those days. Besides the Argosy, another civil transport which retained its name in military guise was the Bristol Britannia, the 'Whispering Giant'. As an aside, Bristol were paid a unique nomenclatural compliment, not only for the 'Whispering Giant' but for the 'Whispering Death' which was the Japanese name for the Beaufighter. Britannias were also built by Short Brothers at Belfast, and a later heavy lift version for the RAF became the Belfast. It was originally suggested as Britannic, but this was disallowed on the sensible view that it could be a code hazard. Short's own suggestion was Strangford, the name of a sea loch in County Down.

Whilst drones (non-piloted surveillance aircraft) will be found in the Total Index, rockets and missiles not having 'wings' in the accepted sense have not been included although they have been given names, many of the British with colour code names. The following letter from Flight gives some indication of these:

'From time to time our readers have expressed interest in such curious names as "Red Dean" and "Yellow Lemon", which have been publicly — if not officially — revealed as describing various British weapons or electronic systems. Without comment, we reproduce the following extract from our American contemporary *Aviation Week*:

'British missile code names originally were based on two words, the first a colour describing the type of guidance system and the second a word assigned to the project. Typical examples were Fairey *Fireflash* which was 'Blue Sky' and de Havilland *Firestreak* which was 'Blue Jay'. Bristol *Bloodhound* was 'Red Duster', English Electric *Thunderbird* was 'Red Shoes,' Vickers infra-red air-to-air Type 888 missile was 'Red Dean'. Other examples: 'Red Hawk' and 'Blue Boar'. Elaborate designation even included systems for component coding but is believed to have broken down in practice and has been abandoned as a designation system.'

Much of this is shrouded in mystery, at least to an author on the outside, but we see that this secret world also has its nicknames. From what I have gathered, however, it seems there was a Surveillance and Target Acquisition System which could be none other than SANTAS, and the aircraft involved was thus the *Sleigh*, its propulsion system being *Rudolph*. One of its precursors was a Coarse Enemy Strength and Position Inference Tracker whose nickname was *Cesspit*, which may have contributed to its destiny, which was to sink without trace.

With the advent of the Vickers VC 10, the world awaited its name, but this was not forthcoming. There was a ruling in BOAC not to name individual aircraft, and in later times with the purchase of many American Boeing aircraft, it is understandable that BOAC became American-orientated with just numbers as a type identity. There was also the consideration that *Britannia* sales might have been hampered or lost because of its 'macho' British name, which might (but does not) account for the fact that it was never bought by Air France! The VC 10 went to the RAF whose policy, as evident from these pages and from the 1310, dictated that a name was required. The ministries and committees went about the task, and the RAF were rather keen on *Vimy* — and that surely would have pleased the French! But it was thought few would now know its World War One history. The AOC, Transport Command, was for *Victoria*, but this was ruled as being too close to *Victor*. Other suggestions were: *Venture, Voyager, Vancouver, Van Dyke, Viceroy, Windsor, Warwick, Winchester, Upavon* and *Valentia* (again!). *Viceroy* went out quickly as India was, or was about to become, independent, and Vickers themselves had apparently opted for *Weybridge*. At a meeting in December 1962, Air Marshal Sir Geoffrey Tuttle quietly remarked, 'Why not just call it the VC10?' This was referred to Vickers, who replied that this would no doubt please BOAC, which, in classical Latin, would seem to be a *non sequiter*. And so both the civil and military VC 10 remained as such.

In a letter to the author, Sir George Edwards, once chief designer at Vickers and later chairman of the British Aircraft Corporation (now British Aerospace), wrote that so far as the VC 10 and the BAC 111 were concerned, they never had names because he had grown tired of thinking up names! It remains a puzzle, at least to anyone interested in names, and recalls the quotation used in the introduction to this book: 'Niceness in Words was always counted the next step to trifling, and so was to be curious about names'.

Another jet aircraft of civil origin to join the RAF was the DH 125, which in 1963 was listed in the RAF as an 'Advanced Trainer' and would thus, presumably, have had an educational name. But in the suggested list there were only two such names, *Don* and *Dominie*, the other being: *Didactic, Didaskalos, Diligent, Director, Durham, Dyad, Dogstar, Halley, Harrow, Hathos* (a Greek Goddess, and the sky deity), *Henry* (the Portuguese prince known as 'The Navigator') and *Jetmaster*; all were only marginally educational. *Don* and *Dominie* — both previously used in the RAF — were the final choice. De Havilland were pleased with *Dominie*, their *Don* Trainer of 1937 not having been a success. *Dominie* as an 'educational' name suggests that this ruling still applied, which poses the question why so many non-educational names were suggested?

We now come to an era with the remarkable development of the Jet Lift Fighter, VTOL (Vertical Take-Off & Landing), in which both vertical and horizontal flight power was provided by one engine with swivelling exhaust nozzles. This began as the P1127 of 1960 with the Rolls-Royce *Pegasus* (of Bristol origin and the second engine of that name), and in 1964 a name had to be considered for this revolutionary concept. The choice was based under three headings:

SYMBOLIC OF ROLE	*Harrier, Musketeer, Hammer, Hostile, Hound, Lancet, Cobra, Plunderer, Boomerang* and *Vindicator*.
SYMBOLIC OF TYPE	*Peregrine, Falcon, Sparrowhawk, Kestrel, Skylark* and (again) *Harrier*.
CLASSICAL	*Hector, Hydra, Heriot* (in feudal law, a death tax), *Heros, Paladin* and *Hotspur* (more historical than classical).

On 16 September 1964, *Kestrel* was decided upon, a name already known to the RAF as a Rolls-Royce engine, and the Miles of that name of 1937 which was to become the *Master*.

The P1154 was a development of the P1127 *Kestrel*, and the choice of name was simplicity itself, *Harrier* was already in the *Kestrel*'s suggested list, and, like the aircraft, was the bigger bird! It is the subject of the last of the twenty-four classics. Until these two VTOL fighters, there had been no RAF 'bird of prey' fighter except the Hawker *Harrier* (a torpedo bomber of 1927) the Martinsyde *Buzzard* of 1918 (which seems to have been an accident and an exception to the rule) the Austin *Osprey* of 1918 (which was never built), and the Hawker *Osprey* of 1930 (which escaped the Rolls-Royce 'rule' by being a *sea*bird of prey).

The Hawker *Osprey* of 1930 can only be considered as a terrible mistake, which probably accounts for the fact that it had a Rolls-Royce *Kestrel* engine. An *Osprey* and a *Kestrel* all in one should have been a world-beater. But if Rolls-Royce's prior claim to the birds of prey led to the non-belligerent birds who lent their names to a long line of fighters, there was an admirable continuity in the many piston engines that were named after birds of prey. Of these, *Merlin* was the classic engine and the classic name, and it should be noted that there has always been a Rolls-Royce engine in the RFC from 1915, and in the RAF up to date.

Bristol was literally a classic epic, based on the Planets and Constellations, in turn named after the classic and mythological figures of Greece and Rome, often the same but sometimes with different names; and if the present story now ends with *Jaguar* and *Tornado*, then there is some continuity with an Armstrong-Siddeley engine of 1920 and a Hawker fighter of 1939.

The future can only be conjecture except for those concerned with naming the aircraft to come, and new types are likely to be few compared to those covered by the 115 years just reviewed. There may yet be another *Jaguar* or *Tornado*, and is not *Eagle* a good name for a multi-national Eurofighter?

There have been two *Eagle* Engines, but not yet an RAF fighter — and it is the king of birds.

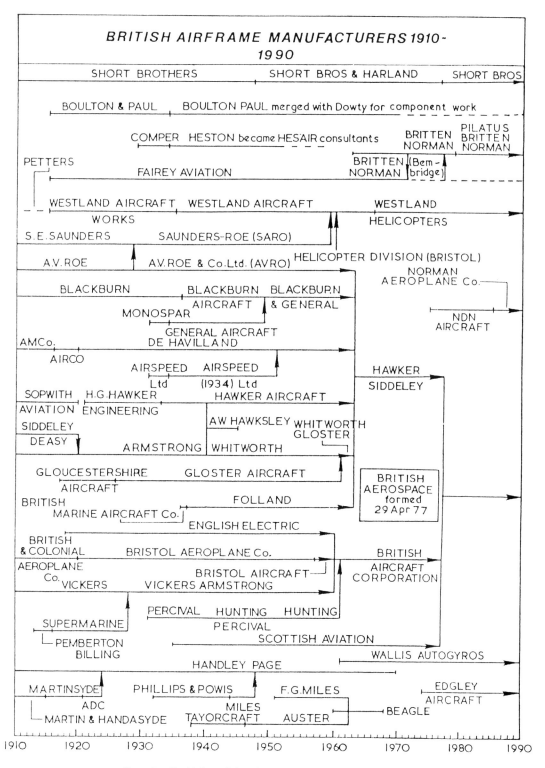

BRITISH AIRFRAME MANUFACTURERS 1910-1990

Reproduced by kind permission of Bruce Robertson, and Patrick Stephens Ltd

Chapter 5 — Classification

Part 1 — Birds

That Man learned to fly was not so much due to his mechanical ingenuity, his love of experiment or his mathematical prowess as to the fact that he just had an inferiority complex. He could walk, dig, jump, run and swim — but fly? And the chip on the shoulder was intolerable until success sprouted between the shoulder blades

> 'Darius was clearly of the opinion
> That the air is also man's dominion
> And that with paddle, or fin or pinion
> We soon or late shall navigate
> The azure as we now sail the sea.
>
> The birds can fly, an' why can't I?
> Must we give in, says he with a grin
> 'T the blue bird an phoebe are smarter'n we be?
> Just fold our hands, and see the swaller
> An' blackbird an' catbird beat us holler. . .?
> Just show me that, –er prove –t the bat
> Hez got more brains than's in my hat —
> An' I'll back down, an' not till then.

— J.T. Trowbridge, *Darius Green and his Flying Machine* (1870)

TO HAVE NAMED his inventions after the birds was Man's natural compliment to the example and source of inspiration. Birds, as symbols and images, have played and still play a graphic part in political and military history. The eagle has long been a symbol of majesty and power, with its origins lost in antiquity. It was used as a regimental ensign by the Romans and as a rallying point for its cohorts, and as fiercely defended against capture as any ensign in later history; the eagle of the empires over history is as ancient a symbol as any, also being used by Charlemagne, successor to the Caesars. The eagle, and the 'double eagle', has been the national crest of Russia, Germany and the Austro-Hungarian Empire, to name but three, and the bald eagle is the symbol of the United States of America.

Another aspect of this is that in ancient civilisations, birds were symbols often raised to the status of deities. One of the early bird gods was Garuda, a mythical golden eagle of Tibet – 'the bird of life, destroyer of all, creator of all'. The Babylonians and Hittities built temples to Eagles, and Horus was a Falcon in Egyptian deity. And to bring the god birds down to earth, the Athenians depicted the Owl on their coins – even then known as Wise and Old. Indeed, the Owl was the companion of Athene, the Goddess of wisdom.

In the heraldry of war, there have been many armorial eagles. There have also been twenty-one ships in the Royal Navy named HMS *Eagle*. Therefore there was an historical precedent, a tradition which the military was to adopt in the names of aircraft. But as has been seen, the RFC used animal rather than bird names, although these were unofficial 'nicknames'. With the formation of the RAF in 1918, so began the 'romantic' era of bird names which was to last until 1927 (not that they have not been used in later times, such as with the present *Harrier*). The Swift (apart from three listed in the Index) is the bird most associated with the RFC and the RAF, for the flying 'brevet' or 'wings' was based on the wings of the Swift. The Swift also appears in the crest of 72 Squadron, RAF.

The origin of the officers' badge of the RAF has been the subject of conjecture over many years — eagle or albatross? It has too large a body and too small a wing span for an albatross, so it may be presumed to be an eagle. Strangely, it originated as a German (French?) brooch, given to his wife by Commander Murray Sueter (later an Admiral) when on holiday in Germany in the summer of 1914. He was CO of the Naval Wing of the Royal Flying Corps (to become the Royal Naval Air Service), and persuaded the Admiralty that active pilots in the RNAS should wear the eagle in the RN cap badge instead of the anchor. This can be seen in photographs of RNAS pilots during World War One.

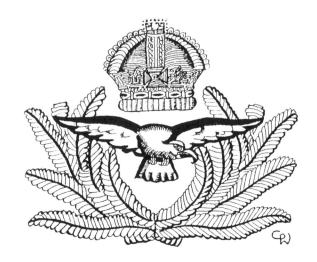

With the formation of the RAF in 1918, the officer class was based on RN practice, and so the RNAS cap badge was taken over for the RAF, but the Admiralty did not consider that the new junior service should have the same number of laurel leaves. Officers of Air rank — Air Commodore and above — have the fuller set of laurel leaves, and as a shoulder badge the eagle was part of the uniform of RAF airmen (other ranks) until comparatively recently. (There is some irony in the fact that a foreign brooch should be the badge of the British enemy in two world wars!)

Chapter 4 detailed the 1918 origins of RAF naming systems, and it will be recalled that fighters came under the 'zoological' definitions of 'Single-seater — insects, birds and reptiles' and 'Two-seater — mammals.' The insects and reptiles disappeared for fighters, and waterfowl was reserved for seaplanes and flying boats, with a further reservation for birds of prey for Rolls-Royce engines. The third 1918 system was in July, being much the same apart from waterfowl being allocated to 'more than one seat'.

A one- or two-letter code was also allocated to the manufacturers, and this was to be the first two letters of the bird name, thus in one word having an aircraft code and also an indication of the maker. So when Boulton Paul produced their 1918 fighter, the search was on in the ornithological encyclopaedias for a 'BO' bird, whence they extracted 'Bobolink', a strange name for a (prototype) RAF fighter, being a North American songbird. Similarly Armstrong-Whitworth's *Ara*, Vickers's *Vireo* and Gloster's *Guan*, hitherto unknown birds to both the makers and the pilots. And not entering RAF service, they remained unknown to most, either as aircraft or as birds.

Up to 1927, any potential service aircraft was given a name, but thereafter only if there was a production order. By 1927 bird names were beginning to run out, particularly amongst waterfowl group. Rolls-Royce, of course, continued with their birds of prey. Their claim to these arose from the production of the *Eagle*, *Falcon* and *Hawk* before the 1918 system. The Index lists 114 bird names, although some of these are duplicated.

Feathered Wings

'Flight,' said the *Eagle*,
'Is our heritage,
Ours from the nucleus,
And always man
Must envy us.'

The owl blinked
With surprise.
'How right you are,
There are more than myself
Apparently wise.'

'Don't worry,' said the *Eagle*,
'In the sky man has
Achieved remarkable things,
But true flight belongs
To feathered wings.
Take the *Hawk*,
Who can flutter suspended
Then drop like a stone;
Or myself — soaring majestic
Aloof and alone

And others of our kind
Supreme as yet
The *Albatross*, *Merlin*
And *Avocet*
And man to his planes
Has given these names,
A tribute indeed to our kind;
And for my dissertation
On things aviation
I hope you really don't mind.'

'Not at all,' said the *Owl*
You've given me delight
In expounding these facets
Of man and bird flight.'
— John Carruthers

A light-hearted poem was composed by the *Aeroplane* magazine on the advent of the Hawker *Hornbill* in 1926:

'Said one to his pal re. the *Hornbill* —
Yon bird will knock spots off the *Fawn*, Bill.
No doubt, Bill replied,
Have you seen the inside?
Those fresh horses must double the corn bill.

The speed-range it had in the air
Appeared to be something quite rare
It tucked up its tail
And crept past like a *snail*,
Then it turned and shot back liked a *hare*'.

The names in italics were not so in the original poem, but their relevance was presumably meant.

Whilst many of the gentler birds have lent their names to military aircraft, there would surely have been limits as to, say, a Nieuport *Nightingale*, but there was such a one in the USA, the Hughes *Nightingale*. Perhaps there was some reticence in the use of the name of this beautiful songbird, for the aircraft was generally known as the 'DGA' — Damn Good Aeroplane'. Neither would have survived the Nomenclature Committees of the Air Ministry. In the Total Index, Chapter 7, under the Notes column, a brief reference is made to other aircraft, civil or military, that have the same name. With some of the more common names, there is not enough (computer) space to include all such names. This is so in the case of birds, the largest name category. The most used names are *Eagle*, *Falcon* and *Hawk;* regrettably, some of the lesser-known aircraft with these names are not recorded, but are comparatively few. (Note that *Eagle*, *Falcon* and *Hawk* were all Rolls-Royce engines before 1918 and the beginning of the RAF naming systems of that year.)

The Rolls-Royce category of birds of prey had its transatlantic equivalent in Curtiss, but they were not all birds of prey. A list reads: *Condor*, *Falcon*, *Hawk*, *Mohawk*[1], *Oriole*, *Robin*, *Shrike*, *Sea Hawk*, *Sparrowhawk*, *Blackhawk*[2], *Nighthawk*, *Raven*, *Swift*, *Tomahawk*[4], *Kittyhawk*[3], *Warhawk*, *Seagull* and *Seamew*. [1] and [2] are Red Indian tribal names, and [3] a place name, but they sound like hawks! [4] is allegorical. There is a 'kittywake', but no bird listed as a 'kittyhawk', which is in fact the place where the Wright brothers in 1903 flew the first controlled and powered flight. That historic aeroplane was the *Flyer* (See Chapter 4, Part 2).

Boulton Paul Bittern

Gloster Gnatsnapper

De Havilland Albatross

Gloster Goldfinch

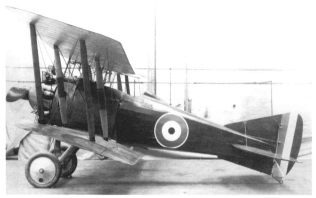

Nieuport Nighthawk

Bristol Bullfinch

Gloster Grebe

Hawker Osprey

Boulton Paul Bobolink

Hawker Hoopoe

Supermarine Seagull

De Havilland Flamingo

Gloster Gorcock

Hawker Heron

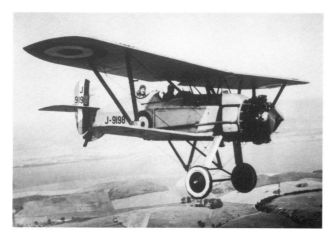

Armstrong Whitworth Siskin

Fairey Gannet

Boulton Paul Partridge

De Havilland 53 'Humming Bird'

Fairey Fulmar

Sopwith Sparrow

Vought-Sikorsky Kingfisher

Westland Wagtail

Parnall Pipit

Parnall Puffin

Gloster Guan

Blackburn Skua

Gloster Gambet

BAT Bantan (Pahlip Jarrett)

Armstrong-Whitworth Starling

Fairey Flycatcher

Avro Avocet

Westland Widgeon

Sopwith Snipe

Hawker Hornbill

Hawker Woodcock

Sopwith Cuckoo

Armstrong-Whitworth Ara

Part 2 — Animals

Roused now by the lash of his own stubborn tail
Our *Lion* new will foreign foes assail. . .'
— John Dryden, *Astraea Redux*, 1660

'Thy spirit, Independence, let me share!
Lord of the *Lion*-heart and Eagle-eye.
The steps I follow with my bosom bare
Nor heed the storm that howls along the sky.'
— Tobias Smollett, 1721–1771

'As it were a ramping and a roaring *Lion*'
— Psalms

'In peace there's nothing so becomes a man
As modest stillness and humility;
But when the blast of war blows in our ears,
Then imitate the action of the *Tiger*.
Stiffen the sinews, summon up the blood. . .'
— William Shakespeare, *Henry V*

As WITH CERTAIN birds such as the eagle, so animals, and particularly the lion and the tiger, represent virtues and strengths that humans wish to emulate.

The February 1918 RAF naming system allocated 'zoological mammals to fighters, two-seater', quickly followed by the March system which changed to 'zoological' for both single- and two-seater types, with mammals being reserved for aircraft used on land or sea to distinguish them from seaplanes or flying boats. From mammals were reserved the cats (Felidae) who were claimed by Armstrong-Siddeley engines.

The July system strove for more clarity, and did indeed simplify matters: now 'zoological, animals' were applied to aircraft with one engine only, and more than one seat. That system lasted until 1921 (the fourth RAF system) when mammals, except Felidae, were allocated to land aeroplanes, multi-seat, up to 6000 lb.

A radical change came in 1927, when birds and animals were perhaps getting a little scarce as names, and reference to that system will show that whilst the appropriate letter could be an animal named with the appropriate first letter, there was no indication as such that it should. Thus, the Hawker *Hornet* had to change to an 'F' and become *Fury*, but it might just as well have been *Fox*, ignoring the fact there was a Fairey 1925 aircraft of that name; but then, duplicated names were no novelty.

With the 1932 system, there was a positive reversion to animals for Bombers, day, again with the exception of Felidae. Marine animals were allocated to the Fleet Air Arm (under RAF command) Spotter Reconnaissance aircraft. For the time being, 1932 saw the end of animals as names, but in 1939 the FAA now reverted to the Admiralty, and FAA names were 'as proposed by Admiralty', who seemed to prefer birds and fishes. Some exceptions with later aircraft include: Piper *Cub*, DH Canada *Chipmunk*, Beagle *Bulldog*, *Westland* Gazelle, North American *Mustang*, Sepecat *Jaguar*, Supermarine *Sea Otter*, DH *Sea Vixen* (no such animal), DH *Vampire* and Supermarine *Walrus*. The two prestige names of 'Lion' and 'Tiger' were reserved for Armstrong-Siddeley, but they have never become RAF aircraft names, although as engine names they have powered many RAF aircraft. ('. . . The blood more stirs/To rouse a Lion than to start a Hare', as Shakespeare observed in *Henry IV*, Part 1).

Bristol Beaver

Blackburn Kangaroo

Sopwith Pup

Fairey Fawn (prototype)

Hawker Duiker

Short Springbok

Parnall Possum

Sopwith Hippo

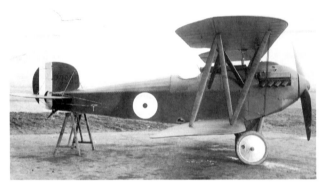

Bristol Badger

Hawker Hedgehog

Avro Antelope

Armstrong-Whitworth Armadillo (Philip Jarett)

Handley Page Hare

Auro Buffalo

Austin Greyhound

Westland Weasel

PV Kitten

Vickers Vampire

Martinsyde Elephant

Part 3 — Fish

'Will he never strike?
no change of rhythm
signals his intent,
fins, tail and gills
move in perfect precision;
then suddenly
lightning swift he moves,
a streak of pewter grey,
grinning jaws crunch evilly,
a Pike has got his prey.'
— John Carruthers

FOR 'MACHINES OPERATING by sea', the February 1918 system offered three options for a fighters: 'single-seater — river fish, two-seater — saltwater fish, and three-seater — shell fish. The March system changed that to 'waterfowl and fishes'

for single-engined seaplanes and flying boats, and this was repeated in the revised July system. 1921's class of nicknames had 'shellfish for a single-seat sea aeroplane (but not amphibious craft), and a multi-seat up to 6000 lb was allocated 'fresh and saltwater fish', that all lasting until 1927. Then fighters (F), torpedo bombers (M) and Fighter Reconnaissance (A) were to have names of maritime significance, a broad choice in which fish were an option not a requirement, for the system was intended to widen the naming potential.

By 1932 piscatorial nomenclature was at an end so far as the RAF was concerned, and again had no place in the 1939 system which was very similar to the 1932. In 1939 the FAA reverted to the Admiralty, and has since remained so. The Fairey *Barracuda* appeared in 1940, a fine hunting and sporting fish; for so fierce and predatory a creature, 'Shufty' seems an undeserved nickname. The 1934 *Swordfish* will be found as a classic, and a later name was the Fairey *Spearfish*.

Note: Strictly, some of the illustrations, such as 'Dolphin', 'Seal' and 'Sea Lion' are not 'fish', but mammals.

Short Sturgeon

Sopwith Dolphin

Fairey Seal

Parnall Perch

Short Gurnard

Black Burn Shark I (Philip Jarrett)

Blackburn Nautilus

Parnall Pike

Sopwith Snapper

Part 4 — Reptiles

THE FEBRUARY 1918 system of naming offered 'reptiles' for single-seat fighters. The March system slightly changed that to 'aircraft for use on land or sea', but excluding seaplanes and flying boats.

The July system repeated this, but with the important exception of 'snakes', which were now reserved for Wolseley engines.

An armoured Fighter of 1917 was the Sopwith *Salamander*. This was designed as a low-level 'trench' attack fighter, and the name was chosen because of the mythical legend that a salamander could survive fire.

The BAT *Basilisk* was similarly a 'trench' armoured fighter. The reptile is a tropical lizard but in mythology it was a creature born of a cock and a dragon, and whose stare and breath were lethal. The shield is part of the crest of the city of Paris.

The 1921 system allocated reptiles, except snakes, to amphibians, and whilst the system lasted until 1927 there is no record of such a name, presumably as a reptile was seen as a land creature and with no association with the sea. There was, of course, the 'sea serpent', but even that element of marine mythology had no appeal, not even in a list of suggested names, so far as is known. A reptile was possible but not used with the 1927 system, and there was no provision for reptiles in the 1932 system, except for the far-fetched improbability of a sea serpent for FAA Spotter Reconnaissance as a 'marine animal'.

Wolseley later gave up snake names, and it is strange that snakes or even the word 'serpent' were not used, for they met the 1932 requirement of 'speed, activity and aggression' and many are indeed lethal! Perhaps the Ministry and manufacturers felt much about snake names as they did about snakes. The snake, certainly, has had a poor public relations image over the ages and has hardly been promoted as a cuddly pet:

'O Thou, who Man of baser earth did make
And who with Eden did devise the Snake,
For all the Sin wherewith the Face of Man
Is blackened, Man's Forgiveness give — and take.'
— Edward Fitzgerald

RAF pilots are, however, made of sterner stuff, and four RAF Squadron crests portrayed snakes. There has never been a crocodile for engine or aircraft, except for the individual name of a Bristol fighter of 1918. This arose from its checked black and white colour scheme, but the resemblance to a crocodile is obscure.

Basilisk (Philip Jarrett)

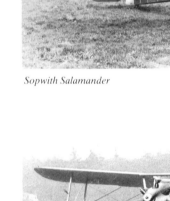

Sopwith Salamander

Westland Pterodactyl

Sopwith Snail

Part 5 — Insects

MORE THAN THREE quarters of the known living species of this world are insects, and nearly a million of them have so far been named. It is thought that there may yet be millions more insects to discover, and these are chiefly in the tropical rain forests.

As fliers, the speeds at which winged insects beat their wings vary widely: a fluttering tiger moth has a wing speed of about ten beats a second whilst a mosquito's wings beat so rapidly — about three hundred times a second — that they emit a high-pitched whine. In aeronautical terms the analogy is somewhat exaggerated, however the comparison is not without interest. As a classic, the *Mosquito* will be found in Chapter 6.

As with birds and animals, so too have insects had religious or mythological associations in various parts of the world, and this was particularly the case in ancient Egypt. Of the many insects, the most revered was the scarab, known to us as the dung beetle. *Scarabiae* is the scientific name for the beetles, and the scarab is also known as the 'sacred beetle'. There does not seem to have been a military 'scarab', but a civil one was made by Supermarine. The Ancient Egyptians regarded the scarab as the symbol of resurrection and immortality, adding stone or wooden ones to the mummified bodies of the dead. The ball of dung was imagined as the sun, and thus this sacred insect was the Egyptian god of dawn, named as 'Khepera'. There was, however, a scarab with military connotations, and that was the American Warner *Super Scarab* engine which will be seen in the Index.

The various moths were the hallmark of de Havilland, and their origin has already been detailed, arising from his interest in moths and butterflies. The 'Gipsy' series of engines were originally associated with the Gipsy Moth, and as a series of engines are in the Classics.

The *Queen Bee* and *Wasp* were radio-controlled target aircraft. The 'queen' prefix certainly distinguished these aircraft from their piloted kin, but it is not known how or why this came about. The aircraft were only produced in small numbers, and the image of thousands of them being bred is really somewhat far-fetched, although some association must probably have been imagined.

Except, perhaps, for the Egyptians, insects do not have an instant attraction to mankind and make very indifferent pets. Animals and birds have the greater attraction, but in technical terms the insects do have a claim to more names being given to aircraft than engines — many of them do actually fly. However splendid the name, that cannot be said of a *Bulldog* or a *Jaguar*.

Queen Wasp

De Havilland Hornet

Avro Spider (Philip Jarrett)

Fairey Firefly

De Havilland Dragonfly

Sopwith Bee

DH 90 Dragonfly

Part 6 — Geography (Land)

THIS SOMEWHAT TERSE title has been chosen to save sub-classifications such as 'Mountain', 'District', 'Country' and so on, with the obvious inference that all such are included in this part. For easy reference, 'Geography — Land' has been extracted from the various RAF naming system from 1918, and follow in chronological order. Note that some names did not originate under the RAF system, and will generally be seen in the Index under 'Maker'. Where an 'xxx' is shown, this indicates that it was an exception to a system then in force — but note that there have been several exceptions to the general rules. The subject is not always neatly bundled up and tidily put away, but perhaps that is part of its fascination.

FEBRUARY 1918 MACHINES OPERATING BY LAND
BOMBER Spec. A2B, A3B
Geographical (Inland)

Size of Machine.	Sub-class word.
Single-seater	Italian towns
Two-seater	Gt. Britain
Three-seater	French towns
Crew exceeding three;	
Wt, under 5 tons	Towns in Colonies and Dependencies
5 to 10 tons	Towns in Asia
10 to 15 tons	Towns in Africa

MARCH 1918 MULTI-ENGINED MACHINES

TYPE OF DESIGN	GROSS WEIGHT LADEN		TWIN ENGINES	
	Over Tons	Up to Tons	Class	Sub-Division
4. Machines for use on land or from Ship's docks	—	5	Geographical Inland Towns	France
5. Do.	5	10		Europe (Except France)
6. Do.	10	20		Great Britain
7. Do.	20	—		—

THREE ENGINES		FOUR ENGINES	
Class	Sub-Division	Class	Sub-Division
Male Historical or Mythological Proper Names connected with:	France	Geographical Names other than towns, rivers, lakes & islands, eg; counties, mountains, tribes, etc.	France
	Europe (Except France)		Europe (Except France)
	Gt. Britain		Gt. Britain
	Asia or Africa		Asia or Africa

JULY 1918 AIRCRAFT WITH MORE THAN ONE ENGINE

Gross weight, laden

	over	up to	
	lb	lb	
3.	—	11,000	Geographical Inland towns in England or Wales
4.	11,000	20,000	Geographical Inland towns in Scotland or Ireland

	1921
TYPE	LAND AEROPLANE
6,000 — 12,000 lb	Inland towns in the British Isles
12,000 — 20,000 lb	Inland towns in the British Empire

The 1927 system called for names to begin with a 'class letter', and 'Geography — Land' was permitted if the name began with the appropriate letter, and was within its particular classification. The system did not specifically call for geographical names.

1932
2. Bombers

(a) Day	
(b) Army Co-operation	
(c) Night	Inland towns of the British Empire or towns associated with the RAF
(d) General Purpose	British historical names.
(e) Transport	General towns [and seaports] of the British Empire

1939
Bombers — Place names — an inland town of the British Empire or associated with British history
Transport — Counties or districts of the British Empire

The 1949 system was almost identical, but for 'British Empire' now read 'British Commonwealth'. Theoretically, there was no change (except where a country may have left the Commonwealth) but now that there were fewer aircraft types, so there were fewer names, and by the time of the 'V' bombers the 'town' tradition was gone. In a way, this was a pity, for it was a further loosening of the bonds between Commonwealth countries.

Part 7 — Geography (Water)

THE SAME GENERAL comments apply to this part as those for the previous part. One point to note is that the earlier naming systems referred to 'seaboard towns' which, if taken literally, need not have been a port. However, this did not seem to be the case, and it was the name of a port that was used and not a 'seaside town'; thus there was a *Southampton* but not a 'Bognor Regis'.

FEBRUARY 1918 MACHINES OPERATING BY SEA
BOMBER Spec. N2B
GEOGRAPHICAL (Seaboard)
As for land machines, but coastal towns in place of inland

MARCH 1918 MULTI-ENGINED MACHINES	
TWIN ENGINES	
Class	Sub-Division
Geographical Inland Towns	France
	Europe (Except France)
	Great Britain
Seaplanes & Flying Boats	
As above, but Seaboard Towns	

JULY 1918 AIRCRAFT WITH MORE THAN ONE ENGINE		
Gross weight, laden over lb up to lb	Geographical	Seaplanes
3. — 11,000	Geographical	Seaboard towns in England or Wales
4. 11,000 20,000	Geographical	Seaboard towns in Scotland or Ireland

1921	SEA AEROPLANE	AMPHIBIAN
6,000 — 12,000 lb	Seaboard towns in the British Isles	Islands in British Isles
12,000 — 20,000 lb	Seaboard towns in the British Empire	Islands in the British Empire

The 1927 system called for a letter prefix in the name, and the following apply to this chapter:

2 Fighters, Fleet	'N' The names of 2, 5 & 12
5 Bombers, Torpedo	'M' to have maritime significance.
12 Fighter Reconnaissance	'O'

If 'maritime significance' included ports, then there would have been Port names beginning with 'N', 'M' and 'O', but this does not seem to have been the case. Examples were *Nimrod* and *Osprey*, and the only flying boat was *Medina* of 1926 which had a civil origin. Thus, so far as flying boats or seaplanes were concerned, this system seems not to have been used. As may be seen in the chapter on naming systems, this 1927 system was not a popular one with either the manufacturers or the RAF.

1932	
(e) Transport	General towns and seaports of the British Empire
3. Flying Boats	Coastal towns and seaports of the British Empire
1939	
Flying Boats	Coastal towns and seaports of the British Empire

US aircraft used by the RAF in World War Two were all named, but with US connotations, and the *Catalina* was such a flying boat. As already noted, the 1949 system saw only the one significant change of 'Empire' to 'Commonwealth'. There has not been a seaplane or flying boat in RAF service since 1959. In their day, they did magnificent service in most seas and oceans around the world, and without them the Battle of the Atlantic would not have been won.

Part 8 — Mythology

'And twenty more such names and men as these
Which never were, nor no man ever saw. . .'
— *The Taming of the Shrew*, Shakespeare

ANCIENT MYTHOLOGY SEEMS so distant from our modern experience that we cannot believe it to be true; 'mythical' nowadays implies 'incredible', not believable. It was not so in their times, and myths from the Bible have literary parallels in Persia, Babylon, Egypt, Greece and Rome. The northern regions such as Germany and Scandinavia have myths aplenty, and thus a mythology; Thor, the Norse god of thunder, is the name for a Douglas missile of 1956 used by the RAF. There are many books on British folklore, some with 200 pages and more, the origins of some of which go back to pagan times. Some names have been used at least twice. The most common origins are Greek and Roman, and their mythology is part of the 'classics' of Western civilisation. They have been popular names for ships, are the source of many of our words and phrases such as 'Herculean', and to bring the story up to date there is even a US spacecraft named *Mercury*. So there can be no surprise that 'mythology' was included in the RAF February 1918 system:

Heavy Armoured Machines	
Proper Names (Male)	
Size of Machine;	Sub-class word
Under two tons ....Mythological Greek two to five tons ....Mythological Roman five to ten tons ....Mythological Eastern & Egyptian ten to twenty tons ....Mythological north Europe	

Patrol & Anti-Submarine Spec. N3A, N3B
Proper Names
As for land machines, but females

Note the specific requirement for Greek, Roman, Egyptian and north European names, and the subtle distinction between male and female aeronautical capabilities. Whilst the Amazons (female warriors of renown) were never anti-submarine, they were certainly on patrol even if they were never heavily armoured.

The system lasted only a month, but some eastern and Egyptian names would have enlivened the aeronautical scene. By March they were 'out' as Asia and Africa were now 'in' — not that any names were forthcoming.

MARCH 1918		
Class	THREE ENGINES Sub-Division	
Male historical or Mythological Proper Names connected with:	France	
	Europe (except France)	
	Great Britain	
	Asia or Africa.	
As above, but female proper names.		

By July 1918 it was no longer 'three engines' but 'with more than one engine' and by aircraft weight; 'male' for land, and 'female' for seaplanes which also meant flying boats.

The exclusion of stars and planets, named after Greek and Roman mythology, was for what was to become Bristol and who subsequently have provided most of the classical names.

JULY 1918 AIRCRAFT WITH MORE THAN ONE ENGINE			
Gross weight, laden over lb up to lb		Aircraft for use on land or from ships' decks	Seaplanes
5. 20,000	45,000	Male historical or mythological proper names (excluding names of stars and planets).	Female historical or mythological proper names (excluding names of stars and planets).

The 1921 system was similar in this respect:

CLASS OF NICKNAME		
Type	Land Aeroplane	Sea Aeroplane
20,000 – 40,000 lb.	Male mythological names	Female mythological names

The 1927 system allowed for mythological names but fitting the 'letter' classification. No names seem to have arisen from this system. *Nimrod* did, but was a 'person' rather than a myth.

And so to 1932:

4. Fleet Air Arm (a) Fighters	Mythological names

The only FAA aircraft listed as mythological is the Blackburn *Roc*, and that was a fabulous giant bird from the 'Arabian Nights.' It has been suggested that the name is a local one for a Yorkshire seabird, and a 'bird' would be in order under the system if the *Roc* was 'Fighter Reconnaissance', but it was a dive bomber for which there was no system provision. There is no reference to such a local name anyway, and so the mythological Roc it remains until advised to the contrary, which has not happened since 1954 when the first article on the subject appeared in the *Aeroplane*, but it is odd that the Blackburn *Skua*, also a dive bomber, is quite positively a bird . . .

After 1932 it seems that mythology became a fading interest. The times were getting too serious for whimsical characters, and in the 1932 system no provision was made for mythology. The admirable exception was Bristol, who from 1918 had remained true to their mythological tradition, and this continued until the present and second *Pegasus*. Bristol is now part of Rolls-Royce, who took no more to names but to letters and numbers, and even the rivers have come to an end. But this changed in 1992 with another *Trent*, albeit now a civil engine.

Mythology itself is not dead, nor will it ever be for it is a part of the human scene; the Greek and Roman gods and goddesses (essentially the same to both cultures but with some different names) remain the heroic as well as the villainous characters they ever were. They have provided some splendid names. Icarus seems to have been carelessly overlooked, but then . . .

"Myths are the Bridges of Time"
Anonymous.

Dragon

Grain Griffin (Philip Jarrett)

Blackburn Roc

Martinside Boreas

Gloster Mars

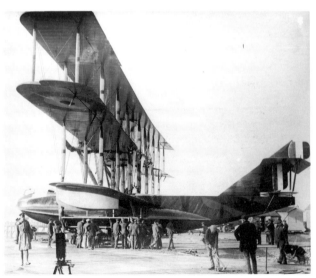

Felixstowe Fury

Lockhead Neptune

Avro Athena

Gloster Mars

Armstrong-Whitworth Apollo

Grahame-White Gannymede

Hawker Hector

Lockheed Hercules (Crown Copyright)

Armstrong-Whitworth Atlas

Part 9 — Astronomy

'Reason has Moons, but Moons not her's
Lie Mirrored on the Sea,
Confounding her Astronomers
But Oh! delighting me!'
— Ralph Hodgson (1871–1962)

THE PREVIOUS PART was concerned with mythology and so far as outer space is concerned the planets, stars and constellations listed in that chapter were named after Greek and Roman characters. Those listed in this chapter do not have such an origin, and thus 'Taurus' is both a constellation and the second sign of the zodiac, and whilst its Latin name means 'the bull', it is not mythological. The same applies to Aries, the Latin word for 'the ram'; in astronomy, the first point of Aries is the prime meridian of the celestial sphere, just as the Greenwich meridian is of the Earth.

The mirrored sea further confounds the distinction between astronomy and astrology, the latter connoting association with the signs of the zodiac. This, with its twelve signs, was devised about 3000 BC by Babylonian priests who observed that the sun, moon and planets seemed to move around the Earth in a yearly course which passed through twelve constellations. The Babylonians also saw that the sun seemed to rise in different parts of the zodiac each month, and on this basis designed a calendar. Astrologers still use the basic concept, although the constellations have been moving apart since those early days.

We are now dealing with astrology rather than astronomy, but starting from the top of the zodiac and going clockwise:

Aries	the ram	Royal Aircraft Factory 1917
Taurus	the bull	Bristol, 1936
Gemini	the twins	Castor and Pollux, names suggested by King George V for the R 100 and R 101
Cancer	the crab	DH6
Leo	the lion	Napier, 1917
Virgo	the virgin	
Libra	the scales	
Scorpio	the scorpion	
Sagittarius	the archer	A centaur is half man, half horse, and the constellation is Centaurus. Bristol 1938.
Capricorn	the goat	
Aquarius	the water carrier	Cherub, Bristol 1925.
Pisces	the fish	Dolphins which is not a fish but a mammal, Sopwith 1917.

In the RAF naming systems, only that of 1921 specifically refers to 'astronomical', and then for civil amphibians! There were none which qualify for this book.

There are more mythological than astronomical names (ignoring the generic term 'fish') but with mythology and astronomy/astrology, there is some confounding which hopefully intrigues the reader.

Part 10 — Weapons

'. . . and famous by my Sword'
— Marquis of Montrose (1612-1650)

WITH THE 'EXCLUSIONS' of the 1918 naming systems, Napier were allocated 'arms and weapons', although the distinction between the two is somewhat subtle. An 'arm' (hence 'army') is a weapon, especially a firearm, but it is also a military unit, such as infantry or cavalry — and there is, of course, the Fleet Air Arm, but it is doubtful that this latter meaning was ever intended for Napier engines. A 'weapon' is any instrument or bodily part used as a means of attack or defence in combat, or any means employed to get the better of another; but in the intended sense of 1918, arm and weapon are virtually the same.

Why Napier was allotted this category of name is not known, for there was apparently no precedent prior to 1918, as there was for Rolls-Royce, Bristol and Armstrong-Siddeley. The previous Napier engines were the *Lion* and *Cub* (the latter was the larger engine), and later there was a *Lioness* (1927) which presumably should have been a weapon? There were five weapons in the Napier armoury. The Culverin is an old-fashioned musket, but the other four were all for close combat.

The Commonwealth (Australia) *Boomerang* trainer is one of the more interesting names. It is the only 'aerodynamic' weapon, invented by the Australian aborigines long before contact with the early explorers of the seventeenth century. To this day, its aerodynamic characteristics baffle the scientists!

Between the wars there was a fighter specification (F 27/29) calling for the mounting of a Coventry Ordnance Works cannon, soon known as the 'COW Gun', and various aircraft were built to this specification. The name conjures up a splendid image.

Napier's greatest weapon was the *Sabre*, a massive beast with twenty-four sleeve-valve cylinders in an 'H' configuration. The noise of the *Sabre* was in itself most formidable, and allied to the guns of the *Tempest* would have been another subject for the attention of Shakespeare's pen.

The only aircraft with weapon names were the *Boomerang* (Australian, but trained RAF pilots) *Javelin* and *Scimitar*. The other *Sabre* was the North American fighter used by the RAF.

Part 11 — People

'A name as it were the distinguishing
mark of a thing'
— Latin legality

THIS PART POSES a slight problem in that 'people' would also include the classical Greeks and Romans who have already been described elsewhere; now the 'mythological' people are excluded, and this is primarily historical, a chapter of 'other than'. 'Other than' was dealt with by the RAF naming systems thus:

March 1918 – three engines — male names, historical (and
mythological) connected with France, Europe,
Great Britain, Asia and Africa
– seaplanes and flying boats — ditto, but female
July 1918 – as above, but now aircraft with more than one
engine (land, male)
– seaplanes — ditto — female
1921 – sea aeroplanes — names of famous historical
persons
1927 – class letter prefix, but no specific requirement
1932 – bombers (d) general — British historical names
1939 – general purpose, torpedo and landplanes —
British historical names
– glider — historic military leaders
1949 – generally as 1939

Whilst seven generals and four admirals are named in the index, it was ruled by Sir Charles Portal when Chief of Air Staff that the names of RAF officers, however distinguished, should not be used. This was possibly a sensible decision in view of the comparatively short time that the RFC and the RAF had been in being, but is in marked contrast to the Royal Navy tradition whereby their ships have had admiral names, such as *Nelson*, *Rodney* and *Anson*. The Army, being based on a regimental or corps basis, tends not to commemorate famous names thus, except such as the 'King's Own. . .' or the 'Prince of Wales's Own. . .' — and their weapons tend not to have 'people' or personal names, which is immediately contradicted by their front line tank, the *Crusader* — also a Short's 1925 seaplane. Similarly 'Brown Bess' was the soldier's affectionate name for his standard Army musket at the time of the Napoleonic wars, but in the view of the War Office she was hardly heroic. Makers' names could also become the aircraft name, or rather nickname, such as 'Caudron', 'Blériot', 'Farman', 'Dunne', 'Avro' and 'Dyott'.

Chapter 4, on naming systems, reported on the 1911 Royal Aircraft Factory system of 'BE', 'FE' and 'SE', being 'Blériot', 'Farman' and 'Santos Dumont' Experimental. They were famous pioneers in their own right, but their reputation was certainly enhanced by what must have been a very unexpected accolade in that the type names of British military aircraft should have French names! Even the remote possibility of a French 'SE' — 'Sopwith' or 'Short' Experimental, or even an 'AE' or 'Avro' experimental, puts a considerable strain on the best of imaginations. Further, the index lists other French designers, a Spanish explorer, a French lieutenant, a Boer general, North American Indians, a Romanian engineer, a Carthaginian general, a Scandinavian pirate, even an Australian designer and a wing commander RAAF at that! What a self-effacing lot we British are, and from the above we may conclude that we are not as insular as we are made out to be.

Avro Shackleton. Named after Sir Ernest Shackleton, Explorer (1874–1922).

Douglas Dakota

General Aircraft Hotspur

Handley-Page Clive

Gloster Gladiator

Vickers Viking

Vickers Jockey

Fairey Gordon

Part 12 — Allegorical

'Which things are an allegory.'
— Galatians (4.24)

'PERTAINING TO, CHARACTERISTIC of or having the nature of, comparison, simile, parallel, contrast, match, pair, representation of a subject to illustrate deeper or more general truths. In short, a very difficult chapter to illustrate, and hopefully the names will illustrate themselves — in allegorical terms.

'Again to the battle, Achaeans!
Our hearts bid the tyrants defiance!
Our land, the first garden of Liberty's tree,
It has been, and yet shall be, the land of the free.'
— Thomas Campbell (1774–1844)

Boulton Paul Defiant

No. 264 (Madras Presidency) Squadron
A Helmet with the Motto: 'We Defy.' A helmet with the visor closed indicates readiness for combat. The Motto derives from the Squadron's aircraft: Defiants.

Part 13 — Meteorology

'Why didst thou promise such a beauteous day,
And make me travel forth without my cloak,
To let base clouds o'ertake me on my way. . .?'
— Shakespeare, Sonnet 34

IN THE RAF naming systems over the years, there was no specific call for meteorological names. Those aircraft that had such names under an RAF system were from 1932 onwards, and were fighters with the requirement for 'general words indicating speed, activity or aggressiveness'. To satisfy this condition, the weather and its many vagaries supplied some splendid names.

The word 'meteorology' comes from the Greek 'meteorologia', 'discussion of astronomical phenomena', and there being a very clear distinction between meteorology and astronomy, the original meaning has been lost. In the eighteenth century the study of the weather was known as 'aeromancy' which might have served well as the title of this book; an attractive combination of 'aeronautics' and 'romance'.

The technical meaning of a name is given in the index, and it is interesting to note three *Cyclone*s, three *Tornado*s and three *Whirlwind*s, but why no *Tempest*? That is entire romance, and just a poetic name, and so is outlawed to 'Miscellaneous'. Of *Hurricane* there is but one, for it stood alone.

Part 14 — Education

''Tis education forms the common mind,
Just as the twig is bent, the tree's inclined'
— Alexander Pope (1688-1744)

THE 1911 ROYAL Aircraft Factory had no particular 'code' for trainers, nor had the February 1918 naming system, and it would seem that at that time this was not a matter of any great import. Such a function was obviously recognised, but not enough to warrant an allocated naming system. Training in the March system would have come under 'more than one seat', to which 'zoological — animals' was allocated, but this equally applied to fighters and bombers, and a seaplane, trainer or otherwise, would be 'waterfowl and fishes'. Even the final July system did not recognise the trainer, being the same as March, and this was exactly followed in 1921.

1927, for all its unpopularity, did recognise a separate trainer class, which was allocated the letter 'T', thus the Avro *Tutor* of 1929. The Hawker *Tomtit* of 1928 was another, also educational but with a bird name. In 1932 came the first specific link to education: 'words indicating tuition, and places of education' were allocated to trainers to which was added in 1939 'but not Air Forces Training Establishments'.

'*Harvard*, eh? — *Balliol* myself, old boy!'

As Dr Johnson remarked: 'There's a woundy luck in names, Sir, an' a Man knew it.' The 'educational' ruling certainly applied up to 1964, as witness the DH *Dominie* (the second of that name).

Avro – the *Cadet* and the *Prefect*

By courtesy of *Aeroplane*

Part 15 — Miscellaneous

'Here stands the shadow of a glorious name. . .'
— Lucan (AD 39–65)

It is interesting to note that out of approximately 250 names, only two are directly from RAF naming systems; that is, from 1918. One was the Westland *Welkin* fighter of 1942, the name being the Anglo-Saxon for the arch or vault of heaven. This hardly indicates speed or aggression, but in view of the fundamental inferno of the outer regions it may be considered to reflect some activity. To make 'the Welkin ring' was to create a great fury of sound, so satisfying the Air Ministry as to adequate activity.

The second was the Hawker *Tempest* fighter of 1939, whose name certainly reflects the attributes laid down by the 1932/39 systems, but it is a poetic word and is not found in the meteorologist's handbook.

All other names are 'Maker' or 'xxx', indicating an exception to the current naming system. Many, of course, were experimental or for evaluation, and it was of great credit to the RAF that it took so wide an interest in so many types of aircraft and engine. That intellectual curiosity, the willingness to encourage manufacturers and even mad inventors, and the determination to find the best that could be afforded was an attitude of mind that was to pay handsome dividends. The RAF was triumphant, but that would have not been possible without research, development, and the 'miscellaneous' preparation.

Part 16 — Nicknames

'Of all eloquence, a nickname is the most concise; of all arguments the most unanswerable.'

'A nickname is the hardest stone that the Devil can throw.'
— William Hazlitt *On Nicknames* (1778-1830).

The attitude of military authority to the use of nicknames has been covered in Chapter 4 'Naming Systems' and coverage will be found especially in parts 2, 3 and 4 of that chapter.

Mindful of the propensity of the soldier, sailor and airman to give a nickname to almost anything in sight, there must be many more than are here recorded. As the literature seems to record only the better known nicknames, this suggests that either they were not considered an important element of history, and/or they were somewhat improper, as indeed some of them were; those that are lost could well have been unprintable or were of local currency and not recorded.

Letters have been published in various aeronautical journals asking for any known nicknames, but whilst the response has been interesting it has produced comparatively few; Time and Memory take their toll of all of us. An article on the subject is copied from the US magazine *Air Force* which also gives some British nicknames. The article is reproduced with their kind permission.

Referring above to the military propensity for nicknames you may be sure they were given for other than aircraft. Cars with aircraft nicknames, or vice versa, have been listed in a previous chapter. Missiles from aircraft also have names such as *Bullpup*, *Bulldog*, *Condor*, *Falcon*, *Griffon*, *Hawk*, *Hornet*, *Kangaroo*, (Sea) *Skua*, *Snapper*, *Viper*, *Kingfisher*, (Sea) *Eagle*, *Bantam*, *Wasp*, *Albatross*, and no doubt more. Assuredly a 'missile', although beneath the waves, is the torpedo, commonly known as a 'fish' (and the torpedo-carrying *Wellington* was the 'Fishington'). Quite frightening was the returning torpedo with the mild but apt name of *Fido* (also an RAF runway fog-dispersing system). Torpedoes do not normally return to aircraft, but aircraft have been known to follow torpedoes. Mines were known as 'vegetables', and quite logically the air-laying operation, or sowing, was 'gardening'.

It is interesting that, as with the other foreign aircraft in this book, the Japanese Imperial Air Force also had names/nicknames for some of their aircraft, and the following are the same names as those used by the British and Americans: 'Flying Dragon', 'Storm Dragon', 'Fire Dragon', 'Peregrine Falcon', 'Sabre', 'Thunderbolt', 'Comet', 'Crane', 'Phoenix', 'Flashing Lightning', 'Swallow' and 'Hurricane'. The Allied code-names included 'Buzzard', 'Goose', and 'Willow', which was an early British airship. The one Japanese aircraft listed with a name and evaluated by the RAF in the Far East was the *Dinah*, but that is an Allied codename. Two other Japanese aircraft were so evaluated but have no name or codename. All other Japanese captured aircraft went to the USA, and to some Far East countries.

And finally a leader page from *Flight* magazine of 1 September 1979 is of interest as regards American names.

Names of the planes

Attention all you military readers — this is not another Spamcan page. A serious defence topic demands your interest.

Relax, it was only a rumour! The F-16 has not been christened *Condor* no doubt to General Dynamics' relief. Protecting the F-16's delicate image from the lascivious assaults of unfeeling journalists must be a full-time job for GD's public relations staff without hanging an Albatross — sorry, *Condor* — round their necks.

We personally feel that an aircraft as beautiful as the F-16 deserves a fitting name. The thought of that Star Wars shape carrying a title which calls to mind a monstrous bird perpetually wheeling round the sky, because it is too dimwitted to land, offends our poetic nature. We mean no insult to the Society for the Prevention of Cruelty to Condors, but hereby launch our campaign to give the F-16 a fitting name.

There's the rub. What is a fitting name?

The Americans are keen on alphanumerics, resisting the allure of magic names like *Sabre*, in preference to 'F-86'. Even Ed Heinemann, designer of the *Skyhawk* refers to his creation as the 'A-4'.

At times the serial has a unique attraction, such as the F-111, which was never named, at least nor printably. At other times numbers are just a cursed nuisance. Those of you less fortunate and talented, perhaps, cannot tell the difference between F-14s, F-15s, F-16s and F-18s. How do you explain to someone over the telephone that an 'eff-one-hundred' is an aircraft while an 'eff-one-hundred' is an engine?

The F-16 is in danger of falling into the F-111 trap; the serial slips off the tongue too easily. We must fight this insidious menace. After all, other American fighters have names; the F-14 *Tomcat* (admittedly this lacks the venom of *Hellcat*); the F-15 *Eagle* (say no more); the F-18 *Hornet* (hmmmm). Excuse us while we consult our copy of Jane's *Plane Names to Bring Tears to Your Eyes* . . . *Albacore, Bobolink, Cubaroo, Gnatsnapper, Knuckleduster, Snargasher, Vildebeest, Warthog* . . .

Warthog? That reminds us. All those of you still suffering shock following the christening of the A-10 *Thunderbolt II* can relax. Warthog is alive and well and living in the A-10 squadrons. *Pig, Porker, Warthog* . . . You can trust pilots to find an apt name.

Aptness is the key to the naming game. Northrop's hooded YG-17 bore the title *Cobra*. The McDonnell Douglas F-15 could merit no other name but *Eagle*. For F-16 there can be only one name, a name which crystallises the F-16's thoroughbred qualities as aptly as it did those of the Second World War's greatest American fighter. Support the campaign to name the F-16. Vote *Mustang* II.

G.W.
Flight
1 September 1979

What They *Really* Called Them

Most airplanes have at least two names — the official one and the one given by the troops.

By Jeffrey P. Rhodes, Aeronautics Editor

Illustrations by Bob Stevens

[Reprinted by permission from *Air Force* magazine. Copyright Air Force Assocation, Arlington, VA, USA.]

After at least four rounds of suggestions and reviews over eight years, the Rockwell B-1 bomber was officially nicknamed *Lancer* this spring. That may catch on as an everyday flight-line reference, or it may not. The airmen who fly and fix airplanes have a long history of deciding for themselves what they will call their machines.

In the list that follows, by no means complete (either in terms of aircraft that have had unofficial nicknames or as a complete list for a given aircraft), some aircraft will be seen to have several "real" (flight-line) nicknames, some affectionate, others derogatory. In some cases, the disrespectful appellations are the work of rivals who fly some other airplane. In other instances, the tough-sounding name was awarded with fondness and used with considerable pride. Still others were given because the airplane was regarded as a "dog".

Aircraft are listed by the date of first flight of the prototype (or specific model), except for such planes as the C-47, which moved over from the commercial world. The dates for those reflect when they joined the military. (Another exception: the SR-71 date is first take-off of the SR-71 — not the A-12 — from the Lockheed Skunk Works.)

Aircraft (Year of First Flight)	Official Nickname	Real Nickname(s)
US Air Force/Army		
Curtiss JN-4 (1914)	None	Jenny
		Canuck (Canadian-built version)
Boeing P-26 (1932)	None	Peashooter
Douglas C-47 (1935)	Skytrain *Dakota*	Gooney Bird
		Placid Plodder
		Dowager Duchess
		Old Methuselah
		Grand Old Lady
	B.E.A. Pionair Class.	(names also applied to DC-3, C-53, and C-117)
North American AT-6 Texan (T-6) (1938)		Awful Terrible Six
		Mosquito (Korean War)
North American B-25 (1939)	Mitchell	Billy's Bomber
Beech C-45 (1940)	Expeditor	Bug Smasher
Martin B-26 (1940)	Marauder	Widow-Maker
		Flying Prostitute (it has no visible means of support)
		Baltimore Whore
Vultee BT-13 (1940)	Valiant	Vibrator
		Bee Tee
North American P-51 (1941) *and the Invader*	Mustang	'Stang
		Peter-Dash-Flash
		Spam Can
Republic P-47 (1941)	Thunderbolt	Jug
		T-Bolt
Ryan PT-22 (1941)	Recruit	Maytag Messerschmitt (Also a generic reference to L-series [Liaison] aircraft)
Cessna UC-78 (1942)	Bobcat	Bamboo Bomber
		Rhapsody in Glue
		San Joaquin Beaufighter
		Useless 78
		Double-Breasted Cub
Douglas A-26 (1942)	Invader	Li'l Racer
		L'il Hummer
Sikorsky R-4 (1942)	Hoverfly	Flying Eggbeater
		Frustrated Palm Tree
Consolidated C-109 (1943)	Liberator	Cee-One-Oh-Boom (several of these cargo B-24s exploded while ferrying fuel over the Hump to China)
Curtiss XP-55 (1943)	Ascender	Ass-Ender (its canards and rear-mounted engine made it appear to be flying backwards)
Fairchild C-87 (1944)	Packet	Crowd Killer
Douglas A-1 (1945)	Skyraider	Spad
		Sandy (A-1H only)
Convair B-36 (1946)	Peacemaker	Aluminium Overcast
		Magnesium Overcast

Aircraft (Year of First Flight)	Official Nickname	Real Nickname(s)
Republic F-84 (1946)	Thunderjet	Hog Lead Sled Lieutenant-Eater
Fairchild C-119 (1947)	Flying Boxcar	Dollar Nineteen Crowd Killer
Lockheed T-33 (1948)	Shooting Star	T-Bird
Northrop F-89 (1948)	Scorpion	FOD Vacuum (because of its low intakes) Stanley Steamer (because of its oversized main landing gear)
Douglas C-124 (1949)	Globemaster II	Aluminium Overcast Old Shaky
North American F-86D (1949)	Sabre	Sabre Dog
Lockheed C-121 (1950)	Constellation	Connie Flying Speed Brake
Republic F-84F (1950)	Thunderstreak	Super Hog Lead Sled Ground-Loving Whore
Boeing B-52 (1952)	Stratofortress	BUFF (Big Ugly Fat Feller — polite form) Monkeyknocker (Vietnam) Coconutnocker (Vietnam)
Vertol CH-21 (1952)	Workhorse	Flying Banana
Convair F-102	Delta Dagger	Deuce
Martin B-57 (1953)	Canberra	Cranberry
North American F-100 (1953)	Super Sabre	Hun Silver Dollar
Cessna T-37 (1954)	Tweet	World's Largest Dog Whistle Converter (converts fuel into noise) Hummer Tweety Bird

Aircraft (Year of First Flight)	Official Nickname	Real Nickname(s)
Lockheed C-130 (1954)	Hercules	Herky Bird Herk Hog (ski-equipped LC-130s are Ski-Hogs)
Lockheed F-104 (1954)	Starfighter	Missile with a Man in it
McDonnell F-101 (1954)	Voodoo	One-Oh-Wonder
Convair TF-102 (1955)	Delta Dagger	Tub (from bulged cockpit)
Lockheed U-2 (1955)	None	Dragon Lady Deuce Black Bird Angel
Republic F-105 (1955)	Thunderchief	Thud Lead Sled Thunderthud Squash Bomber (if all else fails, turn off the engine and squash the target) Triple Threat (it had three ways it could kill the pilot) Ultra Hog Iron Butterfly
Bell UH-1 (1956)	Iroquois	Huey (some versions were called "Slick" or "Hog")
Boeing KC-135 (1956)	Stratotanker	Stratobladder Flying Gas Station Tank GLOB (Ground-Loving Old Bastard)
Convair B-58 (1956)	Hustler	Delta Queen
Convair F-106 (1956)	Delta Dart	Six Sixshooter (with gun pod attached)
Cessna U-3 (1957)	None	Blue Canoe
Kaman HH-43 (1958)	Huskie	Flying S--t-house
McDonnell Douglas F-4 (1958)	Phantom II	Double Ugly Rhino Old Smokey
Northrop T-38 (1959)	Talon	White Rocket
Boeing CH-47 (1961)	Chinook	S--t-hook Hook
Hughes OH-6 (1963)	Cayuse	Loach (from original LOH [Light Observation Helicopter] designation) Egg
Lockheed C-141 (1963)	StarLifter	StarLizard (from its camouflage paint scheme) T-Tailed Mountain Magnet
Cessna T-41 (1964) (military 172 Skyhawk)	Mescalero	Chickenhawk F-172

Aircraft (Year of First Flight)	Official Nickname	Real Nickname(s)	Aircraft (Year of First Flight)	Official Nickname	Real Nickname(s)
Douglas AC-47 (1964)	Skytrain	Puff the Magic Dragon Spooky Dragon (and Dragonship)	McDonnell Douglas F-15 (1972)	Eagle	Great Bird Rodan Big Bird Tennis Court (a match could be played on its fuselage and wings) Aluminium Overcast
General Dynamics F-111 (1964)	None	Aardvark Flying Edsel Widow-Maker Switchblade Swinger	Boeing T-43 (1973)	None	Gator (from navigator) Strike Pig
Lockheed SR-71 (1964)	None	Blackbird Habu (an Okinawan species of snake) Lead Sled	Martin Marietta X-24B (1973)	None	Flying Flatiron
Sikorsky CH-54 (1964)	Tarhe	Skycrane Crane	General Dynamics F-16 (1974)	Fighting Falcon	Electric Jet Viper Lawn Dart Little Hummer
Bell AH-1 (1965)	Huey Cobra	Snake	Rockwell B-1 (1974)	Lancer	Bone (from B-one) Lawn Dart The Jet
LTV A-7 (1965)	Corsair II	SLUF (Short Little Ugly Feller — polite form) Man-Eater	Sikorsky UH-60 (1974)	Black Hawk	Catfish
Northrop M2-F2/M2-F3 (1966/1970)	None	Flying Bathtub Cadillac (from its 1950s-style tail fins)	Grumman EF-111 (1977)	Raven	Sparkvark Electronic Fox
Cessna O-2 (1967)	None	Duck (from the way its landing gear retracted) Blow-Suck (from its powerplant arrangement) Pushme-Pullyu	Lockheed F-117 (1981)	None	The Black Jet Nighthawk Frisbee F-19 (Note: "Wobbly Goblin" is purely a media creation)
Lockheed C-5 (1968)	Galaxy	Fat Albert	Grumman X-29 (1984)	None	Polecat
Martin Marietta X-24A (1970)	None	Flying Potato	**Generic References**		
			All rescue aircraft (SB-17, SB-29, SA-16, etc.)	Various	Dumbo
Fairchild A-10 (1972)	Thunderbolt II	Warthog SLAT (Slow, Low, Aerial Target) Porker Hog	All cargo aircraft	Various	Trashhauler Trashcarrier

Aircraft (Year of First Flight)	Official Nickname	Real Nickname(s)
US Navy/Marine Corps		
Grumman FF-1 (1931)	None	FiFi
Stearman N2S (PT-17) (1934)	Kaydet	Yellow Peril
Consolidated PBY (1935)	Catalina	Pigboat
		P-Boat
		Black Cat (those aircraft involved in a specific, continuing, night mission only)
Naval Aircraft Factory N3N (1935)	None	Yellow Peril
Vought SB2U (1936)	Vindicator	Wind Indicator
		Vibrator
Douglas SBD (A-24) (1938)	Dauntless	Slow But Deadly
North American SNJ (AT-6) (1938)	Texan	J-Bird
Beech SNB (AT-11) (1940)	Kansan	Slow Navy Bomber
Vought F4U (1940)	Corsair	Bent-Wing Bird
Grumman TBF/ General Motors TBM (1941)	Avenger	Turkey
McDonnell F2H (1947)	Banshee	Banjo
		Drut
Beech T-34 (1948)	Mentor	Radial Interceptor
Douglas F3D (F-10) (1948)	Skyknight	Whale
North American AJ-1 (1948)	Savage	Salvage
Vought F7U (1948)	Cutlass	Gutless Cutlass
Douglas F4D (F-6) (1951)	Skyray	Ford (from pronunciation of F-4-D)
Douglas A3D (A-3) (1952)	Skywarrior	All Three Dead (no ejection seats)
Grumman S2F (S-2) (1952)	Tracker	Stoof (from pronunciation of S-2-F)
Lockheed WV-2 (EC-121) (1953)	Warning Star	Willie Victor
Douglas A-4 (1954)	Skyhawk	Scooter
		Heinemann's Hot Rod
		Tinker Toy
		Bantam Bomber
		Mighty Mite
		Skyhog
Vought F-8 (1955)	Crusader	MiG Master
Grumman WF-1 (E-1) (1956)	Tracer	Willie Fudd
		Stoof With a Roof (because of the large radome)
Douglas EA-3 (1958)	Skywarrior	Electric Whale
North American T-2 (1958)	Buckeye	Attack Guppy
Douglas ERA-3 (1960)	Skywarrior	Warbird
Grumman E-2 (1960)	Hawkeye	Hummer
Grumman EA-6 (1963)	Intruder/Prowler	Sterile Arrow

Aircraft (Year of First Flight)	Official Nickname	Real Nickname(s)
McDonnell Douglas/ British Aerospace AV-8 (1966)	Harrier	Jump Jet
		Whistling S--tcan
		Scarier
Grumman F-14 (1970)	Tomcat	Turkey
Lockheed S-3 (1971)	Viking	Hoover (from sound of its turbofan engines)
Sikorsky CH-53E (1974)	Super Stallion	Super S--tter (from its tendency to leak hydraulic fluid)
Foreign		
Bristol Fighter (1916)	None	Brisfit
		Biff
Royal Aircraft Factory R.E.8 (1916)	None	Harry Tate
de Havilland DH-4 (1917)	None	Flaming Coffin (from alleged tendency to burn)
Junkers Ju-52 (1930)	None	Tante Ju (Auntie Junkers)
		Iron Annie
Dornier Do-11 (1932)	None	Fliegender Sarg (Flying Coffin)
Heinkel He-51 (1933)	None	Caza de Cadena (Chain Fighter, from the Nationalists' follow-the-leader strafing tactics in the Spanish Civil War)
Supermarine Walrus (1933)	None	Shagbat
Fairey Swordfish (1934)	None	Stringbag
Avro Anson (1935)	None	Faithful Annie
Dornier Do-17 (1935)	None	Fliegender Bleistift (Flying Pencil)
Hawker Hurricane IIB (1935)	None	Hurribomber
		Hurricat (these were catapulted from merchant ships)
Messerschmitt Bf-109 (1935)	None	Usually called by series name (e.g. Bf-19E was Emil), but Bf-109G (Gustav) also called Beule (Boil) for additional equipment crammed in and faired over

Aircraft (Year of First Flight)	Official Nickname	Real Nickname(s)
Fairey Battle (1936)	None	Fairy Rattle
Hadley Page Hampden (1936)	None	Flying Frying Pan
Vickers Wellington (1936)	None	Wimpy
Westland Lysander (1936)	None	Lizzie
Blohm & Voss BV-138 (1937)	None	*Fliegender Holzschuh* (Flying Wooden Shoe)
Focke-Wulf FW-189 (1938)	*Uhu* (Owl)	*Fliegendes Auge* (Flying Eye)
Fairey Albacore (1939)	None	Applecore
Heinkel He-177 (1939)	*Greif* (Griffon)	*Luftwaffenfeuerzeug* (Luftwaffe's Lighter)
Mitsubishi G4M (1939)	None (Allied code name "Betty")	*Hamaki* (Cigar)
de Havilland Mosquito (1940)	None	Wooden Wonder Mossie
Hawker Typhoon (1940)	None	Tiffie
Fiesler Fi-103 (V-1) (1942)	None	*Kirschkern* (Cherry Stone)
Messerschmitt Me-262 (1942)	*Schwalbe* (Swallow) *Sturmvogel* (Storm Bird)	Turbo
Messerschmitt Me-323 (1942)	*Gigant* (Giant)	*Leukoplastbomber* (Adhesive Tape Bomber — it was mostly canvas)
Dornier Do-335 (1943)	*Pfeil* (Arrow)	*Ameisenbär* (Anteater — it had a long nose)
Gloster Meteor (1943)	None	Meatbox
Focke-Wulf FW-190D (1944)	None	Dora *Ameisenbär* (Anteater)
Avro Shackleton (1949)	None	100,000 Rivets Flying in Loose Formation

Reproduced from *Air Force* Magazine, September 1990.

Part 17 — The Great Unnamed

'Call things by their right names!'
— Robert Hall (1764-1831)

THE SUBJECT OF the book is names and naming systems, and the 'qualification' for any aircraft or engine is that it also had, or has, some military connotation, if only a one-off for evaluation purposes. Thus are included some obscure, indeed very obscure, types, which create the absurdity that there were some well-known squadron types, produced in quantity and with a reputation left behind, yet which do not qualify. Briefly, and for a few chosen aircraft, this part seeks to redress the absurdity, but as with the Classics in Chapter 6, it is an arbitrary choice by the author. Many will no doubt

disagree with the choice, and mindful of this an opinion was sought from various aviation historians. Agreement was pretty general, but any praise or blame is entirely due to the author.

From 1918, of course, it was RAF policy that *all* aircraft should be named, and as will have been seen, much Air Ministry time was given to suggestions and the final choice. It is odd, therefore, that two great aircraft of this part after 1918 should have gone unnamed. Before 1918 the Royal Aircraft Factory made no provision for names, and any 'nicknames' met with military disapproval; in contrast, 1918 to 1927 saw *everything* named, production orders or not. Most odd of all is the lack of recorded nicknames for some aircraft. Engines, somehow, do not lend themselves to such semantic frivolities — they do all the work and the aeroplanes just follow . . .

The 'Classics' and the 'Great Unnamed' really serve the same purpose, and but for this breaking of the eligibility rule, the latter would be omitted from this book. All the unnamed in this chapter served long and well in Britain's flying services, but there remains one aircraft which is on the author's historical conscience in regard to this book. As with the others, it had no name and no nickname — but it would have in time, and could well have been a 'classic'. It was the British Aircraft Corporation *TSR 2*, a supersonic strike and reconnaissance bomber powered by two Bristol *Olympus* engines (the *Concorde* has four) and planned to replace the English Electric *Lightning*. However, this was the British time of 'no more manned fighter aircraft', an absurdity as time has proved, and *TSR 2* was to be the one grudging exception. First flight was in 1964 and it was cancelled in 1965.

Avro 504 (Avro 500) — Monosoupape (1)

Why '500'? After a few early types, the company decided on a systemised type numbering system, and presumably it was a case of where better to start than 500? Why there was never a name for so prolific and important a breed is not known, and perhaps '500' was thought a significant name in its own right. The lack of nicknames (but there must have been many) is also a mystery, and the only one — the 'Mono(soupape) Avro' — is merely a description to differentiate the current from the earlier (*Gnôme*) engines. It is strange because we are dealing with a long-lived aircraft, serving the RNAS, RFC and RAF from 1913 to 1927, and four civil types were even being pressed into RAF service as glider tugs in 1939! There can have been no other aircraft that saw military service at the beginning of *both* World War One and World War Two.

Developed from the Type 500, the 504 was built in secrecy to race in the 1913 Aerial Derby, and took part the next day after its first flight, making a great impression even if having to force-land. In that same year, a 504 reached 15,000 feet, probably a world record but not then recognised as such. It was also ambidextrous, being as nimble on floats as on wheels.

The War Office gave a first order for twelve, delivered in 1914, and the RNAS followed suit with a first order for four. The RFC moved with their contingent to France in August, and the 504 acquired the inglorious distinction of being the first British fighter to be shot down in World War One; revenge was sweet — a German *Albatros* was shot down a

Avro 504N

Royal Aircraft Factory BE 2c — 1914 Blériot Experimental Renault (1)

Its pilot attraction lay in its stability, but this was to prove a great disadvantage for a fighter one of whose essential assets should be that of easy and quick manoeuvre. Where this was not a special requirement, the BE 2 series offered a very stable gun platform, and it was with this characteristic that it found its greatest combat successes in 'Home Defence', shooting down eight Zeppelin airships. As most of these were over land, it would be an event directly in the public eye, and would lead to praise not only for the pilot but also for the BE 2. One such pilot was Lt W. Leefe-Robinson who was awarded the VC.

Royal Aircraft Factory BE2c

month later, one of the first British victories. The RFC aircraft were little used for front-line operations, but the RNAS took part in the first pre-planned bombing raid on the Zeppelin sheds at Friedrichshafen. An audacious and successful mission, it was followed up by a raid on Ostend, which destroyed two U-boats. The 504s were then relegated to Home Defence Squadrons and to training. It became the *Mono Avro* in 1916, and had also become the 504 K, by which famous appellation it is mostly remembered.

In experimental guise, the 504 was one of the first aircraft to be catapult-launched from the deck of a ship. Of greater consequence was its association with the RFC/RAF Gosport School of Flying where a standardised system of pilot training was introduced by Major R. Smith-Barry, and led to the RAF (who from 1918 to 1939 also provided pilots for the FAA) being considered as having the best trained pilots. The Gosport tube will be well remembered, a speaking tube between instructor and pupil which led to many misunderstandings . . .

At the end of the war, eighty 504s were being produced a week, and with the amalgamation of the RFC and RNAS to become the RAF there were 2,999 on charge. By the time production ended and the last was delivered to the RAF in 1927, a total of over 10,000 had been built.

One in military guise is now with the Shuttleworth Trust at Old Warden, and is still flying. Starting with 'A', the last variant was 'M', but it is the 'K' (*Monosoupape*) and the 'N' (*Lynx*) which are associated with RAF training; with the 'N' the famous anti-noseover skid disappeared.

There were many military sales overseas, and the 504 had a very varied civil career. Many thousand had their first flight in the Avro, and the Cobham Flying Circus and the other 'joy riders' really introduced the aeroplane to the British public: now they could actually take part. Many of those who gladly paid their five shillings for a fifteen-minute flight never got over the experience and joined the Royal Air Force.

The 504 was replaced by the Avro *Tutor*, and Avro training aircraft prepared the majority of RAF pilots for the outbreak of World War Two; the *Tiger Moth* and *Magister* were then to take on the task.

A distinction must be made between an Avro *Trainer* and the Avro Strainer. The latter was an early Avro patent for tensioning the interplane bracing wires, and which in the early days was quite a money-spinner for the company. They needed it in those early days.

One of the most striking early examples of widespread mass production, the BE series was produced by at least twenty-two British manufacturers, who completed over 3,500 aircraft. The BE 2c was a considerably better design than its predecessors. It did, however, come in for much criticism in 1916, not entirely warranted, for the statistics of the time showed that it was, in fact, the most durable of the eight types then in service with the RFC. Its mortality rate, or 'wastage' rate as it was put, was seventeen per cent, and that was the lowest of all.

By 1917 it was outclassed by the German *Albatros* and the Halberstadt fighter, and the poor BE 2c was to become known as 'Fokker Fodder'; but the RFC continued to fly and fight in the BE 2 (now also with an 'e', 'f' and 'g'), and for the one compelling reason that at that time there were no new types to take on the challenge. In the 'Bloody April' of 1917, sixty aircraft were lost to enemy action.

The obvious nickname was *Stability Jane*, and there was also *Querk*, so perhaps the Lady was not as demure as history records. The BE 2 series served in the Home Defences (UK), Africa, Aden, Macedonia and India, and then less glamorously as a trainer.

By 1918 few remained in service, but enough to equip three RAF Squadrons. Although now in the RAF, and the 1918 naming system was in force, there was still no name for it. There never was, possibly (a) because it was not worth it for the time remaining, and (b) because there was no one manufacturer to press for one, although the Royal Aircraft Factory had been allocated 'RA' or 'RHA'. On 1 April 1918 it became the 'Establishment' and its name-bestowing powers were no more.

Airco (de Havilland) DH 2 1915 Monosoupape (1)

The single-seat 'gunbus' pusher was, in effect, a scaled-down version of the DH 1, and this configuration was retained owing to official military lack of anticipation of the need for a gun firing through the propeller, thus the gun in front and the engine behind. The Germans were ahead with the Fokker interruptor gear, with which they had a great advantage.

Some 400 DH 2s were delivered to the RFC, and at first were none to successful, the pilot aiming the Lewis gun and not the aircraft as a fixed gun. This lesson learned, pilots had a strong mount with good handling to make a fully aerobatic fighting machine, and to win many victories.

The first major contest was in the Battle of the Somme with continuous fighting against the German Fokker monoplanes, and it was hoped that the DH 2 would end the 'Fokker Scourge'. (Note that Fokker, a Dutchman, had once offered his products to the British Government. . .) No. 24 Squadron flew 774 combats with DH 2s, and destroyed forty-four enemy aircraft, a worthwhile contribution to the war effort. In the UK, a Home Defence DH 2 attacked the Zeppelin L 48, which was an early warning to the Germans that this 'secret' weapon was indeed vulnerable to the aeroplane.

One of the longest aerial combats of the war, in 1916, was between Manfred von Richthofen and Major Hawker in a DH 2, who sadly lost the contest. To balance the story, the leading German ace of the time was Oswald Boelke who lost his life in a fight with the DH 2s — but perhaps only because one of his own squadron collided with him.

When the DH 5 appeared on the Western Front, DH 2s were sent to the Near East, serving in Palestine and Macedonia. At home, a hundred were issued as trainers, and by 1918 their work for the RFC was done. Its task was to be the first British fighter aircraft specifically designed and not just adapted to fight.

In an age when nicknames were in particular vogue among the 'rude soldiery' it is surprising that there appears to be no record of any nicknames for the DH 2; but no doubt there were many. It was not an outstanding fighter, but it nevertheless has its place in military history; it was strong and able and its pilots were certainly willing.

Airco (de Havilland) DH 4 1916 *Eagle* (1)

The connection between Geoffrey de Havilland and Airco (the Aircraft Manufacturing Company) needs some explanation. De Havilland was a designer and test pilot at the Royal Aircraft Factory at Farnborough, and from his drawing-board stemmed the 'DH' series. Whilst the aircraft were manufactured by Airco, they all carried the DH initials and the following numbers. De Havilland himself later joined Airco, and then founded the de Havilland Company in 1920.

The DH 4 first flew in 1916, first with *Puma* engine and later with the *Eagle* which made it the better aeroplane, and this fighter is best remembered as a high performance day bomber! This apparent contradiction may be resolved (?) by the following correspondence: 'Capt. Mayo is returning to England with the DH 4 machine. We have suggested that its chief function should be as a reconnaissance fighter, but it should be able to carry the new 200 lb, or two 112 lb bombs, if necessary. It is now necessary to decide the role of the DH 4.'

Airco (de Havilland) DH 4

It would make an excellent bomber with the new gyroscopic bombsight, and eliminate the BE 2, RE 7, A-W 160 hp Beardmore and the Martinsyde from the programme.' Such seems to have been undue optimism, but in October 1916, Brooke-Popham wrote to Brancker (both to become great names): 'As a reconnaissance fighter, I think it will be a first-rate machine but do not think it is entirely suitable for bomb dropping. It is extremely handy to fly, is quick into turns, with very sensitive fore and aft control, and has a very large speed range.' This is all understandable in that such aircraft could readily be multi-purpose to some extent; to have called the DH *Tiger Moth* a bomber in World War Two would be entirely correct . . . for one particular purpose at one particular time.

An interesting aspect of the DH 4 design was that it could be fitted with any type of suitable engine. It was the first British aircraft to be specifically designated a bomber, but also destroyed a Zeppelin and a U-boat.

Used both by RNAS and RFC, its greatest successes were with the Eagle engine, and in the end that was as a bomber. Some DH 4s were modified to become the DH 9, but this was not so successful as it had a *Puma* rather than an *Eagle* engine. The RAF had 584 DH 4 aircraft on charge in 1918, and the type then served with eight RAF Squadrons. With other 'Factory' aircraft, it was not given a name in 1918. For further explanation, see 'BE 2' in this part.

Finally the DH 4 deserves one particular accolade. It was built in quantity (4,846) in the USA, and was the only US combat aircraft to reach the fighting front in France. It further served well in America, war surplus aircraft being used for the pioneer US Airmail Service.

Airco (de Havilland) DH 9a 1918 *Eagle* (1)

Ninack or *Ninak* was an improvement on the DH 9 which had not proved itself as a warplane, and was rapidly replaced by the DH 9a. Nevertheless, the DH 9 and 9a were sold to some

Airco (de Havilland) DH 9a

16 overseas countries. One, or both, may also have had the nickname of *De Voortreker*.

Although of AIRCO design the 9a was built by a number of UK manufacturers, and mostly by Westland of Yeovil who had already built the DH 4 on which the DH 9 had been based.

The intended engine was the Rolls-Royce *Eagle* which was such an excellent engine that by 1917 it could not meet the demands of the RFC and RNAS. Thus it was that Westlands turned to the American *Liberty*, a good engine but heavier than the *Eagle* and which led to another 9a nickname — the *Devil* as the aircraft was nose heavy and tended to lose height. But it was to be an outstanding strategic Bomber, but this could only be with the *Eagle* and for the 'Long Range Bombing Programme' of 1918 the Admiralty offered its incoming stocks of the engine.

The DH 9a was in service by August and the attacks on Mannheim and Coblenz, amongst other industrial targets, was one of the factors that convinced the German High Command that they had lost command of the air. This then hastened the end of the war and in November the Armistice was signed.

One of the more obscure duties allocated to the DH 9a was then to fight the Bolsheviks in the Russian Revolution. Somewhat ironically, the aircraft was later made in Russia and sold to Afghanistan! It is believed that a postwar US project was for a pressurised cockpit for high altitude flying,

in which case it would have been a first. The US Army Air Corps was already familiar with the DH 4 in France, and planned to build 4,000 DH 9as in the US. Following the Armistice, only four were built.

But it continued in production for the RAF and Auxiliary Squadrons after the war, and served in 24 RAF and Auxiliary Squadrons until 1931.

The end of the war left a vast store of DH 9 and 9a assemblies and spares, some for RAF production, and some of the balance used by Westland to make the *Wapiti* and the *Walrus*, and de Havilland the *Stag*. Odd that the descendants were named, but not the ancestor.

In its time there were many military and civil applications and the RAF carried out some historic long distance flights, and one of the historic beginnings of what was to become commonplace was the regular Cairo-Baghdad mail run. In 1920 the UK presented a number of aircraft to the Canadian and Australian Governments as an 'Imperial gift'. Apart from many workaday operations, notable events were several long distance Australian flights and the first trans-Canada flight.

The final total was 2,187 built in the UK by 7 Manufacturers. In South Africa they served until 1937, one with a *Viper* engine known as the *Mantis* and one with a *Jupiter* as the *M'Pala*. Incredibly, DH 9as were used in anger during the Spanish Civil War.

The DH 9 first flew in 1917 and so would have no 'name' as such, and 9a first flew as an adapted 9 in 1918. The February RAF naming system of that year required a 'Gt. Britain Town', the March and July systems a 'Zoological' name. Perhaps DH and the Air Ministry just didn't have time to catch up with the changes, and hence the DH 9a finds itself in this part.

Royal Aircraft Factory RE 8 1915 RAF 4a (1)

An addendum to the 1911 'Factory' system of designation was 'RE' for 'Reconnaissance Experimental', but once in service it appears that the RAF aircraft were still 'experimental'! With an RAF 4a engine, the RE 8 was a design replacement for the BE 2c (still serving at the end of the war and after) which first flew in 1916, to be used as an Artillery Spotter and Photo-Reconnaissance.

Royal Aircraft Factory RE8

On 16 July 1916, Brigadier Brooke-Popham wrote: 'The flying qualities of the machine are splendid. The airspeed is 103 full out, flying level, and Gooden flew for at least five minutes at forty-seven on the airspeed indicator, and the machine perfectly under control all the time. It is very handy and easily manoeuvred, lands very slowly and pulls up quickly.' If such were its attributes, why is the RE 8 not now produced for the private pilot, and the engine of 140 hp is just about the same as those of current vintage? A comedian of the time was Harry Tate which, rhyming with RE 8, was immediately adopted as a nickname.

Early experience with the RFC in France was disappointing, and much criticism was levelled at the RE 8; but after investigation, it was agreed that the fault lay not so much with the aeroplane as with the inadequate pilot training of the time. Pilots were scarce, casualties high, and there was pressure to train pilots as quickly as possible, some joining their squadrons in France with very low flying hours. If they survived the early sorties, their training was in action. Service continued until the end of the war, and after with the Royal Air Force. *Harry Tate* was known on the Western Front, in France, Italy, Palestine and Mesopotamia, and used in various combat roles.

A total of 2,262 had been delivered up to 31 March 1918 (the last day of the RFC) and another 1,800 to the RAF before the end of the war. 'Jack' Bruce, in his *Aeroplanes of the Royal Flying Corps* (Putnam) writes: 'Its successes were modest and little known, its failures progressively more numerous as the war went on, yet experienced and determined crews proved that the RE 8 would defend itself pugnaciously in combat.' Such comments perhaps question its choice as one of the 'Great Unnamed'. The sheer number produced, and its deployment in various theatres of war at a very critical time, was a consideration of choice. Whilst not the best of aeroplanes, there was no other at the time as good and without it the ascendancy of the enemy air force and artillery would have lasted longer; and had there been fighters to spare as defence escorts, then the RE 8 would have done its job more than adequately well. In itself, it was designed for reconnaissance with one-gun defence, and not as a fighter.

Royal Aircraft Factory SE 5a *Viper* (1)

This was one of the most successful single-seat fighter aircraft of World War One, a title that would be challenged by the Sopwith *Camel*. Having no name (and only a local nickname), it is a 'classic', but here found amongst the 'great Unnamed'.

Developed from the SE 5, it first flew in November 1916; Captain Ball VC flew it for ten minutes on the next day, noting that he 'didn't like it much'. However, it was later to be a most worthy mount for this equally famous jockey and he was to change his opinion. Many of the RAF 'aces' of this period are associated with the SE 5a.

Armament was a fixed, synchronised Vickers and a Lewis firing over the top plane and mounted on a rail so that it could be brought down to change the 100-round drum, or to clear a stoppage. This was no easy task for the pilot, who still had to fly the plane with one hand, so an enlarged windscreen was fitted to help the pilot, which gave rise to the nickname of 'Greenhouse' for this particular type of SE 5a.

Royal Aircraft Factory SE5a

A local nickname at the 'Factory' at Farnborough was *Sepha*, but this does not seem to have been used by the RFC. It is strange that a so well-known and widely produced aircraft should not have had a universal nickname, and that the RAF did not name it in 1918; even the 'makers' did not name it, but this would not have come from Farnborough (now the Establishment) or from the many sub-contractors. The same applies to the other Farnborough types.

The overall design responsibility was that of Folland (later to set up his own company), and Captain Ball led the first flight of six SE 5as on an offensive patrol, and now 'liking it much better'. Large-scale production had been decided in January 1917, but there were engine problems with the Hispano-Suiza and the Sunbeam *Arab*, and the best engine seems to have been the Wolseley *Viper*, with which the SE 5a is generally associated.

It was the most successful of the many 'Farnborough' designs, and served with twenty-four RFC and RAF Squadrons, and 5,205 were built. In October of 1918, the RAF had 2,696 on charge. Thereafter it served, but now on a modest scale, in both military and civilian guise; and today, 1994, there are about twelve SE 5a replicas, a few in flying condition.

Compared to the number of American aircraft that have served the UK flying services, there have been few British aircraft that have served with the US military. One must, then, record the SE 5a (Hispano-Suiza engine), of which there were sixty delivered to the US Army Air Corps. These were assembled in the USA, and said to be largely from spare parts! Was there an American nickname?

Fairey III 1918 *Eagle* (1)

The Fairey III A and B appeared in 1918, and the last (the F) left the RAF in 1935 (just four years before World War Two) so it was an aircraft of long lineage; which prompts the immediate question as to why it never had a name? There is a part answer which leaves two mysteries unanswered. Firstly, the Air Ministry became somewhat annoyed with Fairey because they did not respond to requests to submit a name. Names supposedly being so important to the manufacturer, why did Fairey not only fail to suggest a name, but also not answer Air Ministry letters? Secondly, as a result of this, the Air Ministry decided to take unilateral action and proposed that the Fairey III would henceforth be known as the *Salmon* or *Griffin;* but it continued as the Fairey III! The sequence of events has not been traced.

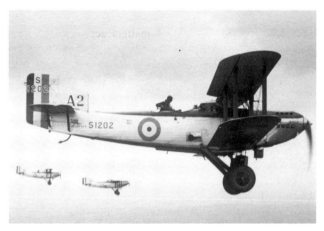

Fairey IIIF

The Fairey III D was a development of the C (which seems logical) and was first delivered to the RAF in November 1918, for them as a land plane and then to the FAA as a seaplane. They were originally fitted with *Eagle* engines but standardised for the most part with the *Lion*. The RAF carried out their first long-distance flights with the III D, one notable flight being in Africa from Cape to Cairo, and with not a single mechanical failure. This was in 1927, and one of the flight pilots was Wing Commander A.T. Harris, later to be 'Bomber' Harris of Bomber Command during World War Two. The III E, a metal version, was nicknamed the *Ferrett*, leading to the III F.

The III F, last of the line, gave excellent service, and was a cleaned-up version of the D. It first flew in 1926 as a two-seat general purpose type, and production ceased in 1932. 691 were built, and the last were used as target tugs in World War Two, recalled from retirement.

In the UK it was used as a day bomber, and the last III in service was retired in Malta in 1935. The IIIF flew many distinguished politicians about the government's business, and there was one flight that deserves special mention — that of the Prime Minister, Mr Ramsay McDonald, as a passenger in the Fairey III F going to the Disarmament Conference in Geneva in 1932.

Was the III F ever known as a *Ramsay*, and why did the III series seem never to have had any universal nickname? The nearest to a nickname was the 'Eversharp Nose' for the clean entry with the Napier *Lion* engine. ('Eversharp' was the name of a pencil with a sharp point.) About 700 were built.

Vickers VC 10 1962 *Conway* (4)

That so renowned a civil transport, later to be an RAF tanker, should have had no name in either sphere is, at least in the terms of this book, a somewhat odd story. So far as it has been pieced together, the story follows.

The name of the earlier Bristol *Britannia* had been criticised in some 'sales' circles as being a marketing problem in selling to foreign countries, and especially in this case to France and America. The point may have been taken by Vickers, but Sir George Edwards (who was then chief designer, and later chairman of the British Aircraft Corporation) has stated that Vickers just got tired of finding new names, and thus the VC 10 (Vickers Commercial) and the BAC III with no name to offend any country or airline.

When the VC 10 was adapted for the RAF, many names were considered and the standard routines were initiated. In the final stages of decision on a shortlist, an Air-Marshal quietly suggested that it have no name but just be VC 10 — which, surprisingly, was equally quietly accepted, with a later comment that this would please BOAC. Why BOAC should be pleased is somewhat puzzling, and going back to the 'code' concept, surely this would have been in keeping with a long-established RAF policy.

Following on a BOAC brochure in 1956, a VC 10 was proposed as the *Vanjet*, a jet-powered *Vanguard*. There was also a VC 11 proposed for British European Airways, but they considered it too big for their routes. Then the designation VC 10 was transferred to a large civil project for BOAC, and which in the event was probably the most popular passenger aircraft of its time. There was also to be a V 1000, but this was cancelled. The RAF also issued a requirement for short field requirements for Transport Command, and this was virtually the same as the BOAC brochure already mentioned.

As the VC 10 wing could not accommodate the big gas-

Vickers VC10

turbine engines of the time, the four Rolls-Royce *Conways* were incorporated into the tail plane and this offered many design advantages, although the new generation of large transport aircraft have opted for wing pylons. The first flight was in June 1962, and BOAC had signed up for thirty-five in 1958. High lift devices gave the VC 10 a superb field performance, so that its take-off and landing distances were comparable to propeller-driven aircraft of that size.

There was also a Super VC 10 for BOAC. The RAF version was for eleven aircraft under a 1960 specification.

Later, in 1984, further VC 10s were recruited from various civil airlines, and they with the earlier batch performed a most important function as fuel tankers. Their worth was amply proven during the Falklands campaign, and during the (1990) Gulf crisis.

Super VC 10s are now (1994) being converted into RAF tankers, having been in storage for a decade.

Whilst the Air Ministry was considering a name for the VC 10, one favourite was that of *Vimy*, after the Vickers bomber of 1918, and so named to commemorate the Battle of Vimy Ridge in France. This, before the decision of no name, was turned down as it was thought that very few of today's generation would be either aware or interested in a battle of long ago. Let us hope that no further battles will be added to the long list in our history.

This book is concerned with type and not with particular individual names, but here an exception is made. VC, stands for Vickers Commercial but also for the Victoria Cross, the highest military decoration in the British Armed Forces. It was thus both imaginative and appropriate that the two types of VC should come together with individual names of RAF VCs of World War One and Two for the militarised aircraft.

Lanoe Hawker, Guy Gibson, Edward Mannock, James McCuden, Albert Ball, Thomas Mottershead, James Nicolson, William Rhodes-Moorhouse, George Thompson, Donald Garland, Thomas Gray, Kenneth Campbell, Hugh Malcolm, David Lord, Arthur Scarf.

Part 18 — Engines

THIS PART DEALS with most of the products of those engine companies whose engine names were 'exceptions' to the July 1918 RAF system of naming aircraft:

Rolls-Royce	— Birds of Prey
Napier	— Arms and Weapons
Armstrong-Siddeley	— Felidae (Cats)
Bristol	— Stars and Planets
Wolseley	— Snakes

Note that the name types did later change: such were Napier with 'deer' names, Rolls-Royce with rivers, and Bristol acquiring the planets. Names of other engine companies were also taken over, on amalgamation or take-over. Whilst the '1918' list covers most of the big engine companies, an exception is de Havilland who were formed as an Aircraft Company in 1920, the engine side in 1926.

Wolseley were later allocated 'Arms and Weapons', and as 'Weapons' is a part on its own (Part 10).

Putting dates to engines has been a difficult task, the literature often being vague or indifferent on that item, and the author is grateful to the information given by Bill Gunston, ex-RAF pilot, one time technical editor of *Flight*, and now a prolific author on matters aeronautical. For a 'genealogical' plan of British Aero Engine manufacturers, see Chapter 3.

Some engines will be found in this chapter in the *Air BP* copy article.

'The Classics' (Chapter 6) give more information on the naming and engine histories of *Monosoupape*, *Gipsy*, *Jupiter*, *Hercules*, *Merlin* and *Avon*.

Also included is an article by the author in *Air BP* (and reproduced with their permission) on 'Fair Names and Famous — British Engines'. Although also covering civil engines, it has a strong military interest and whilst repeating some of the information given in this part, it gives a brief history of the engine companies up to the time of publication of this *Air BP* article, which is now some years old. This means that the listing in it is also far from up-to-date, but the Total Index brings the listing up-to-date to January 1994.

Fair Names and Famous — British Engines

Bearing in mind the astonishing advances in moon exploration made during the past few years, and yet looking back also on nearly seventy years of aviation's technical progress, it seems that there was an unconscious and even 'romantic' anticipation of what was to come. This was not so much in prophecy, which is a conscious act, but in the naming of aircraft and engines, for many of these names expressed the desire to be freed of the Earth's gravity and to find release in space. Maybe even the Royal Air Force, with its 1918 motto of 'Per Ardua ad Astra', was looking forward in prophetic anticipation to the 'seventies.

Often, the names of aircraft and engines have been used more than once in the UK. Recently for example, we have had *Vampire*, *Lightning*, *Fury* and *Dove* for the second or third time. Similarly, in the list of current astronautical hardware names are being used which have a very familiar ring to British ears . . . *Vanguard*, *Pioneer*, *Atlas*, *Mercury*, *Centaur(us)*, *Saturn*, *Scout*, *Thor*, *Titan*, *Meteor*, *Nimbus* and the Russian *Cosmos*.

The purpose of this article is to give a brief history of the naming of British aero-engines. So, as no fewer than five of the names listed above are those of 'Bristol' products, it is appropriate to show first how the astronautical associations of these power plants were really linked with a tradition which began in 1920 and, by coincidence, even earlier.

The British & Colonial Aeroplane Company was founded in February 1910 and began by associating itself with aircraft designed and built by the Zodiac company of France, known also as a constructor of airships. Bristol's first trade-mark was the same as that of the French company — the sign of the Zodiac. In July 1910 Bristol introduced their own design of Zodiac, but with the severance of the French connection four months later changed to the famous 'Bristol' scroll. Today the Zodiac has some remembrance with a mosaic set in the floor of the company's old headquarters known as Filton House in Bristol.

By way of chronological interruption, it must be mentioned that in the early 1930s the signs of the Zodiac (excepting planets and constellations) were reserved officially by the Air Ministry for Wolseley engines; but this was the Morris

(Nuffield) Wolseley firm, linked only in name with the earlier Wolseley of *Adder* and *Python* fame.

Contemporary with the young British & Colonial, and also in Bristol, was the firm of Brasil Straker, of which Roy Fedden was chief engineer. A product of some renown was the Straker Squire motor car, for this was their trade. With the call for aircraft engines in World War One, Brasil Straker embarked upon the manufacture of the Rolls-Royce *Hawk* and *Falcon* and components of *Eagle* engines under government contract and, at the invitation of the Ministry of Munitions, also turned to design. Thus was born the *Mercury*, followed by the *Lucifer*, *Jupiter* and drawing-board *Hercules*, all air-cooled. It is an interesting sidelight of history that the Rolls-Royce licence agreement specifically forbade Brasil Straker to enter into the design of liquid-cooled engines.

Brasil Straker was reorganised at the end of the war as a part of Cosmos Engineering Co, and in 1920 its engine element was taken over by Bristols to form the Engine Division of the Bristol Aeroplane Company — later Bristol Aero Engines Ltd, then Bristol Siddeley, and now the Bristol Division of Rolls-Royce.

If 'Zodiac' and 'Cosmos' were not sufficient in themselves to start a tradition, there is yet another beginning in 1918, but this time it is concerned with aircraft. Primarily because of the 'Brisfits' (Bristol Fighter F2a and 2b) with varying engines, and the consequent difficulties in nomenclature and documentation, the Ministry invited Bristol to suggest a series of distinguishing names for its products. A 'Star' system was put forward as follows:

Bristol Fighter Mercury type (originally Type F2a)	Series I	Rolls-Royce Falcon I
	Series II	Rolls-Royce Falcon II
	Series III	Rolls-Royce Falcon III
	Series IV	Hispano-Suiza (French)
	Series V	Hispano-Suiza (English)
	Series VI	RAF 4.D
	Series VII	Sunbeam
Bristol Monoplane Orion type (originally type M1B or C)	Series I	110hp Le Rhône
	Series II	110hp Clerget
Bristol Fighter Comet type	Series I	Sunbeam Arab
Bristol Fighter Saturn type	Series I	Hispano-Suiza (French
	Series II	Hispano-Suiza (English)

These suggestions were shelved when a system of aircraft nomenclature was introduced for the whole industry in 1918. This included 'reservations' of note, such as 'Animals, except Felidae', and 'Land Birds, except of Prey', which are explained by reference to the later official Air Ministry list of 1921: Rolls-Royce: Birds of Prey, Napier: Arms and Weapons, Armstrong Siddeley: Felidae (Cats), to which was added Canes (Dog tribes) in 1934, Bristol: Planets and Constellations.

It is not to be supposed that Cosmos had any studied connection with Zodiac or the Star names; they just merged into the 'Bristol' tradition with the takeover of Cosmos Engineering: but it was a remarkable coincidence, leading to a tradition which is now unique. An interesting sidelight to this era is that all Bristol engine drawings produced between 1920 and 1942, when Sir Roy Fedden left the company, were

marked F/B for 'Fedden and Butler'.

An even earlier tradition of naming was that of the Sunbeam Motor Company, which became interested in aircraft engines in 1912. After various early designs came the series of named engines, and these (apart from nicknames 'Scouts' and 'Bullets' and the Royal Aircraft Factory system of FE, RE, BE, SE and so on) are among the first in British aviation to have a definite system of designation. It involved not numbers but names, and before the long line of Sunbeam engines came to an end included *Afridi*, *Dyak*, *Maori*, *Cossack*, *Amazon*, *Matabele*, *Sikh*, *Nubian*, *Saracen*, *Malay*, *Bedouin*, *Zulu*, *Gurkha*, *Viking*, *Spartan*, *Tartar* and *Kaffir*.

The choice of such 'tribal' names was possible because some of the earlier engines were destined for use in Royal Navy airships — and to have 'classes' of craft is a naval tradition.

Another early name was that of the Rolls-Royce *Eagle*, which appeared in the spring of 1915. There is no proof, but it seems likely that Claude Johnson deliberately chose it to be the first of a 'class' of engine names. He was then general managing director and, if such credit is really due to him, he chose splendidly and started a tradition of names that has been as fine as the engines themselves.

As already noted, the first official naming system for the Royal Air Force came in 1918. It included 'insects, birds and reptiles' for single-seat fighters and, a little later, 'waterfowl and fishes' for seaplanes and flying boats. Whilst engine name reservations did not become official until 1921, no RAF aircraft has ever borne a name that clashed with the Rolls-Royce series. The company thus established its 'mark' in 1915, and this was respected in the three years (1918-21) before it was laid down as an official choice.

Civil aircraft have had names of birds of prey (as given alongside the Rolls-Royce entries in the index of names) but never those of the Royal Air Force — with one exception, the Martinsyde *Buzzard*, more commonly known as the F4 and reputedly, with a Hispano-Suiza engine, the fastest aircraft of World War One. In quantity production in 1918, the Armistice stopped it seeing war service. The F3 was the same machine with the *Falcon* engine, which was then in short supply. This would have been a 'double bird of prey' although 'Buzzard' was not a true military designation. Naval aircraft have had the names *Skua* and *Osprey*, but these were seabirds of prey, and Rolls-Royce engines were patently related to land birds of prey. Of more significance is that there has always been a Rolls-Royce engine in RAF service since the series started.

The *Kestrel* appeared in 1927 and was for some time known as the 'F' engine. This is believed to have been due to an original intention to repeat the names of the *Falcon* of 1916. The *Kestrel* was followed by an englarged version, the 'H' which became the *Buzzard*. This in turn, was developed to give the 'R' engine for the Schneider Trophy aircraft. Thus three successive engines bore the initials 'FHR'. Was it just coincidence that these could have stood for Frederick Henry Royce?

As in all systems there are exceptions, and so with Rolls-Royce. The *Exe*, *Pennine* and *Boreas* were all 24-cylinder, air-cooled, sleeve-valve engines, and the *Crecy* a Vee 12-cylinder, water-cooled, petrol-injection, sleeve-valve. These are all exceptions in being sleeve-valve and three were air-cooled. The *Exe* apparently got its name from its 'X' configuration, and the *Boreas* (tried out in a *Hurricane*!) possibly because it needed a cold north wind to cool it. No historical reason is known for the choice of these names, but a probable explanation is that they were experimental prototypes and would have become birds of prey on going into military production. All military aircraft prototypes had names up to 1927, but as these were being used up at an uneconomic rate such machines were subsequently allocated only a specification number.

The exception to an exception, and so a return to conformity, was *Eagle* the second — a 24-cylinder 'H' engine with sleeve-valves. This was very similar to the Napier *Sabre* designed by Halford, but did not develop beyond the Rolls-Royce prototype stage. Another manufacturer, William Beardmore & Co Ltd, may also claim to have set a fashion before its time, with *Adriatic*, *Atlantic* and the later *Meteor*, *Typhoon*, *Simoon* and *Tornado* (fitted to the R101 airship). Strangely enough, there was also a Rolls-Royce *Whirlwind*, rather bigger than a *Kestrel* and intended for the Westland *Welkin*, itself a development of the Westland *Whirlwind* fighter.

Adriatic offers another interesting sidelight on history, in that it was an original 120hp Beardmore enlarged by B.H.P. (Sir William Beardmore, Major Halford and T.C. Pullinger) and the Arrol Johnston Co. B.H.P. designs were then taken over by the new Galloway Engineering Co Ltd, and this particular engine was known later as the Galloway *Adriatic*. It was also produced by the Siddeley-Deasey Co (later Armstrong Siddeley) and in turn became the famous *Puma*. Truly, what's in a name?

In the post-Whittle era, only Bristol retained their tradition, although too close a distinction should not be made between what is a planet or constellation or simply mythological. Orion, for instance, was used for the third time, quite apart from the Bristol M1B/C Monoplane proposal. The first occasion was in the mid-'twenties, applied to a high-altitude engine of 450hp with exhaust superchargers, while the second *Orion* was an 18-cylinder proposal to follow the *Centaurus*, and the third an experimental turboprop.

Similarly, *Hercules* was used for the third time, ignoring the de Havilland aircraft of that name. The first was the Cosmos drawing-board engine already mentioned, the second a compression-ignition engine intended for airships, while the third and present *Hercules* performed his many tasks all over the world during and after World War Two.

Looking briefly at related engines, the *Jupiter* was Bristol's first major success and after considerable production evolved into the *Pegasus*, a smaller edition being the *Mercury*. The *Lucifer* was a 3-cylinder engine, using the same *Jupiter* cylinder. The 7-cylinder sleeve-valve *Aquila* was intended for a Vickers fighter, but neither went into production and the *Taurus* was a smaller edition of *Hercules*, *Phoenix* a diesel form of *Pegasus*, and *Draco* the same with fuel injection: both of the latter were fully type tested, but not produced.

At one time it was not known what the naming policy of the Bristol Siddeley consortium would be, but the answer came with the BS53, now known to the word as the second *Pegasus*. The tradition carried on with *Proteus* and *Olympus* — although now under the Rolls-Royce banner.

The other British engine companies changed to new naming systems with the advent of the jet. Rolls-Royce, after piston-engine names that live in history (*Falcon*, *Kestrel*, *Buzzard*, *Peregrine*, *Merlin**, *Vulture* and two *Eagles*)

embarked on the river class (*Derwent*, *Welland*, *Dart*, *Avon*, *Conway*, *Spey*, *Nene* and *Trent*) to signify the continuous flow of air through a gas-turbine.

In the interests of historical completeness, mention must be made of an Air Ministry proposal of 1930 to give river names to training aircraft. The list of suggestions included *Thames*, *Trent*, *Tweed*, *Test*, *Tees*, *Tamar*, *Tor*, *Tavy*, *Torridge* and *Taw*. If this had come about, how different would be the entries in many log books . . .

Armstrong Siddeley passed from Felidae and Canes to the reptiles, such as *Mamba* and *Python*, used long ago by Wolseley with *Viper*, *Adder* and *Python*. It is also interesting to remember that reptiles were reserved for single-seat fighters in 1918, along with birds and insects. Armstrong Siddeley also adopted the *Sapphire*, developed originally by Metropolitan-Vickers as a member of their 'jewel' class, with the *Beryl*.

Napier, after an aggressive history with an armoury of weapons such as *Dagger* and *Sabre*, and originally with *Lion* and *Cub*, wandered peacefully to *Nomad*, *Eland* and *Oryx*. De Havilland, after a faint air of occult with names of Gipsy origin (taken from the original and authentic *Gipsy Moth*), levitated to the frankly supernatural with *Ghost*, *Goblin* and *Sprite*. *Gyron* was allegorical, a 'turning' from the Greek gyros, but a reputable dictionary will also advise you that it is an heraldic triangle concerned with the escutcheon . . .

Alvis entered the aircraft engine field in 1935, with *Leonides*, a constellation and not to be confused with Leonidas, a Spartan king. Blackburn, who took over the Cirrus concern, had *Cirrus*, *Bombardier*, *Musketeer* and *Grenadier*. Blackburn turbojets were of French Turboméca design.

This short history is devoted purely to the naming of British aircraft engines and not to their histories. Thus, the accompanying list is of aircraft engines that have been specifically named: I believe it to be accurate and possibly the first list so compiled. But I may be wrong, and the list of engine names, lengthy though it is, does not claim to be comprehensive.

By contrast, our cousins the Americans seem now to use letters and numbers — convenient if one has a prodigious memory, but dull. British names have not always been appropriate, but they have conveyed a 'personality'. It may not have any part in legend or in mythology, but what a battle was fought between the Bristol *Jupiter* and the Armstrong Siddeley *Jaguar* between the world wars. Now the companies that produced them are one, and Rolls-Royce at that!

But to give the Americans some credit, there were the *Cyclone*, *Wasp* and *Whirlwind* — preceded by a British ABC *Wasp* of World War One, a genuine if disappointing engine. It was a prototype, and whilst still on paper its bigger brother, the *Dragonfly*, attracted an Air Board order for 10,000 engines early in 1917. Major George Bulman, a former director of engine production and now retired, comments emphatically that the *Dragonfly* would have lost the war for the Allies had the fighting continued into 1919. It created mountains of scrap! The Americans also produced the famous *Liberty*, widely used by the British towards the end of World War One and, afterwards, in the DH9A.

One of these days, when we have nuclear power plants in aircraft, may I suggest the names of *Proton* and *Neutron*. In any case, please, no numbers ●

---

*In RAF slang, *Merlin* may have been a 'wizard' engine, but it is, nonetheless, a bird of prey!

Reproduced by kind permission of *Air BP*. First published 1972

FAIR NAMES & FAMOUS BRITISH AERO ENGINES

NOTE: This list was produced in 1972 and covers both 'civil' and 'military' engines. The updated (1994) list is found as Chapter 7, TOTAL INDEX.

Manufacturers are named as they were before the Bristol Siddeley, de Havilland and Rolls-Royce engine company mergers.

Engine name	Manufacturer and notes
ADDER	Wolseley
ADOUR	Rolls-Royce/Turboméca
ADRIATIC	B.H.P./Galloway
AFRIDI	Sunbeam
ALCIDES	Alvis
AMAZON	Sunbeam
ARIES	Wolseley (Morris Motors)
ARTOUSTE	Turboméca, built by Blackburn under licence
AQUILA	Bristol
AQUARIUS	Wolseley (Morris Motors)
ARAB	Sunbeam
ATLANTIC	B.H.P./Galloway
AVON	Rolls-Royce
BEDOUIN	Sunbeam
BERYL	Metropolitan-Vickers. A jewel
BETA	Fairey rocket engine. Also early Army airship and Rollason lightplane
BOMBARDIER	Blackburn
BOREAS	Rolls-Royce
BUZZARD	Rolls-Royce. Also Luton Buzzard and Martinsyde F.4 aircraft
CARDEN	Modified Ford 10 car engine
CATARACT	Pobjoy
CENTAURUS	Bristol
CHEETAH	Armstrong Siddeley
CHERUB	Bristol
CIRRUS	A.D.C./Blackburn. Major & Minor
CIVET	Armstrong Siddeley
CLYDE	Rolls-Royce
CONDOR	Rolls-Royce
CONWAY	Rolls-Royce
COSSACK	Sunbeam
CRECY	Rolls-Royce
CUB	Napier
CUMULUS	Turboméca, built by Blackburn under licence
CULVERIN	Junkers diesel, built by Napier under licence
CUTLASS	Junkers diesel, built by Napier under licence
CYCLONE	Beardmore
DAGGER	Napier
DART	Rolls-Royce
DERWENT	Rolls-Royce
DRACO	Bristol
DRAGONFLY	A.B.C. Also D.H. aircraft
DYAK	Sunbeam
EAGLE (2)	Rolls-Royce. Also British Klemm aircraft
ELAND	Napier
EXE	Rolls-Royce
FALCON	Rolls-Royce. Also Miles aircraft
FELIX	Fairey (Curtiss D-12)
FLYING SQUIRREL	Scott
GADFLY	A.B.C.
GAMMA	Bristol Siddeley rocket engine
GAZELLE	Napier. Also Westland/Aérospatiale helicopter
GENET	Armstrong Siddeley. Also Major
GHOST	de Havilland
GIPSY	de Havilland. Also Major, Minor, Six
GIPSY KING	de Havilland
GIPSY QUEEN	de Havilland
GNAT	A.B.C. Also Folland aircraft
GNOME	de Havilland (General Electric T58)
GOBLIN	de Havilland
GOSHAWK	Rolls-Royce

Engine name	Manufacturer and notes
GRIFFON	Rolls-Royce. Also Griffin (heraldic) – Port Victoria aircraft
GHURKA	Sunbeam
GYRON	de Havilland. Also Junior
HAWK	Rolls-Royce. Also Pilcher glider, and Avro and Miles aircraft
HERCULES	Cosmos Engineering, Bristol (2). Also D.H. aircraft
HORNET	A.B.C.
HYDRA	Bristol (many cylinder heads!)
JAGUAR	Armstrong Siddeley
JANUS	Bristol (back-to-back centrifugal compressors)
JAVELIN	Napier. Also Gloster aircraft
JUPITER	Cosmos/Bristol
KAFFIR	Sunbeam
KESTREL	Rolls-Royce. Also Austin, Miles and Hawker Siddeley aircraft
LADYBIRD	Ministry of Supply. Also De Bruyne aircraft
LEONIDES	Alvis. Also Major
LEOPARD	Armstrong Siddeley
LION	Napier
LIONESS	Napier
LUCIFER	Cosmos/Bristol
LYNX	Armstrong Siddeley. Also Westland helicopter
MAEONIDES	Alvis
MAORI	Sunbeam
MAMBA	Armstrong Siddeley. Also Double Mamba
MANITOU	Sunbeam
MALAY	Sunbeam
MARBORÉ	Turboméca, built by Blackburn under licence
MARTON	Rover
MATABELE	Sunbeam
MAYFLY	Ministry of Supply. Also Lilian Bland aircraft (1911)
MEDWAY	Rolls-Royce
MERCURY	Cosmos/Bristol
MERLIN	Rolls-Royce
METEOR	Beardmore. Also Gloster aircraft
MINIJET	Alvis/Rover
MONOSOUPAPE	Gnome. Also built in UK by Peter Hooker & Co
MONGOOSE	Armstrong Siddeley
MORETON	Rover
MOSQUITO	A.B.C. Also de Havilland aircraft
MUSKETEER	Blackburn
NAIAD	Napier
NENE	Rolls-Royce
NEPTUNE	Bristol
NIAGARA	Pobjoy
NIMBUS	A.D.C. (Halford design), Blackburn
NOMAD	Napier
NUBIAN	Sunbeam
NYMPH	Napier
ODIN	Bristol Siddeley ramjet
OLYMPUS	Bristol
ORÉDON	Bristol Siddeley/Turboméca
ORION (3)	Bristol
ORPHEUS	Bristol
ORYX	Napier
OUNCE	Armstrong Siddeley
PACIFIC	Siddeley-Deasey
PALOUSTE	Turboméca, built by Blackburn under licence
PANTHER	Armstrong Siddeley

Engine name	Manufacturer and notes
PEGASUS (2)	Bristol, piston and VTOL vectored-thrust (BS.53)
PELIDES	Alvis
PENNINE	Rolls-Royce
PEREGRINE	Rolls-Royce. Also Miles aircraft
PERSEUS	Bristol
PHOEBUS	Bristol
PHOENIX	Bristol. Also Heston aircraft
PROTEUS	Bristol. Also Marine Proteus, and Industrial Proteus
PUFFIN	Budworth
PUMA	Siddeley-Deasey. Also Westland/Aérospatiale helicopter
PYTHON	Wolseley, Armstrong Siddeley
RAPIER	Napier
RAVEN	Ministry of Supply/Bristol rocket engine
RYTON	Rover
SABRE	Napier
SAPPHIRE	Armstrong Siddeley
SARACEN	Sunbeam
SATURN	Bristol
SCORPIO	Wolseley (Morris Motors)
SCORPION	A.B.C., Napier rocket engine, also Double and Triple
SERVAL	Armstrong Siddeley (Double Mongoose)
SIKH	Sunbeam
SIMOON	Beardmore
SNARLER	Armstrong Siddeley rocket engine
SOAR	Rolls-Royce
SPARTAN	Sunbeam, Bristol Siddeley rocket engine
SPECTRE	de Havilland rocket engine, also Double Spectre
SPEY	Rolls-Royce
SPRITE	Douglas
STENTOR	Bristol Siddeley rocket engine
STROMBOLI	Peter Hooker & Co
TARTAR	Sunbeam
TAURUS	Bristol
TAY	Rolls-Royce
THESEUS	Bristol
THOR	Bristol ramjet
THRUSH	Burney & Blackburne
TIGER	Armstrong Siddeley
TITAN	Bristol
TOMTIT	Burney & Blackburne. Also Hawker aircraft
TORNADO	Beardmore. Also Hawker aircraft
TRENT	Rolls-Royce
TURMO	Turboméca, built by Blackburn under licence
TWEED	Rolls-Royce
TYPHOON	Beardmore. Also Hawker aircraft
TYNE	Rolls-Royce
VIKING	Sunbeam. Also Vickers-Armstrongs aircraft
VIPER	Wolseley, Armstrong Siddeley
VULTURE	Rolls-Royce (4-bank Peregrine)
WASP	A.B.C. Also Westland helicopter
WELLAND	Rolls-Royce
WHIRLWIND	Beardmore. Also Westland aircraft and helicopter
WOLSTON	Rover
ZEPHYR	Proposed name for Orion, at one time to be built under licence by Curtiss-Wright
ZEUS	Bristol
ZULU	Sunbeam

Armstrong-Siddeley

Tiger! Tiger! burning bright
In the forests of the night.
What immortal hand or eye
Could frame thy fearful symmetry?'
— William Blake (1757–1827)

A WELL ESTABLISHED engineering company, it was later in World War One when the unexpected opportunity arose for Armstrong-Siddeley to undertake aero-engine design and manufacture. This was in 1917 when the Royal Aircraft Factory production of their RAF types was handed over to industry, the RAF8 being taken over by Armstrong-Siddeley to become the *Jaguar*. For some years this was to be one of the most successful engines, but by about 1926 was overtaken by the Bristol *Jupiter*. The BHP (Beardmore, Halford, Pullinger) was also taken over, to become the *Puma*.

Puma cylinder blocks were incorporated in the Tiger engine of 1920, and a two-cylinder version became the small 40 hp *Ounce*, aptly named as a small member of the cat family. The Felidae allocation of name was in July 1918, but as the *Jaguar* and *Puma* had appeared before the Napier *Lion*, *Lioness* and *Cub*, Napier had perforce to take on 'Arms and Weapons'. How *Jaguar* was so named is not evident, and at that time there was no official requirement for a name type, so it was a 'maker's' name. This may be substantiated by the fact that the February and March naming systems made no mention of engine names, the 'exceptions' for engines being published in July of that year when the RAF (now Force, and no longer Factory) was formed.

The index lists a long line of cats, but there was also a *Hyena* which, whilst a cat-like animal and carnivorous, is not a cat. This engine has no RAF connection, so far as it is known.

The *Tiger* was a name of some fame, powering the *Shark*, *Sinai*, *Ensign* and *Whitley*.

ASM (Armstrong-Siddeley Motors) were early involved with the gas turbine, and their first product was the ASX of 1943. To this was added a gearbox, to become the turboprop *Python*, so ASM was now into reptiles! Then followed *Mamba* and *Double Mamba*, and the removal of the *Mamba*'s gearbox produced the *Adder*. There was also an ASM *Viper* of 1951, and further developed by Bristol-Siddeley and Rolls-Royce is still operational in 1990, in the *Dominie* (DH 125). Earlier, in 1947, ASM had taken over the work of Metrovick (Metropolitan Vickers) and in particular the *Sapphire*; now it was gem stones!

Of their own original choice of name, the two cats *Jaguar* and *Cheetah* played a significant part in RAF history. In terms of numbers, *Cheetah* was in front with over 37,200 built, but then it was wartime, with *Anson*, *Consul*, *Courier*, *Envoy* and *Oxford* evaluated or used by the RAF with this engine. ASM lost its identity in 1959.

Note: The *Mongoose* is not a 'cat'.

Bristol

Hercules and Mercury

The Bristol engine names were allocated in the July 1918 system of naming as 'stars and planets', later to become 'constellations'. This simple statement is not as it may seem,

for the Aero Engine Division of the Bristol Aeroplane Company was not formed until 1921, which calls for some explanation.

It begins with a young Roy Fedden who in 1904 was apprenticed to the Bristol Motor Company, and having served his 'time' sought out a Mr John Brasil to interest him in his design for a small two-seater car. As Mr Brasil was an Irishman, Fedden had named the car *Shamrock*, which set him on the right road for names, and also to a job as head of the design team of The Straker Squire Company. Previously the company made steam engines, then took on a German Büssling licence to build motor omnibuses in Bristol (and supplying over 1,000 to London). Then came an interest in cars, and the formation of Brasil-Straker which Fedden joined. The *Shamrock* was a great success, as were the Straker Squire cars. By 1905 Fedden was chief engineer.

In 1915 the factory was commandeered by the Admiralty, and put to work making the Rolls-Royce *Hawk*, *Falcon* and components for the later *Eagle*. The manufacturing licence forbade the design and manufacture of water-cooled engines, so when in 1916 the Admiralty called for designs for an air-cooled engine for RN airships, Fedden and Butler designed the *Mercury*. This, however, lost to the ill-fated *Dragonfly*, which in turn almost lost the war. Then followed the *Jupiter*, *Lucifer* and the drawing-board *Hercules*, all 'constellations' and *before* the 1918 naming systems.

When that system appeared, it was referring to Brasil-Straker as 'Bristol'. November 1918 saw the end of the war, and also the immediate cancellation of production contracts. With many other such companies, Brasil-Straker went into liquidation, and — the first coincidence — was bought by Cosmos Engineering. Cosmos also failed, and Fedden finding no other buyer, the Ministry persuaded the Bristol Aeroplane Company to take over the undertaking, to become the Aero Engine Division.

The second coincidence was that the British and Colonial Aeroplane Company (as it then was) had an early business association with the French Zodiac company. The signs of the zodiac may still be found on the floor of the entrance foyer to Filton House. Zodiac, cosmos and the classical names already given could only lead to more classical names, some perhaps 'immortal' in engineering terms. Ultimately Bristol became Bristol-Siddeley and then Rolls-Royce, but *Olympus* still powers the *Concorde*, *Proteus* the *Britannia*, and *Pegasus* the *Harrier*; All 'shipshape and Bristol fashion'.

de Havilland

The first engine allocation of names was in July 1918, when neither the de Havilland Aircraft Company nor its engine division was in existence. The other engine companies in this chapter came under the 1918 system, which is their passport to this book, but this seems no good reason for the exclusion of de Havilland; on the contrary they played a significant part in the military, as in the civil scene.

Geoffrey de Havilland was an early self-taught pilot and designer, and before World War One he joined the Royal Aircraft Factory at Farnborough with responsibility for the design of the BE 2 (see 'The Great Un-named'). In June 1914 he left the Factory to join the Aircraft Manufacturing Company (AIRCO) to design the long and mostly successful series of de Havilland aircraft. The de Havilland Company was formed in 1920 and the engine division in 1926, when

Halford joined forces to produce the first *Gipsy*, which ran in 1927.

Then followed a long series of Gipsy engines, as may be seen from the DH engine index, and it will be recalled that being a keen lepidopterist Sir Geoffrey (as he was to be) chose the *Gipsy Moth* as an aircraft name. It is thought by some that 'Gipsy' was human, but it was indeed entomological. All the DH piston engines were Gipsies of some sort, such as Major, Six, Minor and so on, but the aircraft of the *Moth* line were named after particular moths such as *Tiger*, *Puss* and *Fox*.

In 1941 DH engines were invited to design a jet fighter, and its engine, the latter designated H (Halford) 1, was later named *Goblin*. This first flew in the DH 100, and was also used in the prototype US *Shooting Star*. The engine company as such was formed in 1944, and then followed *Ghost*, *Gyron* and the *Gyron Junior* which powers the Blackburn *Buccaneer*. Rocket engines were the *Sprite* and *Super Sprite*. Whilst the Greeks and Romans left positive images of their mythological beings and creatures, the supernatural has no such definition. Why the supernatural was chosen is not known; perhaps they were just super engines?

Then came the *Gnome* of 1959; shades of long ago with the many French *Gnôme* engines of World War One which powered a number of RFC and RNAS aircraft. The word in French is the same as in English.

In 1963, DH became part of Hawker-Siddeley Aviation, which in turn was absorbed into the British Aircraft Corporation. It's all big now, but the little *Gipsy* and *Tiger Moth* are still flying.

Napier

'As it were a roaring and rampant Lion'
— New Testament

THE BEGINNING OF the Napier Company was when David Napier moved down from Scotland, and set up as an engineer making printing machinery. This was in 1808, and was apparently successful for in 1903 motor cars were on the production line, to become well-known: a 'Napier' racing car was a name of some respect. It was a logical step from this to the aero-engine, beginning with the building of the RAF 3a and the Sunbeam *Arab*. With apparently no licence restriction on designing and building water-cooled engines (as had been the case with Rolls-Royce towards Brasil-Straker/Cosmos in Bristol), Napier embarked on their own design.

The *Lion* became a very successful engine, going up to 570 hp, and with the 'racing' *Lion* touching 1400 hp, which was more than the standard *Merlin* in 1939. This excellent engine powered some forty-seven aircraft, sixteen in service with the RAF and five with the FAA. It was all but obsolete by about 1930, but note that it was used in RAF air-sea rescue craft in World War Two — well remembered by the Author as indeed roaring and rampant.

With the 1918 RAF naming system, there would appear to have been some clash of interest for the *Lion* was Felidae (Cats) and so was the Armstrong-Siddeley *Puma* of 1917. The *Puma* won the battle — in spite of the proverb that lions do not fear cats — and it was to Armstrong-Siddeley that the RAF awarded the Felidae in July, 1918.

Napier now fought the opposition with 'Arms and Weapons', and there were six such names to follow, the best-known being the *Dagger* and the *Sabre*. But Napier *Lions* did not then disappear as a name, for as noted the engines gave widespread service until the 1930s; there was a *Lioness* in 1927, and there was also a *Cub* of 1920, much bigger than its parent. Another weapon not listed here (as it has no military connotation) was the *Javelin*, the name later used by Gloster.

A change to the Napier names came with the 1950 *Nomad*, and this would have been a 'maker' name system rather than an RAF change. The *Nomad*, a wanderer over long distances, was a compound engine, half diesel and half turboprop and each driving a counter-rotating propeller. Whilst it had an excellent (low) fuel consumption and was intended for the maritime *Shackleton*, the honour went to the Rolls-Royce *Griffon*.

Now fully committed to the gas turbine, Napier produced the *Eland* and *Gazelle*. Others, not here recorded, were the *Oryx* (in the running with *Eland* and *Gazelle*) and *Nymph* and *Naiad*. *Naiad* was yet another borrowing from the Greek classics, being a nymph living in and presiding over brooks, springs and fountains; as it was neither a planet nor a constellation, it did not infringe the 'Bristol' copyright.

In the domain of rockets there was the *Scorpion* (insects!), and the '*Double*' *Scorpion* powered a *Canberra* to 70,000 feet in 1957.

In 1962 Napier was merged with Rolls-Royce; strangely, they had near-parallel histories, from famous cars to famous aero-engines. Whether famous or not, Napier had the historical edge with printing machines.

Rolls-Royce

'They shall mount up with wings as Eagles.'

THIS FAMOUS COMPANY was formed in 1906 by Henry Royce, and the Hon. Charles S. Rolls who in spite of undertaking the marketing and selling had also taken an engineering degree at Oxford. Henry Royce was an engineer *par excellence*, and such was the standard set by the company

At the beginning of World War One the War Office approached Rolls-Royce to make Renault and RAF (Factory) engines under licence, but this was declined. Of immediate interest and agreement was the suggestion that they should design a Rolls-Royce engine as a 'standby' for Sunbeam. The suggestion was made by the Admiralty through Commodore Murray Sueter who, as a Lieutenant-Commander, had been the CO of the Naval Wing of the Royal Flying Corps at its inception in 1912.

The first engine, a V-12 configuration, first ran in 1915, and with its name began the long tradition of birds of prey names (although it was already an established tradition with Rolls-Royce cars, and all had various names).

In 1911 four Rolls-Royce cars were prepared for the Austrian Alpine car trials, and Claude Johnson, the general manager, decided on the name of the *Alpine Eagle*. He, too, had already decided that aero-engines would have names and it was most appropriate to so name their first, and *Eagle* it was. There was also the *Hawk* and *Falcon*, and an enlarged *Eagle* became the *Condor*. These names for piston engines continued up to the advent of the jet engine, and the 'flow' concept led to the many river names such as *Tay*, *Conway* and *Spey*, with *Avon* being one of the classics of this book, and one with *Merlin*. The rivers no longer flow, and Rolls-Royce

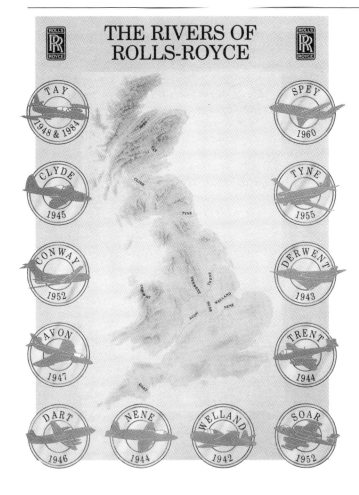

THE RIVERS OF ROLLS-ROYCE

TAY 1948 & 1984
SPEY 1960
CLYDE 1945
TYNE 1955
CONWAY 1952
DERWENT 1943
AVON 1947
TRENT 1944
DART 1946
NENE 1944
WELLAND 1942
SOAR 1952

has gone 'American' with letters and numbers. An exception is the *Tyne*, but now a civil engine.

With the incorporation of Bristol (then Bristol-Siddeley) Rolls-Royce took over the planets and constellations, the classical names of ancient Greece and Rome, and *Pegasus* the winged horse still flies in the *Harrier*. Strangely, there was never a Rolls-Royce *Harrier*; neither has there ever been a Rolls-Royce *Osprey*. This name was 'usurped' by Hawker for the *Osprey* fighter of 1930; Rolls-Royce is presumed not to have objected as it was a *sea* eagle.

Rolls-Royce were not alone in making extensive use of the names of birds of prey. Some of these were used by Miles Aircraft, although for civil aircraft which could, of course, have been pressed into RAF service.

On the other side of the Atlantic, and again for aircraft, Curtiss made extensive use of bird names, and not all of birds of prey: *Eagle*, *Seagull*, *Teal*, *Hawk*, *Falcon*, *Sparrowhawk*, *Shrike*, *Raven*, *Swift*, *Thrush*, *Condor* and *Osprey*. Rolls-Royce, however, was unique — just birds of prey. Generally, aircraft and engine manufacturers zealously guarded their naming systems, and objections were made and sustained. Rolls-Royce 'transgressors' were such as the Hawker *Hawk* which was not built. There has been a Rolls-Royce engine in service in the RAF since 1918.

Wolseley

Python

THIS ONCE WELL-KNOWN motor car company embarked on the design and manufacture of water-cooled aero-engines as early as 1909, with works at Adderley Park in Birmingham. It can only be presumed that the name Adderley was the suggestive force that led to the Wolseley snake names, the first being the *Viper* of 1916, based on the Hispano-Suiza engines.

The *Viper* was the main engine of the famous SE5a (see 'The Classics'), and this fighter also used the ensuing *Adder* which is said to be entirely of Wolseley design, but was probably influenced by the Hispano-Suiza designs. Indeed, the later Wolseley car engines can also trace some ancestry to the Hispano-Suizas. The name *Viper* for an engine was later used by Armstrong-Siddeley.

1918 saw the advent of the *Python*, and with the precedent set by *Viper* and *Adder*, the RAF allocated snakes to Wolseley in the July 1918 naming system. The *Python* appears not to have developed beyond the prototype stage, but was used in one of the Admiralty (AD) flying boats.

Going back to 1911, HMA 1 — His Majesty's Airship No. 1, also known as the *Mayfly* — was powered by a Wolseley engine. Another was used in the Royal Aircraft Factory BE1, which was designed by Geoffrey de Havilland.

At a later date Wolseley were allocated signs of the zodiac (excepting planets and constellations, the latter having already been allocated to Bristol engines). *Aries* seems to have been the only Wolseley engine in this class, but with no known military history.

Possibly due to the great contraction of business after World War One, the company pulled out of the aero-engine market. Wolseley cars were taken over by Morris Motors in 1927. It is interesting that in 1933 Wolseley made a family of small air-cooled radial engines, with sales and service backed by Morris Motors, but nothing seems to have come of this.

Part 19 — United States

'. . . I wouldn't be surprised to see a railroad in the air, or a Yankee in a flyin' ship a-goin' almost anywhere.' — J.H. Yates (1827).

THE MAIN CONTRIBUTION of aircraft by the United States to the British in World War One was of flying boats: the Curtiss *America* (adapted in the UK to become large and small), the *Columbia* (nicknamed 'Canada'), the *Jenny* (more of US than UK fame) and the *Liberty* engine. As regards fighter and bomber aircraft, the US had not given the effort and resources (and perhaps had not the incentive) as had the French and British, for war is a powerful motive for technical invention and improvement.

Thus the US Fighter Squadrons were either French or British, who provided *Camel*s and SE5as and a US Marine Corps Bomber Squadron was equipped with DH9as, which maybe accounts for its use after the war with the US Mail, using a *Liberty* engine.

Between the wars, Britain and America fought several Schneider Trophy competitions, Britain finally holding the trophy with three consecutive wins. This competition forced the pace of development, especially with engines and fuel, and were of material benefit to America, Britain and Italy, and of Germany, who took note.

Come World War Two, the US were better prepared than in World War One, but did not actually enter the war in an official capacity until the Japanese attack on Pearl Harbor in December 1941. Not only did they make a prodigious effort on behalf of their own forces, but with their huge capacity were also able to supply the British RAF and FAA with some fifty-seven types of aircraft (1939-1990). Naming systems were an immediate problem, the US systems being alphanumeric with the occasional name. The Navy and Army seldom chose the same name! Without absorbing the detail (unless you are so inclined), this page from a 1941 edition of the *Aeroplane Spotter* shows the complications that the British wished to avoid:

THE AMERICAN CODE
The Type Designation of Aeroplanes of the US Navy and US Army Air Corps

Many people are confused by the system of numbers instead of names adopted by the United States Navy and Army to designate their Aircraft. A string of letters such as the XSB2C-1 cannot have the same simplicity or glamour as the single name *Spitfire*. Yet, strange as some of them seem, the American system of lettering and numbering is done to a plan and does convey useful information to the initiated.

Until the American systems are fully understood they are bewildering, the more so because the Army and the Navy differ in their designations and the US aircraft constructors have further numerical systems of their own. A further, and completely separate set of figures is allotted to each aeroplane for export sale. Take, for instance, the now familiar Bell *Airacobra*. It is designated the *Airacobra* by its makers and the P-39 by the US Army; in its Naval form it is known as the XFL-1, and for export goes by the title P-400. Another example is the Beechcraft single-motor biplane. One model is designated the D-17R by its makers, the YC-43 by the US Army Air Corps and the GB-1 by the US Navy.

Now let us see what all these symbols mean.

US Navy Designations

Aeroplanes in the US Navy are classified in detail by their code letters and numbers. All heavier-than-air craft in the US Navy have a prefix letter 'V' before the rest of the symbols. Similarly 'Z' signifies a lighter-than-air craft. These letters are omitted in the designation of individual types but used with reference to squadrons.

The reference letters and figures are divided into five separate 'tell-tales'. The first indicates experimental or is omitted, the second indicates the purpose (bomber, transport, etc), the third is the design numbers, the fourth the maker's code number, and the fifth the modification number of the type. Thus XSB2C-1 is:

X	SB	2	C	–	1
Experimental	Purpose (Scout-Bomber)	Design (Second SB by Curtiss to be adopted by Navy)	Maker's code number (C=Curtiss)		Modification number (First model)

Similarly the XF4F-1 is:

X	F	4	F	–	1
Experimental	Purpose (Fighter)	Design (Fourth fighter by Grumman to be adopted by Navy)	Maker's symbol F=Grumman		Modification number (First model)

The letters indicating the purpose of the particular aeroplane in service with the US Navy are as follows. The Americans refer to them as Mission Symbols. They are represented by the first letter before the first figure in the designation. There are 19 different missions in the US Navy. They are:

B = Bomber
BF = Bomber-Fighter
F = Fighter
G = Transport (single-motor)
J = Utility (General-purpose)
JR = Utility Transport
M = Miscellaneous
N = Training
O = Observation
OS = Observation-Scout
P = Patrolplane
PB = Patrol-Bomber
PT = Patrol-Torpedo plane
R = Transport (multi-motor)
S = Scout
SB = Scout-Bomber
SO = Scout-Observation
T = Torpedo plane
TB = Torpedo-Bomber

In each instance where an aeroplane has more than one letter the first letter indicates the primary purpose. Thus there are both OS and SO.

After the first figure in the designation — a figure which indicates how many designs of aeroplane for the particular purpose have been adopted by the Navy from the constructor indicated — there comes the letter denoting the constructor which made the aeroplane. The list is as follows:

A = Brewster
B = Beech
    Boeing
C = Curtiss
D = Douglas
E = Bellanca
F = Grumman
G = Great Lakes
H = Hall-Aluminum
    Stearman-Hammond
J = North American
K = Kinner
    Keystone
    Fairchild
M = Glenn Martin
N = Naval Aircraft Factory
O = Lockheed
P = Pitcairn
Q = Stinson
R = Ford
S = Stearman
T = Northrop
U = Vought-Sikorsky
W = Waco
X = Experimental
Y = Consolidated

Further instances of the use of symbols in the US Navy are:-

PBY-1 (the first Patrol-Bomber to be produced by Consolidated)

PBY-5 (the fifth model of the first Patrol-Bomber produced by Consolidated).

XPB2Y-1 (the first model of an experimental version of the second type of Patrol-Bomber produced by Consolidated).

OS2U-1 (the first model of the second type of Observation-Scout aeroplane to be produced by Vought-Sikorsky).

SBC-4 (the fourth model of the first Scout-Bomber to be produced by Curtiss).

The Air Ministry and Ministry of Aircraft Production in London were anxious for US aircraft to comply with the 1932/39 RAF naming system, but not requiring a 'British' association where that applied to a particular type. Equally, a US *Yorktown* supplied to the UK might have been embarrassing . . .

So the 1939 system as then published foresaw the use of US aircraft in the RAF, and had included the following addendum to the system:

'In the case of American aircraft allotted to Britain, and Canadian aircraft built for MAP, fullest consideration will be given to the wishes of the relevant authorities should they press for the adoption of names not within these categories. Endeavours should be made, however, to follow as closely as possible the basic rules, but names with an American or Canadian flavour will be very appropriate. For instance, American-built transports should not necessarily be named after a county or district of the British Empire, but would preferably be named after a District or State of the United States of America.'

An early list of US names for RAF and FAA service appeared in the *Aeroplane Spotter* in January 1941, and this was eleven months before that first Japanese victory over the Americans.

NEWS OF THE WEEK

Names have been officially approved by the Air Ministry and the Admiralty for most of the types of military aeroplanes which are arriving from the United States in increasing numbers — by sea and by air. The following is the list as it stands at the moment with the new RAF and FAA names, and equivalent American titles:

MAKER AND BRITISH DESIGNATION	AMERICAN NAMES AND NUMBERS		NUMBER AND TYPE OF MOTOR(S)	TYPE
	MAKER'S	US ARMY OR NAVY		
Bell Caribou	P.400 Airacobra	P-39	One Allison	S.S.fighter
Brewster Bermuda	138	SBA-1	One Cyclone	Fighter — dive bomber
Brewster Buffalo	439	F2A-2	One Cyclone	S.S. fighter
Consolidated Catalina	Model 28-5	PBY-5	Two Twin-Wasp	G.R. flying-boat
Consolidated Liberator	Model 32	B-24	Four Twin-Wasp	Heavy bomber
Curtiss Cleveland	Helldiver 77	SBC-4	One Cyclone	Dive bomber
Curtiss Kittihawk	Hawk 87	P-46	One Allison	S.S. fighter
Curtiss Mohawk	Hawk 75-A	P-36A	One Twin-Wasp	S.S. fighter
Curtiss Tomahawk	Hawk 81-A	P-40A	One Allison	S.S. fighter
Douglas Boston I	DB-7	A-20	Two Twin-Wasp	Day bomber
Douglas Boston III	DB-7B	A-20A	Two Double-Row Cyclone	Day bomber
Douglas Digby	DB-280	B-18A	Two Clyclone	heavy bomber
Grumman Martlet	G-36A	F4F-3	One Cyclone	S.S. fleet fighter
Lockheed Hudson	EB-14B	—	Two Cyclone	Reconnaissance-bomber
Lockheed Lightning	322-61	P-38	Two Allison	S.S. fighter
Lockheed Vega Ventura	Vega 37	—	Two Twin-Wasp	Reconnaissance-bomber
Martin Baltimore	187	—	Two	Day bomber
Martin Maryland	167-B4	—	Two Twin-Wasp	Day bomber
North American Harvard I	NA-16-1E	BC-1	One Wasp	Advanced trainer
North American Harvard II	NA-16-3	BC-1A	One wasp	Advanced trainer
North American Mustang	NA-73	—	One Allison	S.S. fighter
North American Yale	NA-64	BT-14	One Whirlwind	Advanced trainer
Vought-Sikorsky Chesapeake	V-156	SB2U-2	One Twin-Wasp Jr	Dive bomber
Vultee Vengeance	72	—	One Allison	S.S. fighter

Several aeroplanes, such as the Boeing B-17B (the so called 'Flying Fortress'), the Consolidated Models 28-5A and 51, the Douglas DB.8A-5, the Northrop A-17A, and the Vultee Vanguard, still remain to be offically named.

By December 1941 (Pearl Harbor) the list had expanded with:

9 JULY 1942
MORE GLAMOUR

Many more aeroplanes of the US Navy have now been given names in addition to numbers. Some of the names come from the same aeroplanes supplied to the RAF. Some are original. The full list now is:

MAKER	MAKER'S NUMBER	BRITISH* NAME	ORIGINAL DESIGNATION	U.S. Navy Name
Boeing	–	–	PBB-1	Sea Ranger I
Brewster	–	–	F2A-1	Buffalo I
Brewster	339	Buffalo I	F2A-2	Buffalo II
Brewster	439	Buffalo II	F2A-3	Buffalo III
Brewster	340	Bermuda I	SB2A-1	Buccaneer I
Chance-Vought	V-156	–	SB2U-1	Vindicator I
Consolidated	28-1	–	PBY-1	Catalina I
Consolidated	28-2	–	PBY-2	Catalina II
Consolidated	28-3	–	PBY-3	Catalina III
Consolidated	28-4	Catalina I	PBY-4	Catalina IV
Consolidated	28-5	Catalina II	PBY-5	Catalina V
Consolidated	29-1	–	XPB2Y-1	Coronado I
Consolidated	29-2	–	PB2Y-2	Coronado II
Curtiss	–	–	SB2C-1	Helldiver I
Curtiss	–	–	SO3C-1	Seagull I
Douglas	–	–	SBD-1	Dauntless I
Douglas	–	–	SBD-2	Dauntless II
Douglas	–	–	SBD-3	Dauntless III
Douglas	–	–	TBD-1	Devastator I
Grumman	G-36A	Martlet I	F4F-2	Wildcat II
Grumman	G-36B	Martlet II	F4F-3	Wildcat III
Grumman	G-36C	Martlet III	F4F-4	Wildcat IV
Grumman	G-36D	Martlet IV	F4F-5	Wildcat V
Grumman	–	–	TBB-1	Avenger I
Martin	162	–	PBM-1	Mariner I
Martin	162	–	PBM-2	Mariner II
Martin	170	–	XPB2M-1	Mars
Vought-Sikorsky	–	–	F4U-1	Corsair I
Vought-Sikorsky	–	–	OS2U-1	Kingfisher I
Vought-Sikorsky	–	–	OS2U-2	Kingfisher II
Vought-Sikorsky	–	–	OS2U-3	Kingfisher III
Vought-Sikorsky	V-156	Chesapeake I	SB2U-2	Vindicator II
Vought-Sikorsky	V-156	Chesapeake II	SB2U-3	Vindicator III

*The aeroplanes listed as supplied to the RAF or FAA usually differ from the American versions in detail

That there was some confusion amongst so many designations and names was not surprising, as witness the following letter to the *Aeroplane Spotter* and the Editor's (Peter Masefield) reply:

NAMES FOR US AEROPLANES

It is high time something was done about the names of American aircraft. With the majority of them, there are alternative names and much confusion is caused. For instance, about a week ago I was out with a friend when an Airacobra passed over. I immediately said 'Airacobra,' but he denied it fiercely and insisted it was a Caribou!

We agree it is a pity that you, and indeed everyone, do not call American aircraft by one name. J.M.P.

Names of American aircraft are certainly confusing. The trouble is that a certain type may have one name in the RAF, a second in the US Navy and a third in the US Army Air Forces. The correct name in any instance is that of the machine in whichever Service it is at the time. The name 'Caribou' for the Airacobra was abandoned by the RAF many months ago. The following are the respective names of the more common US types in service in the British Air Forces:

BRITISH NAME	U.S. ARMY	U.S. NAVY	MAKER'S NUMBER
Bell Airacobra I	P-39D	–	P-400
Boeing Fortress I	B-17c	–	B-299T
Boeing Fortress II	B-17F	–	B-299P
Boeing Fortress IIA	B-17G	–	B-299O
Brewster Bermuda	–	SB2A-2 (Buccaneer)	Brewster 340
Brewster Buffalo II	–	F2A-3 (Buffalo)	Brewster 439
Cessna Crane	AT-17 (Bobcat)	–	T-50T
Consolidated Catalina I	–	PBY-5 (Catalina)	Model 28-5
Consolidated Catalina III	OA-10	PBY-5A	Model 28-5A
Consolidated Coronado I	–	PB2Y-3 (Coronado)	Model 29-3
Consolidated Liberator III	B-24D	–	Model 32-4
Curtiss Cleveland I	–	SBC-4	Curtiss 77
Curtiss Kittyhawk I	P-40g	–	Hawk 87-A3
Curtiss Kittyhawk II	P-40F (Warhawk)	–	Hawk 87-A4
Curtiss Mohawk IV	P-36E	–	Hawk 75-A4
Curtiss Tomahawk IIB	P-40c	–	Hawk 81-A3
Douglas Boston III	A-20c	BD-2	DB-7B
Douglas Dakota I	C-47	R4D-1	DC-3
Douglas Dakota II	C-53	–	DC-3A
Douglas Digby I	B-18A	–	DB-280
Douglas Havoc II	A-26	–	DB-7A
Fairchild Argus I	C-61	–	Fairchild 24W41
Grumman Goose I	OA-9	JRF-2	G-21B
Grumman Gosling I	–	J4F-1	G-44 (Widgeon)
Grumman Martlet IV	–	F4F-3 (Wildcat)	G-36A
Lockheed Hudson III	A-29	–	414-46-01
Lockheed Hudson IV	A-28	–	414-08
Lockheed Lightning I	P-38D (Atalanta)	–	322-61
Lockheed-Vega Ventura I	B-34 (Lexington)	–	Lockheed-Vega 37
Martin Baltimore I	A-30	–	Glenn Martin 187B1
Martin Marauder I	B-26B	–	Glenn Martin 179
Martin Mariner I	–	PBM-3 (Mariner)	Glenn Martin 162
Martin Maryland I	A-22	–	Glen Martin 167B
North American Harvard II	AT-6A	KNJ-3	NA-16-3
North American Yale I	BT-14	–	NA-64
North American Mitchell I	B-25B (Mitchell)	–	NA-62B
North American Mustang I	P-51 (Apache)	–	NA-73
Northrop Nomad	A-17A	BT-1	8A-3P

Republic Thunderbolt I	P-47B (Thunderbolt)	—	Thunderbolt
Vought-Sikorsky Chesapeake	—	SB2U-3 (Vindicator)	V-156
Vought-Sikorsky Kingfisher I	—	OS2U-3 (Kingfisher)	VS-310
Vultee Vengeance I	A-31	TBV-1	Vultee 72
Vultee-Stinson Vigilant I	L-49B	—	O-74

In 1942, the Air Ministry sought to provide a 'total' picture, of the many names and equivalents, both for the UK and the US, and the following is taken from a (then secret) document of the time:

No.847/42. Designation of British, U.S.A. and Canadian Type Aircraft

For the information and guidance of all concerned, the following list details the classification of American, British, and Canadian types of aircraft, together with the British nomenclature (Column 3) of American type aircraft.

2. The list has been agreed by:-

Air Ministry
Admiralty
Ministry of Aircraft Production
U.S.A. Army Air Force
Washington Munitions Assignments Board

3. Periodic amendment lists will be issued as necessary

1	2	3			4	5
		U.S. Aircraft				
Serial No.	Type	U.S. Army Designation	British Designation	U.S. Navy Designation	British Aircraft	Canadian Aircraft
1	Heavy Bombers 4 engine	B.17 B.24	Fortress Liberator		Halifax Lancaster Stirling	Lancaster
2	Heavy Bombers 2 engine				Manchester Warwick	
3	Medium Bombers 2 engine	B.25 B.26 B.34 B.37	Mitchell Marauder Ventura G.R.Ventura		Albemarle Hampden Wellington Whitley	Hampden
4	Light Bombers 2 engine	A.20 A.29 A.30	Boston Hudson Baltimore		Beaufort Blenheim Mosquito	Bolingbroke
5	Light Bombers 1 engine	A.24 A.34 A.31	Bermuda Vengeance	SBD (Dauntless) SB2A SB2C (Helldiver) SBN S.B.2.U. (Vindicator) TBF, TBM (Avenger)	Albacore Barracuda Swordfish	
6	Pursuits 2 engine	P.38 P.70	Lightning Havoc		Beaufighter F.9/40 Mosquito	
7	Pursuit 1 engine	P.39 P.40 P.43 P.47 P.51 P.66	Airacobra Kittyhawk Thunderbolt Mustang		Defiant Hurricane Spitfire Typhoon	Hurricane

1	2	3			4	5
		U.S. Aircraft				
Serial No.	Type	U.S. Army Designation	British Designation	U.S. Navy Designation	British Aircraft	Canadian Aircraft
8	Navy Fighters 1 engine		Martlet	F2A(Buffalo) F4F(Wildcat) F4U(Corsair) F3A FG1 FH1	Firebrand Firefly Fulmar	
9	Flying-boats 4 engine		Coronado	PB2Y	Sunderland	
10	Flying boats 2 engine			PBM (Mariner) PBN		PBY
			Catalina	PBY		
11	Naval Reconnaissance 1 engine			SO3C (Seagull) OS2N (Kingfisher) OS2U (Kingfisher)	Sea Otter Walrus	
12	Heavy Transport 4 engine	DC4 type C54 C54A Constellation		JR2S		
13	Heavy Transport 2 engine	C46	Commando			
14	Medium Transport 2 engine	DC3 type C47 C53 Lodestar Type C59 C60 Hudson Type C63	Dakota Hudson			
15	Light Transport 2 engine	C45	Goose	JRB JRF J4F		
16	Communications 1 engine	C61 L49 L57 L58 L59 L62	Vigilant	GB2 GH1 J2F		Lysander

1	2	3			4	5
		U.S. Aircraft				
Serial No.	Type	U.S. Army Designation	British Designation	U.S. Navy Designation	British Aircraft	Canadian Aircraft
TRAINING AIRCRAFT						
17	Advanced Trainers 2 engine	AT8 AT17 AT9 AT10 AT11 AT13 AT14 AT15 AT18	Crane Crane Hudson	SNB	Anson Botha Oxford	Anson
18	Advanced Trainers 1 engine	AT6 Texan AT19	Harvard	SNJ SNC	Master	Norseman Harvard
19	Basic Trainers	BT13 BT15		SNV		
20	Primary Trainers	PT17 PT19 PT21 PT22		N2S NP1	Dominie Moth Proctor Defiant (T.T.) Lysander (T.T.)	Moth (FT2) Fleet 60 Freshman (PT26)
0.1. 15/9/42.					W.M. Yool, Air Commodore, Director of Organisation	

It could be a maker's name, Navy, Army and British name, but would almost inevitably have a fifth — nickname, and sometimes nicknames. They are noted in this index, space permitting, but the subject of nicknames is covered more fully in Chapter 5, Part 16.

The German Luftwaffe also had nicknames, and some of these are listed for their own and Allied aircraft:

Aeroplane	German Nickname	Translation
The Me.109	*Die eckige 109*	*The square 109*
The Ju.88	*Die drei-finger 88*	*The three-fingered 88*
The He.111	*Der 111 — Spaten*	*The 111 spade*
The Do.17	*Der fleigende bleistift*	*The flying pencil*
The Ju.52	*Die kasten-Ju*	*The box-like Junkers*
The Fi.156 Storch	*Der rechteckige Stork*	*The rectangular Storch*
The Lysander	*Der wespen Lysander*	*The waspish Lysander*
The Hurricane	*Die angerundete Hurricane*	*The rounded Hurricane*
The Spitfire	*Der spitze Spitfire*	*The pointed Spitfire*
The Mohawk	*Die Curtiss-Hummel*	*The Curtiss bumble-bee*
The Blenheim I	*Die kurznasige Blenheim*	*The short-nose Blenheim*
The Blenheim IV	*Die langnases-Blenheim*	*The long-nose Blenheim*
The Whitley	*Die scheunentor-Whitley*	*The barn-door Whitley*
The Hampden	*Die kaulquappen Hampden*	*The tadpole Hampden*
The Wellington	*Die haifisch-Wellington*	*The shark Wellington*
The Lerwick	*Die flegende bulldogge*	*The flying bulldog*
The Hudson	*Die walfisch Hudson*	*The whale Hudson*
The Sunderland	*Das flegende schlachtschiff*	*The flying battleship*

CHAPTER 6 — INTRODUCTION TO THE CLASSICS — THIRTY AIRCRAFT AND SIX ENGINES

1   Sopwith *Camel*
2   Bristol *Fighter*
3   Vickers *Vimy*
4   Bristol *Bulldog*
5   Hawker *Fury*
6   Supermarine *Southampton*
7   Supermarine *Walrus*
8   de Havilland *Tiger Moth*
9   Gloster *Gladiator*
10 Avro *Anson*
11 Westland *Lysander*
12 Vickers *Wellington*
13 Supermarine *Spitfire*
14 Hawker *Hurricane*
15 Fairey *Swordfish*
16 Bristol *Blenheim*
17 Avro *Lancaster*
18 Handley Page *Halifax*
19 Bristol *Beaufighter*
20 Short *Sunderland*
21 de Havilland *Mosquito*
22 Consolidated *Liberator*
23 N. American *Mustang*
24 Hawker *Typhoon*
25 Gloster *Meteor*
26 Hawker *Hunter*
27 Avro *Vulcan*
28 Eng. Electric *Lightning*
29 Hawker *Harrier*
30 Panavia *Tornado*
31 Gnôme *Monosoupape*
32 de Havilland *Gipsy*
33 Bristol *Jupiter*
34 Bristol *Hercules*
35 Rolls-Royce *Merlin*
36 Rolls-Royce *Avon*

THE CHOICE OF these is entirely that of the author, and thus can only be entirely arbitrary and personal, but there was some seventy-five per cent agreement amongst my historian friends, and I can only hope that the twenty-five per cent who disagreed will not become historical enemies. There can be no definitive or authoritative selection, and as in any discussion or argument amongst pilots — or even historians for that matter — ask any ten and you will get eleven options. Indeed, if excellence (in its day), fame and numbers were the criteria, then one should include such as the SE5a fighter of World War One, the Fairey III F of the 1920s, and of recent vintage the VC10. Sadly, they have no name and, oddly, not even a nickname, and having neither should not be a part of this book. To obviate such an absurdity, the rules have been bent and they and others will be found in the 'The Great Unnamed', Chapter 5 Part 17. So, whilst this book seeks to be a comprehensive index, it is not so insofar as unnamed or un-nicknamed aircraft are concerned; but, other than in World War One such aircraft are likely to have been 'experimental' or a manufacturer's private venture, and hopefully there are not too many gaps in this 116 year history.

Engines are somewhat dull as photographs, but respond admirably to the pen of the technical artist, and no one has ever surpassed the mastery of this technical artistry than J.H. Clarke, who then drew for *Aeroplane* magazine. Grateful acknowledgement must be made to *Aeroplane* and to its Editor, Richard Riding, for seeking out some engine drawings and for permission to reproduce them.

In the Total Index, the classic aircraft and engines are listed only with the basic data with no 'notes' other than to refer to this chapter. Thus the 'Classics' and 'The Great Unnamed' pages contain more information as to name, origin of name and technical and historical information than the remaining 1274 aircraft and engines in the Index. It would be possible but impractical to so treat all the names, and the task would probably require another fifty years! If curiosity for further information is aroused, then please refer to the bibliography, and another of the book's aims will have been achieved.

In most cases, the number of existing aircraft of any one type has been noted. These totals cover both original and replica aircraft, and there could additionally be further aircraft, both static and flying, in the United States and Canada (see 'A Cautionary Tale' Chapter 2)

Classic No. 1: The Sopwith *Camel* (1916) — Le Rhône, *Rotary* (1)

As with all World War One military aircraft, the *Camel* as such did not exist and as a nickname was only grudgingly recognised with the formation of the Royal Air Force in 1918. To the hierarchy of the Royal Flying Corps (of the British Army) the nickname was taboo, and an initial letter or letters and a number was deemed to be more than adequate to identify an aircraft, which, of course, ignored the humour and affection that the common soldier or sailor, and now airman, bestowed on his allotted weapon of war; and if *Camel* was not enough, then the nickname soon also had a nickname, and 'Camisole' was known to the many thousands of the RFC.

Why *Camel* in the first place? Two explanations may be found. One has it that the 'hump' in front of the pilot's cockpit (which housed the two machine guns firing through the propeller arc) was an obvious inspiration for the name. The second origin has it that the lack of dihedral angle on the upper wings gave the aircraft a 'humped' and so camel-like appearance. One pilot is on record to the effect that far from looking like a camel, on the ground it looked like a frog.

Such visual versatility was well rewarded, for *Camel* type TF1 was the trench fighter, 2F1 was the ship's *Camel*, and there was also a *Camel* seaplane. The *Camel* was carried on towed barges and carriers, and launched from the R 23 Airship, One *Camel* actually sank a German U-boat, but after the champagne and the congratulations, it was hard to tell the pilot that he had been credited with the destruction of a whale.

The *Camel* can probably claim to carry the most distinguished name and combat record of World War One. This wicked little warplane destroyed 1,294 enemy aircraft and at the time of the Armistice in 1918 there were 2,582 models in the RFC, which was now the RAF. *Camels* of all sorts, from many manufacturers, totalled 5,747. It was not easy to fly, but in the hands of a skilled pilot it was one of the most manoeuvrable of fighters — engine, fuel, guns, ammunition and pilot were closely situated on its centre of gravity. The rotary — as distinct from the later radial — engine caused strong gyroscopic forces and it is recalled that to turn left one used right rudder, and if the control column was let go one was on the way to a loop. That the *Camel* has not been forgotten is evident in that it is the NATO code-name of the Russian Tupolev Tu-104.

The Sopwith *Pup* of 1914 was the immediate ancestor of the *Camel*. It went into service first with the Royal Naval Air Service at the end of 1916, and now (and possibly then) it is to be wondered at that it took only six weeks from first drawing to first flight, and was in service within nine months! The RFC followed later with its orders. The exploits of this extraordinary machine were numerous and legendary, from the shooting down of Zeppelins in the air to destroying them on the ground after taking off from RN ships — possibly the first 'carrier' operation — and it is certainly credited with regaining Allied superiority in the air after a rough time at the hands of the German Air Force.

Whilst the concept of the *Camel* was a team affair, the lead and the inspiration came from Thomas Sopwith (later Sir Thomas) who was one of the earlier British aviators, and who from small beginnings built up an aviation empire that ultimately, after many changes of name, became the British Aerospace of today. After World War One, Sopwith became Hawker and, and the later *Hurricane* was in some respects the *Camel* of its time.

Some swear that a ghost *Camel* appears now and then; it is reputed to be a benevolent phantom, with a pilot who helps others in trouble. A good story, and a tribute to the old gladiator, but who has actually seen the 'Flying Dutchman'? Certainly, the *Camel* travelled widely and saw service not only on Royal Navy ships, but in the UK, France, Italy, the Aegean, Macedonia and Russia (from whence the parody that 'The *Camels* are coming. . .') And a small postscript to history: there was a Gloster *Bamel*, so called as it was supposed to look like half a bear and half a camel!

Sopwith Camel (Replica) (Frank B. Mormillo)

Classic No. 2: The Bristol *Fighter* (1916) — Rolls-Royce *Falcon* (1)

'But few of them knew the secret
Of making my heart rejoice
With a well rigged Bristol *Fighter*
And a two-six-five Rolls-Royce.

Is there a sweeter music
Or a more contented sound
Than the purring clop of her
  broad curved prop
As it gently ticks around?
— Ballad of the Bristol *Fighter*, 1918

The author can only nostalgically agree with the above, for he has been fortunate enough once to share the experience.

In 1916 Captain Frank Barnwell began work on this two-seater fighter which was to become the F2a, and as the F2b in RFC service it gained fame as one of the best fighters of World War One. Such was its reputation that it continued in RAF service until 1932 in an active role, and in the training role with the University air squadrons until 1935.

The *Fighter* shared battle honours with the *Camel* and the SE5a, and soon established a good reputation with RFC pilots, but only after an inauspicious start when it was used in the conventional 'two-seater' style; when fought with as a single-seater, but with a defensive rear gunner (and for which it was designed), then defeat rapidly turned to victory. Strong and manoeuvrable, the 'Biff' or 'Brisfit' became a formidable fighting machine. In 1917, the CO of 48 Squadron, Major Vere-Bettington, wrote: 'Regarding the Bristol, she is a topping fighting two-seater — the best here.'

'Brisfit' is obviously an amalgam of 'Bristol' and 'Fighter', and the illustration (page 129) is of the famous Bristol scroll which was the logo of both aircraft and engines, and started in 1910 (with the British & Colonial Aeroplane Co., later to become the Bristol Aeroplane Co). The 1910 Company was an offshoot of the Bristol Tramway Co, who indeed were to build many *Fighters*, and the scroll is still to be seen on Bristol buses. Contrary to belief, it was the Tramway Co. that borrowed the scroll from the Aeroplane Co. who discontinued it in 1958. By September 1918, the total number built was 4,747, and in only two years that was a remarkable total. Many engines were fitted, including the Sunbeam *Arab*, which in the event was none too reliable, and the *Fighter* is best remembered with the Rolls-Royce *Falcon*. The final total was 5,329 built for eleven countries.

Apart from post work service in the UK, the *Fighter* was also used in Ireland and in India. In its last years in India in Squadron service, such was the military parsimony of the British Government that aircraft were taking off on bare rims, there being no spare tyres; which says something for its very robust design.

Fearing that World War One would continued for a long time, the United States entered into *Fighter* production. Its version was known as the XB-1A, the first being built at Cook Field; another forty then followed, built by Dayton-Wright. The American aircraft had *Liberty* engines, heavier than the *Falcons*, and, as forecast by Bristol, they were nose heavy. As a result the US Army Air Corps considered it a poor aeroplane, but Bristol still consider them as poor at taking good advice.

In retrospect, the Bristol *Fighter* influenced tactics for many years, and was the first aeroplane produced by a 'shadow' industry as it was later known. It has been described as being the greatest two-seat fighter of World War One, with great strength and the ability to dive faster than its contemporaries, to find home when damaged and generally in a class of its own.

Four *Fighters* remain, one flying with the Shuttleworth Trust at Old Warden. The *Falcon* engine is getting a little tired, with spares hard or impossible to come by, but there is good news that a second *Falcon* is being assembled. As with all vintage and veteran aircraft, it is a continuing and dedicated fight, so perhaps the words of Robert Browning are relevant:

'I was ever a Fighter
So — one fight more,
The best and the last.'

Bristol Fighter

Vickers Vimy

Classic No. 3: Vickers *Vimy* (1917) — Rolls-Royce *Eagle* (2)

The Royal Air Force was formed on 1 April 1918, but prior to this the Ministry of Munitions had issued a nomenclature system in February, rapidly followed by an amended system in March. This, again, was amended to the July system when the RAF was in full legal existence. The March system for 'multi-engined machines' allocated various type names depending on weight and the number of engines, and for twin-engined machines the names were to be of France, Europe (excepting France) and Great Britain — the three in order of ascending weight. The French connection was applied to only three RFC/RAF aircraft, the Boulton Paul *Bourges*, the Airco (de Havilland) *Amiens* and the Vickers *Vimy*, originally suggested as *Versailles*.

The aircraft name *Vimy* was chosen in remembrance of the infamous Vimy Ridge, a formidable fortress built into the hill and cliffs by the Germans as part of their front line in France; nearby were the small villages of Vimy and Petit Vimy. The naming systems had allocated the letters 'U' and 'V' to Vickers for naming, and *Vimy* was a good alliteration with Vickers. The 'U' was never used.

The first Battle of Arras began in April 1917, and lasted for some five days. This was a considerable victory for the Allied cause, fought at great cost, and it can be seen as the beginning of the end for the German forces. The Vimy Ridge, contemptuously called the 'Pimple', had strategically over-looked the front lines, and was deemed impregnable, at least by the Germans. Its taking was a very considerable feat of arms by the British 1st and 2nd Armies, including the Canadians, whose association with Vimy has an enduring memory in the Commonwealth, and especially in Canada.

In spite of the effective Gotha raids on London in 1917, the RFC thought heavy bombers were vulnerable and until then had relied on the smaller bomber such as the DH4. However,

that same year saw the HP 0/400 become the future heavy bomber, and also a new design from Vickers, the FB27 which was the become the *Vimy*. Oddly enough, the name seems to have been given in 1917, before the three naming systems referred to! Perhaps it was the name that led to the system?

In the event, *Vimy* was too late for World War One, but then served in nine RAF Bomber Squadrons. Some 285 were built, and the type were in service until 1933. Herein was the beginning of 'Bomber Command'.

France, in a strange way, is also remembered by an engine, the Rolls-Royce *Crecy*, commemorating an English victory in 1346 during the Hundred Years War, but whilst *Vimy*'s name arose from stirring deeds and great battles, does its own record in the RAF give it right of place in this 'classical' section? The answer must be yes, but in contradictory fashion as a civil rather than RAF aircraft, albeit one with an RAF crew: it completed the first non-stop crossing of the Atlantic in 1919, and it is a happy coincidence that the flight started from Nova Scotia, in Canada. The coincidence seems to have been overlooked, more interest being focused on the fact that this epic flight ended in an Irish bog. The two RAF pilots were Alcock and Brown, both knighted by King George V for their achievement.

But the Vimy was memorable for more than the Atlantic crossing, for there were the long-distance flights between England and Australia by the Smith brothers, and in 1920 England to Cape Town. *Vimy* also pioneered the airmail route between Cairo and Baghdad. After the War, *Vimy* served with six RAF Squadrons between 1919 and 1927.

Four *Vimy*'s remain, one at Brooklands, one at the RAF Museum, one at the Science Museum in London, and a flying replica which flew from the UK to Australia. Two Rolls-Royce *Eagle* engines which powered the civil bomber one this epic flight also have claim to fame. *Eagle* engines served in the RAF and FAA for some years after 1919.

Bristol Bulldog

Classic No. 4: The Bristol *Bulldog* (1927) — Bristol *Jupiter* (1)

A single-seat fighter, *Bulldog* first flew in 1927 and had it been named in accordance with the RAF system of that year, its name would have begun with an 'F'; it follows that it was named in accordance with the 1921 system, except that it was not! A single-seat landplane was allocated a land-bird name, but a multi-seat (up to 6000 lb) that of an animal. Here we have another of the exception of the name game, but what its name meant is not open to doubt.

The British *Bulldog* is descended from the Pugnaces (hence 'Pug' as a dog) of the early Britons. By about 1500 it was referred to as the 'Bondogge, a vast, stubborn and eager dogge of heavy burdensome, and body serviceable to bait a bulle, so that two dogges at most were capable of subduing the most untameable bulls' (*The Dogge* — Dr Caius, 1576). There are three other aviation references, the (German) Friesmen *Bulldog* of 1914, the (unofficial) nickname of the Sopwith of 1917, and the Beagle *Bulldog* currently serving in the RAF University Air Squadrons.

Bristol Type 105 (Spec. F9/26) was the winner of an RAF fighter competition, flying against the *Siskin* and *Gamecock*.

The contract to supply the standard RAF Fighter (1929 until 1936) was a matter of keen competition and much pride, and *Bulldog* was certainly **the** single-seat fighter until the advent of the Hawker *Fury* with its liquid-cooled *Kestrel*

engine. Bristol chose its own famed *Jupiter*, air-cooled, reliable, and well tried. The *Kestrel/Fury* combination was of a later era, but *Jupiter/Bulldog* was certainly king of its own era. It was the star aerobatic turn at many an RAF Hendon pageant and the memory lives long with those who remember the 1930s, little thinking of the years that were shortly to come. The *Bulldog* never saw action in the RAF, but to live up to its name had the opportunity in the Finnish Air Force to fight Russian bombers in 1940 — and two were not required to down one bomber. The total built was 443.

Apart from Finland, the *Bulldog* was sold to seven foreign air forces, including the US Navy. A surviving example, being used as an RAF static engineering trainer, was refurbished by Bristol to flying status, but was later lost in an air display accident. (The author played a small part in the refurbishment by finding two Vickers machine-guns.)

As noted, the advent of 1927 saw the end of the bird and animal names, unless they began with 'F' for 'Fighters-Land', or 'N' for 'Fighters-Fleet', so *Bulldog* was one of the last 'mammal (except Felidae)' names.

It should, according to the rules, have been a 'land-bird, except of prey' but with that exclusion there would have been no tenacity or aggression as was conveyed by *Bulldog*. Such must have been in the mind of the air marshals, for just that came about in 1932: fighters names were now required to convey speed, activity and aggressiveness. Perhaps *Bulldog* has another niche in history that has not been recognised, for it was certainly aggressive!

Classic No. 5: The Hawker *Fury* (1931) — Rolls-Royce *Kestrel* (1)

'As when that devilish Iron Engine
Wrought in deepest hell, and framed
 by Furie's skill,
With windy nitre and quick sulphur fraught
And rammed with bullet round, ordained
 to kill.'
— Edmund Spenser (1552–1599)

Somewhat before Hawker's classic of 1929, Spenser refers to the mythological Furies of the classics, and with literary licence we make the association — if only because of the appropriateness of the poem — with the name of the famous RAF fighter. The Furies were the ministers of justice and vengeance on mankind.

The 1929 Hawker *Fury*, indeed, provoked considerable fury between Sir Sidney Camm, Hawker's chief designer, and the Air Ministry over the naming of this fighter; this occurred in 1927, before the first flight, but when the aircraft had already been named and with Air Ministry approval. That was the Hawker *Hornet*, named under the 1921 system (except that a hornet is not the bird that it was supposed to be — another exception, but understandable as a hornet is somewhat more aggressive). Anyhow, along came the 1927 system which decreed that land fighters should begin with 'F', and on this the Air Council was having no exception. Thus was used what was to become the renowned name of *Fury*. 'Fighter — Fleet' names were to begin with 'N', and hence the

Nimrod, which was the navalised version of the *Fury*. The name seemed to be popular, notwithstanding Hawker's fury, for there was the Felixstowe *Fury*, a five-engined flying boat of 1918, this of 1929, another Hawker of 1944, and also the North American FJ-1 jet fighter of the US Navy, and the *Fury* of 1944 had its FAA counterpart in the *Sea Fury*.

One of the last of the biplane and fixed undercarriage fighters of the RAF, a 'way of life' carried on only by the Gloster *Gladiator*, the *Fury* was the standard fighter (serving with seven RAF Fighter Squadrons) until the advent of the *Spitfire* and *Hurricane*. There were several versions: 'Persian', 'Iranian', 'Spanish' and 'High Speed'. A later monoplane (not built) was to be named *Hotspur*, all of which led to the *Hurricane*. The name *Fury* was also used by the North American fighter bombers of 1956. (see also the Felixstowe *Fury* of 1917).

As with the previous *Bulldog*, *Fury* was the star of the RAF Hendon pageants. Whilst it never saw action in RAF service, it was the ideal 'trainer' for what was to follow with the advent of World War Two in 1939. Many a Battle of Britain pilot had been trained, or had experience of the *Fury*, and it too can make some claim towards ensuring the Victory that was to come. Without the *Fury*, there may well have not been enough experience or training for the *Spitfire*s and *Hurricane*s.

From a first flight in 1930 to its becoming obsolete in 1939 was no mean span of time for a first line fighter. Some *Fury* pilots thought it the most beautiful biplane ever built, and others that it was the most perfect fighter that could be built.

Hawket Fury

Supermarine Southampton

Classic No. 6: The Supermarine *Southampton* (1921) — Napier *Lion* (2)

The name came under the RAF 'Class of Nickname' system of July 1918, whereby a seaplane up to 11,000 lb and with more than one engine was to be named as a seaboard town in England or Wales.

Whilst the *Southampton* first flew in 1925, the name equally qualified under the 1921 system, the only difference being that it was now a 'sea aeroplane' to be named after a seaboard town in the British Isles. In practice, all flying boats were named after ports (while officially still being seaboard towns!) in the British Empire. The Southampton to which we refer is in the County of Hampshire, but were you to be in New York (USA) you might be somewhat surprised to find that it was in Suffolk County. The Hampshire port has lost some of its previous glamour with the passing of the great ocean liners plying their trade across the Atlantic to the Americas. It remains a busy trade port, but in the Middle Ages was reckoned to be second only to London, and Southampton Water was then known as Hampton Water.

The flying boat name not only fitted the RAF naming system, but was appropriate as the manufacturers, Supermarine, had their works at Woolston on Southampton Water. This had been started before World War One by a Mr Pemberton-Billing, who produced some early and reputable boats, but who then decided that being a Member of Parliament was more fun than making aircraft and so sold the business, which then became Supermarine, the name taken from the telegraphic address. Supermarine Aviation Co. Ltd were allocated 'SU' and 'SW' as name prefixes in 1918, but presumably 'Southampton' was good enough. (Note that the *Southampton* was derived from the civil *Swan*, which was Supermarine's first post-war flying boat, and in turn was developed into the *Scapa*. *Southampton*'s hull was originally of wood, but later of long-lasting aluminium.)

Service in the RAF was from 1925 until 1936, and apart from its other virtues, this is one good reason for its inclusion in this 'Classics' chapter. Designed by R.J. Mitchell, later to win particular fame as the designer of the *Spitfire*, the *Southampton* served with six RAF Squadrons, one of which was at Singapore.

The claim to fame of the *Southampton* was a series of long-distance flights by groups of these flying boats over parts of the then British Empire. One of these groups in 1927 flew from Felixstowe to Australia via Singapore and Hong Kong, and then returned to Singapore, a total of over 27,000 miles. With a goodwill tour of the Baltic in 1927, came the name of the *Baltic Boat*.

Whilst serving an 'Empire' political purpose, with attendant publicity for the RAF, the operational aspect was put to good purpose with Coastal Command in World War Two. But there was, perhaps, an even more important function, that of surveying future air routes for civil aircraft to connect the British Empire. These did, indeed, materialise in the form of the Empire routes served by the later Short 'Empire' flying boats. So the *Southampton*s served a purpose beyond that of being RAF service flying boats. Apart from the later Empire routes, the Short 'C' class boats also pioneered the non-stop flights across the Atlantic. There is thus a certain irony, not even suspected at the time, that the long-distance feats of the *Southampton* in the 1920s and 1930s were the beginning of the end of the ocean liners, one of whose major ports was Southampton. One *Southampton* survives.

Supermarine Walrus

Classic No. 7: The Supermarine *Walrus* (1933) — Bristol *Pegasus* (1)

Pegasus was the classical 'winged horse': so, if horses could fly, then why not the walrus, which promptly did. It is doubtful if the Air Ministry had this in mind when the decreed in 1932 that any Fleet Air Arm, Spotter Reconnaissance, was to have the name of a marine animal.

In spite of its aquatic habitat, the walrus is indeed an animal, although the Dutch insisted on calling it a 'walvish' or whale fish. More accurate was his name in Old English, the 'horschwoel' or horse whale, which at least recognised that he was not a fish. So there is some diversity in the name of this mammal, as there was in the nicknames bestowed on the aircraft, such as 'Shagbat', 'Pusser's Duck' and 'Steam Pigeon', but that was after it had been, quite properly, known as the 'Seagull V' and served in the Royal Australian Air Force; it did not become *Walrus* until 1935. (Note also that there was a Westland *Walrus* of 1920, a conversion of the DH9a, which served in the FAA from 1924 with the endearing nickname of 'Tadpole'.)

It should here be recalled that whilst the Royal Navy was responsible for their own aviation from 1914, it became an RAF affair in 1918 and so lasted until 1939 with the outbreak of World War Two. Thus the official names here discussed were of RAF rather than RN origin, although it was official policy to invite suggestions from the manufacturer prior to liaising with the Admiralty.

Whilst other purposes were in mind, the immediate one was for the *Walrus* to be capable of being catapulted from a warship. But first, as noted, the Seagull V was bought by Australia in 1933 after the first flight, and the RAF *Walrus* did not begin sea trials on HMS *Repulse* and HMS *Valiant* until 1935. With the war and RN control of its own aviation destiny, the *Walrus* served in both the RAF and the FAA (now RN), and some 746 were built, 461 by Saunders-Roe.

As diverse as its names and nicknames was its military talent in many theatres of war, from being a dive bomber(!) in Norway in 1940 to playing the benevolent role of Air-Sea Rescue, to which role many an allied and enemy pilot owed his life. In this role it served with eleven RAF Squadrons. The year 1940 saw the arrival of the *Sea Otter*, which was to later replace the *Walrus*.

To finish with the theme with which we started, and to quote from Lewis Carroll:
> 'The time has come, the Walrus said,
> To talk of many things;
> Of shoes, and ships, and sealing wax,
> Of cabbages and kings,
> Of why the sea is boiling hot
> And whether pigs have wings.'

Two *Walruses* survive, in the RNAS Museum at Yeovilton and in the RAF Museum.

Classic No. 8: The de Havilland *Tiger Moth* (1931) — *Gipsy Major* (1)

Arctiidae — 'stout body and ample wings. A medium-sized, typically colourful moth, the larvae being hairy and known as the "Woolly Bear".'

The line of de Havilland *Moths* comes from Sir Geoffrey de Havilland who was a Lepidopterist (one who studies moths). Besides the tiger moth, there is a tiger beetle, fish, heron and shark. Indeed, there was a DH *Heron* and a Blackburn *Shark*, but definitely not lepidoptera.

'Tiger' and 'Tiggy' were the nicknames, but the Australians had a higher opinion — to them it was the 'Tigerschmidt', and the early days of World War One did see them with guns, and even bombs.

Tiger Moth was not a new name, for there was an earlier DH diminutive monoplane racer of that name in 1927. The fin and rudder are all but identical to the 1931 model. It was developed from the *Moth* and *Gipsy Moth* (having a Gipsy engine), and the latter was not only famous in its own right but in particular because it was flown by Amy Johnson and also Francis Chichester on their epic flights to Australia. As will be seen, there was a strange affinity between this aeroplane and Australia.

The early *Moths* were the foundation of the British light aircraft movement, and the *Tiger* itself, the most famous of the line, was a basic military trainer serving throughout World War Two with the RAF and the Empire training schools. The total of 8,800 built leaves small doubt as to their military importance, even if stemming from modest civil beginnings. To some it was an awful aeroplane, but they missed the point — it soon sorted you out, and it was said that if you could fly a Tiger then you could fly anything! This was not altogether true, because some who survived the *Tiger* could come unstuck with the *Harvard* and *Oxford* or *Anson*.

The *Tiger*, and to a lesser extent the *Maggie* (Miles *Magister*), trained many tens of thousands on their onward journey from EFTS (Elementary Flying Training School) to SFTS (Service Flying Training School) where they would obtain their wings.

The early *Moth* had an upright engine with the crankshaft at the bottom, and so with a small propeller clearance from the ground. The *Puss Moth* had an inverted engine which solved the problem, and such was the installation in the *Tigers*. It was originally the DH 60T or 'trainer', but then the Dh 82A and the *Tiger Moth*. Large-scale production began at Stag Lane, later at Hatfield, and eventually models were sold to no less than twenty-five countries. By the beginning of the war 1,150 had been built at Hatfield, and many of the civil aircraft were pressed into the RAF in 1939. 227 had also been made in Canada.

With the advent of the *Mosquito* (an insect, if not a moth) production was transferred to Morris Motors. By 1945, 8,000 plus had been built in the UK and overseas and Australia was shipping them to Rhodesia and South Africa.

With the shortage of *Gipsy Major* engines due to the Battle of the Atlantic, Canadian *Tigers* used the Menasco *Pirate*, and to cope with the extreme winter temperatures a cockpit canopy and heating was fitted. With wheels, floats and skis there was no stopping in training. The USA bought 200, and handed them over to the RCAF, so the 'Tigger' was as well-known 'over there' as 'over here'.

As part of its war record, it was even an (uncomfortable) ambulance in Burma, taking just one stretcher. With the end of the war a *Tiger* plus a spare engine could be bought for £50. Today — and there are still some — it would cost about £30,000, but the value of the pound has, of course, greatly changed.

The RAF continued with its tried and trusty *Moths* in the RAFVR and the University Squadrons until the advent of the DH Canada *Chipmunk*, but the FAA *Tigers* saw even longer service as glider tugs.

In New Zealand they found a new role as crop sprayers, and not to be outdone in innovation, in the UK they were fitted with a canopy for the front seat and became the 'Taxi Tigers'! A more drastic conversion in the UK was a side-by-side with a canopy, and known as the 'Jackaroo'. With the continuing fervour for a genuine *Tiger*, 'Jackaroos' were turned back to their original form.

It is interesting to note that the Australian 'Tigerschmidt' should become the 'Jackaroo' for that is the Australian term for a young helper on a cattle or sheep farm. Australia has yet another connection: de Havilland Australia manufactured drones, and with a proper regard for history three types were named *Enmoth*, *Beemoth* and *Promoth*.

DH Tiger Moth

Classic No. 9: The Gloster
Gladiator (1934) — *Mercury* (1)

This well named biplane fighter marked the end of an era in the RAF which began with the biplanes of the 1911 Air Battalion, Royal Engineers which became the RFC in 1912, but while *Gladiator* first flew in 1934, it was still in service to the end of 1946. The last of the RAF's biplane fighters (replacing the Bristol *Bulldog)*, it is ironic and interesting that the first of their jet fighters, the *Meteor*, should also have been produced by Gloster.

The building of the *Gladiator* was a Gloster board decision to fill the time gap before the new era monoplane fighters would be available in quantity. Production was speeded up by using as many *Gauntlet* components as possible, and the first aircraft were ready for squadron service by 1937; whilst the *Gladiator* was a four-gun fighter compared to the eight-gun *Hurricane* and *Spitfire*, to many of the defeated enemy it was an academic difference. At the time of the Munich crisis in 1938, the RAF had six *Gladiator*, three *Hurricane* and no *Spitfire* squadrons, which reflects some credit on the Gloster board, and not much on the politicians.

Its first action was during the blitz retreat in France, and then in Norway where they will long be remembered for their spirited defence against the German advance from off the ice-covered Lake Lesjaskog, which the Luftwaffe effectively bombed. All the *Gladiator*s were lost. They had been launched from the carrier HMS *Glorious*, which then brought back the crews and replacement aircraft to cover the retreat of Allied forces at Narvik. After some desperate fighting, the *Gladiator*s and *Hurricane*s landed back on the carrier which was then tragically sunk with only two RAF survivors.

After the Battle of Britain, their next theatre of war was North Africa and Greece. The highest scoring RAF pilot of World War Two, S/Ldr St. J. Pattle, DFC, is credited with forty victories, of which fifteen were with a *Gladiator* in these battles. One 'accepted' the surrender of an Italian submarine, and in a period of six weeks they destroyed fifty-eight enemy aircraft for the loss of only eight. One, piloted by P/O Jacobsen, attacked six of the enemy; forced a Ju88 into a mountain; shot down three He 111 bombers, maybe a fourth, and all in one day. Without these antiquated biplanes, the military outcome may well have been more difficult and further prolonged.

By 1941 the Me 109 had arrived in North Africa, and aircraft were then seconded to Malta; these aircraft formed the only defence of the island when Italy entered the war. Later when desperate for fighters, six crated *Sea Gladiator*s were found and put into the service. The three survivors were the renowned *Faith*, *Hope* and *Charity*, and one survives in a Malta museum. The *Sea Gladiators* served in eight FAA Squadrons, flew from five RN Carriers, and also played a part in the Battle of Malta. A grand total of 474 was built, went to 15 countries, and they put up a magnificent fight for the Finnish Air Force against the Russian invasion of 1940.

In monoplane-dominated wars, it was just an old-fashioned biplane; but then so was the *Swordfish*. One flying *Gladiator* is preserved by the Shuttleworth Trust at Old Warden.

Gloster Gladiator

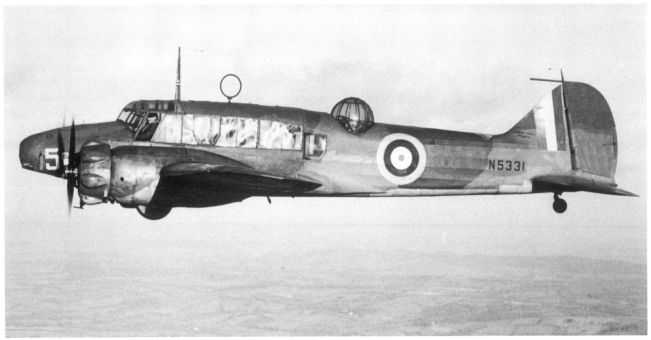

Auro Anson

Classic No. 10: The Avro *Anson* (1933) — Armstrong Siddeley *Cheetah* (2)

Lord George Anson (1697-1762), British Admiral of the Fleet, circumnavigator, and one of the founders of the naval profession that was to have no equal, gave his name to this aircraft. It was originally conceived by Imperial Airways in 1933 as a small civil transport. Whilst still in the design stage, the Air Ministry issued a specification for coastal patrol, and this was all but identical to the Imperial Airways requirement, and few drawing changes were needed. The Air Ministry ordered one prototype. It is sometimes said that the aircraft was developed from the *Avalon*, but this is a part truth. The two civil planes had individual names, *Avalon* and *Avatar*, the latter a Hindu deity that descended to Earth in human form. The name was very soon changed to *Ava*. Now Avalon is fabled as an island paradise in the western seas where King Arthur and other heroes are buried. As there was an Avro *Ava* in 1921, presumably the names were of Avro origin, but then Imperial Airways named their own aircraft(?) (Incidentally, *Avalon* and *Ava* had very successful civil careers. The RAF were impressed, so they pressed both into RAF service in 1941. Ironically, they were then handed over to the FAA).

First flown in 1935, and after official trials and some few modifications, the name was officially *Anson*. The Admiralty had reservations on using RN naval names of fame, but it was too late. Not to use such names was a later Admiralty/Air Ministry agreement.

The first *Anson* was delivered to the RAF in 1936, its first monoplane with retractable undercarriage. Another irony was that six were ordered by Iraq, and had to be destroyed by the RAF in the Rashid Ali rebellion of 1941. Designed for coastal reconnaissance and not a fighter nor yet a bomber (although in the Middle East was so adapted), it could be surprisingly pugnacious. In 1940 *Anson*s damaged a U-boat,

shot down a flying boat, three Me 109 fighters, a seaplane and a bomber. The great Admiral Anson would have been delighted.

Those named after him were the backbone of Coastal Command until the arrival of the Lockheed *Hudson*, and in the UK they were then relegated to the more pacific duties of training; overseas, they replaced Junkers 52s of the SAAF for coastal patrols off the East African coast and one was on floats was an SAAF trainer for the Sunderland flying boat. Earlier in the war, escaped Dutch pilots had formed a squadron in Coastal Command, and after the war Holland was presented with some *Anson*s to form the beginning of a new Royal Netherlands Air Force. At this time RAF *Anson*s were doing sterling work as transports in, and to/from Europe. They played a great part in the Commonwealth Air Training Scheme, and Winston Churchill said that this vast enterprise laid the foundations of victory. Noting their worth, Canada requested *Anson*s for anti-sub duties. At this time the U-boat was in the ascendant and the aircraft could not be shipped from the UK, so Canada adapted some trainers and also made their own, first with Jacobs and then with Wright *Whirlwind* engines — it became known as the *Blowpipe*. Later, UK-made aircraft were shipped over. In the Canadian Navy and Air Force the *Blowpipe* served until the late 1950s, and they were also used as civil transports.

RAF *Anson*s urgently required in Egypt were delivered in clandestine fashion with civil registrations and in Imperial Airways colours, flying to Lisbon and then down to West Africa and across to Egypt. In post-war years they sold to many countries including the UK and served with many aviation companies; and even more were transferred from the RAF to the FAA!

The last flying *Anson* was in Australia in 1987, fifty-two years after the first flight. 11,020 were built. FAITHFUL ANNIE, which trained so many Commonwealth multi-engined pilots (and navigators, and air gunners, and W/T operators), was never averse to a good fight.

Classic No. 11: The Westland *Lysander* (1936) — Bristol *Mercury* (1)

'Some talk of Alexander and some of Hercules
Of Hector and *Lysander*, and such great
    names as these. . .'
— marching song of the Grenadier Guards

LYSANDER (d 395 BC) was the son of a Spartan admiral, and became one himself in 407 BC, winning a series of naval battles over the years. Building up the Spartan Empire, he was to become the most powerful man of his time in Greece. After a complex and violent career as politician, admiral and general, he was killed at the siege of Haliartus. The term 'spartan' derives from the Spartan, a citizen-soldier of the State who lived a frugal existence, his life dedicated to the military arts. The dictionary defines 'spartan' as of Spartan character, of fortitude and self-discipline.

The 1932 nomenclature system allocated classical names to 'Bombers, Army Co-operation', but why *Lysander* in particular was chosen is not known. The matter is of no great import, for to the British it was affectionately known as *Lizzie*, whilst the more respectful Luftwaffe knew it as *Die Wespe*, the *Wasp*.

Its first flight was in 1936, and the *Lysander* was the first monoplane to serve in Army Co-operation Squadrons, entering the RAF in 1938. The short landing and take-off capability made it entirely suitable for this role, but many

others with similar functions were to come the RAF's way so perhaps its particular claim to fame would be the clandestine 'spy running' operations into occupied France. France was already well-known country, for the *Lysander* served in numbers up to the retreat from Dunkirk and some eighty aircraft were lost during the blitz in the Low Countries and France. There is an historic first and last to recall here: a *Lysander* in 1939 shot down the first Heinkel bomber in BEF (British Expeditionary Force) territory, and was the last RAF aircraft to leave Europe after Dunkirk. Some thirty RAF Squadrons were equipped with the 'three marks', and apart from service in the UK and over France, it was also used in Italy, Greece, Egypt and Palestine. (Greece being *Lysander* country, it poses the thought as to whether the historical connection over 2,300 years was ever a subject of conversation among pilots and ground crew. It is improbable, but what would the Spartan admiral have thought?) One *Lysander* was known as the *Delanne*, a twin tandem wing to support a new turret; more unofficially it was known as the *Pregnant Perch*!

Later roles of this versatile aircraft included air-sea rescue and target towing, and as noted, the spy runs to France and the close co-operation with the French Resistance which played an important part in the run-up to the Allied invasion. In this the *Wasp* had a more vicious sting than in direct combat with the Luftwaffe. The spy-droppers were based in Bedfordshire, and the 'milk run' eventually totalled over 400 operations. The aircraft was then known as the *Black Lysander*. RAF service finished in 1946, and only three *Lysander*s are known to survive. 1,424 were built.

Westland Lysander

Classic No. 12: the Vickers *Wellington* (1936) — Bristol *Pegasus* (2)

The first flight of the *Wellington* was in 1936, making it subject to the 1939 naming system which specified 'and inland town in the British Empire, or associated with British history'. There are three towns with the name, one in Somerset, another in Shropshire and a third in New Zealand (although this last is a 'seaside town'). That deals with the geographical aspect, but note that back in 1935 there had been the Vickers *Wellesley* and that Sir Arthur Wellesley was to become the Duke of Wellington, the 'Iron Duke'. Thus Vickers could assure the Air Ministry that they had complied not only with the rules, but with both alternatives. Wellington the general was the choice, although his association with either of the two English towns is not clear.

The Duke made his military reputation in India, later in the Peninsula War against Napoleon, and finally in his ultimate defeat of the emperor of Waterloo. The hero of his day, Wellington was to serve as both commander-in-chief of the British Army and as Prime Minister; despite this aristocratic background, the aircraft was known as *Wimpey*, a contemporary American cartoon character with a fondness for hamburgers!

The *Wellington* was designed by Barnes-Wallis, with the new structural technique of geodetic construction, simply explained as a lattice of girders helically wound to the required shape. In its time, this was a great success: strong and light, it readily absorbed battle damage and was easy to repair. Many a damaged *Wimpey* came home against all the laws of probability and it had twice the range called for in the RAF specification, B9/32.

Joining the RAF in 1937, *Wellington*s, in company with *Blenheim*s, made the first attack on Germany — warships at Brünsbuttel — the day after war was declared (3 September 1939). They bore the brunt of the early bombing campaigns until the advent of the four-engined 'heavies' in 1943, but continued in Italy and in the Far East. They also served with Coastal Command as anti-U-boat, torpedo bombers and as minesweepers carrying a huge 'de-gaussing' ring to set off magnetic mines. Carrying a lifeboat for air-sea rescue was but another chapter in its long and varied life.

Adding to the campaign list, *Wellington*s also took part in the North African campaign and from there laid mines in the Danube near Budapest. With regard to the Far East, they were the first RAF long-range bombers to take part.

A sight that baffled a few pilots was that of a *Wellington* happily flying across the sky with no visible means of support — both propellers were still! Reports of this phenomenon were just not believed until it was revealed that the required thrust came from a Whittle W2B jet on trials and fixed in the rear turret. The *Wellington* with a torpedo ('Fish') was known as the *Fishington*. A great mine-layer (and destroyer), it is interesting that mines were known as 'vegetables' and the operation as 'gardening'. With radar installations, *Wellington*s were sometimes known as *Sticklebacks* (radar antennae) or *Goofington*.

11,461 *Wellington*s were built (one in twenty-four hours) and served in fifty-eight RAF Squadrons, continuing after the war as a trainer and being finally retired in 1953, a span of eighteen years. From the *Wellington* stemmed the *Warwick* and the *Windsor*. Three now remain.

Wellington

Classic No. 13: The Supermarine *Spitfire* (1936) — Rolls-Royce *Merlin* (1)

'Spitfire': 'a thing which emits or vomits fire, especially a cannon. 'Fire-spitting': 'irascible, displaying anger or hot temper.' 'Spitfire': 'a cat in an angry state, the 'spitfire' or storm jib of a sailing ship'.

As background to the origin of the aircraft name, in 1932 the Air Ministry decided on a system of naming which broke with past traditions and required an impression of 'speed, activity and aggression'. Before this there had been issued specification F7/30 calling for an 'interceptor' with the Rolls-Royce steam-cooled *Goshawk* engine, for which most manufacturers tendered. The Vickers F7/30 which flew in 1932 was given the name *Spitfire*, although this was unofficial so far as the Air Ministry was concerned.

There are two versions as to the origin, one being that Sir Robert McLean, Chairman of Vickers (who took over Supermarine in 1928), had a daughter who was somewhat of a tomboy, a 'spitfire'. The suggestion was not well received, and Mitchell, the chief designer, is said to have stated that it was bloody silly name, but *Spitfire* it became.

Mostly because of the engine, *Spitfire* (1) was abandoned, and Mitchell set himself the task of designing something better. This was a 'PV', or 'private venture', as was the PV12 Rolls-Royce engine. Specification F37/34 'blessed' the PV, and the engine was to become the *Merlin*. What name for this new fighter? *Shrew* was one suggestion. Despite the same objections, Sir Robert's original suggestion prevailed, and *Spitfire* (2) it became. Another version is that the suggestion was that of General Manager, Sir James Bird, who is alleged to have announced the name to Mitchell, who replied that it could be called 'Spit Blood' for all he cared! The last word shall be that of Mrs Ann Penrose, daughter of Sir Robert McLean, who writes: '... time was running short; after much discussion, I floated the idea [of Spitfire] amongst some rather ordinary names.' The appellation was not entirely new, for there is a photograph of an RFC RE 8 (Harry Tate) with the individual name of *Spitfire*.

The history of the *Spitfire* is so well-known that it seems almost superfluous to record it yet again. As regards names however, it is ironic that what was to become the most widely known name of any aircraft of any age should have had so contentious a beginning. The 1923 system, of which this name was so classic an example, also heralded a new era, for it was the first time that the significance or 'psychological impact' of a fighter name was considered. The birds and the animals had a charm of their own, but the war was a new scene. The first sign of this had been the Hawker *Fury*, but the only official requirement was that a fighter should begin in 'F'.

There were 21 operational marks of *Spitfire*, and some 500 listed squadrons that fought with them, but as several squadrons used different marks, the actual number of squadrons is smaller than 500; but it indicates the enormous contribution made to the Allied effort (including other air forces with the RAF) by the *Spitfire*, and this may again be seen with a grand total of 22,890 built.

The *Spitfire* Mk 21 was an advanced design, with the Griffon engine (but the combination was not new), and there was a considerable opinion that a new name should be found, even the surprising view that *Spitfire* was 'old hat' and a new name would raise the morale of the RAF! There was much discussion in the Air Ministry and from a long list of names, *Spiteful* (later used) and *St George* was put forward, preference being given to the latter. Air Chief-Marshal Sir Charles Portal, was not impressed and declared that *Spitfire* was a noble and well-proven name, and would remain.

From the later number and its overall performance in many roles and in many theatres of war, the *Spitfire* earned its reputation, but to some this was thought to be overdone so far as the Battle of Britain was concerned, for approximately twice as many *Hurricanes* shot down approximately three times the number of Luftwaffe fighters and bombers.

It is the *Spitfire*, however, that seems to have captured the imagination of the post-war generations. *Spit* and *Spitty* were the common nicknames.

There was, indeed, a 'Speed Spitfire', one specially modified to try for the world speed record, but abandoned with the advent of war in 1939 (in which respect one quotes Lord Amhurst (1762) on his mistress: 'Not so fast, I beg of you, my dear little spitfire'.) Unlike the *Hurricanes*, quite a number of *Spitfires* survive, both in the UK and in the United States. One USA interest would be the Eagle Squadron of the RAF which flew *Spitfires*, the pilots being American who volunteered before the USA entered the War. In total, about seventy-five *Spitfires* exist (only a few are airworthy) in the UK, with others in the USA.

It is interesting, but not surprising, to find that the name had some fame even before the advent of the flying-machine. One of the 'Firefly' class locomotives of the Great Western Railway was named *Spitfire*, and gave excellent service between 1840 and 1878. Another was the London & North Eastern Railway *Spitfire*, a Whitworth type locomotive which ran for many years up to 1920, but the name appeared long before that with a Royal Navy galley of 1778. In fact, there were twelve RN fighting ships with the name *Spitfire*, one being a destroyer or 1912. The last of the line was *Spitfire* III, an RN yacht active to 1946, which could at least claim to have been a contemporary of the aircraft. RAF torpedo recovery tenders also attracted names, and two in 1986 were *Spitfire* and *Hurricane*.

Classic No. 14: *The Hawker Hurricane* (1935) — Rolls-Royce *Merlin* (1)

'Hurricane': 'a violent tropical cyclone originating in the Gulf of Mexico or Caribbean Sea, with the wind exceeding 32.7 metres per second (73 mph) or Force 12 on the Beaufort scale. From the Caribbean, and later Spanish 'Huracan'.

Also known as tropical cyclones or typhoons, hurricanes can reach speeds of 200 mph and contain as much energy as 400 twenty-megaton bombs. With these statistical exactitudes in mind, it was a well-chosen name, and joins *Spitfire* in the ranks of the most famous names in the RAF, if not in the world. The name was allocated under the same 1932 system as *Spitfire*.

There was a clear lineage from *Fury* (originally *Hornet*) to the proposed *Fury* monoplane, Interceptor (with the Rolls-Royce PV-12 to become *Merlin*) and so to *Hurricane*. Thus was founded a meteorological or 'wind and fury' tradition, a fighter family to be followed by *Tempest*, *Typhoon* and *Tornado* (no 'Whirlwind', as that had been appropriated by Westland).

The *Hurricane* was the RAF's first multi-gun fighter and entered squadron service in 1937. As with the earlier Hawker fighters, it was a steel tube structure with a fabric covering, having the advantage of easy, well-proven manufacture and the ability to take heavy punishment. Unless it was a lucky hit, a bullet or shell just made a hole which, at least in the fabric, could be patched over.

Sir Thomas Sopwith and his board at Hawkers foresaw that World War Two was inevitable, and entirely at their own risk laid down an order for no less than 400 *Hurricanes*. Had they waited for a formal government order, the outcome of the Battle of Britain and thus of the war could well have been very different. To the far-sighted Hawker men, Winston Churchill should also have given the thanks of the nation.

On 8 August 1940, a *Hurricane* fired the first shot of the Battle of Britain, and in the ensuing battle *Hurricanes*, with twice the number of fighters compared to the *Spitfire*, shot down three times as many enemy aircraft, a total of 860. The only VC awarded to Fighter Command was to Flight Lieutenant Nicholson, flying a *Hurricane*.

The 'Hurribird', 'Hurribomber' and the genial nickname of *Hurriback* saw service in many marks, and after the Battle of Britain possibly the most enduring memory is of the *Hurricane* armed with mighty cannons as a most effective tank buster, as Field-Marshal Rommel and the Afrika Korps learned to their cost.

The grand total built was 14,527, serving in no less than 153 RAF Squadrons. In terms of speed the *Hurricane* was slower than the *Spitfire*, but in 1939 startled the world in a flight from Northolt to Edinburgh and back at an average speed of 408 mph — admittedly with a good tail wind for part of the time.

There was also the *Sea Hurricane* or 'Hurricat', which was catapulted off merchant ships as convoy protection. The pilots were brave men, for the only way back was to parachute into the sea, and for some that was above the Arctic circle with little chance of survival. In those Norwegian waters *Hurricanes* improbably but successfully took off from HMS *Glorious*. With the retreat from Norway, the two squadrons were ordered to destroy their aircraft, but they actually landed them back on *Glorious*, which sadly was soon to be sunk.

One more name should be mentioned, that of Sir Sydney Camm, who designed all in this long line of Hawker fighters carrying through to *Hunter* and *Harrier*. Sixteen *Hurricanes* are known to exist in the UK.

Hurricane was the name of an RAE light aircraft of 1923, and the proposed name for the Hawker P 1121 which became the *Harrier*.

Hawker Hurricane

Classic No. 15: The Fairey *Swordfish* (1934) — Bristol *Pegasus* (1)

'Swordfish': 'One of the Xiphiidae, a pelagic fish whose terrible weapon is formed by the coalescence and prolongation of the maxillary and intermaxillary bone beyond the jaw, being very hard.'

The Fleet Air Arm of the Royal Navy would quite agree with the above definition, for the *Swordfish*'s weapon was indeed terrible, and in naval parlance a torpedo was a 'fish'; furthermore, the name comes from the Anglo-Saxon 'strang' meaning 'strong' and the Gaelic 'balg' or 'bolg' meaning 'a pair of bellows, a blister or a bag'. So there you have it, a 'strang bag' or a 'strongbag'. The aircraft was indeed strong, but 'stringbag' it was, the string referring to the many interplane wires of this big biplane. Its reputation preceded it, for as George Wabbe (1754-1832) wrote in his book on fish: 'It is a sly old fish, too cunning for the hook'.

In the 1932 system the FAA was given names of estuaries, seas and oceans for torpedo bombers, and marine animals for spotter reconnaissance, to neither of which does the name *Swordfish* belong. It was almost obsolete before it began, and was totally out of keeping with the modern, fast and streamlined types about to come into service, noting that it first flew in 1934. It was certainly an exception to the rule, and many consider it to have been the best naval aircraft of World War Two. Its considerable success arose from its strength, manoeuvrability, load-carrying capability and its low landing and take-off speeds, making it ideal for carrier operations. Like the mythical Hercules, the many tasks allotted to it were in the 'impossible' class, yet this improbable and antiquated old biplane with but one engine was wholly responsible for the devastating night attack on the Italian Fleet at Taranto, from which Italian naval power in the Mediterranean never recovered. The attack had a profound effect on the North African campaigns. Who would have ventured that the *Swordfish* would make a torpedo attack on the mighty *Bismarck* damaging the rudders, one of the first vital steps in her final destruction?

The great feats of Taranto and the sinking of the *Bismarck* were collective squadron efforts, but there was one *Swordfish* in Norway which in 1940 had one glorious day all to itself: it spotted for the guns of HMS *Warspite* which destroyed seven German destroyers, then bombed and sank a U-boat, and rounded off a busy day by finishing off an already damaged destroyer. The pilot's logbook should be part of the nation's military archives, and the Royal Navy's pride. To add yet another chapter to the long story, the first raid on Italy was carried out by a *Swordfish* over Genoa, and in the Mediterranean over a period of nine months, some twenty-seven aircraft sank 50,000 tons of enemy shipping.

The Fairey Aviation Company no longer exists. Whilst it made a long line of aircraft with naval connections, this surely must have been the jewel in the crown. In all, 2,391 were built, 692 by Fairey and the balance, from 1940, by Blackburn at Brough. Not surprisingly, the Blackburn aircraft were known as *Blackfish*. The *Swordfish* was eventually superseded by the *Albacore*, but was still going strong when the *Albacore* had been retired!

Five *Swordfish* remain, two belonging to the RNAS Museum at Yeovilton and always a popular visitor on the annual airshow round. A second flying example took to the air in Canada in 1992.

Fairey Swordfish

Bristol Blenheim

Classic No. 16: The Bristol *Blenheim* (1936) — Bristol *Mercury* (2)

Blindheim is a village on the banks of the River Danube in Bavaria, and it was here in 1704 that the English and Austrian armies under the command of the Duke of Marlborough defeated the French and the Bavarians; in England this became known as the Battle of Blenheim. Such was the victory that a grateful nation erected and presented to the Duke the Palace of Blenheim in Oxfordshire. A descendant was Sir Winston Churchill, who was born at Blenheim Palace, and who wrote a classic biography of his illustrious ancestor.

Thus was named an illustrious aircraft, but to be pedantic, in no way did it meet the requirements of the 1932 naming system. The name complied with the 1939 system, but the *Blenheim* first flew in 1936 and deliveries to the RAF were already under way by 1937. In 1934 Bristol exhibited at the Paris Air Show a monoplane civil transport with two *Aquila* engines, known as 'The Captain's GIG', referring to Captain Frank Barnwell, the Chief Designer. This came to the attention of Lord Rothermere of the *Daily Mail* who ordered a variant that became Type 142. Tested by the RAF at Martlesham Heath, it was found at 14,000 ft to have a top speed fifty mph faster than the *Gladiator!* Now with *Mercury* engines, Lord Rothermere presented 'Britain First' to the nation, and production orders for the militarised *Blenheim* soon followed.

The first operational flight of the RAF in World War Two was a reconnaissance mission by a *Blenheim* to the island of Sylt, a German seaplane base, and *Blenheim*s in various forms of development were still in service at the end of the war. In 1939 the 'short-nosed' *Blenheim* I was superseded by IV with the 'long nose' to allow better accommodation of the navigator.

*Blenheim*s played a valiant part in France in between 1939 and 1940, but suffered heavy losses in low-level attacks against the advancing German armies in the blitzkreig against the lowlands and France. As a bomber the *Blenheim* served with distinction in the Middle East, and was also used by Coastal Command. They also fought to stem the Japanese advance in the far East. The *Blenheim* is generally associated with the defence of Malta in 1941 and early 1942, but it was wholly in the attack, carrying the war to the enemy shipping carrying supplies from Italy to Field-Marshal Rommel in North Africa.

Far removed from its intended role, in 1940 the *Blenheim* was converted to a long-range and night fighter, awaiting the arrival of *Beaufighter* for this purpose. It was still a front line bomber, and one of its most notable operations was a low-level daylight raid on Cologne in 1941 with a total of fifty-four aircraft. Retired from front line service in 1942, it continued in an essential role as an operational trainer until the end of the war.

The *Blenheim* IV, as the 'long nose' version was known, was proposed as the *Bolingbroke*, but the name was reserved for the Fairchild-built aircraft in Canada. Another version was the *Bisley*, but this then reverted to type as *Blenheim* IV. Another version of the *Blenheim* led to the *Beaufort*, itself in turn being modified to become the incomparable *Beaufighter* (also in this Classics chapter).

The total built was 4,544, with others sent to Finland (where one remains in the Finnish Air Force Museum), Turkey, Greece, Yugoslavia and Romania. Two *Blenheim*s remain in the UK, both now at Duxford, one being rebuilt after a crash at Denham. Several were offered by the Finnish Air Force, but receiving a belated response they were consigned to the scrap heap for salvage.

Avro Lancaster

Classic No. 17: The Avro *Lancaster* (1941) — Rolls-Royce *Merlin* (4)

The *Lancaster* first flew in 1941 and was subject to the 1939 naming system which specified 'place-names — an inland town or the British Empire or associated with British history'.

In this case the name satisfied both conditions, the capital town of Lancashire being undoubtedly in the British Empire and also associated with British history over many centuries. An historical link is the War of the Roses, a dynastic struggle (1455-58) between the House of Lancaster and the House of York for the English crown. That this enmity was long forgotten and forgiven is evident from the transport version of the *Lancaster* being called the *York*.

The *Lancaster*'s forerunner was the *Manchester*, a sturdy and well-designed airframe but with the unreliable Rolls-Royce *Vulture* engine which, in effect, was two *Kestrels* on a common crankshaft. With four Rolls-Royce *Merlins*, *Lancaster* was to become the foremost RAF bomber of World War Two, and some would claim of any air force of that time.

'Lanc' or 'Lankie' was a great load carrier, and was the only bomber to carry the 12,000 lb 'Tall Boy' which sank the *Admiral Tirpitz* in Norway; but this was just a little training along the way, for *Lancaster*s then carried the 22,000 lb (ten tons!) 'Grand Slam' which wreaked havoc on the enemy, one particular sortie entirely destroying the Bielefeld viaduct. Perhaps the most spectacular operation with *Lancaster*s was that of 617 ('Dambusters') Squadron which attacked the Möhne and Eder dams with spherical bouncing bombs designed by Barnes-Wallis of Vickers.

This supreme bomber made its debut in 1942 with a daylight raid on Augsberg, but then generally was on night operations, taking part in the 'thousand bomber' raids of 1942 and in all the subsequent campaigns, including the battles of the Ruhr, Hamburg and Berlin. The bombing of the German Experimental Station at Peenemunde in the Baltic (which made the V2 'secret' weapon) was a significant attack, and

but for this the outcome, or at least the length of the war might well have been different. In its spare time, the *Lancaster* was also a minelayer and went on anti-U-boat patrols.

Air Chief-Marshal 'Bomber' Harris declared that the *Lancaster* 'was the prime weapon of victory', and as commander-in-chief of Bomber Command his word, like the bomber, carried great weight. *Lancaster*s dropped 608,000 tons of bombs, flew 156,192 operational sorties, and served in eighty-four RAF Squadrons. 7,337 were built, requiring 29,348 *Merlin* or *Hercules* engines. If the number of engines used is the criterion, then the runner-up is the *Spitfire* with 20,351 engines: the *Lancaster* has statistical top marks in World War Two. Numbers alone do not necessarily equate with efficiency or effectiveness, and a further set of figures is enlightening; the 'bomb to loss' ratio of World War Two:

LANCASTER	132 tons for each one lost
HALIFAX	56 tons for each one lost
STIRLING	41 tons for each one lost

A scaled-up version of the *Lancaster* became the *Lincoln*, with a civilian version known as the *Lancastrian*, and the *York* followed with the same wings and engines. A variant of the *Lancaster* were the 'Upkeep', conversions being made by Vickers.

A static *Lancaster* may be found in the RAF Museum at Hendon, and one flying *Lancaster* of the RAF Battle of Britain Memorial Flight, with attendant *Hurricane* and *Spitfire*, is seen each summer season over many parts of the UK. One further flying *Lancaster* is in Canada.

Why *Lancaster*, or *Manchester*? The latter is the location of A.V. Roe Ltd (as was, and now part of British Aerospace); as *Manchester* was not a 'success' (at least the engines were not), Avro wished to change the name, and thus *Lancaster*, not very far away and the capital town of the county. As may be seen in the Index, there was an Avro *Manchester* bomber in 1918.

Classic No. 18: The Handley Page *Halifax* (1939) — Rolls-Royce *Merlin* (4)

Handley Page alliterates with *Halifax*, and in the March 1918 naming system this requirement was 'mandatory' and then abandoned, but it was a tradition with most, and certainly with Handley Page.

As a town in the British Empire or associated with British history, there are the alternatives of Halifax in Yorkshire, a small seaside town in Queensland (Australia) or the city and port in Nova Scotia (Canada). Was it Yorkshire or Nova Scotia? In the absence of positive information there is a happy solution in that in 1749 the Earl of Halifax founded Halifax in Nova Scotia, with the obvious inference that it was not directly named after its Yorkshire counterpart.

This heavy bomber was designed to the same RAF specification, B13/36, as the Avro *Manchester*, and was similarly designed for the Rolls-Royce *Vulture*. With some foresight the design was changed to four *Merlins*, powering *Halifax* I & II; III, IV, V, VII and VIII had *Hercules* engines.

Whilst somewhat overshadowed by the *Lancaster* in retrospect, and maybe also by post-war 'mythology', the *Halifax* played a very significant part in the heavy bomber operations in which the third heavy bomber, the Short *Stirling*, played a lesser part. Coming into RAF service just after the *Stirling*, the *Halifax* made the first four-engine bomber foray into Germany, bombing Hamburg in March 1941, and, of course, carrying on with this task over Germany for much of the war. Targets were also to be found in occupied France, with one famous raid on the *Gniesnau* and *Scharnhorst* battleships at Brest. From late 1942 they also served with Coastal Command, and also as glider tugs for parachute operations, with experimental electronics work, and also did a fair trade in dropping weapons and supplies to partisan groups.

There is a record of one *Halifax* which, in spite of its nickname of 'Friday The 13th', survived 128 missions; 'Halibag' was tough and could take as well as give its share of punishment. A post-war version of the *Halifax* was a transport/reconnaissance concept, the type staying with the RAF until 1952; with a first flight in 1939, that was a service span of thirteen years. The transport contemporaries were the Handley Page *Hastings* and *Hermes*.

With the later reorganisation and amalgamations of the British Aircraft Industry, Handley Page ceased to be. In this short review of the *Halifax*, it should be recalled that a 'Handley Page' was a household word for a heavy bomber, this going back to the end of World War One. From that time until 1952 there had been an almost unbroken line of military 'Handley Pages'. They are all recorded in the Index.

A total of 161 *Halifax*es were on the civil register after World War Two, and as the *Halton* played a great part in the Berlin airlift. Halton is an RAF station, so the name would not have been allowed for a military aircraft under RAF rules of nomenclature (but there were exceptions).

Altogether 6,176 were built, and in 89 RAF Squadrons they carried out 82,000 bomber missions. One *Halifax* is to be found in the RAF Museum.

Handley Page Halifax

Bristol Beaufighter (Philip Jarrett)

Classic No. 19: The Bristol *Beaufighter* (1939) — Bristol *Hercules* (2)

That the *Beaufighter* could carry bombs, rockets, cannon, machine-guns and torpedoes would not have been known to William Walton (1858 — ?), but he summed up such formidable firepower in just a few lines: '*Who hath found another so shod with fire, so crowned with thunder, and so armed with wrath divine?*'

It seems the name would not meet the 1939 system, but it is well within the requirement of 'speed, activity and aggression' even if it was a made-up name. It was developed from the *Beaufort*, a torpedo bomber, with the Bristol concept of producing a fighter from the *Beaufort* with only a new fuselage. The 'Beau'-prefix suggested a handsome, fine image, a 'great fighter' and even a 'Beau Geste', the fighting hero of the Foreign Legion. With a less romantic image it was the 'Beau' to the Allies, and 'Whispering Death' to the Japanese, and in its guise as a torpedo bomber it was the 'Torbeau', which gives the clue that it would not be possible to classify the *Beaufighter* in any one role; it had many.

The Bristol *Beaufort* was named after the Duke of Beaufort, whose ancestral home was nearby in Gloucestershire. The first dukedom began in 1390 and ended in 1470. The second was revised in 1682 and continues to this day.

The *Beaufighter* first flew in 1939 and entered service in 1940, to serve until the end of the war with eighty-four RAF Squadrons. 5,564 were built in the UK and a further 364 in Australia to be used in the Pacific theatre by the RAAF. Whilst carrying two large air-cooled engines, it was as fast as the *Hurricane*. With a temporary shortage of Hercules engines, the *Merlin* was substituted, which required extra fin area. This not being entirely successful, the tailplane was given a large dihedral angle (12°) which entirely solved the directional stability problem. This new stability was too much for a fighter, but made for an excellent and stable platform for bombs, rockets and torpedoes against any ship, tank or target that foolishly got in the way. The firepower of the Beau could be devastating, of which the Japanese in Burma and Malaya soon became aware; and, judging by their nickname of 'Whispering Death', by the time it was heard it was probably too late . . .

The feats and accomplishments of the *Beaufighter* were legion, but to many, and particularly the Parisians, one unique and joyous mission was the dropping of a large tricolour flag by the Arc de Triomphe in the Champs D'Elysée. This was in 1942, with three years of occupation ahead.

The *Beaufighter* not only served for six years of war, but continued in the RAF to 1960, a span of exactly twenty years. There is one last *Beaufighter* to be found in the RAF Museum, and no other that is known.

Classic No. 20: The Short Sunderland *(1937) — Bristol Pegasus* (4)

If the fame of an aircraft may be judged by the number of its nicknames, *Sunderland* was well on the way: nicknames included 'Monty' 'Tyne Boat' and 'Wonderland'. To the Luftwaffe and the German Navy it merited no less than two nicknames: the 'Flying Porcupine' and the 'Flying Battleship'; generally, Coastal Command aircraft were known as 'Kipper Kites'. 'Tyne Boat' clearly indicates that it was Sunderland (on the Tyne), and as a 'seaboard town' in the British Empire entirely satisfied the 1921 and 1932 naming systems, together with the time-honoured alliteration of 'S'.

In 1936 the first of the 'C' or Empire flying boats flew from the River Medway — Rochester being the home of Short Brothers — and the move to Belfast took place after the war. The militarised version was the *Sunderland*, first flown in 1937 and having the same engines. *Tyne* engines would have been interesting, but were a post-war jet development by Rolls-Royce. It was the first flying boat to be fitted with power-operated gun turrets, and hence the 'porcupine' image, possibly arising from one occasion when a *Sunderland* shot down three Junker 88s.

With the outbreak of war, four 'C' Boats were pressed into RAF service: *Cleo*, *Cordelia*, *Cabot* and *Caribou* — not warlike names, but as this book records, only a minority of RAF names have been of a bellicose nature. The *Sunderland* was one of the most useful of aircraft in RAF service, and apart from the three Junkers 88s was credited with the sinking of twenty-nine U-boats, and could claim to be the backbone of Coastal Command.

In 1939 two *Sunderland*s saved the entire crew of a torpedoed British 'Tramp' some seventy miles off the Scilly Islands. On another occasion, in a single-handed fight against six Junkers 88s, one was shot down and another was forced to land in the sea. In the 1940 Norwegian campaign, they played an invaluable role in reporting enemy Fleet movements to the Royal Navy, and transporting senior officers and urgent stores. They saw service in the North Sea, Atlantic, West Africa and the Indian Ocean, and after World War Two in the Korean War, being based in Japan; and with the crises of the Berlin airlift, the *Sunderland* played its part landing on a nearby lake. Whilst water was convenient, it wasn't essential; a RAAF *Sunderland* in trouble was landed on an airfield, with very little damage, and a few RAF boats landed on the seashore, all to fly again.

Total production was 749, serving in twenty-two RAF Squadrons, and the last was flown home from the Far East in 1959, a span of twenty-two years.

From an experimental scale model — the Short *Shrimp* — was built a large *Sunderland* with four 2000 hp Bristol *Centaurus* engines. This was the *Shetland*, but whilst the two (one destroyed by fire) proved to be excellent in the air and on the water, it was too late to be used by the RAF, and too large to have an immediate attraction as a civil passenger flying boat.

The civil version of the *Sunderland* was the *Sandringham*, which had a successful career (another was the *Hythe*, of which 749 were built). The day of the big flying boat was coming to an end, it being aerodynamically inferior to the new generation of airliners which also required less maintenance, and unlike the earlier years, the military around the world had provided civil aviation with many square miles of concrete; but the 'C' Empire, and the later 'G' or 'golden' boats (e.g. *Golden Hind*) and the *Sunderland* played an enormous part in the aviation scene of those times. One *Sunderland* remains, in the RAF Museum at Hendon.

Short Sunderland

DH Mosquito

Classic No. 21: de Havilland *Mosquito* (1940) — Rolls-Royce *Merlin* (2)

The 1939 categories of nomenclature called for names portraying speed, activity and aggression, which the *Mosquito* fitted most admirably even though the mosquito is hardly speedy, which was the hallmark of the *Mosquito*. No matter, a mosquito is small and this was a *Mosquito* attribute, and all in all it was a most appropriate and either a famous or notorious name, depending on which side you were on. The name itself is the diminutive of the Spanish 'mosca', from the Latin 'musca', a fly.

The 'Wooden Wonder' (part of it was made of balsa wood) followed on from the experience gained from the DH *Albatross*. In the early days it was known as 'Freeman's Folly', Air-Marshal Sir Wilfred Freeman then being the Air Council Member for Research and Development, and who backed the project in spite of much misgiving elsewhere. It took eleven months from the start of design to the first flight. Other nicknames were 'Mossy', 'Mosque' and 'Skeeter', and a later Vickers-built variant had the codename of 'Highball'. No.248 Squadron had a variant with a particularly nasty bite (Molins 57mm cannon), and this was known as the 'Tsetse', an insect of Central Africa, and the cause of sleeping sickness.

First flown in 1940 and entering RAF service in 1941, the *Mosquito* carried no defensive armament, relying entirely on its speed, but yet at the same time could carry a large bomb-load for its size — indeed, a larger bomb-load than the four-engined US *Flying Fortress*. A particularly valuable load of a less destructive nature was ball-bearings flown back from Sweden by 'civil' *Mosquito*s. These clandestine trips across the North Sea and Norway were also a convenient transport for VIPs, their accommodation being the none-too-convenient bomb bay with a minimum of creature comforts.

One of the most successful aircraft of World War Two, the *Mosquito* started its operational life in 1941 in photo-reconnaissance, becoming in turn a day and night bomber, night fighter, anti-shipping fighter-bomber and the guide dog of the bombers following the Pathfinders dropping markers on enemy targets, and dropping not a few 4000 lb 'cookies'. Opening up Gestapo HQs was a speciality, and the raid on

Amiens jail to free Allied prisoners was a masterpiece of planning and precision bombing. *Mosquito*s visited Berlin 170 times, and their loss rate was one in 200 sorties. At the time of the V1 'Doodlebug' raids on England towards the end of the war, *Mosquito*s are on record as having shot down over 500 in just two months, thus not only inflicting great damage but also preventing it.

Apart from shooting down the V1 flying bombs, it was also imperative to destroy the launching sites in enemy-held territory. The *Mosquito* was also central to these missions, and the following figures indicate just how effective a fighting aircraft it was (the figures show the number of tons of bombs taken to destroy one V1 launch site):

Mosquito	39.8
Mitchell	219.0
Marauder	182.0
Fortress	165.4

The *Mosquito* was also amazingly strong, and in one crash-landing wrote off three *Beaufighters;* the *Mosquito* was flying again in six weeks! Field-Marshal Goering is quoted as saying: 'I turn yellow and green when I see the *Mosquito*. The British knock together a beautiful wooden aircraft which every piano factory over there is making. They have the geniuses, I have the nincompoops.'

Not only was the *Mosquito* paramount in Europe, but it also came to the notice of the Japanese in Burma. Speed triumphed over defensive armament, and this 'Wooden Wonder' was the fastest aircraft in the RAF from 1941 to early 1944. Production ceased in 1950 with 7,781 built in forty variants, and RAF service came to an end in 1955. It had served in ninety-seven RAF Squadrons, and twelve Air Forces. (212 were built in Australia).

A 'small' *Mosquito* was built after the war to become the DH *Hornet* but was not used by the RAF. It served with the Fleet Air Arm, known as the *Sea Hornet*, and is claimed to have been the fastest standard propeller aircraft in the British Services. A *Mosquito* is to be found in the RAF Museum and at the de Havilland Museum. Two or three are still airworthy worldwide, and the UK total is eleven.

As another historical aside on the name *Mosquito*. There was a Brooklands, the Gurney Brice 'Box on Wheels', also a helicopter and an Italian lightplane.

Classic No. 22: The Consolidated-Vultee *Liberator* (1939) — *Twin Wasp* (4)

'No Fame I slight, nor for her favours call,
She comes unlooked, if she comes at all.'
— Alexander Pope, 1688-1744

To judge by literature, films and TV, it was the Boeing B-17 *Flying Fortress* that was the bomber of fame of World War Two, whilst the B-24 *Liberator* was but a poor second, if remembered at all by the general public. While I have no wish to disparage the *Fortress* which deservedly came first, and played a vital role at great cost, it must be noted that the total numbers built were 12,731 compared to the *Liberator*'s 18,118 — the largest production total of any US aircraft in World War Two. It was also faster, had a longer range and carried twice the war load. A good analogy may be that of the *Spitfire* which is popularly the fighter of the Battle of Britain, but there were twice the number of *Hurricanes* at that time, whose guns shot down three times the number of enemy aircraft. Again, this is not a disparagement of the *Spitfire* in any way, and in due course they were to outnumber the *Hurricanes*. (22,890 to 14,527).

The *Liberator*'s great success was in part due to the Davis wing, the patent licence of which was held by Consolidated-Vultee. This allowed higher lift at lower angles of attack and so with the reduced drag gave longer range. In its maritime role (at reduced weight) it had a range of 2290 nm, and it was this particular asset which enabled Coastal Command of the RAF to close the critical 'Atlantic Gap' being dominated by the German U-boats. Whilst not making a claim for all the success in the long battle, the long-range, load capacity and the homing torpedo contributed to significant German losses. In the first half of 1942, there were twenty-eight which then dramatically rose to eighty-one in the second half.

A total of 2,000 *Liberator*s went to the RAF, the first batches being transferred from French orders at the fall of France in 1940. At the other end of the world there was the staggering number of 6,000 in the Pacific area at the end of the war. The first venture in Europe was in 1943 in the company of *Fortresses* in raids on U-boat pens in Wilhelmshaven and Bremen, but there were many spectaculars: the Romanian oilfields, Italy, Germany, the Pacific, Atlantic and the Indian Ocean with both the American and British Air Forces, all of which called for speed, load and range. Its roles were obviously many, but as military support there was cargo, personnel and fuel (a load of 2,900 US gallons) to deliver. They were part of the Atlantic Ferry Service, and four were 'loaned' to BOAC. Presumably they could not be spared, for they were called to the colours (RAF) in 1942.

A Very Important Plane for Very Important People, Sir Winston Churchill had his own much travelled 'Commando' and another VIP was Madame Chiang-Kai-Shek of China, whose aircraft later made its way back to the US. A US Navy version had an (enlarged) single fin and rudder instead of the standard two, and so had to have a difference name (the *Privateer*).

Nicknames of the *Liberator* were many, and apart from the RAF 'Electronic Salmon Can', it was also known as 'Lady Be Good', 'Lady Corinne', 'Blue Streak' and certainly many others forgotten or not recorded.

The last was built in 1945, so it was in production for the (European) war years, and only a few aircraft can make that claim. It is appropriate to note that a rebuilt *Liberator* in 1992 made a visit to Britain. The RAF must have fond memories, for two *Nimrod*s accompanied 'Diamond Lill' across the water from Iceland to be met with a flight of *Tornados* over England. Whilst remembering the 'Memphis Belle', forget not 'Diamond Lill'.

B-24 Liberator

Classic No. 23: The North American *Mustang* (1940) — Rolls-Royce *Merlin*

'Mustang': 'a breed of horse which developed naturally in North America, descended from the Spanish horses introduced by the Conquistadors. They gradually moved north from South America.'

Many aircraft and engines, mostly French in World War One and American in World War Two, have served with distinction in the British Forces: many, indeed, in larger numbers than some British names in this chapter. The three chosen as 'classics' so far as the UK is concerned (and in the author's arbitrary opinion) are the French Monosoupape engine without which the UK and France could hardly have started to fight back in World War One, and North American *Mustang* without which the Allies could hardly have finished World War Two (somewhat of an exaggeration, but it would have certainly taken longer and at greater cost) — and the *Liberator*.

The *Mustang* was built to a British specification and for a 'European' fighter that the US were not then in a position to provide. This was in 1940. North American undertook to build the requirement in 120 days, and in spite of the care needed with the laminar flow wing, this was achieved in 117 days! A US stipulation was that two, with the original name of *Apache*, were to be given free of charge to the US Army Air Corps. After Pearl Harbor, some of the British order were requisitioned with US insignia painted over the RAF camouflage; pleased with their new fighter, 310 in 1942 were the first of many US orders. The final overall total, US and UK, was 15,586. Australia also built 266, and imported eighty-five.

The *Mustang* reached the RAF in 1941, but whilst it had an adequate performance at low level with the Allison engine and was thus used for low-level strikes, a high-level requirement was also sought. This was achieved with the Rolls-Royce *Merlin*, and an outstanding fighter made its debut. US Packard *Merlins* were also built in quantity — another great US contribution.

When compared with contemporary Allied fighters, the *Mustang* had the advantage of good performance with long range, using drop tanks. All, of course, had their own specific roles, but the *Mustang* was supreme as the long-range single-seat fighter. Capable of over 1,500 miles, it could make it to Berlin and back. At one period when the Luftwaffe was bombing the UK and providing fighter cover, *Mustangs* followed the fighters and bombers back, even beyond Berlin, and contributed to the German loss of over 1,000 aircraft in four months.

The 8th Army Air Force and the RAF bombers were given great protection by their respective *Mustang* escort squadrons. The nickname of 'Flying Undertaker' is apt: it attended many enemy funerals, but Allied bomber losses were also heavy. Without escorting *Mustangs* and, later, *Spitfires* their losses would have been greater and a German victory more likely. Other nicknames included 'Stang' and 'Spam Can'. Twin *Mustangs* were also used, as in Korea, and were known as 'Betty Jo'.

Extensively used in northern Europe (General Eisenhower, Supreme Allied Commander, flew in a two-seat *Mustang* over the Normandy invasion beaches) and with the Desert Air Force in the invasion of Italy, they wreaked havoc on the enemy and with comparatively few losses. With its high speed, it was also capable of catching the V-1 or 'Doodlebug', and 10,000 of these were launched against England. A *Mustang* was the first Allied fighter to meet the advancing Russians.

Extensively used in the Pacific, they were typically, in 1945, escorting US bombers over Japan and Tokyo — a repeat of their European success story — and were the first US fighters (including Twin *Mustangs*) to the Korean war. Here they were giving the MiG jet fighters a hard time, and with several victories (250 'Twins' were built). As a measure of its value to the UK, it was to serve with twenty-seven RAF Squadrons.

Mustangs were in US service until 1951, and later with the Reserve and National Guard Squadrons; fitted with a Rolls-Royce *Griffon*, one gained the world piston-engine speed record in 1978 at 499 mph. The airframe still had the capacity to take a Rolls-Royce turbo-prop engine, the *Dart*, and also the Lycoming TP 1. It then became the *Enforcer*. This was later made by the Piper Corporation, but as the *Cavalier*.

The name was too good to be left alone. A French post-World War Two name for a *Mustang* replica was *Gnatsum*, or 'Mustang' reversed; and a US aerobatic replica of 1948 was the Bushby *Mustang*, followed in 1976 with kits for a *Mustang* and a 'midget' *Mustang*.

Several *Mustangs* are still to be found in the US, some as high-speed racers.

The Rolls-Royce connection was invaluable: *Merlin*, *Griffon* and *Dart*, and another reason for inclusion in the 'Classics'. As a long-range escort fighter, the *Mustang* was the best of World War Two. It was beautiful to fly, deadly to its enemies and the only US-made fighter specified by the RAF.

North American Mustang (RAF Museum, Hendon)

Hawker Typhoon

Classic No. 24: The Hawker *Typhoon* (1940) — Napier *Sabre*

'Typhoon' is defined as a small but intense tropical cyclone of the western Pacific and China Seas, and known in China as 'Dafun', a great wind. In Greek mythology there was a monster named Typhon, son of Typhoeus who was Father of the Winds. Typhon was a 100-headed monster.

The *Typhoon* was nicknamed 'Tiffy' and was later 'Tiffy of 2nd TAF', for which the explanation will follow. With bombs it was the 'Bombphoon' and with rockets the 'Rockphoon'. Its first flight was in 1940 with the new Sabre 24-cylinder 'H' engine with sleeve valves, which was to have many teething troubles, amongst others, in the early days. However, with the need for concentrated manufacture on the *Hurricane*, production ceased after the fall of France, not to recommence until 1941.

Apart from engine problems, in part caused by the then standard of constant speed units, the *Typhoon* was one of the first to encounter compressibility or 'shock wave' affects at high speed and altitude. This was partly due to the thick wing, a lesson learned with the *Tempest* of the same basic design but with a thin wing. All in all it was not a promising interceptor fighter at height or at high speed, and production was almost stopped. One test pilot said that 'as an aeroplane it was the most bloody ever'! However, just as the ugly duckling became a beautiful swan so the *Typhoon* soon found its form and its fame in the 2nd Tactical Air Force as a ground attack fighter. It revelled and excelled in this role and with four cannon and eight rockets was reputed to have the firepower of a Royal Navy cruiser. It had excellent low-level perform-

ance, great strength and obviously was a good weight-lifter as witness the previous paragraph. In fact, it was devastating, as noted by the Panzer Divisions, for the armour-piercing rockets would penetrate any armour then known.

In 1943 *Typhoon*s attached the Wehrmacht Army HQ at Doordrecht in Holland, with over fifty fatalities among the staff officers in the building. It was also this aircraft, that on a strafing mission wounded Field-Marshal Rommel in his staff car. Train engines supplied many of the *Typhoon*'s victims, with the holding up or denial of supplies and reinforcements to the front lines, and it was one of the contributory causes for the defeat and retreat of the German armies in France, Belgium and Holland.

It was the first fighter with a 2000 hp engine to go into RAF service, and in its trial days as an interceptor fighter achieved a speed of almost 400 mph at altitude. Such speed was not needed nor could it be achieved at low level, but it had enough for the purpose and could sweep in on an unsuspecting target. No.609 squadron destroyed one hundred locomotives in a few months for the loss of only two aircraft; in addition, between 1941 and 1943, *Typhoon*s shot down sixty enemy aircraft.

Few aircraft, either civilian or military, can have had such an inauspicious beginning, but by the great efforts of designers, manufacturers and test pilots, improved to help win a mighty war. The grand total built was 3,317 and 'Tiffie' was flown by thirty RAF Squadrons. One *Typhoon* survives at the RAF Museum. In an earlier age there had been the Beardmore *Typhoon* engine, and there was also the German *Taifun*.

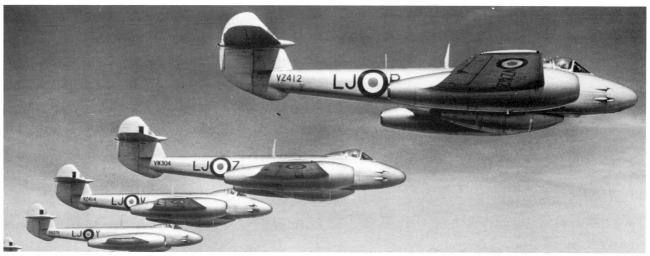

Gloster Meteor

Classic No. 25: The Gloster *Meteor* (1943) — *Derwent* (2)

'Here — here's his place
Where METEORs shoot, clouds form,
LIGHTNINGs are loosened,
STARs come and go.
— Robert Browning

'Meteor': 'the luminous tail or streak when a meteoroid, probably no bigger than a grain of sand, is made incandescent by friction with the Earth's atmosphere. Also known as the 'Shooting Star', the name of an early US jet fighter. It is estimated that 100 million meteors enter the Earth's atmosphere every day.'

If large enough to penetrate the Earth's atmosphere, then it is a meteorite, and so qualifies for the 1932, 1939 and 1949 RAF naming systems as being 'aggressive'. There were previous aeronautical *Meteor*s — the Halton Aero Club of 1929, Seagrave *Saro* of 1931 and the Beardmore engine.

Much effort went into finding a name, and early suggestions were: *Tempest, Thunderbolt, Cyclone, Avenger, Skyrocket, Dauntless, Vortex* and *Tyrant*. From all these was chosen *Rampage*, but that was shortlived and they went back to *Thunderbolt*. But no, there was now the US P-47 of that name, so it was back to the original list, and in 1942 it was called *Meteor*.

Nicknames of 'Meat Box', 'Meat Hook' and 'The Reaper' suggest some lethality, but what of the 'Whittle Daunt Potato Lifter'? Whittle developed the first British jet engine, and Daunt was the pilot who flew the prototype in 1943. The agricultural allusion is obscure.

When the first Air Ministry order was placed in 1941 it was for the 'Gloster Whittle aeroplane', which at least paid tribute to that great pioneer, noting the RAF ruling that names of officers should never be used; but Air Ministry were no doubt referring to the engine. The first engines were made by Rover and then taken over by Rolls-Royce. *Welland* was the first of the Rolls-Royce river names, but later aircraft were fitted with the DH *Goblin*.

1944 saw the first deliveries to an RAF Squadron, and made their first kills with the V-1 'Doodlebugs'. Early in 1945, two squadrons with *Meteor*s were stationed at Nijmegen in Holland but saw no action, for by now there was nothing to combat. After World War Two it was the RAF's standard fighter, and was a great success in Korea against the Russian MiGs, but more at low rather than high level.

It was the RAF's first jet fighter, the first to be in action, and the world's first turbo-prop powered by a propeller-turbine engine, the *Trent* (thus the *Trent Meteor*). The Fleet Air Arm was also interested, and touch-and-go trials took place on an RN carrier, where it showed good decklanding ability. However, there was to be no 'Sea' *Meteor*, and the FAA Squadrons were land-based.

In 1945 two *Meteor*s were delivered to the reformed RAF high speed flight. One, named *Britannia*, set a world speed record of 606 mph, soon raised to 616 mph. The *Meteor* was to serve in thirty-two RAF Squadrons in many marks and various guises. One was as a two-seat trainer, first produced in civil guise, to then become the *Meteor Trainer*, also used by the FAA and many overseas countries. Officially, this was the *Meteor* T. Export sales totalled 1,183. The *Meteor* also proved the concept of the Martin-Baker ejection seat. This was in 1947, first with a dummy and then for real. The first 'ejectee' was indeed a brave man, and the lives of many pilots have been saved from many types of aircraft. Another of its uses was for experiments with a prone pilot, which required a lengthened nose, and so there was the Prone Pilot *Meteor*. A long-nose version was also used operationally with the need to carry more radar.

In 1955 there appeared the 'Pilotless' experiment, successful and very valuable for later civil and military developments. This then led to the target drone, of which there were 200, and some went to Australia to the Woomera Weapons Research Establishment. One would expect a pithy Australian nickname, but there seems to have been no more than U Mk 15 and 16, the 'U' standing for 'un-manned'. As was inevitable, there were target tugs, usually the first sign that the halcyon days are over.

An aside on naming is that No. 500 (County of Kent) Squadron, was the only *Meteor* Squadron to have individual names such as *Canterbury* and *Rochester*. Another *Meteor*, but as long ago as 1930, was a specially designed aeroplane by Blackburn, and built to the order of Sir Henry Seagrave, a breaker of world sea and land speed records; a good omen for the air.

From 1942 to 1955, a grand total of 3,530 was built, plus 330 in Holland, of which thirty assemblies went to Belgium. In many respects the *Meteor* went a long way at high speeds for its time, and achieved many 'firsts'.

Classic No. 26: The Hawker *Hunter* (1951) — Rolls-Royce *Avon* (2)

The Hawker P 1067 first flew in 1951, and an Air Ministry memo of February 1952 reads: 'F3/48 Hunter' is most appropriate, and we recommend that it be adopted.' As usual, much effort had gone into the name, and it was chosen from a shortlist comprising *Harrier*, *Hustler* and *Hunter*. *Hunter* was Hawker's wish, but the Secretary of State was rather keen on *Falcon*. The *Harrier* suggestion would have formed an ornithological pair with the Supermarine *Swift*.

'Hunter' is a word with a wide scope of meaning. Nimrod, an Assyrian King, was the mighty hunter of the Bible. It is also appropriate as *Nimrod* was a Hawker fighter of 1931 used in the Fleet Air Arm. The name is again that of the militarised DH *Comet*.

This most elegant and successful of fighters replaced the *Meteor* and entered RAF service in 1954. About 1,000 were built, and they served in some thirty-eight RAF Squadrons, as well as being exported all over the world. Production ended in 1960, but probably a unique happening in aviation military history is that the *Hunter* is still eagerly sought by many air forces, and an old aeroplane capable of refurbishment commands a ready market — a great tribute to what was 'Hawker' and to Sir Sidney Camm and his team.

It was, and is, used as a fighter, ground attack, tactical reconnaissance and as a trainer. Whilst all was well on the night, the 'rehearsals' were subject to many problems, including the fitting of the *Avon* engines, and a new phenomenon of engine 'flameout' whilst the Aden cannons were fired. This was an aerodynamic problem of some complexity, but the solution by Rolls-Royce was very simple — when the firing button was pushed, it also cut out the fuel supply for that period.

The popularity of the *Hunter* was also shared by the general public, it being a great favourite at the bi-annual Farnborough shows. Squadron Leader Neville Duke breaking the sound barrier over the main runway literally shook those who were there. These stunts are no longer permitted and the present Farnborough Shows seem almost tame affairs. It was certainly fast in its day, being the first RAF aircraft to exceed Mach 1 (about 750 mph at sea level and faster with increased altitude) and exceeded 1.03. To put this capability in to practical terms, the *Hunter* in 1952 made London to Brussels in just twenty-five minutes.

Its public popularity was also established by the Black Arrows RAF Aerobatic which was the forerunner of the Red Arrows. The *Hunter* was a line fighter, but the RAF then decided that the aerobatic team would be equipped by trainers, such as the present *Hawk*.

Another small but significant tribute must be paid to the *Hunter* and that was its use in ETPS, the Empire Test Pilots School, where it was used for inverted spinning. This is an unpleasant manoeuvre for the pilot, but a great tribute to the stamina of the aeroplane: one recalls a *Hunter* doing something like twenty-three spins at a Farnborough Show.

Hunters saw action with the RAF in the Aden Protectorate (as was) and in Kuwait, and the last left the RAF in 1976. Without access to the records of many air forces, the number of *Hunters* still flying is unknown. An Israeli Industries 'drone' or 'UAV' (Unmanned Air Vehicle) named the *Hunter* is due to go into US Army service in 1994. The FAA still flies them from Yeovilton but with civilian pilots under contract and on specific MoD projects.

For such a well-known and respected aircraft, it is strange that there were not more nicknames. The only one known is 'Meathook' the 'meat' presumably being any enemy who came into the sights of those four Aden cannon.

Of all these thirty classic aircraft, the *Hunter* holds the remnant record with 130 (2,000 plus were built).

Hawker Hunter

Avro Vulcan

Classic No. 27: The Avro *Vulcan* (1952) — Bristol *Olympus* (4)

'Vulcan': in Roman mythology was the god of fire. He was also the god of furnaces and metal-forming and is associated with the forge; he was married to Venus, the goddess of love.

The first of the three 'V' bombers (there was also the Short *Sperrin* which did not go into production) was the Vickers *Valiant*, with the obvious alliteration. The second was to be the Handley Page, for which the short list of names was *Victor*, *Vulcan*, *Vanquisher* and *Vehement* — none of them suggested by the manufacturers. The decision to have a 'V' name was taken after the *Valiant* had been named. When it came to the turn of the Avro 698 (built to specification B35/46), the list of names was lengthy and had been prepared before the 'V' decision: *Artemis*, *Arqus*, *Arcturus*, *Aries*, *Arthur*, *Agravaine*, *Apollyon*, *Alcock*, *Acendant*, *Adamant*, *Attila*, and the non-alliterative *Sidney*, *Raleigh*, *Drake*, *Grenville*, *Ottawa* and *Bowland*.

Avro were keen on *Ottawa*, but in October 1952 the Air Council decreed that the *Vulcan* it would be. During its deliberations, a memo was considered from an Air-Marshal who listed some alternatives:

(1) Bomber airfields, such as Marham, Waddington, Hemswell, Coningsby and Binbrook.
(2) Famous officers in the RAF e.g. Trenchard.
(3) Follow the tone set by the *Valiant*, and choose from *Vulan*, *Vanquisher* and *Vehement*.

All this was getting a little complicated but the allocated names were Vickers *Valiant*, Handley Page *Victor* and Avro *Vulcan*.

First flown in 1952, the *Vulcan* was the first in the world to enter service as a delta wing heavy bomber. There had been a pre-war Northrop 'Flying Wing' but this was not a delta, and also a civil Vickers *Vulcan* airliner of 1922. Designed to have a very long range at high altitude, and to carry ten tons of bombs, it was powered by the mighty Bristol *Olympus* engines. Mount Olympus in *Greece* (being the home of the gods, *Vulcan* must be thought to have felt at home). The acquaintance was further renewed with a later *Olympus* tested in the *Vulcan* for the civil Concorde. Avro had another direct connection with its own product as the *Vulcan* carried the Avro 'Blue Steel' cruise missile.

Vulcan saw active service in the Falklands war, destroying Argentinian aircraft on the ground. The start of the flight was from the Ascension Islands, and the two *Vulcans* were refuelled in the air for the long flight across the south Atlantic.

Stationed in the UK, it was standard procedure for four *Vulcans* to be at immediate readiness, and to be airborne in two minutes from the start of the engines. On one occasion, seven were airborne in the same two minutes! In the days of the now passed Cold War when preparation and the utmost vigilance was the order of the day, this almost immediate readiness did not pass unnoticed. *Vulcans* served in ten RAF Squadrons, and were withdrawn in 1984.

It is gratifying, if a surprise, to report that fifteen are recorded as being in the UK. The last flying *Vulcan* was grounded in 1993, but is preserved for taxying only.

Classic No. 28: The English Electric *Lightning* (1958) — Rolls-Royce *Avon* (2)

Meteorologically speaking, lightning is an atmospheric discharge of many millions of volts, heating the surrounding air to more than 16,000°C (28,800°F) — three times hotter than the surface of the sun. The explosive expansion of the heated air causes a shock wave and thus the noise of thunder. 'Forked' lightning is the incandescent path of the electrical discharge seeking the easiest path to earth, and thus striking some terrestrial object, all of which, albeit indirectly and to a lesser degree, justifies the name of a very lethal fighter. In mythology, lightning was one of the attributes of the god Zeus and the later Roman Jupiter, who held a bolt of lightning and from whence the word 'thunderbolt'; thrown once, it was a warning, twice the final warning, and thrice a fiery retribution, which supposedly kept the Greeks and Romans in good order.

The US *Lightning* was widely used in World War Two, but the UK production order was cancelled after evaluation. The two-seater version was known as 'Chain Lightning'. The *Thunderbolt*, however, was a US fighter of some renown in the RAF.

The prototype P1A first flew in 1954, and the production PIB in 1957, originally the *Sapphire* and later with *Avon* engines. The P1A posed particular design problems, one being the 60° sweep-back of the wings, and to investigate this the Short SB5 was designed and built. Only small changes were required to PIA and, the design figures were fully vindicated. Some of these calculation equations were processed by an early computer at the National Physics Laboratory, possibly the first serious computer application of this kind, noting that the *Lightning* was designed for a top speed above Mach 2. Not only was that achieved but Mach 1 could be reached without engine 'reheat' — the pumping of fuel directly into the jet efflux. Another 'first' associated with *Lighting* was the use of a ground simulator.

The chosen name was announced at the 1958 SBAC show at Farnborough, and as usual had been the subject of intense nomenclatural activity. English Electric themselves suggested *Flash, Defender, Rapier, Scimitar, Scorpion, Harrier, Arrow, Eagle, Challenger, Astra* and *Lightning*. *Flight* magazine, back in 1954, had suggestions for the P1A: *Arrow, Assegai, Fiend, Wraith, Terror, Excalibur, Champion, Strongbow, Crossbow, Virago, Warrior* and *Paladin*, and within the Air Ministry there were many other suggestions. The Air Council finally decided on *Lightning* in October 1956, but that the name should not be published until 1957, following on the ruling that the name was not to be used until full production of the aircraft had been authorised.

Pilots loved the *Lightning*, but for the mechanics it was something of a nightmare with two mighty *Olympus* engines, one above the other, and with a very tight fit for the many bits and pieces that make up a modern jet fighter. Fuel was thus limited, considering the thirst of the two engines, and so range was an ever constant consideration. Nevertheless, those based at Leuchars in Scotland never failed to intercept the Soviet long-range bombers on their frequent patrols of the North Sea and the Iceland/Shetlands gap.

The *Lightning* went into RAF Squadron service in 1960, served with ten squadrons, and was retired in 1988. 388 were built, including those sold to Saudi Arabia and Kuwait; from those, twenty-five are known to be in the UK.

No doubt with all this in mind, the English poet Shelley (1792-1822) wrote:

'Sublime on the towers
Of my skiey bowers
Lightning my pilot sits
In a cavern under
Is fitted the Thunder. . .'

English Electric Lighting

Classic No. 29: The Hawker *Harrier* (1966) — Bristol *Pegasus*

This bird of prey is of the 'Circus' family of narrow-winged hawks, and 'Circus Pygargus' will be readily recognised as the Montague Harrier, some other species being Common, Ringtail, and Marsh. It is also a dog of prey, the harrier being a small breed of hounds originally used to hunt hares. In human terms it is a long-distance runner; all good attributes, and the hovering *Harrier* is especially apt as a name. Hawkers had previously used the name for the 1927 torpedo bomber with the Bristol *Jupiter* engine; so Bristol again powers a *Harrier*, and *Pegasus* is also apt as being the Greek mythological winged horse who carried the thunderbolts of Zeus, whose Roman counterpart was Jupiter!

The *Harrier* was originally the *Kestrel*. Now whilst a bird of prey is an obvious name for an RAF fighter, this had not been the case until the advent of these two names, for in 1918 it was ruled that Rolls-Royce engines would be allocated the birds of prey, this only ceasing with the advent of the jet engine, when Rolls-Royce turned to river names. Prior to 1918 they had produced the *Falcon* and *Eagle*, which set the precedent. There have been two exceptions, and both from Hawker — the *Harrier* already noted and the *Osprey* — and this was 'allowed' as both were sea rather than land aircraft, and the Osprey is a sea and river bird.

The story begins in the 1950s when a Frenchman, Michael Wibault, designed a VTOL (vertical take-off and landing) combat aircraft. Others followed, but practical success was made possible with the Bristol BE35 with four rotatable nozzles, which became the *Pegasus* which first ran in 1959.

The P1127, to become *Kestrel* before *Harrier*, was Sir Sydney Camm's last fighter, designed in close collaboration with Sir Stanley Hooker who moved from Rolls-Royce to Bristol, and later back to Rolls-Royce when it took over Bristol-Siddeley engines. The P 1127 first flew in 1964 as the *Kestrel;* service with the RAF began in 1965, with evaluation by NATO Air Force pilots. Thus in 1966, six surviving *Kestrels* were shipped to the USA for trials, and in 1969 the US Marines were authorised to buy 'AV-82's. Spain became interested, but because of its dispute over Gibraltar ordered their aircraft from the USA. Then came the *Sea Harrier*, first flown from HMS *Hermes* in 1978, payload being most usefully increased by the 'ski jump' running take-off. The effectiveness of this and of the aircraft was proven by its splendid record in the Falklands conflict, not least in its capability to take on the latest supersonic French fighters of the Argentinian Air Force. In 2,300 sorties the *Harrier* shot down twenty-four enemy aircraft, and sank three ships.

It also serves in the Indian Navy, and that same HMS *Hermes* is now the *Viraat*. The USA through McDonald-Douglas, planned and carried through some radical changes which doubled the payload/range performance, and in 1981 Britain and the UK signed a joint manufacturing agreement.

The *Harrier* plays an essential role in the RAF/NATO defence system in Germany (West, as was), and no air show would succeed without such a 'star'.

Of all the aircraft with which the late Sir Thomas Sopwith was concerned, from pre-World War One as Sopwith through the Hawker days, the *Harrier* was his favourite.

A US/Spanish/Italian *Harrier* (if not eventually known by that name) is in hand with Italy as the next possible operator. Japan could become another, so whatever the name the *Harrier* will be seen in many air forces for many years to come.

Apart from being an exceptional aircraft, it is the only one of two of the thirty classics of this book to be still in RAF service.

Hawker Harrier

Classic No. 30: The Panavia *Tornado* (1979) — Turbo Union RB-199

Meteorologically speaking, tornadoes are the most violent and destructive disturbances in the atmosphere, but are quite small by atmospheric standards and only affect limited areas. It is seen as a writhing column of cloud apparently suspended from a thick black cloud and reaching down to earth, rotating at high speed with local pressure falling to about half normal. At sea it is known as a 'water spout'. Wind speed in the core can reach up to 300 knots.

The 'Flying Flicknife', a military masterpiece, found sudden and surely lasting fame in the Gulf War where it so adequately carried out its varied tasks — the crews became heroes overnight. In terms of role precedence, *Tornado* was an imaginative but to some a foolhardy concept, and if not foolhardy then many thought it a very risky undertaking. Its original concept and definition was MRCA — a multi-role combat aircraft — which ran counter to the general military thinking of specialised function: fighters were fighters and bombers were bombers, and seldom had the dual role been a success. Now MRCA was to be general and yet highly specialised, a contradiction in terms.

It was proposed as a 'Wild Weasel' to replace no less than the *Phantom*, *Vulcan*, *Jaguar*, *Buccaneer* and *Canberra*, and that surely was a nonsense for a start, but MRCA, later *Tornado*, confounded the cynics who predicted that an aircraft designed to fulfil all roles would be master of none. To the contrary, it became the undisputed leader among low-level, all-weather interdictors and strike aircraft, hitting pinpoint targets with unerring precision.

The next improbability was that it was not only to be multi-role, but multi-national in manufacture and multi-air force in operation, thus the Panavia Consortium (the wings were built in Italy, centre fuselage in Germany, and the rear and front fuselage in Britain). The three manufacturers were Avitalia, MBB (Messerschmitt Bulkow Blohm) and British Aerospace. The air forces were British, Italian and German, and sales have also been made to Saudi Arabia and Kuwait.

The 'swing-wing' concept had been proposed in 1945 by Barnes-Wallis of Vickers, (two models were named 'Swallow' and 'Wild Goose') but the first to fly was the US F-111 which, being a prototype of this new concept, had many teething troubles. It was a competitor to the *Tornado* and a cause of some anxiety to Panavia, already burdened with the doubts and improbabilities expressed by others. Its first flight was in 1974, and TTTE (Tornado Tri-National Training Establishment) fully evaluated the aircraft, and trained the early crews. A nice touch was a combined 'roundel' of the three air force insignia. In inter-USAF/RAF bombing competitions, the *Tornado* established some superiority over the F-111, both in accuracy and in general performance, but the US Under-Secretary of Defense declared: 'I just don't think it's a good plane. The *Tornado* is the nearest goddamned thing for unsurvivability that there is!'

The advantage of the *Tornado* is in part explained by the 'swinging' underwing weapon pylons which always face into the airflow irrespective of the angle of the wings. Standard armament is one 27mm Mauser cannon, four Skyflash and four Sidewinder missiles, but a variety of combinations of weapons and sensor pods can be carried, all of which were put to very good service in the Gulf war. The wing angle is fully forwarded for slow flight and fully back for fast flight, with intermediate settings as required. Maximum speed at low level is translated from Mach 1.2 at sea level as approximately 900 mph, and Mach 2.2 at optimum high level as 1,650 mph. Low-level flying is at 200 feet, riding the ground contours with forward-looking onboard radar and thus flying under enemy radar.

Such performance requires very sophisticated avionics, and with the other avionic capabilities, including 'fly-by-wire', it is perhaps not surprising that each *Tornado* costs about £18m — which in terms of achievement in war could be cheap at the price. Ground performance is equally impressive — airborne in about 1 km, and stopping with engine reverse in 365 metres, which is about 1200 ft. The variable geometry wing makes for a comfortable crew ride, whether at top speed at low or high level. It is not a 'dog fighter' in the conventional sense, but has a weapons platform which, with long-range radar identification, can shoot down an enemy aircraft up to thirty miles away. At low level with cluster bombs to break up enemy runways, this was an essential first step early air superiority.

The name itself is common in English, Italian and German. Previous *Tornados* were the North American (1947), Beardmore (1929), Hawker (1939) and an Italian/Brazilian jet fighter of 1990 known as the 'Pocket Tornado'.

Panavia Tornado

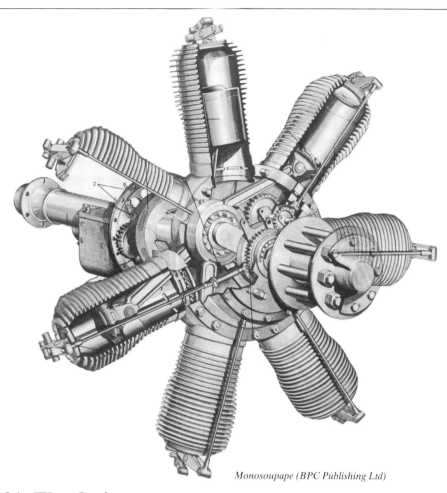

Monosoupape (BPC Publishing Ltd)

Classic No. 31: The *Gnôme Monosoupape* (1912)

As with all piston engines, the cooling is achieved either with water or with air. The water-cooled engine is reasonable for slow running, but tends to be heavy, complex, and vulnerable to bullets — and thus it was about 1907. The air-cooled engine had a metallurgical problem as a speed of about 80 mph was inadequate for the higher power engines then being made. Instead, then, of a fixed or 'radial' air-cooled engine, why not a 'rotary' or turning engine with the crankshaft fixed and the engine rotating? The cylinders could then be cooled by both the forward speed of the aircraft and the rotary motion of the engine which would also act as its own flywheel. These were the thoughts of the French Sequin brothers. They helped win World War One.

The advantages were comparative simplicity and a good power:weight ratio, but a singular disadvantage was the gyroscopic effect of the rotating mass of the engine. As noted in the *Camel* classic, right rudder was needed for a left turn, and with hands off the control column the aircraft would tend to do a loop; but once mastered and in the hands of a good pilot, the gyroscopic effect could be put to good effect.

The earlier *Gnômes* had stemmed from designs as far back as 1892, but a recurring problem had been the two rocker/rod valve systems for inlet and outlet ports. The Monosoupape, or 'single valve', had the conventional outlet valve, but the inlet was now a hold drilled in each cylinder, being covered and uncovered by the travel of the piston — a kind of half two stroke. It was immediately recognised as an advance on previous *Gnôme* models, and the first to buy one was Paulhan; it was flown in a Voisin. A nine-cylinder,

100 hp Monosoupape was fitted in the 1914 Sopwith *Tabloid* Schneider Trophy racer at Monte Carlo; not only did the *Tabloid* win outright, but Howard Pixton did two extra laps at full power, averaging 92 mph which was a record for seaplanes.

Another of those times was Henri Farman (actually an Englishman) who was so impressed with the new engine that he bought and installed one whilst part way through a Rheims meeting. With the Monosoupape, he went on to win the Grand Prix de Distance as well at the Grand Prix de Passages!

The engine as described appeared in 1912, and whilst close tolerance engineering was essential, the power:weight ratio and the comparative mechanical simplicity were bonus points. Whilst previous *Gnômes* had a conventional throttle arrangement, the Monosoupape had a mixture or 'fuel' adjustment lever, and there was only one engine speed — flat out — which was controlled by a 'blip' ignition switch on the control column, cutting out the firing and so power sequence on a cylinder or cylinders. Lubrication was by castor oil, some of it being exhausted as unburned, and which was reputed to have a very beneficial effect on pilots' digestive systems. To many RFC and RNAS pilots the smell of castor oil was inseparable from flying.

There was a shortage of Monosoupapes for the Avro 504 and *Tabloid*s. The firm of Peter Hooker Ltd, engineers, was taken over and reorganised for production beginning with one per week and quickly rising to ten per week! There were, of course, other *Gnôme* models used during World War One, but some fifteen Monosoupape types are recorded between 1913 and 1926, and the standard RAF trainer, the Avro 504 K, lasted until 1935.

Classic No. 32: The de Havilland *Gipsy* (1927)

Sir Geoffrey de Havilland was a keen lepidopterist, a student of moths and butterflies, and one aircraft to become famous was the Moth. For this particular engine he was anxious to have the name *Gipsy* (there being a *Gipsy Moth*) so that the ensemble of engine and DH 60 would be known as *Gipsy Moth*. With the Gipsy there were various developments with different affixed names, the total so far as this book is concerned being fifty-six. Drawings have appeared showing a human 'gipsy' but this is not correct, even if the engine in its various forms was widely travelled.

Halford, a very gifted engineer, first produced the *Gipsy '4'* by taking one cylinder bank of a World War One Renault V8, and making a new crankcase. By 1946 this simple beginning had been developed into a 145 hp *Gipsy Major*. The first production engine appeared in 1928, and in that year the pilot Hubert Broad stayed aloft with this engine for twenty-four hours, covering 1,440 miles. He recalled that he became so bored that he read a complete novel. The 'clean sheet of paper' recorded its first line in 1927, so the change from a V8 to a straight '4' was only a matter of one year. One of its early mounts was the DH 71, the first and monoplane racer *Tiger Moth*. The engine was specially tuned to reach 135 hp.

In 1929 a *Gipsy* was chosen at random from stock, sealed, and run continuously for 600 hours, no mean test for an engine of any sort or power. It was then stripped down to its component parts, examined and fitted with replacement parts; these cost the company £7, eleven shillings and sixpence . . .

In 1932 the '4' had been stretched to '6' and the *Gipsy Six*

powered the DH *Comet* which in its class won the Mac Robertson race from the UK to Australia. Then followed the *Gipsy Minor* of 75 hp and the *Gipsy Queen* of 90 hp, respectively in 1937 and 1938. Also in 1938 the *Gipsy King* appeared as a V12 inverted engine.

'Inversion' was already established practice, for the original *Gipsy* had been an upright engine, that is with the crankshaft and the direct drive propeller at the bottom, and was so installed in the *Moth*. This put the propeller tips somewhat close to the ground, the problem being neatly solved in the *Gipsy III* by turning it upside down. No longer having a 'wet' oil sump, the oil was circulated from outside the engine and cooled in a 'hump' on the fuselage just behind the engine. It was this configuration that powered the second, and well-known RAF *Tiger Moth* in which the majority of RAF pilots in World War Two learned to fly.

In all forms, 27,654 *Gipsies* were delivered and the index ranges from 1932 to 1946 so far as the book is concerned as 'first flights' The DH *Gipsy* series was extensive, comprising: *Gipsy, Gipsy Minor, Gipsy Major, Gipsy Six, Gipsy Queen* and *Gipsy King*. There was also a *Water Gipsy* (shades of A.P. Herbert), but this was an outboard motor and thus named was used in various forms other than those on water, including motorcycles.

Ralph Hodgson (1871-1962) wrote:

> 'Time, you old Gipsy Man,
> Will you not stay,
> Put up your Caravan,
> Just for one Day?'

No, for the *Gipsy* is still travelling round the world, and there must be many thousands of this remarkable engine still powering a variety of aircraft.

THE GYPSY SERIES II AERO-MOTOR

Classic No. 33: The Bristol *Jupiter* (1919)

In the 1918 RAF system(s) of nomenclature there were reservations for engine names; Bristol, Wolseley, Rolls-Royce and Armstrong-Siddeley being so honoured. Bristol were allocated starts and planets (later constellations), but as will be seen, 'Bristol' had earlier meant Brasil-Straker and Cosmos Engineering. Perhaps it was the 'Cosmos' that started it all? The planets and constellations (illustrations in Chapter 21) are mostly named after Greek and Roman gods and goddesses. With the exception of the *Cherub* engine, all Bristol engines were mythologically named, and the Rolls-Royce *Pegasus* (the second) was of 'Bristol' origin.

Jupiter — alias the Greek Zeus — was the Roman father of heaven, 'Diovis Pater', Rome's special patron and protector, and as the god of justice and virtue was also guardian of the law. Astronomically speaking, Jupiter is the fifth plant from the sun, and the most massive in the solar system, having a mass 318 times that of the Earth.

Roy Fedden (later Sir Roy) was originally connected with Brasil-Straker, manufacturers of high-class cars, and he himself was a racing driver of some renown. The firm moved from London to Fishponds, Bristol, and being an engineering company was offered production orders for Rolls-Royce engines, with the legal proviso that they did not engage in the design of liquid-cooled engines, which prompted Fedden, an entrepreneurial engineer, to look to the design of air-cooled engines. Thus was designed the *Mercury*, *Jupiter*, *Lucifer*, and *Hercules* engines, only the latter remaining as a drawing-board engine. Cosmos as a group went into liquidation, and the Fishponds factory was without money or orders. Efforts by Fedden to sell to other companies such as Vickers were not successful, but the Ministry was very interested in the *Jupiter* and prevailed upon the Bristol Aeroplane Company, who then took over Cosmos as the Aero Engine division.

It first ran in 1918, and developed 475 hp at 662 lb, setting a world record for a completely equipped engine at about 1.4hp/lb. Rolls-Royce did offer Fedden a job, which he did not accept as Rolls had been somewhat disparaging about his engine. But Rolls later apologised: 'I am delighted that you have proved me wrong.'

Jupiter had many new features including four valves per cylinder and, at a potential 500 hp, it offered more than any present or near future specification requirement. Fedden had promised his board a potential 500 hp, 650 lb and at a cost of not more than £200,000; by September 1921 only £3,000 of the budget was left, and the board were ready to abandon the project, but then *Jupiter* passed the 100-hour type test, the first engine to do so, at a nominal 385 hp and tested to a maximum of 400 hp. *Jupiter*'s flight trials were first in the Bristol *Badger*, and it was also used in the Sopwith *Schneider* for the 1919 Schneider Trophy Race. The race was abandoned, but this was the fastest entry.

Fedden was insistent upon constant testing and retesting and the trying out of new ideas but only in the most stringent conditions, in keeping with the old saying of 'shipshape and Bristol fashion'. Thus *Jupiter* was continually being improved, and in 1923 the Ministry placed an order for eighty-one engines and the future was assured. A licence was granted to Gnôme et Rhône, and many *Jupiters* were to be built on the continent. At the time of the 1929 Paris Aero show, there was a 'scandale *Jupiter*' when it was realised that almost eighty per cent of military aircraft were *Jupiter*-powered!

In 1926 Imperial Airways had ordered the *Jupiter* for the DH66 *Hercules* followed by the later HP 42 — *Heracles*, *Hengist*, *Horsa* etc. It was by now an almost standard engine in many countries, and for the next decade was probably the most important aero engine in the world. The list of aircraft powered by this engine is long and varied, but a brief statistic notes that in the decade from 1923 there were twenty-seven foreign licences and over 7,100 engines built powering 262 different types of aircraft. Forty-eight are listed in this book's index. It was even used by the Russians in World War Two as the *Mirs*, the equivalent for *Jupiter*. The only rival to Bristol's *Jupiter* was the Armstrong-Siddeley *Jaguar*, but the *Jupiter* won the final round of the contest in 1924 by powering an aircraft to more than 30,000 feet; by then Fedden was focusing his attention on the sleeve-valved engine, and his famous *Hercules* will be found in this Chapter.

In 1919, Brigadier-General J.G. Weir, Technical Controller, Ministry of Munitions, wrote to Fedden: '. . . you should press on in all haste to perfect the *Jupiter* which I feel sure has a considerable future in front of it . . .' The deal with Bristol was worth £15,000, and in later years it was the financial mainstay of the company. It is surprising that there has not been a second *Jupiter*, but it was developed into the *Mercury*. The *Jupiter* powered forty-nine RAF and FAA aircraft types.

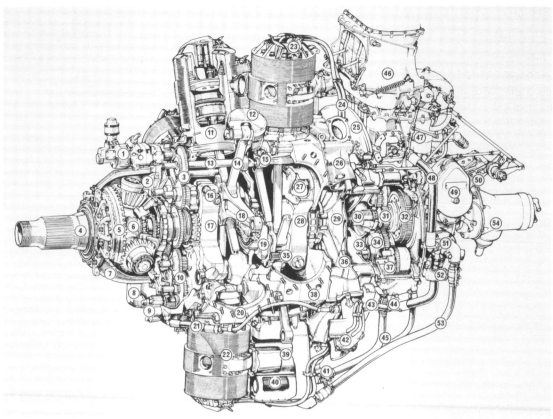

Bristol Hercules

Classic No. 34: The Bristol *Hercules* (1935)

The Roman version of Heracles, Hercules was a widely venerated and popular god. He was famous for his mythical exploits, starting when he strangled two serpents in his cradle, and his prodigious strength was to be put further to the test in his manhood. To atone for the murder of his wife and children, the Delphic oracle sent him to Eurystheus, King of Argos, who set Hercules the 'Twelve Labours', all supposedly impossible but which he accomplished to create a legend known to this day. When he came to die, on a funeral pyre of his own making, he was carried off to Mount Olympus, home of the gods. This was on a cloud sent by Zeus (the Greek Jupiter) who was his father, and there Hercules received the gift of immortality. Herculaneum, named after him, was an ancient town on the slopes of Mount Vesuvius. The town was totally destroyed by the volcanic eruption of AD 79, and remained undiscovered until 1709. The astronomical Hercules is a constellation in the northern hemisphere near Lyra and the Corona Borealis.

Hercules was the drawing-board name of an engine designed by Brasil Straker, later Cosmos, and then the Aero Engine Division of the Bristol Aeroplane Company (see *Jupiter* in this chapter). The 'second' *Hercules*, of 1935, was the development of previous sleeve-valve engines. If the Rolls-Royce *Merlin* was the racehorse of World War Two, then *Hercules* was the workhorse, but even that compliment would be unfair, for the engine also powered the 1944 Hawker *Fury* which was no laggard when it came to a turn of speed.

The engine was developed over many marks (series) and in eight years showed a power increase of thirty per cent at a weight expense of ten per cent. By the end of the war power had been boosted to 1800 hp, and post-war this was sent up to 2020 hp. The engineering of a two-row radial, sleeve-valve engine was a remarkable accomplishment by Sir Roy Fedden and his team, and his drive and engineering skills have already been noted in the *Jupiter* classic. It is interesting to note that when the Ministry of Munitions tried to interest engine manufacturers in a supercharged engine, the only response was from Cosmos, soon to become 'Bristol'.

Of the Bristol sleeve-valve engines, *Hercules* was the most successful and led to the larger and more powerful *Centaurus*, there having been, of course, the earlier and smaller *Taurus*. Although there were sleeve-valve engines other than Bristol's, it was only at Filton that a truly successful engineering technique was developed for the manufacture of sleeve-valve engines, and there was no American equivalent.

The best-known applications of *Hercules* were in the *Stirling*, *Wellington*, and *Beaufighter*, a long gap since work began on the sleeve valve in 1926. Over 100,000 Bristol engines were produced during World War Two, and of these 57,400 were *Hercules*. The *Centaurus* total was 2,500 but production continued after the war, the engine reaching a power of 2375 hp!

Hercules continued in service in the RAF until the 1960s, and is still the powerplant of several veteran aircraft in the UK and the USA.

Hercules has been a well-used name: DH 67 of 1929, German Ju 352 of 1943, Howard Hughes flying boat of 1947 known as the 'Spruce Goose', and the 1954 Lockheed military transport.

Classic No. 35: The Rolls-Royce *Merlin* (1933)

Before 1918 Rolls-Royce had produced three aero engines — namely the *Eagle*, *Hawk* and *Falcon* . . . and that these came to be named after Birds of Prey was due to the R-R *ALPINE EAGLE* car of 1911. This created a precedent, so that when the RAF was formed in 1918 the main engine companies were allotted their own naming systems within the overall system as 'exceptions'. The birds of prey names lasted with Rolls-Royce until the advent of the jet engine, when it changed to rivers.

To many, even to RAF pilots during and after World War Two, Merlin was thought to be the wizard of Arthurian legend, in spite of the previous names that had gone before. In fact it is Britain's smallest bird of prey, being little larger than a thrush, and flies fast and low to catch its prey: *'being of rapid flight and great courage, possesses all the attributes and character of the falcon. Bold as well as powerful is this little bird in proportion to its size, and so tenacious is it of its prey, that it is very difficult to make it quit anything that is has taken'* Yarrell's *British Birds*, 1856). The aeronautical association is not unique, for Miles Aircraft had a series of birds of prey names, including *Merlin* in 1935.

In 1932 Rolls-Royce decided that future fighters would require more powerful engines; the *Kestrel* was becoming outmoded, and the *Buzzard* was too heavy and large — something larger than the *Kestrel* and about 750 hp was required. Rolls-Royce then embarked on a private venture, the PV 12, the Air Ministry advising that there were no funds available, and two engines were built at company risk. This was justified as Hawker was designing the *Hurricane* and Supermarine was embarking on the *Spitfire* line. Government support was later forthcoming and the PV 12 then became the *Merlin*. By 1934 it was developing 790 hp at 16,250 feet. Later in that year, with a new cylinder head, power rose to 950 hp at 11,000 feet. Flight testing was in a *Hart*, and cooling was changed to glycol. The first production engine, issued to *Hurricane* and *Spitfire* Squadrons, reached 1030 hp at 12,250 feet, now with a two-speed supercharger and glycol/water

cooling. The extra power had also been achieved with 100-octane fuel, used with the 'R' engine employed to gain the outright win of the Schneider Trophy in the Supermarine 6B. Engine, fuel and airframe all played a part in the development to Merlin and *Spitfire*. The fuel contribution was largely the work of Air Commodore 'Rod' Banks, and the supercharger improvements that of Doctor Stanley Hooker, later to be chief engineer of Rolls-Royce.

The part that the *Merlin* played in the Battle of Britain was vital, for however brilliant the aircraft or however brave and skilful the pilots, without the *Merlin* there would have been no victory. The name has also been used for eight Royal Navy ships.

Another fighter aircraft with which the *Merlin* is closely associated is the American (British designed) P-51 or *Mustang*. With a US Allison engine, the top speed was 350 mph; with a Merlin there was a dramatic rise to 430 mph, and the fighter went on to become one of the celebrated aircraft — still flying in civil form in the United States. L.J.R. Selricht (*The Power to Fly*, 1971) said that 'The Rolls-Royce *Merlin* was simply an astonishing engine. There have undoubtedly been aero engines that were better designed, and some that were better made, but beyond a shadow of doubt there has never been another engine more thoroughly, continuously, aggressively successful and amazingly developed than the *Merlin*.'

From the 1030 hp of 1939, power rose to 1175 hp, and towards the end of the war the engine was giving a dependable 1660. Some models went to 1750 hp, and there was even a 2000 hp model. The RAF and FAA flew *Merlins* in twenty-nine different aircraft. It might be noted that *Merlin* was the name of a 1933 civil glider, and that it was previously known as the *Kestrel*. A more modern *Merlin* is the US Swearinger Transport of 1962, and the new European Helicopter Industries helicopter *Merlin*. It was also a tank engine but then known as the *Meteor*.

55,235 were built in the USA by Packard and Ford, and the total USA and UK production was a staggering figure of about 160,000!

RR Merlin (Rolls-Royce PLC)

Classic No. 36: The Rolls-Royce *Avon* (1946)

Avon is the Celtic word for a river which explains the duplication of the name, there being twelve River Avons in the UK together with a Loch Avon and an Avon Water. To complete the picture, there is also a River Avon in Australia and one in the USA. The English county of Avon is of recent times, being taken from what was the city and county of Bristol and parts of Somerset and Gloucestershire. It is probable that Rolls-Royce had the Upper Avon in mind, this rising near Naseby in Northamptonshire and flowing ninety-six miles through Stratford-on-Avon to the River Severn at Tewkesbury. The Lower Avon rises near Tetbury in Gloucestershire and flows some seventy-five miles through Bath and Bristol to the Severn estuary at Avonmouth. As Rolls-Royce took over the Bristol engine factory at Filton, this would have been a later justification for the name. Rolls-Royce chose the 'river' series to suggest 'flow', even if this was gaseous in the event rather than hydrous, and supposedly rivers are more axial than centrifugal?

The *Avon* started life as the AJ 65 (axial jet), indicating that the forward, compressor element of the engine was axial (in line) rather than centrifugal, the CR type pioneered by Whittle. The prototype was tested in 1946, but with disappointing results. It refused to accelerate, and broke its first-stage compressor blades; but these were the early days of jet propulsion, with many problems to overcome. Blade design was very critical, and at the after-end the power turbine had to contend with a flame temperature of about 1830°C.

Lord Hives, of Rolls-Rolls, hoped that the *Avon* would be the *Merlin* of the jet age, but early evidence of this was then hard to see. On a matter of statistics, the *Avons* built by Rolls-Royce (and there were others) numbered 10,433, whilst the *Merlin* total was about 160,000 — all of which is really incomparable, the jet achieving many times the power of the piston engine, and the *Avon* itself had a larger increase of power over time compared with the *Merlin*.

From a poor start, many developments led to the first production engines being delivered in 1950, now known as the RA3. A proposed successor to the *Avon* was to be named *Thames*, and it is perhaps surprising that of the many Rolls-Royce rivers this first of English rivers had not been used. As the Ministries resided in London, perhaps Derby thought the better of it.

By 1952 the *Avon* was a competitive engine, with much redesigning, including compressor aerodynamics. One unexpected problem was with the *Hunter*, the *Avon* engine stalling when the guns were fired! The unexpected solution was the firing button simultaneously reducing the fuel pressure to the burners. By 1953 the *Avon* was a power in the land, and powered the *Hunter* which broke the world speed record in that year with 727.6 mph, followed by the *Swift* (also with an *Avon*) which recorded 737.7 mph. Only three years later, the Fairey *Delta* 2, with an *Avon*, raised this to 1,132 mph — half as fast again.

The engine was planned for the *Canberra*, but from 1950 was used by several RAF combat aircraft. Apart from the *Hunter*, *Swift* and *Canberra*, it was the powerplant of the *Vulcan*, *Valiant*, *Sea Vixen*, *Lightning* and some *Sabres*. In the civil field, the *Avon* powered the *Comet* and the French *Caravelle*, and the original test flights were in the *Lancastrian* with the jet thundering away alongside three bemused *Merlins*, which perhaps was an indirect tribute to Lord Hives.

If three world speed records were not enough, *Avon* lays claim to the first Polar Intercontinental Jet Flight in a *Canberra*, and also the first non-stop Atlantic flight by a jet. At the time of writing (1993) the *Avon* is forty-seven-years-old, one indication of its merits, but it must now be considered a very different engine from its beginnings in 1946. It still powers the *Hunter* and *Canberra*, and the *Lansen* and *Draken* of the Royal Swedish Air Force, the *Avons* built under licence by Swedish Flugmotor. A turbofan development of the *Avon* was the *Conway*, powering the Handley Page *Victor* which was so successfully deployed as a 'tanker' in the 1990/91 Gulf war. Quite a lively lineage from such as inauspicious start.

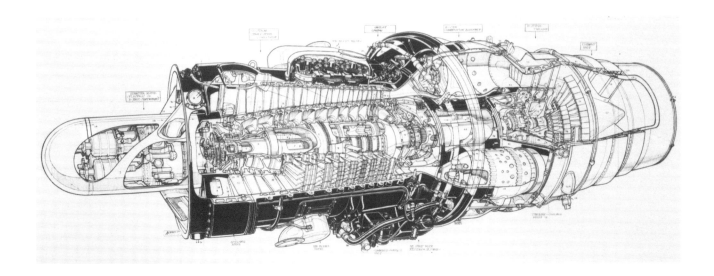

CHAPTER 7 — TOTAL INDEX (1878–1994)

The column title of 'System' refers to the Royal Aircraft Factory 1911 system, Royal Air Force systems of 1918 (3), 1921, 1927, 1932, 1939, or 'maker'. Where 'xxx' is shown, this indicates that although with a military connotation, the aircraft name did not conform to the current RAF naming system. As a quick reference, and to save going back to Chapter 4 and its various parts, the above are reproduced as a 'header' to the Total Index. The 1949 system is not reproduced, being the same as the 1939, but with two small changes: the 'Empire' is now the 'British Commonwealth' and helicopters as 'trees'.

1911 — with later amendments

SE Santos Experimental, after Santos Dumont, the originator of the 'Canard' or tail-first type of aeroplane. The SE1 was the only one of this category, the subsequent designs being the single-seat tractor scout formula. For this reason the designation was subsequently modified to 'Scout Experimental'.

FE Farman Experimental, of pusher biplane formula.

RE Reconnaissance Experimental of two-seat tractor biplane formula.

TE Tatin Experimental monoplane formula with pusher propeller behind tail. (This was never actually used and later came to mean 'Two-seater experimental e.g. TE1 of 1916)

BS Blériot Scout — a combination of the Blériot and Santos formulae in single-seat scout form. (BS1 — designed and flown by Geoffrey de Havilland. After a crash, was rebuilt to become the SE2)

H was a prefix for all sea-aeroplanes, denoting Hydro, as HRE2

Other designations were *CR — coastal experimental* — and *AE — armoured experimental*.

1918(1)						
			TDI 506 14 February 1918			
			MACHINES OPERATING BY LAND			
	FIGHTER		BOMBER			
Military Duty	Spec.A.1.A.,A.1.C.,A.2.A., A.2.D.,A.4.A.		Spec.A.2.B.,A.3.B.		Heavy Armoured Machines.	
Class Word	Zoological, Vegetable, and Mineral (Terrestrial)		Geographical (Inland)		Proper Names (Male)	
	Size of Machine	Sub-class word	Size of Machine	Sub-class word	Size of Machine	Sub-class word
	Single-seater...	ZOOLOGICAL Inspects, birds and reptiles.	Single-seater... Two-seater...	Italian towns Gt. Britain towns	Under 2 tons...	Mythological Greek
	Two-seater...	Mammals BOTANICAL	Three-seater... Crew exceeding 3;	French towns.	2 to 5 tons... 5 to 10 tons...	Mythological Roman. Mythological Eastern & Egyptian
	Three-seater... Four-seater... Five-seater...	Flowers Shrubs Trees	Wt, under 5 tons...	Towns in Colonies and Dependencies	10 to 20 tons...	Mythological Northern Europe Europe
	Over 5 seats...	MINERAL Metals & Rocks	5 to 10 tons... 10 to 15 tons...	Towns in Asia Towns in Africa		
			MACHINES OPERATING BY SEA			
Military Duty Class Word	FIGHTER Spec. N.1.A.,N.1.B.,N.2.A ZOOLOGICAL (Marine)		BOMBER Spec. N.2.B GEOGRAPHICAL (Seaboard)		PATROL & ANTI-SUBMARINE Spec. N.3.A.,N.3.B PROPER NAMES	
	Size of Machine. Single-seater... Two-seater... Three-seater...	Sub-class word. River Fish Saltwater Fish Shell Fish	As for land machines, but coastal towns in place of inland.		As for land machines, but females.	

TDI506A 13 March 1918	APPENDIX A(a) NOMENCLATURE OF EXPERIMENTAL DESIGNS SINGLE-ENGINED MACHINES	1918(2)

| TYPE OF DESIGN | CLASS OF NAME | SUB-DIVISION | |
		AIRCRAFT FOR USE ON LAND OR FROM SHIPS' DECKS	SEAPLANES & FLYING BOATS
1. Single Seater	Zoological	Insects, reptiles & land birds.	—
2. More than one seat	Zoological	Mammals	Waterfowl & Fishes

MULTI-ENGINED MACHINES								
TYPE OF DESIGN	GROSS WEIGHT LADEN		TWIN ENGINES		THREE ENGINES		FOUR ENGINES	
	Over Tons	Up to Tons	Class	Sub-Division	Class	Sub-Division	Class	Sub-Division
4. Machines for use on land or from Ships' decks	—	5	Geographical Inland Towns.	France.	Male Historical or Mythological Proper Names connected with:	France.	Geographical Names other than towns, rivers, lakes & islands, eg. countries, mountains, tribes, etc.	France.
5. Do.	5	10		Europe (Except France)		Europe (Except France)		Europe (Except France)
6. Do.	10	20		Gt. Britain.		Gt. Britain.		Gt. Britain.
7. Do.	20	—		—		Asia or Africa.		Asia or Africa.
Seaplanes & flying boats	Type as above.		As above, but Seaboard Towns.		As above, but Female Proper Names.		As above, but Rivers, Lakes or Islands.	

1918(3)	TABLE B CLASS OF NICKNAME TO DENOTE TYPE OF DESIGN	July 1918

Type of Design		Class of Name	Aircraft for use on land or from ships' decks	Seaplanes
AIRCRAFT WITH ONE ENGINE ONLY				
1. Single-seater		Zoological	Reptiles (except snakes)	—
			Land birds (except birds of prey)	—
2. More than one seat		Zoological	Mammals (except felidae)	Waterfowl Fishes
AIRCRAFT WITH MORE THAN ONE ENGINE				
Gross weight, laden over lbs. up to lbs.				
3.	— 11,000	Geographical	Inland towns in England or Wales.	Seaboard towns in England. or Wales.
4.	11,000 20,000	Geographical	Inland towns in Scotland or Ireland.	Seaboard towns in Scotland or Ireland.
AIRCRAFT WITH MORE THAN ONE ENGINE				
Gross weight, laden over lbs. up to lbs.				
5.	20,000 45,000	Proper names	Male historical or mythological proper names (excluding names of stars and planets)	Female historical or mythological proper names (excluding names of stars and planets)
6.	45,000 —	Attributes	Terminating in 'ous', 'ant' or 'ent'.	Terminating in 'ic', 'al' or 'er'.

NOTE: The names excluded from the above are reserved for denoting engine designs

Rolls-Royce	— Birds of Prey
Napier	— Arms & Weapons
Armstrong-Siddeley	— Felidae (Cats)
Wolseley	— Snakes
Bristol	— Stars & Planets

	1921 CLASS OF NICKNAME		
TYPE	**LAND AEROPLANE**	**SEA AEROPLANE**	**AMPHIBIAN**
Single-Seat	Land-birds (except of prey)	Shell Fish	Reptiles (except snakes)
Multi-seat (up to 6,000lb)	Mammals (except Felidae)	Fresh and Salt water fish	Water fowl (deleted about 1925)
6,000 — 12,000lb	Inland towns in the British Isles	Seaboard towns in the British Isles.	Islands in the British Isles
12,000 — 20,000lb	Inland towns in the British Empire	Seaboard towns in the British Empire	Islands in the British Empire
20,000 — 40,000lb	Male mythological names.	Female mythological names	Ancient geographical names
40,000lb and over	Attributes ending in 'ous', 'ant' and 'ent'	Attributes ending in 'al', 'es' and 'ic'	Attributes with other endings.
Civil Aircraft	Historical names (other than those of people)	Names of famous historical persons	Astronomical names

	1932	
Class	**Category of nomenclature**	
1. Fighters	General words indicating speed, activity or aggressiveness.	
2. Bombers:		
(a) Day	Animals (except felidae).	
(b) Army co-operation	Classical names.	
(c) Night	Inland towns of the British Empire or towns associated with the RAF.	
(d) General purpose	British historical names.	
(e) Transport	General towns and seaports of the British Empire.	
3. Flying Boats	Coastal towns and seaports of the British Empire.	
4. Fleet Air Arm:		
(a) Fighters	Mythological names.	
(b) Fighter Reconnaissance	Names of sea birds.	
(c) Torpedo Bombers	Names of oceans, seas and estuaries.	
(d) Spotter Reconnaissance	Names of marine animals.	
5. Training	Words indicating tuition, and places of education.	

An addendum to this concerned engines:

Rolls-Royce	Land-birds of prey	e.g. Kestrel, Buzzard
Armstrong-Siddeley	Felidae (Cats)	e.g. Jaguar, Panther
Bristol	Planets & Constellations	e.g. Jupiter, Pegasus
Napier	Arms & Weapons	e.g. Rapier

	1927 NOMENCLATURE		
No.	**AIRCRAFT TYPES**	**CLASS LETTER**	**SYSTEM**
1.	Fighters — Land	F	(a) all names to commence with appropriate 'class' letter.
2.	Fighters — Fleet	N	
3.	Bombers Single-engined	P	
4.	Bombers Multiple	B	
5.	Bombers Torpedo	M	(b) the names of 2, 5 & 12 to have maritime significance
6.	Army Co-operation	A	
7.	Spotter & Reconnaissance (FAA)	S	
8.	Coastal Reconnaissance	R	(c) the names of remainder to have non-maritime significance.
9.	Troop Carriers	C	
10.	Training Aircraft	T	
11.	General Purpose Aircraft	G	
12.	Fighter Reconnaissance	O	(d) names already in use not to be used.

	1939	
Fighters	General words indicating speed, activity or aggressiveness.	
Bombers	Place-names — an inland town of the British Empire or associated with British history.	
Army Co-operation	Classical words.	
General Purpose Torpedo	British historical names (including general reconnaissance land planes).	
Transport	Counties or district of the British Empire.	
Flying Boats	Coastal towns and seaports of the British Empire.	
Trainers and Target Tugs	Words indicating tuition and places of education (but not Air Force training Establishments).	
Gliders	Historic military leaders.	
Naval Aircraft	As proposed by the Admiralty.	

'In the case of American aircraft allotted to Britain, and Canadian aircraft built for MAP, fullest consideration will be given to the wishes of the relevant authorities should they press for the adoption of names not within these categories. Endeavours should be made, however, to follow as closely as possible the basic rules, but names with an American or Canadian flavour will be very appropriate. For instance, American-built transports should not necessarily be named after a county or district of the British Empire, but would preferably be named after a district or State of the United States of America.

Maker	Name	Year	Type	Nickname	System	Classification	Service	Engine	Type	Notes
F B A	A & B	1914	Flying Boat	FLYING BANANA	Maker	Miscellaneous	RNAS	MONOSOUPAPE	PR1	Small French trainer craft. F B A = Franco British Aviation. Nickname from the yellow varnished hull. 115 built for the RNAS.
Saunders-Roe	A 10	1929	Fighter	MULTI GUN	Maker	Miscellaneous	(RAF)	Rolls-Royce	PL1	A portent of things to be . . . and 4 guns was an important innovation. The eng was later named the KESTREL. Long trials but no production order.
Saunders-Roe	A 14	1929	Flying Boat	METAL HULL	Maker	Miscellaneous	(RAF)	LION	PL2	Wooden hulls were disallowed, which led, in part, to the demise of the VALKYRIE. A14 was a metal equivalent with Supermarine SOUTHAMPTON wings. Some hull problems, but led to the CUTTY SARK, CLOUD, WINDHOVER & LONDON.
Saunders-Roe	A 33	1938	Flying Boat	MONOSPAR	Maker	Miscellaneous	(RAF)	PERSEUS	PR4	MONOSPAR, an org wing design by General A/c Ltd. Large cantilever wing with 4 engs, and mounted clear of the hull to minimise drag. Wing failed on take off, and an RAF contract for 11 cancelled.
Saunders-Roe	A 37	1939	Flying Boat	SHRIMP	Maker	Miscellaneous	(RAF)	NIAGARA	PR4	Edible crustacian. Scale experiment for the SHETLAND as a SUNDERLAND replacement. Test trials until 1949. Said to be "virtually viceless". One only. Engs almost to exact scale of proposed HERCULES.
Gloster	ACE	1948	Fighter	GORMLESS FLYING SHELL	1939	Allegorical	(RAF)	DERWENT	JT2	ACE was an unofficial name for an experimental Fighter project to Spen. F 4/48, and which was to become the JAVELIN. The name ACE was also used for the Gloster E1/44.
Grob	ACRO (TWIN)	1979	Glider	VIKING	Maker	Miscellaneous	(RAF)			Prefix – topmost, extreme etc; such as ACROBAT. From Greek "akro". German manufacture. The II version named VIKING by the RAF.
Blackburn	AD SCOUT	1915	Fighter	SPARROW	Maker	Miscellaneous	(RNAS)	MONOSOUPAPE	PR1	Designed by the Air Dept. Admiralty, this was designed for the Davis 2 pdr gun – which was never fired! Ungainly with a high fuselage fixed to the top wing, it was overweight and difficult to fly. 4 built and scrapped. Dev into TRIPLANE.
Wolesey	ADDER	1915	Engine		Maker	Reptile	RAF		PL	Family of various venomous snakes, including the VIPER.
Armstrong Siddeley	ADDER	1948	Engine		Maker	Reptile	(RAF)		JT	Dev from the MAMBA.
Bentley	ADMIRALTY ROTARY (AR)	1915	Engine		R N	Miscellaneous	RFC		PR	Later BR = BENTLEY ROTARY. Designed by W R Bentley for the Admiralty and produced by several Companies.
Rolls-Royce	ADOUR	1966	Engine		Maker	Geography-Water	RAF		JT	Rivers – ADOUR in France and ADUR in England. Engine under licence from Turbomeca/France.
Beardmore	ADRIATIC	1916	Bomber		Maker	Geography-Water	(RFC)	ADRIATIC	PL2	A/c and eng with the same name, or Type WB 1 with a B H P eng.
BHP Galloway	ADRIATIC	1917	Engine		Maker	Geography-Water	RNAS		PL	Northern arm of the Mediterranean between Italy and the Balkan Peninsula. B H P = Beardmore-Halford-Pullinger.
Royal Aircraft Factory	AERIAL TARGET	1917	Drone		x x x	Miscellaneous	(RFC)	GNAT	PR1	Named to camouflage its true intention being a small pilotless a/c v Zeppelins or as a flying bomb. 6 built but the first 2 crashed. 1 rebuilt but never flew? Broken up in 1934!
Miles	AEROVAN	1945	Experimental	VAN MINI-FREIGHTER.	Maker	Miscellaneous	(RAF)	CIRRUS MAJOR	PL2	One ton aerial truck. Some civil success. Air Ministry "disapproved" of design in wartime, which led to lost sales in the peace. 50 built and used by 9 countries. A 4-eng development was the prototype MERCHANTMAN.
Austin	AFB. 1	1917	Fighter	BALL	x x x	People	(RFC)	HISPANO-SUIZA	PL1	Suggested by Capt. Albert Ball VC, who was killed before aircraft completed. 2 built. Name intended as AUSTIN-Ball but finally BALL? AFB is not A F Ball but Austin Fighter BIPLANE.
Auster	AIGLET	1951	Trainer		Maker	Miscellaneous	RAF	GIPSY MAJOR	PL1	Aiglet/Aglet=decoration. French military=Aiguillette.
Cierva	AIR HORSE	1948	Helicopter		Maker	Miscellaneous	(RAF)	MERLIN	PL1	Not Pegasus! 3 Rotors. 2 ton load, possibly the world's largest helicopter at the time but unsuccesful. 1st prototype crashed and 2nd never flew. The project was inherited from G & J Weir & Co.
Bell	AIRACOBRA	1938	Fighter		1939	Allegorical	RAF	ALLISON	PL1	USA. Sometime RAF CARIBOU. Half going to Russia. Unloved a/c. with the eng behind and a shaft to the propellor. First tricycle u/c to land on a British Carrier. Dev into the KINGCOBRA. Both = 8854 built.
Bell	AIRACOMET	1942	Fighter		Maker	Miscellaneous	(RAF)	GENERAL ELECTRIC	JT1	This was the USA's 1st jet eng a/c, the eng being a US version of the British Whittle type as used in the Gloster PIONEER. Britain's 1st jet. For secrecy, the AIRACOMET was given a removeable propellor!

Maker	Name	Nickname	Year	Type	System	Classification	Service	Engine	Type	Notes
Eng & Research Co(Erco)	AIRCOUPE		1937	Transport	Maker	Miscellaneous	(RAF)	CONTINENTAL	PL1	Org ERCOUPE (coupe, as car), then AIR COUPE built by Air Products. Civil "easy to fly" with only 2 controls, later 3. Later manf Alon/Mooney as MOONEY ALON. Popular US & UK. and many still exist.
Blackburn	AIREDALE	WOOF	1925	Recon	x x x	Geography-Land	(FAA)	JAGUAR	PR1	Yorkshire town but the name should have had maritime sinifigance. Intended replacement for BLACKBURN and BISON. First post WW I monoplane for the FAA but only 2 prototypes. (Also Beagle AIREDALE – dog! 1961)
Cessna	AIRMASTER		1938	Transport	Maker	Allegorical	RAF	CONTINENTAL	PL1	One of a long list of Cessna light a/c developments. 40 built, and one impressed into the RAF in 1941.
Armstrong Whitworth	AJAX		1925	Bomber	1921	Mythological	(RAF)	JAGUAR	PR1	Greek hero of the Trojan War. All but indentical to the ATLAS and different name presumably to distinguish operational role. 5 built.
Fairey	ALBACORE		1938	Torp. Bomber	x x x	Fish	FAA	TAURUS	PR1	Large marine fish-source of tinned Tuna. Name should have been ocean, sea or estuary. Successful a/c and one of the last combat Biplanes. 800 built. Malta, Matapan, Norway and the Tirpitz, Atlantic and Africa.
De Havilland	ALBATROSS	ALBAFOO	1937	Transport	Maker	Bird	RAF	GIPSY QUEEN	PL4	Ocean wanderer with the biggest wing span of any bird. Wooden structure and ancestor of the MOSQUITO. Org civil. beautiful design. 7 built and 2 impressed by RAF (Also Grumman 1947. Czech Aero 1986. Sardea eng)
Armstrong Whitworth	ALBERMARLE	DUMBO *	1940	Transport	1932	People	RAF	HERCULES	PR2	General Monk was First Duke 1660. A/c designed by Bristol and similar to BLENHEIM with Tricycle u/c. * said to fly like a young elephant. Designed as a Bomber but served as Trooper & Glider Tug. 602 built.
Alcock	ALCOCK SCOUT	SOPWITH MOUSE MOUSE	1917	Fighter	x x x	People	(RNAS)	MONOSOUPAPE	PR1	Part Sopwith TRIPANE and PUP. Desiged by Lt. of Alcock & Brown fame in the VIMY first flight of the Atlantic. Also known as Sopwith A1 SCOUT. One only and lost in a ground accident.
Avro	ALDERSHOT		1921	Bomber	1921	Geography-Land	RAF	CONDOR	PL1	Home of the British Army. The first RAF a/c to be named after a British town. 15 built, and served in only one Squadron. Phased out in 1926 with the new era of twin heavy bombers. 17 built. See ANDOVER.
Messerschmidt	ALDON		1934	Transport	RAF	Miscellaneous.	RAF	HIRTH	PL1	See Messerschmitt Me 108, TAIFUN. Why the RAF gave the name ALDON is not known, nor is its meaning. 3 impressed into the RAF in 1940.
Sud Aviation	ALOUETTE		1959	Helicopter	Maker	Bird	ARMY	ARTOUSTE	TP1	French – Skylark. Org civil. Served with 42 Countries, and also built under license by India, Romania and Switzerland. 1305 built of which 963 military.
Sunbeam	AMAZON		1916	Engine	Maker	People	RNAS		PL	S. American River. Powered HM Airship C. 14 (Coastal). 77 built.
Airco(de Havilland)	AMIENS	KITE HAWK	1918	Bomber	1918	Geography-Land	RFC	EAGLE	PL2	One of three a/c as a French Town, as BOURGES and VIMY. 266 built and one saw service in WW I – the day before the Armistice! Also used in anger in the Middle East and India. RAF service until 1923. Org DH 3.
Avro	ANDOVER (1st)		1923	Ambulance	1921	Geography-Land	RAF	CONDOR	PL1	Ambulances did not have a naming system so the "Bomber" classification had to suffice. Dev from the ALDERSHOT Bomber and 4 built, one civil taken over from Imperial Airways. Red Cross + RAF colours.
Avro	ANDOVER (2nd)		1960	Transport	1939	Geography-Land	RAF	DART	TP2	Town-Hampshire. Dev from civil 748, and the last Avro design before merging with Hawker-Siddeley Group. Also used by New Zealand. About 370 built, inc civil orders and some built in India. Now Br Aerospace.
Air Navigation & Eng Co	ANEC		1923	Transport	Maker	Miscellaneous	(RAF)	CHERUB	PR1	ANEC = Company name. Purchased for trials at Martlesham Heath. One of a series of small a/c.
Avro	ANSON	FAITHFUL ANNIE	1933	Rec+Trainer	1932	People	RAF/FAA	CHEETAH	PR2	See the CLASSICS – Chapter 6
Avro	ANTELOPE	BOUNDER	1928	Gen. Purpose	1921	Animal	RAF	KESTREL	PL1	1929 variant as HAWK. One only. Lost out to the HART but went for service trials and used by RAE to 1933. Experiments with variable pitch propellors.
Armstrong Whitworth	APE	MONKEY	1926	Experimental	1921	Animal	(RAF)	LYNX	PR1	Tall u/c for stall landings and a pivoted tailplane made for the infinetly adjustable a/c. 3 to RAE for various tests until 1929. Not very popular.
Armstrong Whitworth	APOLLO		1949	Transport	Maker	Mythological	(RAF)	MAMBA	TP4	Most Greek of Gods, of manly beauty. A/c org named ACHILLES, then AVON but Rolls-Royce objected and then APPOLO. 2 prototypes, 1 to RAE and 1 to Empire Test Pilot School. (Also US space craft, 1961)

Maker	Name	Year	Type	Nickname	System	Classification	Service	Engine	Type	Notes
Bristol	AQUILA	1934	Engine		1918	Astronomy	RAF		PR	Latin Eagle/Vulture, a Constellation in the N. Hemisphere.
Arado	Ar 232	2191	Transport	TAUSENDFUSSSLER	Maker	Miscellaneous	RAF	BRAMO	#P4	German=Millipede, from 10 loading wheels in bottom fuselage, raised & lowered by hydraulic u/c.22 built but few saw active service. Captured a/c put to good transport work by the RAF.
Arado	Ar 234	1943	Bomber	BLITZ	Maker	Meteorological	(RAF)	JUNKERS	JT2	German=Lightning. Captured in 1945 and evaluated at Farnborough. The Luftwaffe's 1st jet bomber, a very good a/c and an operational success but hampered by lack of fuel to the Squadrons. 214 built.
Hafner	AR III	1935	Autogyro	GYROPLANE	Maker	Miscellaneous	(RAF)	POBJOY	PR1	Raoul Hafner, an Austrian, was there involved in early autogyro experiments, later moving to England. This model went to Farnborough, and was scrapped during WW II. From this was dev Hafner's Bristol SYCAMORE.
Armstrong Whitworth	ARA	1918	Fighter		1918	Bird	(RAF)	DRAGONFLY	PR1	Family name of the Macaw Parrots. An excellent performance, in spite of the dreaded engine prototypes and then Armstrong-Whitworth closed down its aviation department.
Sunbeam	ARAB	1916	Engine		Maker	People	RFC/RNAS		PL	One of a series of Tribal names.
Armstrong Whitworth	ARGOSY	1959	Transport	WHISTLING WHEELBARROW	Maker	Miscellaneous	RAF	DART	TP4	Poetic – a ship or vessel. Second choice of name was COVENTRY. 56 for the RAF and as a BEA Freighter. Also used by Canada, Australia and New Zealand. Excellent service, with many humanitarian flights. 19 civil.
Fairchild	ARGUS	1932	Transport		Maker	Mythology	RAF	RANGER	PL1	Fabled person with 100 eyes. USA FORWARDER (one to the RAF) 1008 built and also used by Australia. USA and Canada. (Also Canadair ARGUS. Maritime Patrol of 1957)
Opel	ARGUS	1919	Engine		Maker	Miscellaneous	(RAF)		PL	See above. German eng purchased for trials.
Thorn	ARGUS	1979	Drone		Maker	Mythology	(ARMY)	WESLAKE	PL2	Giant with 100 eyes, guardian of Io and later slain by Hermes. Trials at RAE, Farnborough.
Armstrong Whitworth	ARIES	1918	Bomber		1927	Astronomy	(RAF)	JAGUAR	PR1	The RAM-Sign of the Zodiac. First Point of Aries=Celestial Prime Meridian. A variant to improve on ATLAS and AJAX but one only.
Armstrong Whitworth	ARMADILLO	1918	Fighter		1918	Animal	(RFC)	BENTLEY	PR1	Armoured burrowing animal and a very appropriate name for an armoured Fighter. A humped fairing over the engine cowling housed 2 Vickers guns but allowed little visibility when landing/taking off. 1 built.
Army Balloon Factory	ARMY AEROPLANE NO 1	1908	Experimental		x x x	Miscellaneous	(ARMY)	ANTOINETTE	PL1	Designed and tested by 'Colonel' Cody, presented to War Office. The first sustained aeroplane flight in England on 16 October, 1908. The establishment were not pleased, withdrawing support from Cody and Dunne.
Army Balloon Factory	ARMY AIRSHIP NO 1	1907	Airship	NULLI SECUNDUS*	Maker	Miscellaneous	ARMY	ANTOINETTE	PL1	* Racehorse owned by Edward VII. Rebuilt as ALPHA. Greek First. Also 2nd NULLI SECUNDUS. After various mishaps, she was found unmanageable and the project was dropped. SECOND TO NONE?
Blackburn	ARTOUSTE	1955	Engine		Maker	Miscellaneous	RAF		TP	French local name. Auxiliary power unit licensed by Turbomeca.
Gloster	AS 31	1929	Transport	SURVEY	Maker	Miscellaneous	(RAF)	JUPITER	PR2	To examine-eg:land survey. Org of D H design. but made by Gloster. The 1st was civil. and the 2nd for the RAF for radio experiments with the RAE until 1936. The civil version sold to S Africa. last seen in 1942!
Avro	ASHTON	1950	Test	ASHCAN	Maker	Geography-Land	(RAF)	NENE	JT4	Ashton-under-Lyne, Manchester. Eng Test. Developed from TUDOR 8. 6 built.
Blackburn	ASTAZOU	1958	Engine		Maker	Miscellaneous	RAF		TP	Peak in the Pyrenees Mountains. Later Rolls-Royce. Built under licence from Turbomeca. France.
Grob	ASTIR	1928	Glider		Maker	Miscellaneous	(AIR CADETS)			German make, but English name = to be awake. on the move, or was a German made up word? Also TWIN and SPEED ASTIR.
Army Balloon Factory	ASTRA TORRES	1912	Airship		Maker	People	RNAS	GREEN	PL	French. Louis TORRES. Spanish Explorer. 1606, named TORRES STRAITS. Officially, Naval Airship No 3. Also Nos 8, 10 & 16 (1912-1916).
Brush Electrical Eng	ASTRAL	1917	Bomber		Maker	Astronomy	(RNAS)	ANZANI	PL2	Latin 'astrum'=star. Pertaining to the stars, as the RAF motto 'Per Ardua ad Astra'. Henri Farman type.

Maker	Name	Year	Type	Nickname	System	Classification	Service	Engine	Type	Notes
Armstrong Whitworth	ATALANTA	1932	Transport		Maker	Mythology	RAF	DOUBLE MONGOOSE	PR4	Greek maiden who would marry any man who outran her. 5 a/c of Imperial Airways impressed into the Indian Air Force (RAF). 8 built.
Fairey	ATALANTA	1923	Flying Boat		Maker	Mythology	(RAF)	CONDOR	PL4	Greek huntress who challenged suitors to a foot race, won by Hipponeus. A/c a large boat, but only two built, the other named TITANIA. In their time they were the largest Flying Boats in the world with a wing span of 139 ft.
Avro	ATHENA	1948	Trainer		Maker	Mythology	(RAF)	MERLIN	PL1	Greek Godess of Wisdom. 22 Built. First flew with the MAMBA and DART (TPs) but thereafter with MERLINs.
Galloway	ATLANTIC	1918	Engine		Maker	Geography-Water	RAF		PL	Ocean between Europe/Africa and America. Pooled for mass production it was known as the Siddeley PACIFIC. (Also civil a/c – ATLANTIC, Sopwith and Boulton Paul, both 1918. (BP adaption of BOURGES)
Short	ATLANTIC	1919	Torp. Bomber		Maker	Geography-Water	FAA	EAGLE	PL1	Failed Transatlantic attempt. Dev of SHIRL. (Also French Breguet maritime ATLANTIC, 1961, US Wassmer 1973)
Armstrong Whitworth	ATLAS	1925	Army Co-op		1921	Mythological	RAF	JAGUAR	PR1	Supported the Heavens with his head and hands. Served with the RAF as Army Co-op and Trainer, the latter up to 1935 – but later in Canada and also used by China. 478 Built. Served in 6 RAF Squadrons. See AJAX.
Supermarine	ATTACKER	1946	Fighter Bomb		1932	Allegorical	FAA	NENE	JT1	See SEA ATTACKER
Hawker	AUDAX	1931	Army Co-op	ART WITH THE 'OOK	1927	Allegorical	RAF	KESTREL	PL1	Latin-audacious, bold, daring. South African AF version was HARTBEEST. Basically a HART, hence 'ART and the 'OOK was the message hook. Widely used. 750 built and later a Trainer Sold to 3 other countries. One Audax with 2 wing m/c guns was the HORRIBLE.
Taylorcraft/Auster	AUSTER	1938	Spotter	AUSTERITY (CIVIL)	Maker	Mythology	RAF/FAA/ARMY	GIPSY MAJOR	PL1	Latin – the South Wind. Org USA Taylorcraft, later Auster A/c Co. in the UK. Served in 19 RAF Sqdns and 1663 built. Essential work as artillery 'spotters' and light transport in WW II. Also civil.
Auster	AUTOCAR	1949	Transport		Maker	Miscellaneous	RAF	GIPSY MAJOR	PL1	Sent to Malaya for pest control. AUSTER variant.
Auster	AUTOCRAT	1945	Spotter		Maker	Allegorical	RAF	GIPSY MAJOR	PL1	Arrogant, domineering, ruler with absolute power, tyrant.
Avro	AUTOGIRO	1926	Autogiro	ROTA	Maker	Miscellaneous	RAF	GENET	PR1	Design of Juan de la Cierva. First built in Madrid and then by Avro. Also C30 of 1934 and C40 of 1938. C30s delivered to the RAF known as ROTAs. Both types used for radar calibration up to 1945.
Avro	AVA	1924	Torp Bomber		Maker	Miscellaneous	(RAF)	CONDOR	PL2	An enormous a/c for its time and 2 built. Name a mystery, but AVATAR= Hindoo for a diety in human form, an individual name for a 1936 Avro similar to the ANSON. AVATAR was soon changed to AVA! Again in 1924?
Avro	AVENGER	1926	Fighter		1921	Allegorical	(RAF)	LION	PL1	Contemporary and in competition with the GORCOCK and HORNBILL, none of the three received RAF orders. Also, with the VIVID, was offered to Rumania. The one prototype then to Air Service Training until 1931.
Grumman	AVENGER	1941	Torp Bomber	PREGNANT TURKEY (USA)	1939	Allegorical	FAA	CYCLONE	PR1	USA. 1943-44 Br name of TARPON, a game fish. AVENGER reintroduced 1944 Most potent Torp Bomber of WW II, and 9839 built. Won its spurs at the Battle of Midway in 1943, and many memorable actions with the FAA.
Avro	AVIAN	1927	Transport		Maker	Miscellaneous	(RAF)	GENET	PR1	Made up name. Orginally a light weight civil a/c. About 80 built, of which 10 impressed into the RAF as ground instruction machines. Also an experimental (RAF) autogiro.
Avro	AVOCET	1925	Fighter		1921	Bird	RAF/(FAA)	LYNX	PR1	Long legged shore bird with upturned beak, now rare in the UK. Trainer for Schneider Trophy and RAE experimental work. Designed as a "naval fighter". 2 built.
Rolls-Royce	AVON	1946	Engine		Maker	Geography-Water	RAF		JT	See the CLASSICS – Chapter 6
Armstrong Whitworth	AWANA	1923	Transport		1918	Geography-Land	(RAF)	LION	PL2	Town in New Zealand (or a place name on an old Oriental trade route?) A large troop-carrier with a wing span of 100 ft +. In competition with the Vickers VICTORIA, ruled to be the more robust. 2 built.

Maker	Name	Year	Type	Nickname	System	Classification	Service	Engine	Type	Notes
English Electric	AYR	1925	Flying Boat		1925	Geography-Land	(FAA)	LION	PL1	Scottish Port. Experimental a/c with the lower wing acting as floats. Not a success and the a/c never managed to be airborne. 2 prototypes but the second not completed.
Blackburn	B 48	1947	Fighter	FIRECREST*	Maker	Miscellaneous	(RAF)	CENTAURUS	PR1	Based on the FIREBRAND as a Torpedo Fighter with the intention to re-engine with a propellor turbine. 2 prototypes, 1 retained by Balckburn for research. * Company name which would have become official with a production order.
Sopwith	B1	1917	Bomber	BOMBER	Maker	Miscellaneous	(RAF)	Hispano-Suiza	PL1	Experimental Bomber. 2 built.
Br. Aerial Transport	BABOON	1918	Trainer	MONKEY	1918	Animal	(RAF)	WASP	PR1	FK24. Frits Koolhoven (Dutch) design 6 ordered, but only 1 built, later civil.
Samuel White	BABY	1916	Seaplane		Maker	Allegorical	RNAS	MONOSOUPAPE	PR1	Also known as WIGHT (Isle of) BABY. 3 built but after service trials, considered to be outclassed by new designs (also US Ace).
Sopwith	BABY	1915	Fighter		x x x	Allegorical	RNAS/ RAF	CLERGET	PR1	Dev of SCHNEIDER-one as JABBERWOCK. Also built as BLACKBURN BABY and BABY SEAPLANE. 100 built. Very active war-with the intrepid carrier "Ben-my-Chree", Turkey & Palestine and Zep bases in Europe. Some BABY!
Baden-Powell	BADEN POWELL	1894		Kite	Maker	People	ARMY			Man lifting Kite. Capt B F S B-P was brother of the Founder of the Boy Scouts (aso B-P Glider, 1904, but no military connotation).
Bristol	BADGER	1919	Fighter	BARNWELL'S WEEKENDER*	1918	Animal	(RAF)	DRAGONFLY	PR1	Body stripes=badge. Eng test bed for JUPITER and others. Redesigned with a PUMA eng as a civil a/c, known as * But BADGER was important, both as a design and test bed (NATO code for USSR Tu-16)
Blackburn	BAFFIN	1932	Torp Bomber		1932	Geography-Land	FAA	PEGASUS	PR1	English navigator (1584-1622), named BAFFIN Sea & Island, Canada. Dev from RIPON. 29 BAFFINs + 68 converted as RIPONs. RAF until 1936 and 29 converted RIPONs in New Zealand to 1941.
Bristol	BAGSHOT	1927	Fighter		1918	Geography-Land	(RAF)	JUPITER	PR2	Town in Surrey. COW Gun Fighter. Orginally, BLUDGEON. Failed wing led to improved wing design incorporated in the BOMBAY. Experimental flying until 1931.
Boulton-Paul	BALLIOL	1947	Trainer		1932	Education	RAF	MERLIN	PL1	Scottish King and an Oxford College at which the Managing Director had been a student. A later development with the MAMBA engine became the world first single turbo-prop aircraft. 210 built, 162 to the RAF.
Martin	BALTIMORE	1941	Bomber	THE BALT	1939	Geography-Land	RAF/FAA	CYCLONE	PR2	USA City in Maryland and a/c was a development of the MARYLAND. Served in the Mediterracean and N. Africa until the end of WWII. Designed to RAF requirements and also used by the S African AF. 400 built.
Target Technology Ltd	BANSHEE	1983	Drone		Maker	Mythology	RAF	WESTLAKE AERO ENGINES	PR1	Female spirit in Gaelic mythology. presentiment of death. Payload version as SPECTRE. Reccon as HAWKEYE and in USA as VINDICATOR. Used in 11 Air Forces. About 1700 built-1991
Br Aerial Transport	BANTAM	1918	Fighter	LITTLE BAT	1918	Bird	RAF	WASP	PR1	Small, agressive fowl-also Boxer. Maneuvrable and had a fine performance of 138 mph at ground level. Dev from the smaller BAT. Possibly only 9 built, but 2 never flew due to lack of WASP engs. (also US Northrop, 1948)
Fairey	BARRACUDA	1940	Torp Bomber	SHUFTY BARROW	R N	Fish	FAA	MERLIN	PL1	Species of voracious tropical fish. A/c famous for 1944 Tirpitz attack and had a successful operational career, especially on carriers in the Pacific. 2540 built and retired in 1950. More of a dive bomber . . .
Various	BARRAGE BALLOON	1937	Balloon	GOSSAGE		Miscellaneous	RAF/RN			WW II standard Barrage Balloon. Air Marshal Sir Leslie Gossage was C in C. Balloon Command. RAF.
Br Aerial Transport	BASILISK	1918	Fighter		1918	Reptile	(RFC)	DRAGONFLY	PR1	Lizard. Mythical name of a creature born of a serpent and a cock's egg. Enlarged BANTAM. An excellent a/c, but like many other a/c of this period was doomed by its engine. 1st flight Sept – Armistice Nov!
Beagle	BASSETT	1961	Transport		Maker	Animal	RAF	CONTINENTAL	PL2	Bassett Hound, a hunting dog. Also suggested as BULLDOG and HOUND. 20 built and served until late 1970s when many were sold to the civil market.

Maker	Name	Year	Type	Nickname	System	Classification	Service	Engine	Type	Notes
Sopwith	BAT BOAT	1913	Flying Boat		Maker	Miscellaneous	RNAS	AUSTRO-DAIMLER	PL1	First successful Br Flying Boat. Name from the ' Night Mail ' by Rudyard Kipling. Org BB had a short naval career. 3 larger BBs with Sampson eng-1 to RNAS, then to Greece. 1 to German Navy, 1 SARACEN eng to RNAS.
Fairey	BATTLE	1936	Bomber	GREENHOUSE	1932	Geography-Land	RAF	MERLIN	PL1	Town near Hastings (Battle of1066). Also FAIRLY RATTLE. 2419 built. Although outclassed by the German Luftwaffe, did yeoman service in France in 1940. Also BATTLE TRAINER. Used by 16 RAF Sqds + RCAF.
Morane-Saulnier	Type BB	1915	Fighter	BEBE BABY	x x x	Miscellaneous	RFC	LE RHONE	PR1	French. A biplane dev of the Morane BULLET used by the French and then ordered by the RFC. Noted as neither worthy of blame or praise. 80 + to the RFC and on active service until 1917, thereafter as trainers.* BB = BEBE (Fr) and so BABY (Br)
Army Aircraft Factory BE 1		1911	Trainer	SILENT ARMY AEROPLANE	Maker	Miscellaneous	(ARMY)	WOLSELEY	PR1	1st UK a/c with Cert. Airworthiness, & to experiment with 'wireless'. Said to have been a 'repair' of a VOISON, but a means to obtain official permission to produce their own design!
Royal Aircraft Factory BE 2		1914	Fighter/Recn	QUERK FOKKER FODDER	1911	Miscellaneous	RFC/RNAS	RENAULT	PL1	See Chapter 5 Part 17 – the Great Un-named
Royal Aircraft Factory BE 3		1912	Recon	GOLDFISH	1911	Miscellaneous	RFC	GNOME	PR1	Bleriot Experimental. "Type"as BE 3 to 8, all different a/c with the "Factory". RFC Squadrons and Central Flying School. BE3 was hard worked, inc trials with signalling flags and then progressed to wireless!
Royal Aircraft Factory BE 8		1912	Trainer	BLOATER	1911	Miscellaneous	RFC	GNOME	PR1	Built by several Manufacturers. 'Bloater', a herring smoked & salted 72 built and served with 5 RFC Squadrons in France and 2 training in the UK.
Royal Aircraft Factory BE 9		1915	Fighter	PULPIT	Maker	Miscellaneous	RFC	RAF 1A	PL1	Name from the Gunner's front Cockpit, immediately in front of the propellor. The one prototype saw one action in France, but "this type of aeroplane cannot be recommended". (Report by Major-Gen. Trenchard)
Blackburn	BEAGLE	1928	Torp Bomber		1918	Animal	(RAF)	JUPITER	PR1	Dog-any of a breed of small hound. One prototype under development or test until 1932 (aso NATO code for USSR 11-28).
Bristol	BEAUFIGHTER	1939	Fighter	BEAU WHISPERING DEATH *	x x x	Allegorical	RAF/FAA	HERCULES	PR2	See the CLASSICS – Chapter 6. * Also TORBEAU and BEAUBOMBER.
Bristol	BEAUFORT	1938	Torp Bomber		x x x	People	RAF	TAURUS	PR2	Name does not fit 1932 System. Named after Duke of BEAUFORT, whose ancestral home is at BADMINTON, near Bristol. See BEAUFIGHTER & Chap 6. RAF Standard Torp Bomber to 1943. 2129 built, inc 700 in Australia.
Bristol	BEAVER	1927	Fighter		1921	Animal	(RAF)	JUPITER	PR1	The Dam builder, amphibious rodent of Eurasia and America. Dev from the BOARHOUND. Competition won by the Fairey III. However, the Mexican AF bought 2 BEAVERS (and 10 FIGHTERS). Excellent service in Mexico.
De Havilland(Canada) BEAVER		1947	Transport		Maker	Animal	ARMY	WASP JUNIOR	PR1	Org 'bush' a/c. US purchased 980, and British Army Air Corps 46. Very rugged – wheels, skis & floats. Used by 24 Countries. Later limited production of the TURBO BEAVER.
Sopwith	BEE	1917	Fighter	TADPOLE	Maker	Insect	(RNAS)	(RNAS)	PR1	Of the order Hymenoptera, with little to suggest a tadpole. . . Small pilot runabout but submitted to the Admiralty for operation from small RN Ships? (Also Baynes BEE, Russian PCHELIJA = LITTLE BEE, 1958)
Short	BELFAST	1964	Transport		1939	Geography-Land	RAF	TYNE	TP4	Based on BRITANNIA and earlier named BRITTANIC. Suggested BLENHEIM. Later civil as heavy-lift a/c. 10 Built. RAF service ceased 1976. Some to Rolls-Royce and 3 to Heavy Lift Cargo Airlines.
Bristol	BELVEDERE	1952	Helicopter	FLYING LONGHOUSE *	x x x	Miscellaneous	RAF	GAZELLE	TP2	1949 RAF name should be 'Tree'! Raised Turret to view scenery. BEL= beautiful. VEDERE-to see. London Pub and King Edward VIII's Fort B. Prod'n taken over by Westland and total of 26 built. * in Borneo.
Bristol	BERKELEY	1925	Bomber		1921	Geography-Land	(RAF)	CONDOR	PL1	Town in Gloucestershire. Found as too large for a single-engined Bomber and RAF decided that Night Bombers to have twin engines, it went for RAE trials. 2 built and 1 still flying in 1930.

Maker	Name	Year	Type	Nickname	System	Classification	Service	Engine	Type	Notes
Brewster	BERMUDA	1940	Dive Bomber	BLASTER*	1939	Geography-Land	FAA	CYCLONE	PR1	British Colony (since 1609) in the Caribbean. Maker=BUCCANEER and * US Navy = HELLDIVER. About 160 delivered to the RAF & FAA but the BEAST was not liked. Some were used as target towers. 771 built.
Metropolitan-Vickers	BERYL	1944	Engine			Jewel	RAF		JT	First of the precious stone series. Source of Beryllium.
Army Balloon Factory	BETA	1910	Airship		x x x	Miscellaneous	ARMY	GREEN	PL1	Greek 'B': Rebuild of BABY and officially Dirigible No 3. Also BETA II but taken over by the RN, to become H M Airship No 17! Brief service in France and then a trainer until 1916. (Also US Robinson & Northrop)
Blackburn	BEVERLEY	1955	Transport	BARRACK BLOCK	1949	Geography-Land	RAF	CENTAURUS	PR4	Yorkshire Town. Prototype known as UNIVERSAL FREIGHTER. Also suggested as BISON, BULLOCK, HOLDALL & BOXCAR. Unaesthetic but very successful in 5 Squadrons. 47 built. Last retired in 1967. Also PREGANT PORTIA.
Hillson	BI-MONO	1941	Experimental	SCRAP WING	x x x	Miscellaneous	(RAF)	GIPSY SIX	PL1	Designed as mono or biplane. the upper plane being released after take off. Built in 72 days, flights were quite successful. A HURRICANE was converted for further trials, but never flew.
Sopwith	BIPLANE	1913	Trainer		Maker	Miscellaneous	RFC/RNAS	MONOSOUPAPE	PR1	Sopwith's beginnings. Specifically ordered for the Admiralty, but came to the attention of the War Office and 9 to Military Wing, RFC. No war service, but a few RNAS a/c went to France.
Breguet	BIPLANE G, L & U.	1911	Transport	CRUISER TINWHISTLE*	Maker	Miscellaneous	RFC	GNOME	PR1	French designer and manufacturer. Org wood fuselage, later metal = * An "unwholesome beast". 1 for Air Battalion, and 6 to RFC. G=Gnome L = Renault & U=Samson engs. Service in RFC Squadrons until 1914.
Bristol	BISLEY	1940	Fighter Bomb		1939	Geography-Land	RAF	MERCURY	PR2	Army Rifle Range. Temporary name for BLENHEIM V.
Avro	BISON	1921	Recon	FLEET SPOTTER	1918	Animal	RAF/FAA	LION	PL1	BISON is N. American but generally as BUFFALO. 56 Built. 'Fleet Spotter' requirement. "As ungainly as the animal" (Also NATO code for USSR May-4)
Boulton-Paul	BITTERN	1927	Fighter		1918	Bird	(RAF)	LYNX	PR2	Family of wading birds. Rare in UK. Little larger than some single engine fighters. The BITTERN was innovative with many features, including side gun turrets. A night fighter concept that was cancelled. 2 built.
Blackburn	BLACKBURD	1917	Torp Bomber	ABOMINABLE	Maker	Bird	(RNAS)	EAGLE	PL1	Alteration, but also an old Scots spelling. Designed for ease of production but an ugly bird. Innovative, with wheels or skis. 3 only (also Lockheed BLACKBIRD. fastest ever military a/c)
Blackburn	BLACKBURN	1922	Recon	BULL	1921	Geography-Land	FAA	LION	PL1	Yorkshire Town. 'Ugly as the contemporary BISON.' Also a Trainer. DART wings with new fuselage and served 1923-31, being replaced by the Fairey IIIF. 59 built. Carrier and land based + seaplane.
Burney & Blackburn	BLACKBURNE	1924	Engine		Maker	Miscellaneous	(RAF)		PR	Combination of Blackburn & Burney.
Westland-Sikorsky	BLACKHAWK	1970	Helicopter		Maker	People	(RAF)	GENERAL ELECTRIC	TP2	N American Red Indian Tribe. Used by USAF, and in 1970 held the world helicopter speed record of 221 kts. 75 ordered by Saudi Arabia as part of a large British military order. 1 RAF demonstrator, 1987 Paris Show.
Aero Technik	BLANIK	1964	Glider		Maker	Geography-Land	R N			Czech. Historic Mountain associated with Czech mythology. Also known as the Omnipol B, but Omnipol was the State Trading Company.
Bristol	BLENHEIM	1936	Bomber		1936	Geography-Land	RAF	MERCURY	PR2	See the CLASSICS – Chapter 6.
Bleriot	BLERIOT XI	1911	Recon	GNOME BLERIOT	x x x	People	RFC/RNAS	GNOME	PR1	Based on 'Channel' m/c and orginal civil trainers. Some impressed into the RAF in 1914 and saw service in France, serving with 4 Squadrons. About 60 built, some still flying as trainers until 1918.
Bleriot	BLERIOT XII	1910	Recon	MAN KILLER	x x x	People.	ARMY	ENV	PR1	BLERIOT, pilot & inventor and made first powered a/c crossing of the English Channel. Org owned by Claude Grahame-White and named the WHITE EAGLE. Brief service with the Royal Engineers.
Bleriot	BLERIOT XXI	1911	Transport		Maker	Miscellaneous	ARMY	MONOSOUPAPE	PR1	Org entered for the 1911 Larkhill (Salisbury Plain) Army Trials, and taken over by the Air Battalion, Royal Engineers. One only, but used for extensive military trials, inc the "wireless".

Maker	Name	Year	Type	Nickname	System	Classification	Service	Engine	Type	Notes
Short	BLIMP	1914	Airships		x x x	Miscellaneous	RFC/RNAS	VARIOUS	–	Name given by Horace Short. Series of BLIMPS 1914-1918. Said to be Type A=Rigid and B=Limp?
Bristol	BLOODHOUND	1925	Fighter		1921	Animal	(RAF)	JUPITER	PR1	Hound with a keen sense of smell. 3 to the RAF for trials and gave good service. Of more importance was the performance and reliability of the JUPITER engine which impressed Imperial Airways, with later orders.
Blackburn	BLUEBIRD	1931	Trainer		Maker	Bird	RAF	CIRRUS MAJOR	PL1	Irenadie-the leaf bird family. One of the most beautiful of forest birds is Fairy BLUEBIRD. but this is Blackburn. 42 built for RAF. (Also DH 4 Trainer, and French Caudron 1927 transport OIAEAU BLEU)
Bristol	BOARHOUND	1925	Gen Purpose		1921	Animal	(RAF)	JUPITER	PR1	Large Hound, such as the Great Dane for hunting Boar. RAE tests gave the advanage to the ATLAS. BOARHOUND then re-designed to become BEAVER. Chile required a 2-seat fighter/bomber as the BORZOI but not built.
Air Department	BOAT	1914	Flying Boat		Maker	Miscellaneous	(RNAS)	HISPANO-SUIZA	PL1	Air Department of the Admiralty. Two prototypes, with many problems, and the project abandoned. Later AD Boats converted by Supermarine as the civil CHANNEL Boats (1919), and some sold abroad.
Boulton-Paul	BOBOLINK	1918	Fighter	BOBBIE	1918	Bird	(RFC/RAF)	BENTLEY BR2	PR1	North American song bird, and the aircraft originally named as HAWK! The 1918 naming system required a bird with Boulton-Paul prefix code of BO. So BOBOLINK. An acrobat of repute but only 6 built.
Reid & Sigrist	BOBSLEIGH	1945	Trainer		Maker	Miscellaneous	RAF	GIPSY MAJOR	PL2	Racing snow sledge. Converted from the DESFORD for prone-pilot trials.
Boulton-Paul	BODMIN	1924	Postal		1921	Geography-Land	RAF	LION	PL2	Cornish Town. Org name as BODEGAR. Innovative, central engines driving 2 propellors between the mainplanes. 2 built, one crashed. Experimental in spite of "postal" (which really meant a Bomber) and valuable lessons learned.
Bristol	BOLINGBROKE	1941	Bomber		1939	People	RAF	TWIN WASP	PR2	Lord BOLINGBROKE. 18C, Tory Statesman Canadian built BLENHEIM.
Boulton-Paul	BOLTON	1922	Recon		1921	Geography-Land	(RAF)	LION	PL2	Lancashire town. Dev of the BOURGES. Whilst very manoeuvrable and with several innovative features, there was only the one prototype.
Blackburn	BOMBARDIER	1946	Engine		Maker	Miscellaneous	RAF		PL	A soldier who operated a bombard. Now aircrew-Bomb Aimer. Engine later manufactured by Blackburn.
Bristol	BOMBAY	1935	Bomber		1932	Geography-Land	RAF	PEGASUS	PR2	Indian City. (Org BEDFORD). Also Troop Carrier. Used BAGSHOT re-designed wing. Some as transports UK/France 1940. Mostly as Bombers in the Middle East but carried 6000 Allied casualties. 50 built.
Dyott	BOMBER	1916	Bomber	DYOTT	Maker	People	(RNAS)	BEARDMORE	PL2	Designed by Mr G M Dyott, but built by Hewitt & Blondeau.
Samuel White	BOMBER	1916	Seaplane		Maker	Miscellaneous	(RNAS)	Rolls-Royce	PL1	As a landplane=WIGHT CONVERTED.
Short	BOMBER (LANDPLANE)	1916	Bomber		Maker	Allegorical	RFC/RNAS	Rolls-Royce	PL1	Urgent need for a long range bomber led to the Short 184 on wheels. RNAS service at Zeebrugge & Saar Valley. RFC request and RNAS offered 15. Saw limited but vital action. Excellent service for a stopgap! 83 built.
Commonwealth	BOOMERANG	1942	Fighter	BOOMA *	Maker	Weapon	RAAF/RAF	TWIN WASP	PR1	Australian, training RAF & RAAF. * Australian nickname. 'Emergency' Fighter based on the WIRRAWAY. Little used as a Fighter but good service in ground-attack role. c250 built.
A/c Disposal Company	BOREAS	1926	Fighter		Maker	Mythological	(RAF)	HISPANO-SUIZA	PL1	Greek mythology-the North Wind. An adaption of the Martinsyde F4. The name was found in an Air Minsitry list of the time but seems to be otherwise unknown. There are some other such "mysteries".
Borel	BOREL	1910	Seaplane		x x x	People	(RN)	GNOME	PR1	French Lieutenant. First French Seaplane purchased by the UK.
Douglas	BOSTON	1938	Bomber		1939	Geography-Land	RAF/FAA	TWIN WASP	PR2	USA. Massachusetts, Capital & Port. French orders diverted to the UK in 1940. Night Fighter as HAVOC with Leight Light. 581 to RAF. Used by 7 Air Forces. First operational tricycle u/c in the RAF.
Blackburn	BOTHA	1938	Torp Bomber	WHY BOTHER?	1939	People	RAF	PERSEUS	PR2	Boer General & first Prime Minister of the Union of South Africa. Under-powered with a military load, it had a short Squadron life but was then used in many training and towing roles. 676 built.

143

Maker	Name	Year	Type	Nickname	System	Classification	Service	Engine	Type	Notes
Boulton-Paul	BOURGES	1918	Bomber		1918	Geography-Land	(RAF)	DRAGONFLY	PR2	French Town – as AMIENS and VIMY. Designed as a 'Fighter Bomber' but whilst BOURGES III was the fastest twin-engine a/c flying, it was then too late. The war was over. Two civil a/c dev as the ATLANTIC, but abandoned.
Bristol	BOXKITE	1909	Recon		Maker	Miscellaneous	ARMY/RFC/RN	GNOME	PR1	Bristol's first aircraft, a copy of the French Farman biplane. 78 built and first used by the Army Air Batalion. Then with the RFC in 1910 and also saw service with the RNAS until 1916.
Grahame-White	BOXKITE	1912	Trainer	BI-RUDDER BUS	Maker	Miscellaneous	RFC/RNAS	GNOME	PR1	Used at Hendon by the Grahame-White Flying School. Purchased by the Military Wing of the RFC, in which it accomplished 10 minutes flying! Reconstructed and no further record.
Vickers	BOXKITE	1912	Trainer		Maker	Miscellaneous	RFC	GNOME	PR1	A variant known as the PUMKIN was based on a Farman fuselage. 2 taken over by the RFC in 1914 but used for only a few months. Vickers first venture into aviation with the Vickers School, closed with the war.
Army Balloon Factory	BR. ARMY AIRSHIP NO 3	1909	Airship	BABY	x x x	Allegorical	ARMY	R E P	PR1	Remade as BETA I & II R E P = Robert Esnault-Pelterie.
Bristol	BRAEMAR	1918	Bomber		1918	Geography-Land	(RAF)	PUMA	PL4	Scottish Town. Large Triplane design to bomb BERLIN. 3 built, last converted to the civil PULLMAN. The TRAMP was a smaller type. 2 built but not flown. The 3 were advanced designs but 1918 and after were hard years.
Bristol	BRANDON	1924	Transport	ABANDON	1921	Geography-Land	RAF	JUPITER	PR1	Suffolk town and strictly the name class for Bombers. Dev from the TEN SEATER and to the RAF as an ambulance based at Halton with ANDOVER ambulances. One only.
Royal A/c Establishment	BRENNAN	1922	Helicopter		Maker	People	(RAF)	BENTLEY	PR1	Louis BRENNAN, prolific British inventor. A/c built at the direction of Winston Churchill, but killed by a Committee who saw no future for the helicopter. 1st free flight 1924
Bristol	BRIGAND	1944	Bomber		1932	Allegorical	RAF	CENTAURUS	PR2	Robber. Bandit. Similar to the BUCKINGHAM. 147 built and used in the Middle East, Burma and Malaya. Also later Trainer to 1958. See also BUCKINGHAM & BUCKMASTER but only BRIGAND saw active service.
Bristol	BRITAIN FIRST	1935	Experimental		x x x	Allegorical	(RAF)	MERCURY	PR2	Type 142 was a private venture and known as the CAPTAIN'S JIG (the Captain being Barnwell, Chief Designer). 143 donated to the RAF by the Daily Mail and faster than the Fighters! Became BLENHEIM.
Bristol	BRITANNIA	1952	Transport	WHISPERING GIANT	Maker	Allegorical	RAF	PROTEUS	TP4	Orginally a Province of Rome and also an allegorical figure. Civil airliner adapted for RAF Transport Command. 83 built. (Also 1910 Triplane known as the STAIRCASE). Canadair RCAF version = YUKON, with the TYNE engs.
Royal Aircraft Factory	BS 1/SE 2	1913	Fighter	BULLET	x x x	Miscellaneous	RFC	GNOME	PR1	Farnborough called it a 'Scout', which highlights the confusion over the many 'Scouts' and 'Bullets'! Very fast but crashed. Rebuilt as BS 2 but changed as SE 2.
Bucker	Bu 131	1934	Trainer	JUNGMANN	Maker	Trainer	(RAF)	ARGUD	PL1	German – young man. Luftwaffe elementary Trainer. 1 stolen from France in 1941 by 2 French pilots and flown to the UK. But not further flow-damaged by souvenir hunters! Post WW II built in Spain.
Bucker	Bu 181	1938	Trainer	BESTMANN	Maker	Miscellaneous	(RAF)	HIRTH	PR1	German = Best Man. About 45 taken over by the RAF, and used on transport/communication duties 1945-46. Also produced in Switzerland and Spain for their Air Forces.
Blackburn	BUCCANEER	1958	Rec Bomber	BANANA BOMBER BRICK	1949	Allegorical	FAA/RAF	GYRON JUNIOR	JT2	1000 public competition suggestions, inc Phantom, Jupiter, Bayonet-and Zube! Orginally FAA and then RAF. 209 built. Obsolescent but used in 1991 Gulf War for bomb laser marking. Declared obsolete in 1944. Also BUCK. (Also Brewster 1941)
Bristol	BUCKINGHAM	1943	Bomber		1939	Geography-Land	RAF	CENTAURUS	PR2	County Town of Buckinghamshire. Earlier project as BEAUMONT to succeed the BLEMHEIM. 54 built for Far East operations but too late. A few modified as fast courier transports. See BRIGAND/BUCKMASTER.

Maker	Name	Year	Type	Nickname	System	Classification	Service	Engine	Type	Notes
Bristol	BUCKMASTER	1944	Trainer	BUCK	x x x	Miscellaneous	(RAF)	CENTAURUS	PR2	102 BUCKINGHAMs converted as an advanced trainer for the BRIGAND. Some served as transports at ADEN and in the RAF until 1956. See also BUCKINGHAM and BRIGAND.
Avro	BUFFALO	1924	Torp Bomber	COW	1921	Animal	(RAF)	LION	PL1	Purchased by Air Ministry for trials as proposed replacement for Blackburn DART. Also Seaplane.
Brewster	BUFFALO	1937	Fighter	PEANUT SPECIAL (USA)	Maker	Animal	RAF/FAA	CYCLONE	PR1	USA Fleet Fighter. About 500 built, 38 to the UK, the balance to 5 other countries. USed by UK in the Far East but with little success.
Sopwith	BUFFALO	1918	Fighter		1918	Animal	(RAF)	BENTLEY BR2	PR1	(BUFFALO = American BISON). An armoured Trench Fighter appearing in late 1918. 2 built. 1 had operational trials in France but too late with the Armistice in November. Good name – the Buffalo is hostile!
Boulton-Paul	BUGLE	1927	Bomber		1927	Miscellaneous	(RAF)	LION	PL2	'Bombers Multiple' = with more than one eng to have letter B. Dev from BOURGES and BODMIN line. 5 built but in spite of being manouevrable and fast with a good load the RAF decided not to order 2-eng Bombers, the policy was then for heavy night Bombers.
Bristol	BULLDOG	1927	Fighter		x x x	Animal	RAF	JUPITER	PR1	See the CLASSICS – Chapter 6.
Scottish Aviation	BULLDOG	1969	Trainer		Maker	Animal	RAF	LYCOMING	PL1	Dog tradition of BEAGLE Aircraft, org Manufacturers. Standard Trainer of the RAF University Air Sqdns. Bought by 10 Countries. About 350 built. One prototype with retractable u/c = BULLFINCH.
Sopwith	BULLDOG	1917	Fighter		x x x	Animal	RFC	CLERGET	PR1	Related to the HIPPO and similar to the SNIPE, there was no production order. A second prototype was then engined with the DRAGONFLY which was a failure.
Bristol	BULLFINCH	1923	Fighter		1918	Bird	(RAF)	JUPITER	PR1	Single-seat monoplane & two seat biplane, thus both Bird and Animal name. PLATYPUS and PEGASUS disallowed, so BullFINCH and BULLfinch! 2 built. (Also Scottish Aviation BULLFINCH. 1976, as BULLDOG variant) BULLFINCH, 1976, as BULLDOG variant).
Bristol	BULLPUP	1928	Fighter	PUPPY	1921	Animal	(RAF)	MERCURY	PR1	Small BULLDOG Fighter. Designed for the MERCURY (later used) but mostly flown with the JUPITER. After RAF assesment, leased to Bristol as an engine test-bed and flying to 1935. (Also US Buhl-Veuille, 1926)
Martinsyde	BUZZARD	1916	Fighter	MUSTARDSYDE (YELLOW)	1918	Bird	RAF	FALCON	PL1	Double Bird of Prey! Rolls-Royce naming system official in 1918. Martin & Handasyde Ltd. The single seat F3 was reputed to be the fastest fighter of WW I. 338 built. Used by 8 countries. BIG FELLA in Ireland and "Atlantic" entry as RAYMOR.
Rolls-Royce	BUZZARD	1927	Engine		1918	Bird	RAF		PL	Bird of Prey. Eng an enlarged KESTREL. Only 100 built but was the basis for a Schneider Trophy engine.
Army Balloon Factory	BR. ARMY AIRSHIP No 3	1909	Airship	BABY	x x x	Miscellaneous	Army	R E P	PR1	Remade as BETA I & II. REP = Robert Esnault Peltrie, eng designer.
Blohm & Voss	Bv 222	1938	Flying Boat	WIKING	Maker	People	(RAF)	JUMO	PR6	German = VIKING. Captured in Norway and evaluated at Calshot. Org civil, designed for a proposed Atlantic service by Deutsche Lufthansa.
Weir	C 9	1944	Helicopter	DRAIN PIPE	Maker	Miscellaneous	(RAF)	GIPSY SIX	PL1	A Weir experimental design. (Weir took over the Cierva Company). Used an offset jet pipe instead of the conventional anti-torque rear rotor
Short	C CLASS	1935	Flying Boat	EMPIRE	Maker	Miscellaneous	RAF	PEGASUS	PR4	4 impressed ex Imperial Airways – CLEO, CORDELIA, CABOT and CARIBOU for maritime duties but now with RAF serial numbers. The RAF military version was the SUNDERLAND.
Albatros	C I	1912	Reccon.	ALBATROSS	Maker	Bird	(RN)	MERCEDES	PL1	Ocean wanderer with the biggest wing span of any bird. Purchased from Germany. The later C III was used as a Fighter/Bomber by the German Air Force.
Rumpler Flugzeug-Werke	C IV	1916	Reccon	LIBELLENFORM*	Maker	Miscellaneous	(RFC)	Benz	PL1	* German DRAGONFLY from shape of lower wing. High altitude reccon and successful against the Allies in the Middle East. 1 flown to the UK for evaluation. The later C VII, the RUBILT, was supreme above 20,000 ft.
Admiralty	C STAR	1917	Airship		1917	Miscellaneous	RNAS	RENAULT	PL2	Developed from COASTAL type. (C) Fwd eng=Berliet/Aft eng=Renault.

Maker	Name	Year	Type	Nickname	System	Classification	Service	Engine	Type	Notes
Blackburn	C. A. A5C	1932	Transport	DUNCAN SISTERS	Maker	Miscellaneous	RAF	JAGUAR	PR2	Duncan=Designer. Sisters=Singers. 2 identical a/c, but one MONOPLANE and one Biplane(also as MAILPLANE). No conclusive results. The MONOPLANE served with the RAF until 1938.
Avro	CADET	1931	Trainer		Maker	Education	(RAF)	GENET MAJOR	PR1	Trainee Officer. Smaller version of the TUTOR. No RAF order but 17 were bought by Air Service Training for ab initio flying. Later RAF colours but civil markings. 7 to Irish Army Air Corps and 34 to RAAF. 106 built.
Slingsby	CADET	1936	Glider		Maker	People	AIR CADETS			Org with the Germanic type name of KADET. Widely used by the Air Training Corps, and by many Gliding Clubs in the UK and abroad. KADETs and CADETs totalled 431+Kits. (Also Mooney(ALON) and French Robin)
General Aircraft	CAGNET	1938	Army Co-op		Maker	Miscellaneous	(RAF)	CIRRUS MINOR	PL1	Based on CYGNET, with the Civil Air Guard in mind = CAG, a pre WW II org to produce civilian pilots as a potential military pool in case of war. One impressed into the RAF for the School of Arms Co-op.
Short	CALCUTTA	1928	Flying Boat	DEOLALI TAP (?)	1921	Geography-Water	(RAF)	JUPITER	PR3	Indian Port & City. Conforming to the RAF naming system, the design was for a civil a/c and was used by Imperial Airways in pioneering the Empire routes. 5 built + 5 French. RAF evaluation, leading to RANGOON.
Airspeed	CAMBRIDGE	1941	Trainer		1939	Education	(RAF)	MERCURY	PR1	University. Single engine CAMBRIDGE to complement the twin engine OXFORD. Two prototypes. Org suggested as SUPER COURIER. Overweight and ignominous role on the ground fanning flames for practice a/c fires . . .
Sopwith	CAMEL	1916	Fighter	CAMISOLE	x x x	Animal	RFC/ RNAS	LE RHONE	PR1	See CLASSICS. Chapter 6.
Fairey	CAMPANIA	1916	Seaplane		Maker	Geography-Land	RNAS	EAGLE	PL1	Region of Italy and name of a Cunard liner purchased by Admiralty in 1914 to convert to seaplane carrier. A/c named after the Ship. Excellent service with the Navy, including Russia. First from a carrier. 142 built.
English Electric(BAeS)	CANBERRA	1949	Bomber	CRANBERRY (USA)	1949	Geography-Land	RAF/FAA	AVON	JT2	RAF's first jet bomber and served to 1992. 1461 built, including USA and 1376 to the RAF. Wing based on the Gloster METEOR. In all, used by 10 Air Forces – obviously a great a/c. (Name of the DH GIANT MOTH, 1926)
De Havilland	CANBERRA	1931	Bomber		1918	Geography-Land	(RAF)	JUPITER	PR3	Federal capital of Australia. With long delays, completion was by the Gloster A/c Co. Many problems, and only the one prototype built.
Consolidated	CANSO	1935	Flying Boat		Maker	Miscellaneous	RAF	TWIN WASP	PR2	CANadian ConSOlidated. CATALINA built by Boeing in Canada.
Slingsby	CAPSTAN	1961	Glider		Maker	Miscellaneous	RN			Rope, cable or chain winding machine usually associated with ships. Successor to the EAGLE. Also POWERED CAPSTAN. Suggested that perhaps CAPSTAN Cigarettes?
Admiralty	CAQUOT	1915	Balloon		Maker	People	RNAS/ RFC			Design of Capt. CAQUOT, French Army. Kite Balloon. With the RFC from 1916.
Bell	CARIBOU	1939	Fighter		1939	Miscellaneous	RAF	ALLISON	PL1	USA AIRACOBRA. A few in the RAF but of the 9558 built, half to Russia.
Baynes	CARRIER WING	1943	Glider	BAT	Maker	Miscellaneous	(RAF)			Also known as BAYNE'S BAT. Exp scale model Glider to carry a Tank as the fuselage. Built by Slingsby as the BAYNES CARRIER WING and success as a glider. No suitable tank, but the glider further tested by the RAE.
Consolidated	CATALINA	1935	Flying Boat	CAT. RUSTBUCKET. DUMBO	1939	Geography-Water	RAF	TWIN WASP	PR2	Port-Newfoundland, Canada. SLOW BOAT PBY, PBN-1=NOMAD. PIG BOAT, P-BOAT, FLYING PLANK and BLACK CAT when on night operations. See also CANSO. Slow but very long range over many oceans. 2378 built, for 9 Countries.
Royal Aircraft Factory	CE 1	1918	Flying Boat	DOUBLE ELEPHANT	1911	Miscellaneous	RAF	MAORI	PL1	Farnborough nickname, possibly from the double boom and/or folding wings. CE = Coastal Experimental. Only two built. Also known as COASTAL

Maker	Name	Year	Type	Nickname	System	Classification	Service	Engine	Type	Notes
Bristol	CENTAURUS	1938	Engine		x x x	Mythology	RAF/FAA		PR	A Constellation in the S Hemisphere From the Greek Centaur, half man and half horse. This powerful, 2-row sleeve valve eng., dev from HERCULES, was a great success and powered 11 a/c recorded in these pages.
Short	CHAMOIS	1927	Army Co-op.	GOAT	1921	Animal	(ARMY)	JUPITER	PR1	A goat antelope. Dev from SPRINGBOK. Metal, immensely strong and could be flown like a fighter. Underpowered, which could be remedied but the advantages of metal were slow to be accepted. 2 built.
Aeronca	CHAMPION	1941	Transport	CHAMP	Maker	Allegorical	RAF	CONTINENTAL	PL1	With an RAF serial number, this a/c is listed as the CHIEF but which did not fly until 1947. The listed a/c is thus likely to be the above, of which 10,000+ were built for the US Army. 1 RAF impressed in India.
Armstrong Siddeley	CHEETAH	1929	Engine		1918	Animal	RAF		PR	Naming system of Felidae, the Cats, allocated to A-S in 1918. Over 37,200 engines built. Org the LYNX MAJOR. Widely used and until the end of the ANSON. (Also S African Fighter, 1985 and US Gulfstream)
Chenu	CHENU	1910	Engine		Maker	People	RNAS		PR	French designer.
Bristol	CHERUB	1924	Engine		Maker	Miscellaneous	(RAF)		PR	Winged celestial being or child. Small horizontally opposed, 2 cyl engine for light a/c. Powered 4 a/c, recorded in this book.
Vought-Sikorsky	CHESAPEAKE	1936	Dive Bomber	CHEESECAKE	1939	Geography-Water	FAA	TWIN WASP JUNIOR	PR1	CHESAPEAKE Bay, USA Eastern seaboard with BALTIMORE as main Port. U.S. Marines as VINDICATOR. 50 to the FAA and used for operational training as unsuitable for carriers but so used by the US in the Pacific.
Boeing-Vertol	CHINOOK	1961	Helicopter	HOOK WOCKA-WOCKA	Maker	People	RAF	LYCOMING	TP2	N. American Indian tribe. Also an East coast Wind. Dev from Piasecki through Boeing-Vertol to Boeing Helicopters. Sold to 9 Countries and with RAF Army Co-operation Sqdns. Twin rotors. Used in the Gulf War.
De Havilland(Canada)	CHIPMUNK	1946	Trainer	CHIPPY	Maker	Animal	RAF/FAA ARMY	GIPSY MAJOR	PL1	Small 'squirrel' of N. America and N. Asia but with striped back. Designed in Canada and RAF standard Elementary Trainer. 1283 Built and sold to 10 Countries. Portugal built 60. Many still in civil use.
Northrop	CHUKAR	1968	Drone		Maker	Bird	RN	WILLIAMS RESEARCH	JT	Old World Partridge (Hindi = chakor). 10 to RN.
Sopwith	CIRCUIT SEAPLANE	1913	Seaplane		Maker	Miscellaneous	RN	GREEN	PL1	Org built for the "Circuit of Britain" competition and acquired for the Navy.
Blackburn	CIRRUS	1925	Engine			Meteorology	RAF		PL	High layer cloud-ice crystals. The org Cirrus Aero Eng Company was taken over by Blackburn in 1934. Main types were the CIRRUS MAJOR and MINOR.
Schempp-Hirth	CIRRUS	1967	Glider		Maker	Meteorology	(RAF) (ARMY)			Cloud. German glider for evaluation
De Havilland	CIRRUS MOTH	1925	Transport		Maker	Miscellaneous	RAF	CIRRUS	PL1	CIRRUS engine in a DH MOTH.
Hannoverke Wagon Fabrik	CL II	1916	Fighter	HANNOVERs *	Maker	Miscellaneous	(RFC)	Argus	PL1	* RFC nickname. "Wagon" = org railway wagon manufacturer! Strong and could take punishment. 1000 + built. Unusual biplane elevators. Often mistaken for an Albatros until "the gunner popped up from his office". Well respected by the RFC.
Halberstadt Flug/Werke	CL II	1916	Fighter	STRAFFER	Maker	Miscellaneous	(RFC)	MERCEDES	PL1	Low level, strafing with guns, bombs and grenades. Great part in German counter attack at Battle of Cambrai, and made havoc of a British Division at Peronne. 2-seat "communal" cockpit with good crew communication. Tough and seemed immune.
Cranwell Aero Club	CLA 3	1923	Trainer	CRANWELL	Maker	Miscellaneous	(RAF)	CHERUB	PR1	A monoplane developed from the CLA biplane, designed for the 1924 Lymne Light Aircraft Trials. Not strictly (RAF), but appeared in RAF colours. Flown until 1929 by Flt/Lt Comper, who them formed his Company.
Clement-Bayard	CLEMENT-BAYARD	1910	Airship		Maker	People	(ARMY)	CLEMENT	PL4	French. Name =a/c + engines. Subscribed for by readers of the 'Daily Mail'.

Maker	Name	Year	Type	Nickname	System	Classification	Service	Engine	Type	Notes
Curtiss	CLEVELAND	1937	Dive Bomber		1939	Geography-Land	RAF	CYCLONE	PR1	USA – 17 Towns (2 in Australia and 1 English County). Org US HELLDIVER. Biplane and 90 delivered to the RAF from the US Navy. Found not suitable for combat, used as instructional airframes.
Handley Page	CLIVE	1928	Transport		1927	People	RAF	JUPITER	PR2	Robert, Baron Clive of Plassey – 'Clive of India' (1725-74). A/c org suggested as CHITRAL (to confuse the enemy?) and adapted from HINAIDI as the transport version. 3 built.
Saunders-Roe	CLOUD	1930	Flying Boat		Maker	Meteorology	RAF	SERVAL	PR2	Similar to civil CUTTY SARK. 21 built, 16 for the RAF. Specified for "flying, navigation and bombing training" RAF service until 1939.
Rolls-Royce	CLYDE	1945	Engine		1918	Geography-River	RAF		JT	Scottish River. Engine performed well but no production. Installed in the Westland WYVERN as a test bed.
Cunlifie Owen	CLYDE CLIPPER	1939	Transport		Maker	Miscellaneous	(RAF)	PERSEUS	PR2	The second of the type impessed by the RAF, and passed to the Free French Air Force as a troop and freight transport in French Equatorial Africa.
Bristol	COANDA MILITARY	1913	Trainer		Maker	People	(RFC/RNAS)	GNOME	PR1	Romanian Engineer ('Coanda Effect') Designer for Bristol. Entered for the Larkhill Military trials and two to the RFC. But little flying due to the ban on monoplanes. Later batches converted to biplanes.
Admiralty	COASTAL	1915	Airship		R N	Miscellaneous	RNAS	MAORI	PL2	C (Coastal) Class. Also (improved) COASTAL STAR Class.
Sopwith	COBHAM	1918	Bomber		1918	Geography-Land	(RAF)	PUMA	PR2	Surrey Town. Triplane Bomber. Wartime design and too late for WW I and project abandoned in 1920. 2 built.
Short	COCKLE	1924	Flying Boat		1924	Fish	(FAA)	CHERUB	PR2	Mollusc, also a weed. Also civil Short MUSSEL (1926) COCKLES and . . . Org known as SATELLITE and name later used. A small flying boat to test a metal hull. RAF and tested at Felixstowe. Later a civil a/c.
Cody	CODY (V)	1912	Trainer	MILITARY	Maker	People	(ARMY)	AUSTRO-DAIMLER	PL1	'Colonel' F S Cody, the first man to fly a 'successful' powered a/c in Britain. Org American but naturalised a UK citizen in 1909. See Chap 4, Part 3, for Cody types + CATHEDRAL.
Cody	CODY KITE	1902	Kite		Maker	People	(R N)			Trials on HMS HECTOR. 1903 & 1908.
Curtiss (Canada)	COLUMBIA	1915	Bomber	CANADA	Maker	Geography-Land	(RFC/RNAS)	CURTISS VX	PL2	West Coast Province. A/c Canadian built, a landplane based on the H1 flying boat. Said to be "bizarre", but had a Sperry autopilot, promptly removed by the RFC. Order for 100 cancelled. 1 to RFC and 1 to RNAS.
De Havilland	COMET	1934	Racer	BURBERRY	Maker	Astronomy	(RAF)	GIPSY SIX	PL2	Won MacRobertson Race to Australia. With later DH ALBATROSS, influenced design of DH MOSQUITO. The nickname (Flying suit) was a later, 1935, name. Restored and flown in the late 80s. COMET remains a very historic a/c.
De Havilland	COMET	1949	Transport		Maker	Astronomy	RAF	AVON	JT4	Celestial Body. A/c adapted from civil (BOAC) COMET. See also D H NIMROD. COMETs of all marks = 114 Built and the COMET 4 had an excellent military and civil record. A very significant a/c.
Westland	COMMANDO	1973	Helicopter		Maker	Allegorical	R N MARINES	GNOME	TP1	Dev from WESSEX. 15 to Royal Marines for assaults from RN Ships, and used in the Falklands war, and later in Borneo. Retired in 1965.
Curtis	COMMANDO	1940	Transport		Maker	People	RAF	CURTISS-WRIGHT	PR2	Org Boer(S African)name for a small independent striking force. 3341 built, and widely used in many parts of the world. Many used post WW II as civil transports.
Avro	COMMODORE	1933	Transport		Maker	Miscellaneous	(RAF)	LYNX	PR1	RN COMMODORE is an appointment. RAF Air COMMODORE is a rank. One impressed into the RAF in 1939.
Breguet	CONCOURS	1915	Trainer		Maker	Miscellaneous	(RNAS)	SUNBEAM	PL1	Superb, worthy of exhibition. French Concours d'Elegance. 68 built and 2 to RNAS.
Rolls-Royce	CONDOR	1918	Engine		1918	Bird	RAF		PL	S American Bird of Prey. Eng an enlarged EAGLE. R-R would not agree to Trenchard's demand for multi-manufacture so, "no more CONDORs". (Also WW II German Bomber, Russian An-124, 1931 Curtiss and 1988 Boeing). 327 built.
Dittmar	CONDOR	1932	Glider		Maker	Bird	AIR CADETS			S American Bird of Prey. German, with first known glider flight at high altitude in cumulo-nimbus (thunder) cloud. (Also Us McCready GOSSAMER CONDOR, man powered a/c, 1977, and UK Rollason light a/c, 1961)

Maker	Name	Year	Type	Nickname	System	Classification	Service	Engine	Type	Notes
Airspeed	CONSUL	1937	Transport		Maker	Allegorical	RAF	CHEETAH	PR2	Converted from military OXFORD, in turn converted from civil ENVOY. About 100 built and served in several countries.
Samuel White	CONVERTED SEAPLANE	1916	Seaplane		Maker	Miscellaneous	RNAS	EAGLE	PL1	Adapted WIGHT BOMBER. First kill of a U-Boat in the English Channel. Small number built.
Rolls-Royce	CONWAY	1953	Engine		Maker	Geography-Water	RAF		JT	River CONWY in Wales. Tested in the ASHTON.
Phoenix Dynamo	CORK	1918	Flying Boat		1918	Geography-Water	(RAF)	EAGLE	PL2	Irish Port – Ireland then being Electric as the KINGSTON. 2 prototypes showed promise but suffered various mishaps. English Electric developed the CORK as the KINGSTON.
Fairchild	CORNELL	1937	Trainer		1939	Education	RAF/RCAF	RANGER	PL1	American University. 2500 supplied for the RAF Empire Training Scheme in Canada and Rhodesia. Also RAAF. 7500 built.
Consolidated	CORONADO	1937	Flying Boat		1939	Geography-Water	RAF	TWIN WASP	PR4	Port in San Diego, USA. Also nearby Los Coronados Islands off Mexico. 215 built and 10 to the RAF for freight services Montreal-Iceland, Newfoundland-Scotland, W Indies and Africa. Withdrawn 1945.
Vought	CORSAIR (1st)	1928	Fighter		Maker	Miscellaneous	(RAF)	WASP	PR1	Pirate Ship. US Navy. 6 sold to Peru, and paid for in guano! 2 to Japan, and one to the RAF for evaluation 1933 – 36.
Vought	CORSAIR (2nd)	1934	Fighter		Maker	People	(RAF)	WASP	PR1	One purchased by the RAF for tests at Martlesham Heath.
Vought-Sikorsky	CORSAIR (3rd)	1940	Fighter	BENT WING BIRD	Maker	Miscellaneous	FAA	DOUBLE WASP	PR1	Pirate Ship, particularly of the Barbary Coast. 12,582 built. USA. Fine Carrier fighter, with many kills in many theatres of war, inc Korea. Served with 4 Air Forces. Also WHISTLING DEATH and OLD HOSE NOSE.
Sunbeam	COSSACK	1915	Engine		Maker	People	RNAS		PL	USSR, noted as cavalry. One of a series of 'Tribal' class engines. Gave name to Handley Page Bomber with COSSACK engines.
Airspeed	COURIER	1934	Transport	COLONIAL *	Maker	Miscellaneous	RAF	LYNX	PR1	Messenger on urgent or diplomatic business. Frequent newspaper name. 9 impressed in 1939 into the RAF. First British production a/c with a retractable undercarriage. 126 built * with the CHEETAH eng. (Also Helio STOL, 1949)
Fiat	CR 42	1939	Fighter	FALCO	Maker	Bird	(RAF)	FIAT	PR1	Italian=FALCON. Used by Italy and 3 Continental Air forces. 1784 built. On a UK raid from France in 1940 one landed intact, and was evaluated at Farnborough. This FALCO still exists as an RAF ground exhibit.
Cessna	CRANE	1943	Trainer		Maker	Bird	RCAF	Lycoming	PL1	Some 14 species of large wading birds. US name of BOBCAT. CRANE for RAF training in Canada.
Short	CROMARTY	1921	Flying Boat		1918	Geography-Water	RAF	CONDOR	PL2	Scottish Port on Loch CROMARTY. Following sub-contract manufacture of PORTE Boats, this was Short's first Flying Boat. A short life, being wrecked in the Scillies and not economical to repair.
Spartan	CRUISER	1935	Transport		Maker	Allegorical	RAF	GIPSY MAJOR	PL3	Small civil airliner, on internal routes in the UK, Yugoslavia, Egypt, Czechoslovakia and India. One impressed into the RAF in 1939.
Saro-Percival	CRUISER	1933	Transport	MAILPLANE	Maker	Allegorical	RAF	GIPSY MAJOR	PL3	Known as the SPARTAN CRUISER. The design was sold by Percival to Spartan who moved to Cowes, and the a/c was built by Saro. 14 built, and 1 RAF impressed. 1 licence built in Yugoslavia.
Short	CRUSADER	1927	Seaplane	* BRISTOW CRUSADER	Maker	People	(RAF)	MERCURY	PT1	Org Soldier engaged in the Crusades in the Middle Ages against the Muslims in the Holy Land. CRUSADER was a 1927 Schneider Trophy entrant but aileron controls crossed and a/c crashed. *Project Supervisor.
Unknown	CRUSADER	1879	Balloon		x x x	Allegorical	ARMY			War Office Purchase. Individual name but still a type! Donated by Col. Templer (maker not known) for instruction by the Royal Engineers.
Piper	CUB	1930	Transport	BIRD DOG	Maker	Animal	RAF	LYCOMING	PL1	Young of an animal. Org and still civil and widely used by US Forces, also for reconnaisance and gunnery spotting. 19 CUB COUPEs impressed into the RAF in 1940. (Also NATO code for USSR An-12 and China Y-8)
Napier	CUB	1919	Engine		Maker	Animal	(RAF)		PL	In 1918, Napier allocated Arms & Weapons for military engines but previous LION of 1917. 'Son' of the LION but a 1000 hp eng!

Maker	Name	Year	Type	Nickname	System	Classification	Service	Engine	Type	Notes
Piper	CUB COUPE	1937	Transport	CUB	Maker	Miscellaneous	RAF	CONTINENTAL	PL1	One of the very successful line of CUBS, still being made and flown by many. 1250 built from 1938 + recent production. 1 impressed into the RAF In civil or military form, was the basic trainer for many US pilots.
Blackburn	CUBAROO	1924	Torp Bomber		Maker	Miscellaneous	(RAF)	CUB	PL1	Probably the largest single engine a/c built. Whilst a new design, the name suggested the KANGAROO with a CUB engine. With fuel and torpedo it weighed 9 tons! 2 only, the RAF deciding on twin eng Bombers.
Sopwith	CUCKOO	1917	Torp Bomber		x x x	Bird	RNAS	ARAB	PL1	First Torp A/c to take off from a Ship. Production by Blackburn. 350 ordered but only 232 delivered and used until 1923. An important a/c in naval aviation and 6 given by the UK to the Japanese Navy.
Napier	CULVERIN	1935	Engine		1918	Weapon	(RAF)		PL	Early type of Musket. Diesel Engine built under licence from Junkers of Germany.
Blackburn	CUMULUS	1962	Engine		Maker	Meteorology	RAF		AUX	Heap Cloud. Licensed from French Turbomeca.
Britten-Norman	CUSHIONCRAFT	1959	Hovercraft		Maker	Miscellaneous	(RAF)	Rolls-Royce	PL1	'Cushioncraft' sometimes a generic term for Hovercraft. Models CC 1-4. CC 2 evaluated RAE Bedford. R-R car engine.
Napier	CUTLASS	1935	Engine		1918	Weapon	(RAF)		PL	Naval sword. Diesel. Junkers Lic. (Also US Chance Vought Navy Fighter of 1951).
Saunders-Roe	CUTTY SARK	1929	Flying Boat		Maker	Miscellaneous	(RAF)	GENET	PR2	Famous Tea Clipper. named after a Scottish Witch. 3 different engs with various configurations. 1 for RAF evaluation. but all sold as civil a/c. 15 built, 11 as amphibians.
Beardmore	CYCLONE	1920	Engine		Maker	Meteorology	(RAF)		PL	Atmospheric depression.
Wright	CYCLONE	1925	Engine		Maker	Meteorology	RAF/FAA		PR	Widely used UK & US Forces. One of the classic US aero engines.
General Aircraft	CYGNET	1937	Trainer	SWANNY	Maker	Bird	RAF	GIPSY MAJOR	PL1	Baby Swan. RAF Tricycle u/c Trainer. org for training for the BOSTON. Org an Airspeed 'bicycle' design purchased by General Aircraft. About 10 built and 5 impressed into the RAF (Also Hawker light a/c, 1924).
Caproni	Ca 1	1914	Bomber	BIPLANE	Maker	Miscellaneous	(RNAS)	FIAT	PL3	Italian. To be flown to UK. but got no further than Dijon. The engs were removed and the a/c handed over to the French. Built under licence in France and 150+ built in Italy.
Caproni	Ca 24	1915	Bomber	GIGANTE	Maker	Allegorical	RNAS	ISOTTA-FRASCHINI	PL3	Italian=GIANT. Large Triplane with twin booms. Rugged. slow but an effective bomber. 60 built and 6 to the RNAS in Italy as "Caproni Flight". One to the Western Front and all returned to Italian AF.
Caproni	Ca 309	1936	Bomber	GHIBLI	Maker	Miscellaneous	RAF	ALFA ROMEO	PL2	Italian = the Desert Wind. Dev from the civil BOREA (from Greek BOREAS, the North Wind). Light reconnaisance bomber, and considered their best. 243 built, serving with the Co-Belligerent Air Force after Italy's surrender and as RAF transports.
Caproni	Ca 42	1918	Bomber	TRIPLANE	Maker	Miscellaneous	RNAS	FIAT	PL3	Dev from the Ca 1 BIPLANE. and used by the RNAS in Italy.
Caproni	Ca 45	1916	Bomber	CAPRONI	Maker	Miscellaneous	RAF	ISOTTA-FRASCHINI	PL4	A big triplane bomber. 6 acquired by the RAF in Italy, an ally in the war against the Austrians. The bombers were returned to Italian Forces in 1918.
Cant	Ca Z. 501	1938	Flying Boat	GABBIANO	Maker	Bird	(RAF)	PIAGGIO	PR1	Italian = GULL. Widely used and well strutted, continued in the war but now against the Germans as part of the 1943 Co-Belligerent Air Force. Also MAMM AIUTO= Mother Help Me, in air/sea rescue role.
Blair-Atholl	D 1 & 4.	1907	Experimental	DUNNE	Maker	People	(RFC)	GNOME	PR1	Designed by Lt J W Dunne, and funded by the War Office. D1 glider, and powered D8 had wide press coverage in secret trails in Scotland! The Blair Atholl Syndicate 8 & 12(1912) built by Shorts. 2 for RFC trials.
Halberstadter Flug/ Werk	D III	1916	Reccon	FERNERKUNDER *	Maker	Miscellaneous	(RFC/ RAF)	Daimler Benz	PL1	* German=knows the mountains, glaciers ie recon a/c. Noted for photo intelligence at the Battle of the Somme and respected by the Allies. Several captured and 1 flown to the UK for evaluation.
Albatros Werke	D III	1916	Fighter	VEE STRUTTER *	Masker	Miscellaneous	(RFC)	MERCEDES	PL1	*RFC nickname. Famous with the German JASTA (Hunting) Squadrons and the mount of most of the German "aces" inc Baron von Richtofen. Large production and the highest rate of fire at the time. Feared enemy in the air and on the ground.

Maker	Name	Year	Type	Nickname	System	Classification	Service	Engine	Type	Notes
Fokker (Holland)	D VII	1917	Fighter	RAZOR EDGE*FOKKER	Maker	Miscellaneous	(RFC/RAF)	MERCEDES	PL1	* German, rectangular fuselage with sharp edge. (D VII monoplane was the FLYING RAZOR) Most famous of WWI German a/c and the subject of "eulogistic propaganda". An Armistice clause required all D VIIs to be handed over but some "emigrated". Postwar service in the Dutch East Indies
Napier	DAGGER	1933		Engine	1918	Weapon	RAF		PL	A short stabbing sword. 'H' type engine. (Also US Convair DAGGER delta jet fighter, 1956).
Slingsby	DAGLING PRIMARY	1930	Glider	GRASSHOPPER * N V M S	Maker	Miscellaneous	AIR CADETS			German ZOGLING design + Mr R F DAGNALL (who founded RFD Ltd) = DAGLING. * NVMS=No Visible Means of Support! A (very) open design with the pilot's seat on a single keel "fuselage". A 1st glider for many.
Douglas	DAKOTA	1935	Transport	DAK GOONEY BIRD	1939	People	RAF	CYCLONE	PR2	American Indian Tribe & District. Org civil DC3. Widely used US and UK Forces (RAF until 1950) and over 21, 000 built, many still in service. Also US Army LOADSTER and SKYTRAIN. (Nato code for USSR DAKOTA=CAB, and US Piper light a/c).
Blackburn	DART	1921	Torp Bomber		Maker	Geography-Water	FAA/(RAF)	LION	PL1	River to Dartmouth. Dev from the SWIFT and some civil a/c of this name. FAA-59, RAF-1 + some civil, inc use as trainer. Dual version known as the VELOS. (US Convair SEA DART, jet seaplane Fighter, 1954)
Rolls-Royce	DART	1946	Engine		Maker	Geography-Water	RAF		TP	With the advent of the jet engine. Rolls-Royce turned to River names. Engine widely used, civil & military. First commercial use in the Vickers VISCOUNT. (Also Canadian SILVER DART of 1949)
Douglas	DAUNTLESS	1938	Dive Bomber		Maker	Allegorical	FAA/RAF	CYCLONE	PR1	Undaunted, defiant. USA. 5937 built. 6 for FAA not used operationally. Most successful US Dive Bomber of WW II, with invaluable service at the Battle of Midway, turning the tide of the Pacific War. 1 to RAF.
Breguet	DE BOMBE	1915	Bomber		Maker	Miscellaneous	(RNAS)	LE RHONE	PR2	French. Specific name. 2 built.
Breguet	DE CHASSE	1915	Fighter		Maker	Miscellaneous	(RNAS)	CANTON-UNNE	PR1	Also French. Also specific. 14 built.
Armstrong-Siddeley	DEERHOUND	1936	Engine		Maker	Animal	(RAF)		PR	Scottish breed of hound. Large exper engine, later scrapped. Dev 1115 hp. The later and larger BOARHOUND dev 2250 hp but never flew. Both dev from the MASTIFF and HYENA.
Brittan-Norman	DEFENDER	1965	Recon		Maker	Allegorical	(ARMY)	LYCOMING	PL2	Dev from ISLANDER and with Airborne Stand-off Radar, known as DEFENDER/ASTOR system. For export known as MASTOR. B-N now owned by Swiss Pilatus. (US Helicopter, 1990)
Boulton-Paul	DEFIANT	1937	Fighter		1932	Allegorical	RAF/FAA	MERLIN	PL1	Turret Fighter-4 m/c guns. Dunkirk, May 29, 1940-destroyed 37 enemy a/c without loss but glory shortlived, although also used as a Night Fighter. Widely used as Target Tower. 1064 built. BP's best known a/c. (Also USA Rutan, 1978)
Dornier	DELFIN	1923	Flying Boat		Maker	Fish	(RAF)	B M W	PL	German design and build=Dolphin. Imported. and reassembled by Handley Page for RAF trials.
Army Balloon Factory	DELTA	1912	Airship		Maker	Miscellaneous	ARMY/RN	GREEN	PL1	Greek D-4th Airship. In Oct, 1913, Early trials with the "wireless" and successful up to 30 miles. To the RN in 1913, and seems to have flown no more. (Also US Northrop lightplane)
Hawker	DEMON	1930	Fighter		1932	Allegorical	RAF	KESTREL	PL1	Devil or evil being. Variant of the HART. and similar to HIND. Also TURRET DEMON. 239 delivered, + 64 for Australia. 'Obsolete' in 1939 but last still flying in 1944. Org HART 2-seat FIGHTER. DEMON in 1932.
De Havilland	DENBIGH	1924	Bomber		1921	Geography-Land	(RAF)	PUMA	PR1	Town in Clwyd. Wales. A mystery? D H have no record, but noted in Air Ministry list of 1924. Org name of DONCASTER, but with PUMA engine'? Or "Project of D of R Type 3a" – not completed?
De Havilland	DERBY	1925	Bomber		1918	Geography-Land	(RAF)	LION	PL1	County Town of Derbyshire, and home of Rolls-Royce Ltd. 1st military a/c of the "new" De Havilland Co. 2 built but RAF trials only.

Maker	Name	Year	Type	Nickname	System	Classification	Service	Engine	Type	Notes
Rolls-Royce	DERWENT	1944	Engine		Maker	Grography-Water	RAF		TP	Celtic-'clear water' and name of several English Rivers. World's first Turbo-prop. Later developed as CLYDE.
Desoutter	DESOUTTER	1937	Transport		Maker	People	RAF	CIRRUS	PL4	French Designer. 5 impressed into the RAF.
De Havilland	DEVON	1946	Transport		Maker	Geography-Land	RAF/FAA	GIPSY QUEEN	PL2	County. Military name for the DOVE, a widely used civil transport. 30 to the RAF as DEVONs, and 13 to the FAA as SEA DEVONs. DOVE + DEVON = 528 built.
D F S	DFS 108-30	1945	Glider	KRANICH	Maker	Bird	(Air Cadets)			German = Crane. Held 9 World and many National records. Also World Championship for 2-seat Gliders.
Airco(de Havilland)	DH 1	1915	Fighter	SCOOTER	x x x	Miscellaneous	(RFC)	GNOME	PR1	Also name for the Martinsyde ELEPHANT in the Middle East. Airco= Aircraft Company with de Havilland as Designer/Pilot, org with RAF, Farnborough. 73 built.
Airco(de Havilland)	DH 18	1919	Transport	ARO	Maker	Miscellaneous	(RAF)	LION	PL1	Farnborough nickname from from org civil registration of G-EARO. Various tests 1924-26.
Airco(de Havilland)	DH 2	1915	Fighter	SCOUT	Maker	Miscellaneous	RFC	MONOSOUPAPE	PR1	See Chapter 5 Part 17 – The Great Unnamed.
Airco(de Havilland)	DH 4	1916	Bomber	FLAMING COFFIN	RFC	Maker	RFC/ RNAS	EAGLE	PL1	See Chap 5 Part 17 – the Great Un-named.
de Havilland	DH 54	1925	Transport	HIGHCLERE	Maker	Miscellaneous	(RAF)	CONDOR	PL1	HIGHCLERE, village & castle in Hampshire. Whilst recorded as a nickname perhaps an intended military name (1921 system)? One only, and destroyed by a falling hangar roof in a snow storm.
Airco(de Havilland)	DH 6	1916	Trainer	SKYHOOK. IDIOT'S DELIGHT	Maker	Miscellaneous	RFC/ RNAS	RAF 1A	PL1	Also CRAB, CLUTCHING HAND, DUNG HUNTER, SIXTY, FLYING COFFIN, and CLOCKWORK MOUSE. Obviously a very popular a/c, with possibly a record number of Nicknames. 2282 built. "Built by the mile, and cut off to order" A trainer, but nearly sank a sub!
De Havilland	DH 67	1929	Transport	HERCULES	Maker	Miscellaneous	RAF	JUPITER	PRF	Adapted from the DH 66 HERCULES, a civil airliner, and hence the misplaced nickname. 2 built, one to the SAAF and one to the RAF for radio trails.
De Havilland	DH 86	1934	Transport	EXPRESS CATHEDRAL	Maker	Allegorical	(RAF)	GIPSY SIX	PL4	Speedy (?) Basically a 4 engined RAPIDE, org designed for Australia and used by several Airlines, inc British and Imperial Airways. Some RAF impressed by RAF as Ambulance/Flying Classroom. Also RAAF. 62 built.
Airco(de Havilland)	DH 9	1917	Bomber	DEVIL NINACK	Maker	Miscellaneous	RFC/ RNAS	LIBERTY	PL1	See the GREAT UN-NAMED – Chapter 5 Part 17
Airco(de Havilland)	DH 9A	1917	Fighter	NINE-ACK NINACK	Maker	Miscellaneous	RAF	LIBERTY	PL1	In RAF service to 1931. Also US Mail, and LIBERTY = American Eng. ACK=a in the military code of the time. 1383 built. Played a great part in 'policing' the Middle East Protectorates.
Douglas	DIGBY	1937	Bomber		1939	Geography-Land	RAF	CYCLONE	PR2	DIGBY is a town in Nova Scotia, Canada (also an RAF Station) Org US name of BOLO. 20 to the RCAF, a few as RAF eng test beds. 1st US a/c with with a fully desiged air/ground radar. Many lost at Pearl Harbour.
De Havilland	DINGO	1924	Fighter		1921	Animal	(RAF)	JUPITER	PR1	Australian wild Dog. A variant of the DORMOUSE (!) which had a Jaguar eng.
Schempp-Hirth	DISCUS	1987	Glider		Maker	Miscellaneous	RAF/ ARMY			A disc thrown for distance at athletic competitions. Also a S American freshwater fish, so named from its circular flat body. (RAF Gliding & Soaring Association)
Sopwith	DOLPHIN	1917	Fighter	BLOCKBUSTER	Maker	Fish	RFC	HISPANO-SUIZA	PL1	Strictly, a Mammal. Followed CAMEL . . . 1st Sopwith design with a water-cooled eng. 1532 built, but only 621 saw service before the end of WW II. Not popular with pilots. Some built in France. (Also DH92, 1936-scrapped)
De Havilland	DOMINIE (1st)	1933	Transport		1932	Education	RAF/FAA	GIPSY QUEEN	PL2	Schoolmaster. Military RAPIDE. Used as transport and radio trainer, and even one as coastal recon with 2 Vickers guns! 300 RAPIDES, and 284 DOMINIEs to the RAF. In service to 1955, and balance sold as civil a/c.
De Havilland	DOMINIE (2nd)	1962	Trainer	JET DRAGON * HAWKER	1949	Education	RAF/FAA	VIPER	JT2	Many suggested names, including HENRY (the Navigator). Org civil BIZ JET, very successful. RAF with world wide sales. RAF as navigation trainer and communications, and FAA for radar development of SEA HARRIER. * after HAWKER-Siddeley, and Sir Harry HAWKER.

Maker	Name	Year	Type	Nickname	System	Classification	Service	Engine	Type	Notes
De Havilland	DON	1937	Trainer		1932	Education	(RAF)	GIPSY KING	PL1	University Lecturer. 50 built, but not a success, and the suggestion of DON for the 1949 DOMINIE not agreed. Some flew as communications a/c for a short while, but relegated as instructional airframes. 30 built.
De Havilland	DONCASTER	1921	Experimental		1918	Geography-Land	(RAF)	LION	PL1	Yorkshire Town. 2 Built, the first for military long range trials, the second as a civil airliner which found no buyer. An ungainly a/c but valuable for research.
De Havilland	DORMOUSE	1923	Fighter		1921	Animal	(RAF)	JAGUAR	PR1	Family of small rodents. DINGO with a JUPITER Eng. Both types = 3 Built, one being used by the RAF for radio trials.
Wright	DOUBLE CYCLONE	1933	Engine		Maker	Meteorology	RAF		PR	See CYCLONE. USA.
Armstrong Siddeley	DOUBLE MAMBA	1948	Engine		Maker	Reptile	FAA		TP2	African family of venomous snakes. Org name of SERVAL.
De Havilland	DOUBLE SPECTRE	1959	Engine		R A F	Miscellaneous	RAF		RKT	Occult – a ghost.
Pratt & Whitney	DOUBLE WASP	1937	Engine		Maker	Insect	RAF		PR	Insect, doubly vicious.
Sopwith	DOVE	1919	Fighter		1918	Bird	(RAF)	LE RHONE	PR1	Sopwith's 1st post-war design, in effect a two seat PUP. 10 built, and after WW II one survivor was converted back to a PUP which is now with the Shuttleworth Trust.
Fokker (Holland)	DR I	1916	Fighter	DREIDECKER	Maker	Miscellaneopus	(RFC)	Oberursel	PR1	A fearsome Fighter leading to air superiority over the RFC at the time – "Fokker Fodder" and was inspired by the Sopwith Triplane. Good speed and agility. Werner Voss claimed 48 Allied a/c and Richtofen was killed in a DR I in 1918. 320 built. Also with Swedish Le Rhone (THULIN) engs.
Airships Ltd	DRACHEN	1914	Balloon		Maker	Mythology	R N			Dragon. German Kite Balloon. Series of Balloons, made by Airships Ltd and Wm. Beardmore. Successfully used as artillery spotters in France, and call RN units taken over by the RFC in 1916.
Sopwith	DRAGON	1919	Fighter		x x x	Mythology	(RAF)	DRAGONFLY	PR1	Should be an 'animal'. SNIPE with this Eng. Org DRAGONFLY SNIPE. 200 built awaiting the (disastrous) eng but only 6 completed. 1 to USA, and 2 to R A E for eng trials (Also US Douglas bomber, and Elizade eng).
De Havilland	DRAGON	1932	Transport		Maker	Mythology	RAF	GIPSY MAJOR	PL2	Built to the order of Hillman Airways for the London-Paris run. Very successful 'airliner' and used by 7 Countries. 53 UK and 87 Australian built. RAF impressed 17 as trainers in 1939. 18 military types overseas.
De Havilland	DRAGON RAPIDE	1934	Transport	RAPIDE	Maker	Mythology	RAF	GIPSY SIX	PL2	DH.89 Dev from DRAGON. Widely used. 737 built. 46 impressed into the RAF as transports and wireless trainers Org known as DRAGON SIX. Variant as DOMINIE. With the RAF until the 70's Some civil a/c still flying (1994)
A B C	DRAGONFLY	1917	Engine	CENSORED	Maker	Insect	RFC		PR	Included as the worst eng of WWI. Claiming a good power/weight ratio, and ordered in quantity for both fighters and bombers. It was soon red hot, crankshafts broke, and was the downfall of many new a/c.
De Havilland	DRAGONFLY	1936	Transport		Maker	Insect	RAF	GIPSY MAJOR	PR2	Smaller DH DRAGON. 67 Built, and 15 impressed into the RAF in 1939. 6 used by the RCAF. (Also Cessna, 1967, and Swedish DRACHEN Fighter=DRAGON)
Westland	DRAGONFLY	1948	Helicopter		Maker	Insect	RAF/FAA	LEONIDES	PR1	USA Sikorsky. 1st helicopter built in the UK for the RAF. Superseded by WHIRLWIND. 149 built. Dev into WIDGEON. Also used by Italy, Japan, Thailand and Australia. UK service until 1956.
Westland	DREADNOUGHT	1923	Experimental		Maker	Allegorical	(RAF)	LION	PL1	Also known as the POSTAL. 'Fear not' but crashed on 1st flight. An a/c ahead of its time.
Hawker	DUIKER	1922	Recon		Maker	Animal	(RAF)	JUPITER	PR1	African Buck. First 'Hawker' (prev Sopwith) aircraft. Parasol monoplane and the one prototype evaluated by the RAF.
Sunbeam	DYAK	1914	Engine		Maker	People	RFC		PL	A member of any of the various people of Borneo and the Sulu Sea Islands – the Tribal class engs. 100 ordered, but one only fitted to an Avro 504 K.
Dornier	Do 17	1936	Bomber	FLYING PENCIL*	Maker	Miscellaneous	(RAF)	DAIMLER-BENZ	PL2	RAF Nickname from the long thin fuselage. Standard Luftwaffe bomber and widely used on all fronts, inc Battle of Britain and the night bombing of UK cities. One force landed in the UK in 1944. * Also German nickname.

Maker	Name	Year	Type	Nickname	System	Classification	Service	Engine	Type	Notes
Dornier	Do 335	1943	Fighter	PFEIL	Maker	Miscellaneous	(RAF)	DAIMLER BENZ	PLE	German = ARROW. Captured from the Luftwaffe and evaluated at Farnborough. One eng/prop in the nose, and second in the tail. A push-pull 2-seat Fighter Bomber. A formidable fighter, but with many problems.
Gloster	E 28/39	1941	Experimental	WEAVER WHITTLE PIONEER	Maker	Miscellaneous	(RAF)	WHITTLE	JT1	1st UK Jet engined a/c. The 1st jet a/c was the Heinkel 178 of 1939, and adequate support for Whittle may well have reversed the position. (WEAVER may have been a project code?) 2 built.
Gloster	E. 1/44	1947	Fighter	ACE NENE MACHINE	Maker	Miscellaneous	(RAF)	NENE	JT1	A singe-seat jet fighter designed as an "insurance" for the METEOR. ACE was the official Gloster name, but seems not to have been used. 4 ordered, 2 built. See also Gloster ACE, 1948.
British Aircraft	EAGLE	1936	Transport		Maker	Bird	RAF	GIPSY MAJOR	PL1	1 impressed into the RAF in India (Also Us Eagle EAGLE helicopter, US Fisher Fighter, 1943)
Slingsby	EAGLE	1954	Glider		Maker	Bird	(AIR CADETS)			Designed as a high performance 2-seat glider for the ATC. Mk4 known as the REGAL. Suggested that the name came from the EAGLE magazine (Also US Curtiss, 1920, AmEagle AMERICAN EAGLE, 1975, Cessna GOLDEN EAGLE)
Rolls-Royce	EAGLE (1st)	1915	Engine		Maker	Bird	RFC/RAF		PL	Bird of Prey. As with FALCON, named before, and led to 1918 RAF system 1914 Mercedes racing engine cylinders as basis for design of EAGLE, HAWK and FALCON. (Also Polish ORLIK 1986 = Spotted Eagle)
Roll-Royce	EAGLE (2nd)	1943	Engine		1918	Bird	RAF		PL	Repeat of a famous name (Also Klemm and Slingsby EAGLES, both civil, US McDonell jet fighter 1973, known as the STRIKE EAGLE, Australian WINJEEL = YOUNG EAGLE, 1951, and BAeS missile SEA EAGLE, 1960) 15 built.
Vickers	EFB. 1	1913	Fighter	DESTROYER (GUN BUS)	Maker	Allegorical	–	WOLSELEY	PL1	Strictly, not eligible for this book but included as first British gun design. Crashed on first flight, but led to the later GUNBUS of fame.
Napier	ELAND	1952	Engine		Maker	Animal	RAF		JT	Largest of African Antelopes.
Lockheed	ELECTRA	1934	Transport		Maker	Mythology	RAF	WASP JUNIOR	PR2	Daughter of Agamemnon and Clytemtra. Org civil, impressed USA and 8 RAF ex BEA. 158 built. Chamberlain flight to meet Hitler. RAF service Middle East. SUPER ELECTRA became HUDSON and VENTURA (org LEXINGTON)
Armstrong Whitworth	ENSIGN	1938	Transport		Maker	Miscellaneous	RAF	TIGER	PR4	Flag or symbol. Ordered and named by Imperial Airways for Empire routes. Whilst working for the RAF, the a/c were flown by civil pilots. One was captured by the Luftwaffe in France 15 built with E names. 2 impressed.
Airspeed	ENVOY	1934	Transport		Maker	Miscellaneous	RAF/FAA	CHEETAH	PR2	Ambassador or Messenger. A/c twin eng dev of 1934 COURIER. 11 acquired by the RAF, one converted for the King's Flight. The 'model' for the later OXFORD. 3 ENVOYS used by the S A AF. 51 built.
Elliot	EON PRIMARY	1948	Glider	GRASSHOPPER	Maker	Miscellaneous	AIR CADETS		PL1	EON = Elliots of Newbury.
Army Balloon Factory	EPSILON I & II	1913	Airship		Maker	Miscellaneous	(ARMY/ RN)	GREEN	PL1	Greek alphabet 'E' – fifth. This was the last (and unfinished) Farnborough design, the RN taking over responsibility for airships in 1913, and being thought better than a/c for anti U-Boat duties.
Vickers	ES 1	1914	Fighter	BARNWELL BULLET	Maker	Miscellaneous	RFC	CLERGET	PR1	ES = Experimental Scout, also known as SCOUT. The first model with MONOSOUPAPE eng, but subject to fire and cancelled. 7 built. BARNWELL was the designer (as was his brother at Bristol)
Army Balloon Factory	ETA	1913	Airship		Maker	Miscellaneous	ARMY/ RNAS	CANTON-UNNE	PL2	Greek alphabet = seventh. Only one month with the ABF, and thence to the RN. Wrecked on her way to France in 1914.
Elliot	ETON	1948	Glider		Maker	Geography-Land	AIR CADETS			District of Windsor, and famous Public School. Manf by EON=Elliot of Newbury. Dev from the PRIMARY.
BAe, DASA, CASA, Aeritlia	EUROFIGHTER 2000	1994	Fighter		Maker	Miscellaneous	RAF	EUROJET	JTF	Whilst its name is as a "fighter" this comparatively small swept-wing canard is a multi-role concept to replace the RAF JAGUAR and TORNADO. 2000 is the anticipated year of RAF service. 1st flight in Germany. The shape of things to be . . .

Maker	Name	Year	Type	Nickname	System	Classification	Service	Engine	Type	Notes
Rolls-Royce	EXE	1936	Engine		Maker	Engine	EAF		PL	R-R exception. X configuration, and River EXE (but rivers for the later jet engs) Successfully flown in the. BATTLE, but no prod order with need for MERLINs. Aircooled & sleeve valves, related to PENNINE and CRECY.
Spartan	EXECUTIVE	1936	Transport		Maker	Allegorical	(RAF)	WASP JUNIOR	PR1	Managerial authority. Govt. Dept. US 4/5 seat civil monoplane, later dev as 2-seat ZEUS. About 200 built, and one RAF impressed.
Beech	EXPEDITER	1937	Transport	BUG SMASHER (USA)	Maker	Allegorical	RAF/FAA	WASP JUNIOR	PR2	USA, org civil. Used in many roles with 5 countries, and with the USA also as the KANSAN and NAVIGATOR. 9,100 built, of which 7,521 were military. The FAA had over 300 as "Admirals' Barges".
Short	EXPERIMENTAL SCOUT	1918	Seaplane	CAMEL SHORT	Maker	Miscellaneous	(RNAS)	EAGLE	PL1	CAMEL as this seaplane had the same lack of dihedral on the top wing. The EAGLE was on loan for another a/c and forbidden for this a/c, but made an excellent machine. However, bureaucracy triumphed – no order.
Wright	F	1914	Fighter	TIN COW	Maker	Miscellaneous	(RFC)	WRIGHT	PL1	Dev from the FLYER, and one to the US Army who found it "dismal". One to the RFC, but whether it ever flew with them is unknown, but scrapped in 1915. TIN COW as it was designed as an "Armoured Fighter".
Martinsyde	F 1	1917	Fighter	FATHER	Maker	Miscellaneous	(RFC)	Rolls-Royce	PL1	Works nickname.
Blackburn	F 1	1927	Fighter	BLACKCOCK	Maker	Miscellaneous	( )	JAGUAR	PR1	BLACKCOCK sometimes given as an a/c name, but was a family of names for 1 type with different engines – MERCURY, FALCON and JAGUAR. TURCOCK (for Turkey) was the one prototype, but destroyed before delivery.
Fairey	F 2	1916	Bomber	FOLDER BIPLANE	Maker	Miscellaneous	(RNAS)	FALCON	PL2	1st twin-eng a/c fitted with folding wings and Fairey's first design. One prototype only and the Admiralty became disinterested. Org planned eng was the BROTHERHOOD of which there is no record, but possibly a GREEN built under licence
Farman (Henri)	F 20	1911	Fighter	FARMAN	Maker	Miscellaneous	RFC/RNAS	LE RHONE	PR1	Of some note, as being a 1913 experiment in the use of machine guns, and being a "gunbus" pusher. Short operational career in France, but did sterling work as a trainer to the end of 1917. 443 buit.
Farman (Henri)	F 22	1911	Trainer	WAKE UP, ENGLAND!	Maker	Miscellaneous	(RFC)	GNOME	PR1	Named by Claude Grahame-White, as part of a national campaign. Bought for the Military Wing of the RFC, but used more as a Parliamentary statistic than as an aeroplane. Both wheels and floats.
Farman (Henri)	F 27	1914	Recomm	HENRY FARMAN	Maker	People	RFC/RNAS	CANTON-UNNE	PR1	Whilst a nickname, it was also an official designation! A "gunbus" pusher, and being all steel was very suitable for the tropics. Served in S W and E Africa, Aden and India. 64 for the RFC, some ex RNAS.
Various	F 29/27	1928	Fighter	COWGUN FIGHTER	x x x	Weapon	(RAF)	VARIOUS	PR1	COW=Coventry Ordnance Works. Exp Cannon Fighter. 7 Manufacturers build to this Spec but scrapped.
Martinsyde	F 3	1917	Fighter	MOTHER	Maker	Miscellaneous	(RFC)	FALCON	PL1	Works nickname. See FATHER (nickname)
Howard Flanders	F 4	1911	Trainer	FLANDERS	Maker	People	(RFC)	RENAULT	PL1	English Designer. 4 ordered for the Military Wing of the RFC, but owing to the monoplane ban were delivered to Farnborough. Engs were removed, no more was heard of the F4, and no RFC pilot is known to have flown them.
Farman	F 40	1916	Fighter	HORACE	Maker	People	RNAS	RENAULT	PL1	First joint design by the Brothers Henri and Maurice–thus the nickname of HORACE. Whilst French Co's the brothers were English!
Donnet-Leveque	F B A	1912	Flying Boat	FRANCO	Maker	Miscellaneous	RNAS	GNOME	PR1	D-L was a French Naval Lieutenant. 1st British Services Flying Boat purchased from France. D-L later as FBA = Franco-British Aviation.
Westland	F. 20/27	1928	Fighter	INTERCEPTOR	Maker	Miscellaneous	(RAF)	MERCURY	PR1	Unusual at Martlesham Heath in 1931, but Air Ministry had now decided that future fighters should have the KESTREL eng.
Hawker	if. 20/27	1928	Fighter	INTERCEPTOR	Maker	Miscellaneous	(RAF)	JUPITER	PR1	A private venture biplane for the "Interceptor" competition. Later with a MERCURY to improve performance, but academic interest only and at Farnborough until 1931.
Admiralty/Felixstowe	F. 2A	1917	Flying Boat	BABY PORTE	Maker	Miscellaneous	RNAS/RAF	EAGLE	PL3	BABY – large a/c! PORTE from Cdr PORTE RN, who developed the AMERICA (Curtiss) to LARGE & SMALL AMERICA, and the F. 2A. Widely used and taken over by the RAF 1918–23. About 300 built. Also FELIXSTOWE.

Maker	Name	Year	Type	Nickname	System	Classification	Service	Engine	Type	Notes
Gloster	F. 5/34	1937	Fighter	UNNAMED FIGHTER	RAF	Miscellaneous	(RAF)	MERCURY	PR1	F. 5/34 was the specification to which the HURRICANE and SPITFIRE was built. The Gloster had a good performance by now the other two types were in full production. 2 built.
Blackburn	F. 7/30	1934	Fighter	INTERCEPTOR	Maker	Miscellaneous	(RAF)	GOSHAWK	PL1	Mid-wing biplane, with the engine steam condensor between fuselage & lower wing. Quick overheating, difficult to taxi and with a doubtful engine the type was abandoned without being flown.
Westland	F. 7/30	1934	Fighter	INTERCEPTOR	Maker	Miscellaneous	(RAF)	GOSHAWK	PL1	A private venture. biplane with a covered cockpit and central eng for the "Interceptor" competition. But no winners with the steam-cooled eng (adapted form the KESTREL) and the eng abandoned.
Bristol	F. 7/30	1934	Fighter	INTERCEPTOR	Maker	Miscellaneous	(RAF)	GOSHAWK	PL1	Conventional biplane, and had no cooling problem with the GOSHAWK! With its demise, Bristol again tendered with a MERCURY. But with wing flexing problems, the type was abandoned.
Fokker (Holland)	F. VII-3.M.	1924	Transport	FOKKER	Maker	Miscellaneous	(RAF)	LYNX	PR3	Dutch airliner, used by the Air Ministry with an experimental MONOSPAR wing. The LYNX engines were also modifications. The wing was a feature of the MONOSPAR range of a/c in the 1930s.
Westland	F29/27	1930	Fighter	COW	RAF	Miscellaneous	(RAF)	MERCURY	PR1	COW = Coventry Ordnance Works. The RAF were interested in a COW large calibre cannon in fighters, and ordered a/c from Westland and Vickers. Not successful, and the one Westland airframe was used for instruction.
Fairey	FAERIE QUEEN	1926	Drone		Maker	People	RAF			All radio controlled Targets were – QUEEN. Shakespeare's Faerie Queen, but a/c later changed to FAIRY QUEEN. Mod from Fairey III F, and type's 1st flight in 1926. The III series began in 1918.
Fairey	FAIREY	1917	Drone		x x x	Miscellaneous	(RAF)	EAGLE	PL1	Spencer's FAERIE QUEEN. RAF name exception-Fairey IIIF as a radio Target a/c, as later QUEEN WASP/BEE.
Rolls-Royce	FALCON	1916	Engine		Maker	Bird of Prey	RFC/RAF		PL	Bird of Prey. R-R name before 1918 system of Birds of Prey for R-R. Most famously, engined the Bristol FIGHTER. (Also Dassault-Breguet jet transport, 1976, Swedish FALKEN trainer, 1928, and Curtiss, 1923)2185 built.
Slingsby	FALCON	1939	Glider		Maker	Bird	AIR CADETS			Bird of Prey. FALCON 3 as above, and FALCON 4 of 1946 was prototype only (Also Italian Reggiane FALCO, 1938. Polish Sokol=FALCON helicopter, 1989 Gen. Dynamics FLYING FALCON, Italian Aeromere FALCO, 1955)
Miles	FALCON MAJOR	1934	Transport		Maker	Bird	RAF	GIPSY MAJOR	PL1	Miles 1st cabin a/c, popular overseas and sold to 7 countries. 19 built. and 2 impressed into the RAF.
Miles	FALCON SIX	1935	Experimental	PREGNANT PERCY. PREGGY	Maker	Bird of Prey	(RAF)	GIPSY SIX	PL1	Name from the eng, and dev into NIGHTHAWK. 1935 1st, 2nd & 3rd in the Kings Cup Air Race. 1936 UK-Capetown record. 17 built, 1 to RAE for experiments with thin laminar flow wings, and known as GILLETTE FALCON.
Northrop	FALCONER	1955	Drone	PEEPING TOM *	Maker	Allegorical	ARMY	MCCOLLOUGH	PL1	In production 1958-1965. and total of 1450 built. App 50 to the British Army as *
Flight Refuelling	FALCONET	1982	Drone		Maker	Bird	ARMY	AMES INDUSTRIAL	JT1	Small or young Falcon. Launched from a circular, centrifugal runway.
Slingsby	FALKE	1968	Glider		Maker	Bird	AIR CADETS	VOLKSWAGEN	PR1	German for Falcon. Motor Glider, under licence from Scheibe.
Fairey	FANTOME/FEROCE	1935	Fighter	SCOUT	Maker	Occult	(RAF)	HISPANO-SUIZA	PL1	French 'Phantom'. Designed for the Belgian Air Force, where also known as FEROCE. Armament trials with RAF Also known as SINGLE SEAT, and HISPANO SCOUT. 2 as FEROCE sold to Russia. 4 built.
Fairey	FAWN	1923	Recon.		1921	Animal	RAF	LION	PL1	Young Deer. Landplane development of the PINTAIL. 75 built, and served in 5 RAF Squadrons. Anything but as graceful as a Fawn, and said to have the aerodynamic qualities of a half brick – a specification fault.
Vickers	FB 16D	1915	Fighter	HART SCOUT POT BELLY	Maker	Miscellaneous	(RFC)	HISPANO-SUIZA.	PL1	HART as an (unsatisfactory) eng. Tried with various emgs, and rebuilt. One of the fastest a/c of its time but one prototype only.

156

Maker	Name	Year	Type	Nickname	System	Classification	Service	Engine	Type	Notes
Vickers	FB 19	1916	Fighter	POT BELLY	Maker	Miscellaneous	RFC	LE RHONE	PR1	Also SCOUT and BULLET. 17 built. One to France(?), some to Russia and the balance to Home Defence. Said to be ineffective. (Also Northrop BLACK BULLET fighter, 1940, and Bristol Racer as BULLET, 1920)
Vickers	FB 7	1915	Fighter	HOWARD FLANDERS	Maker	Miscellaneous	(RFC)	MONOSOUPAPE	PR2	Howard Flanders was the designer. With "gunbus" experience, Vickers sought to produce a larger one with cannon and 2 engs. appearing more as a bomber. Reported as a "horrid a/c" 2 ordered but only 1 delivered.
Fairey	FD 2	1954	Experimental	DELTA TWO*	Maker	Miscellaneous	(RAF)	AVON	JT1	'DELTA' wing. World Speed Record, and first over 1000 mph with 1132 mph. 2 built and both extensively used for high speed research with delta wings, with data for CONCORDE. Dev from the smaller DELTA 1 of 1951. * FD 1 = BEAST, FD 2 = BEAUTY.
Royal Aircraft Factory	FE 2A	1911	Fighter	FIGHTER (Mk 1)	1911	Miscellaneous	RFC	BEARDMORE	PL1	Single seat "gunbus" pusher. All 12 went to France, and were used by 3 Squadrons. Not very successful, and withdrawn in favour of the FE 2b.
Royal Aircraft Factory	FE 2B C & H	1916	Fighter	FEE	1911	Miscellaneous	RFC	BEARDMORE	PL1	Also BATTLEPLANE. 2-seat Pusher with fwd Gunner. Served to end of WW I. 1939 built. (inc FE2a) and 250 FE2d. f, g & h = experimental. Standard Fighter, and night Bomber. Also night Fighter v Zeppelins.
Royal Aircraft Factory	FE 2D	1916	Fighter	FEE-D	1911	Miscellaneous	FRC	Rolls-Royce	PL1	Basically an FE 2c, but a more powerful eng. The first delivery was also its last, being behind enemy lines. 71 built, used by 10 Squadrons, and was well thought of in France.
Royal Aircraft Factory	FE 3	1913	Fighter	ARMED EXPERIMENTAL	1911	Miscellaneous	(RFC)	CHENU	PL1	An ingenious a/c with the tail boom fitting to the (rear engine) propellor boss and also with a COW (Coventry Ordnance Works) cannon, but they never dared fire it! One only.
Royal Aircraft Factory	FE 8	1915	Fighter	SPINNING INCINERATOR *	Maker	Miscellaneous	RFC	MONOSOUPAPE	PR1	Served with 4 Squadrons and also as a home trainer. Bad reputation as a "spinner", probably due to lack of spin training. Many casualties from enemy action and a/c withdrawn in 1917. 295 built. Last = 1-seat pusher. * Also SPINNING JENNY
Fairey	FELIX	1925	Engine		Maker	Animal	(RAF)		PL	Latin for 'happy'. Org Curtiss D. 12
Royal Navy	FELIXSTOWE	1916	Flying Boat	THE INCIDENCE BOAT *	Maker	Geography-Water	RFC	EAGLE	PL2	Built at FELIXSTOWE. Dev from Curtis AMERICA series. * Whilst generally noted, this may have been the individual nickname of one experimental a/c.
Curtiss	FELIXSTOWE FURY	1917	Flying Boat	PORTE SUPER BABY	R N	Allegorical	(RAF)	EAGLE	PL5	See Hawker FURY for name info. FELIXSTOWE = E. Coast RN Station. Curtis Type 7 Boat with 4PL Renault emgs suggested by Cdr. PORTE. Only 1 delivered and crashed on take off in 1919. 19 cancelled.
Fairey	FERRET	1925	Recon.		1921	Animal	(FAA)	JUPITER	PR1	Domesticated Stoat. Fairey's 1st all metal type. 3 built, but in spite of good RAF reports, there were no orders. The FERRET, in effect, was a metal version of the Type III.
Airspeed	FERRY	1932	Transport		Maker	Miscellaneous	RAF	GIPSY MAJOR	PL3	Prototype was named YOUTH OF BRITAIN I and later impressed into the RAF. Successful and 6 built. Cobham Circus, small airlines and in the Himalayas to transport pilgrims as the DRAGOMAN = interpreter or guide.
Fieseler	Fi 156	1936	Recon	STORCH.	Maker	Bird	(RAF)	ARGUS	PL1	German = Stork. Captured 1945 and evaluated at Farnbrough. Served in the Luftwaffe from 1937. About 2700 built, and remarkably versatile for low and slow flying. German rescue of Mussolini when captive in a mountain fortress.
Bristol	FIGHTER	1916	Fighter	BRISFIT BIFF	Maker	Allegorical	RFC/RAF	FALCON	PL1	See the CLASSICS, Chapter 6. 5308 built. Used by 11 Countries.
Fleet	FINCH	1937	Trainer		Maker	Bird	RCAF	RANGER	PL1	Small song Bird. USA a/c, built in Canada, training RCAF and RAF.
Blackburn	FIREBRAND	1942	Fighter	BRICK	R N	Allegorical	FAA	CENTAURUS	PR1	RN system of FIRE prefix. Later dev is FIRECREST. Org designed for the SABRE eng, which was then in short supply. 223 built. A weighty but powerful single-seat Torp. Fighter. Replaced by the Westland WYVERN.
Norman Aeroplane Co.	FIRECRACKER	1982	Trainer		Maker	Allegorical	(RAF)	PRATT & WHITNEY	TP1	Firework. Built to an RAF requirement for a turbo prop advanced trainer with jet qualities. A great flying machine, and 2 built, but lost out to the Short (Brazilian) TUCANO One private FIRECRACKER in the USA.

Maker	Name	Year	Type	Nickname	System	Classification	Service	Engine	Type	Notes
Slingsby	FIREFLY	1982	Trainer		Maker	Insect	(RAF) USAF	Lycoming	PL1	17 used for elementary training under contract to the RAF by Hunting Aircraft and registered as civil a/c. Quantity production for the USAF.
Fairey	FIREFLY (1st)	1929	Fighter		1925	Insect	RAF/FAA	KESTREL	PL1	Also FIREFLY SEAPLANE. 1931 Schneider Trophy Trainer. Standard Belgian Fighter used in 1940 against the Luftwaffe. 76 built, 25 for Belgium (also manufacture) and served in the RAF until 1932.
Fairey	FIREFLY (2nd)	1941	Fighter		R N	Insect	FAA	GRIFFON	PL1	FIRE Prefix. Also FIREFLY TRAINER. In WW II 1st Br a/c to fly over Tokyo, 1945. Dev from the FULMAR. 1707 built. Served Norway (Tirpitz). Sumatra, Far East and Korea. (Also Slingsby, 1982)
Armstrong Whitworth	FK 10	1916	Fighter	QUADRUPLANE	Maker	Miscellaneous	(RFC) RNAS	Clerget	PR1	Dev from FK9 (Fritz Koolhoven) 8 ordered, but only 3 built. An effort to do better than the Sopwith TRIPLANE! But 3 wings were better, and the FK 10s were finally used for ground target practice.
Br Aerial Transport	FK 22	1917	Fighter	BAT	Maker	Miscellaneous	(RFC)	WASP	PR1	Small biplane, pilot looking over the top wing. FK = Fredk Koolhoven, designer. 6 proptypes had a short career, due to the unreliable eng.
Armstrong Whitworth	FK 3	1915	Recon	LITTLE ACK	Maker	Miscellaneous	RFC	RAF 1A	PL1	LITTLE ACK to distinguish from the BIG ACK (FK 8). ACK = Armstrong-Whitworth, and also A in WW I military alphabet. Operational in Macedonia, otherwise trainers UK and Egypt. 488 built.
Armstrong Whitworth	FK 8	1916	Fighter	BIG ACK	Maker	Miscellaneous	RFC	BEARDMORE	PL1	Also ACKUS MAGNUS SUPERBUS. See also LITTLE ACK. Fought in 8 different roles in France and of great value in the German offensive of 1918. Also served in Macedonia and Palestine. 1143 built.
De Havilland	FLAMINGO	1938	Transport		1932	Bird	RAF/FAA	PERSEUS	PR2	Wading birds of the family Phoenicopteridae. From the Latin 'flamma', a flame (pink/red). 16 Built. and 3 impressed into the RAF in 1939. Flew Churchill, 1940, to rally the French. One used by FAA until 1954. (Also Spanish CASA and German MBB).
Airspeed	FLEET SHADOWER	1938	Recon	SHADOW	x x x	Miscellaneous	(RAF)	NIAGARA	PR4	4 engs & folding wings! High lift devices used in HORSA. Designed to cruise at 38 k, and stalled at 33k. The one prototype was not successful.
General Aircraft	FLEET SHADOWER	1938	Recon		x x x	Miscellaneous	(RAF)	NIAGRA	4PR	Name as above. Same spec and history
Fairey	FLEETWING	1929	Fighter		1927	Allegorical	FAA	KESTREL	PL1	No such bird. FAA version of the FOX and Seaplane Trainer for 1929 Schneider Trophy Race. Wooden wings and the RAF required metal, so no production orders. One only, both as land and sea plane.
British Aerospace	FLYBAC	1984	Drone		Maker	Miscellaneous	(RAF)	WEBRA	PL1	RAE evaluation with Br Aerospace. About 20 built.
Fairey	FLYCATCHER	1922	Fighter	FLY BUTTON	1921	Bird	FAA	JAGUAR	PR1	Std FAA Fighter, 1923-35. Also seaplane and amphibian. Served in RN Carriers. and also turret launched. Aerobatic, even with floats! 197 built, and a very popular a/c. Eng and propellor made a caphonic din!
Wright	FLYER	1903	Transport		Maker	Miscellaneous	(RFC)	WRIGHT	PL1	The first successful powered a/c. Short Bros built 6 later models, of which one was bought by the Hon C S Rolls, who sold it to the War Office in 1909 for £1,000. No known subsequent flight. Rolls killed 1910.
Boeing	FLYING FORTRESS	1935	Bomber	FORTRESS	Maker	Miscellaneous	RAF	CYCLONE	PR4	USA. WWII classic. US Army 8th AF daylight bombing of the Continent. Mostly RAF Coastal Command. Whilst the B-52 STRATOFORTRESS had many pungent nicknames, the B-17 was treated with great respect. 8685 built. A few still survive in the USA.
Cunliffe-Owen	FLYING WING	1939	Transport		Maker	Miscellaneous	(RAF)	PERSEUS	PR2	Experimental, but only a few built. Centre wing as part of fuselage to allow more space. Some transport work as a civil a/c.
Short	FOLDER SEAPLANE	1912	Seaplane		Maker	Miscellaneous	RNAS	GNOME	PR1	1st British successful torpedo drop in anger on Christmas Day, Cuxhaven. 2 led the Royal Fleet Review, 1914. 19 to the RNAS. Various actions, inc search for the Cruiser Konigsberg in East Africa. Some lost from HMS Hermes.
Fairey	FOX 1 & 1A (1ST)	1925	Bomber	SHINY 12	1921	Animal	RAF	KESTREL	PL1	Vulpes and related genera. Org private venture with Curtiss FELIX eng. and 50 mph faster than the RAF's FAWN. 28 built for the RAF and the nickname applied to 12 Squadron. An excellent flying machine.
Fairey	FOX II-VII (2ND)	1926	Bomber	KANGAROU MONO-FOX	Maker	Miscellaneous	(RAF)	KESTREL	PL1	With no invitation, Fairey submitted a late entry for a new Bomber. The prototype was released for demonstration in Belgium-32 served, UK and Belgian made. 9 survived, but not 1 Me 109!

Maker	Name	Year	Type	Nickname	System	Classification	Service	Engine	Type	Notes
De Havilland	FOX MOTH	1932	Transport		Maker	Insect	RN/FAA	GIPSY	PL1	From Sir Geoffrey de Havilland's interest in Moths and Butterflies. Org civil a/c, and 154 built. Basic TIGER MOTH, with outside pilot and 3 inside passengers. Some impressed in 1939 (Also Rumanian AIRFOX 1984)
Fairey	FREMANTLE	1924	Seaplane		1921	Geography	RAF	CONDOR	PL1	Seaport City in W Australia. Planned for the 1st round the world flight but not attempted as already done by 3 Douglas a/c. One of the largest 1-eng seaplanes built. To RAE for radio-navigatoon experiments. Org design was as a Fleet Spotter.
Bristol	FREIGHTER	1945	Transport	FRIGHTENER	Maker	Allegorical	RAF	HERCULES	PR2	Load carrier with nose doors, and capable of carrying cars or similar vehicles. Used for radar trials and reverted to civil status. Sold to 6 Airforces, and many civil operators. 214 built. Also known as CARTER PATTERSON, and civil = WAYFARER.
Fairey	FULMAR	1940	Fighter		1932	Bird	FAA	MERLIN	PL1	Seagull, squirts stinking oil over intruders. A/c similar to BATTLE, and dev into (2nd) FIREFLY. Whilst 602 built, it was handicapped by its 2-seat layout. Versions as night Fighters and long range recon.
Hawker	FURY (1st) (Org HORNET)	1931	Fighter		1927	Allegorical	RAF	KESTREL	PL1	See the CLASSICS – Chapter 6.
Hawker	FURY (2nd)	1944	Fighter		1939	Allegorical	RAF	CENTAURUS	PR1	Dev from the TEMPEST. Org as Tempest Light Fighter (Centaurus). 4 prototypes only – to become the SEA FURY. (Also North American FURY, 1946)
Focke Achgelis	Fa 223	1943	Helicopter	DRACHE	Maker	Miscellaneous	(RAF)	BRAMO	PR1	German = KITE. A side-by-side twin rotor. Captured 1945 and the first helicopter to cross the English Channel.
Focke-Achgelis	Fa 330	1938	Autogyro	BACHSTELTZE	Maker	Bird	(RAF)			German BACHSTELTZE = WAGTAIL. This small craft was a "U-Booysauge" or U-Boat Eye. Clever, but generally not successful. About 40 built and one captured by the RAF – and known as the FLYING DUTCHMAN. At sea it was towed by a U-Boat.
Siebel	Fh 104	1938	Transport	HALLORE	Maker	Miscellaneous	(RAF)	HIRTH	PR2	German = Citizen of Halle. 5 seater, 46 built. One captured, and used in 1945 in the communications role in the UK.
Flettner	Fl 282B	1941	Helicopter	KOLIBRI	Maker	Miscellaneous	(RAF)	BRAMO	PR1	German = HUMMINGBIRD. 2 blade intermeshing rotor. Allies considered this a "masterpiece" in comparison with others of this time. Used by the German Navy, and captured a/c evaluated by the RAF.
Focke-Wulf	Fw 189	1941	Bomber	UHU or EULE	Maker	Miscellaneous	(RAF)	ARGUS	PL2	German = OWL. Twin boom light bomber and ground attack, mostly used on the Russian front. 846 built, and 10 captured. In RAF service 1945-46. (Also nickname of the Heinkel 219) Also FLIEGENDE AUGE = Flying Eye.
Focke Wulf	Fw 190	1940	Fighter	WURGER	Maker	Miscellaneous	(RAF)	BMW	PR1	German=BUTCHER BIRD, type of Shrike. The Luftwaffe's finest fighter and in the early years only outclassed by the SPITFIRE's rate of turn. 100 SPITFIREs lost in one month. A 190 captured in 1942 and secrets found.
Focke-Wulf	Fw 200	1938	Transport	CONDOR	Maker	Bird	RAF	HORNET (BMW)	PR4	War prize 1941 as Danish Airlines DANIA. In BOAC as WOLF, and impressed into the RAF. Luftwaffe long range Reccon Bomber. Also captured 1945. Org civil with Lufthansa and 276 built for the Luftwaffe.
Focke-Wulf	Fw 58	1935	Transport	WEIHE	Maker	Bird	RAF	ARGUS	PL2	German=Kite. Captured 1945, and was evaluated at Farnborough. About 4500 built between 1935-42, and used in many roles. 8 others used by the RAF for communications (?)
Handley Page	G	1913	Trainer	HP	Maker	Miscellaneous	RNAS	ANZANI	PR1	Very similar to the German TAUBE. Biplane, one only, and taken over by the RNAS in 1914. It flew but put to no particular purpose.
Martinsyde	G 100 & 102	1915	Fighter	ELEPHANT, JUMBO, SCOOTER*	Maker	Animal	RFC	BEARDMORE	PL1	Pachydermate, related to the Mouse. A/c also known as BEARDMORE, and generally all Martinsyde a/c known as TINSIDES. * in the Middle East. SLOPPY LIZZIE to the Royal Aircraft Factory. Very successful. 101 built.
Short	G CLASS	1937	Flying Boat		Maker	Miscellaneous	RAF	HERCULES	PR4	Larger version of the C Class. 3 impressed by the RAF ex Imperial Airways – GOLDEN HORN, GOLDEN FLEECE and GOLDEN HIND, but now with RAF serial numbers. With 119 Squadron, Coastal Command.

Maker	Name	Year	Type	Nickname	System	Classification	Service	Engine	Type	Notes
Caudron	G III	1913	Reconn	SCHOOL	Maker	Education	RFC	LE RHONE	PR1	French(brothers). 2849 built, and used by Belgium, France, UK, Italy, Russia and the USA. Also flown as a Fighter/Bomber. Served in France, Mesopotomia and in E Africa seeking the German cruiser Konigsberg. Also British Caudron.
Flugbau Friedrichshafen	G III	1916	Bomber	GOTHA*	Maker	Miscellaneous	(RFC)	MERCEDES	PL2	* Strictly the contemporary Gothaer G V but became a generic term for a German heavy bomber, as HANDLEY PAGE referred to any heavy British Bomber. A long range night Bomber which also joined the G V on English raids. One shot down by AA fire over England and repaired.
Caudron	G IV	1915	Reccon	TWIN CAUDRON	Maker	Miscellaneous	RNAS/(RFC)	LE RHONE	PR2	Whilst 1358 built in France, with others in the UK and Italy, and used in France. Italy, Aegean and Russia, only 2 were ordered by the RFC. And there were no further orders.
Blackburn	G P	1916	Seaplane	GENERAL PURPOSE	Maker	Miscellaneous	(RNAS)	NUBIAN	PL2	The GP was basically the TWIN of 1915, but now with a single fuselage 2 built but with no further orders. However, the GP as a landplane became the KANGAROO, used by the RAF
Gothaer Wagonfabrik	G V	1916	Bober	GOTHA*	Maker	Miscellaneous	(RFC)	MERCEDES	PL2	The GOTHS were an early Germanic tribe later displaced by the Huns. With the Zeppelins GOTHAs brought the 1st air raids on England, leading to the withdrawal of Fighters from France for home defence. By day and then night the RFC succeeded. * term used for all big German Bombers.
Weir	GADFLY	1939	Helicopter		Maker	Insect	(RAF)	GIPSY SIX	PL1	One of a family, including the Horsefly, that bite animals. An experimental helicopter which led to later designs. (Also 1929 small monoplane by Henderson-Glenny)
General Aircraft	GAL 55	1943	Glider	TRIXIE	Maker	Miscellaneous	(RAF)			Nickname from the Specification TX.3/43. Small Glider designed as a Glider Pilot Regiment trainer for the HORSA. 2 built.
Gloster	GAMBET	1928	Fighter		x x x	Bird	(FAA)	JUPITER	PR1	Game Bird. Dev from GOLDFINCH. Sold to Japan in 1929, and foundation of their future air power. Operated only by the Imperial Japanese Navy, and 300 there built.
Gloster	GAMECOCK	1925	Fighter	FIGHTING COCK	1921	Bird	RAF	JUPITER	PR1	As the nickname. Dev of GROUSE/GREBE. 82 to the RAF, and served to 1935 as its last wooden fighter. As the Finnish KUKKO fought the Russians in 1941. 125 built. To strengthen the wing a V Strut was known as FOLLAND's (Designer) COCK's CRADLE.
Army Airship Factory	GAMMA	1910	Airship		Maker	Miscellaneous	ARMY/RN	GREEN	PL1	Greek 'C' (third), but Military Airship no 18! Rebuilt NULLI SECUNDUS. Also DIRIGIBLE No 2 . . . Then GAMMA II, to the RN in 1914 and damaged at the 1914 Spithead Review. (Also US Northrop light a/c)
Gnome	GAMMA	1911	Engine		Maker	Miscellaneous	RFC/RNAS		PR	Third letter of the Greek alphabet. This 50 hp eng was used in 19 a/c types and noted as "Gnome". GAMMA-GAMMA was the 140 hp eng! Cooling was a problem and both G and G-G could quickly seize.
Fairey	GANNET	1949	Recon	DAMMIT	R.N	Bird	FAA	DOUBLE MAMBA	TP1	Later prodn by Westland, and Early Warning (AEW). Coupled TPs so that one engine could be closed down for cruise. About 300 built, and also sold to Australia. Indonesia and W Germany. (Also Gloster 1923)
Grahame-White	GANNYMEDE	1918	Bomber		1918	Mythology	(RFC)	MAORI	PL2	Greek-Cupbearer to Zeus. A monster twin fuselage bomber, but too late for WW I, and the one "civilised".
Gloster	GAUNTLET	1929	Fighter		1932	Allegorical	RAF	MERCURY	PR1	Challenge, to throw down a GAUNTLET, from the Roman Gladiators. Dev from GREBE & GAMECOCK. 'A superb little Interceptor' and served in WW II until 1940. Sold to 6 countries, and 228 built. Dev as the GLADIATOR.
Napier	GAZELLE	1955	Engine		Maker	Animal	RAF		JT	Napier 'Arms & Weapons' ceased with the advent of jet engs.
Westland/Aerospatiale *	GAZELLE	1967	Helicopter	WHISTLING CHICKEN LEG	Maker	Animal	RAF/FAA/ARMY	RAF/ASTAZOU	TP1	Also used by Royal Marines. 294 built. Served in 1991 Gulf War. War. French Army gunship as the CANON. Sold to 6 Air Forces. *later Eurocopter.
Airco(de Havilland)	GAZELLE	1918	Bomber		1918	Animal	(RAF)	ATLANTIC	PL1	Family of small Antelopes. Basically a DH 9a. Only 1 Built.

Maker	Name	Year	Type	Nickname	System	Classification	Service	Engine	Type	Notes
Armstrong Siddeley	GENET	1925	Engine		1918	Animal	RAF		PR	One of the Felidae-cats. The GENET MAJOR appeared in 1928, to become the CIVET.
De Havilland	GENET MOTH	1925	Trainer		Maker	Miscellaneous	RAF	GENET	PR1	Standard DH MOTH with GENET Eng.
De Havilland	GHOST	1946	Engine		Maker	Occult	RAF		JT	An apparition, spirit of the dead. The 2nd DH GHOST, the 1st being a piston eng of 1928. The jet eng was very successful, some a/c being the VAMPIRE, VIXEN and COMET.
Kennedy	GIANT	1917	Bomber	WHACKER	Maker	Allegorical	(RFC)	SALMSON	PR4	Made by Fairey and the Gramophone Co. 142 ft span, but very underpowered. Kennedy worked with Sikorsky in Russia on large a/c. (Also 1911 COLLOSOPPLANE known as ELEPHANTOPLANE)
De Havilland	GIPSY	1927	Engine		Maker	Insect	RAF		PL	See the CLASSICS – Chapter 6.
De Havilland	GIPSY KING	1932	Engine		Maker	Insect	RAF		PL	"King" indicated a bigger GIPSY engine
De Havilland	GIPSY MAJOR	1931	Engine	DRIPSY MAJOR *	Maker	Insect	RAF		PL	Also bigger. * As in DRIPSY MAJOR TIGGIE (TIGER MOTH).
De Havilland	GIPSY MINOR	1931	Engine		Maker	Insect	RAF		PL	Now a smaller GIPSY.
De Havilland	GIPSY MOTH	1925	Transport	MOTH	Maker	Insect	RAF	GIPSY	PL1	Lymantria dispar. A/c founded the UK light a/c movement, and led to the TIGER MOTH RAF Std Trainer. 696 Built. The a/c that made the British Empire airminded'. A few still survive.
De Havilland	GIPSY QUEEN	1933	Engine		Maker	Insect	RAF		PL	Bigger GIPSY. RAF name for GIPSY SIX.
De Havilland	GIPSY SIX	1933	Engine		Maker	Insect	RAF		PL	Dev from GIPSY 'four' cylinders. RAF name of GIPSY QUEEN.
Gloster	GLADIATOR	1934	Fighter	GLAD, MULTI-GUN FIGHTER	1932	People	RAF	MERCURY	PR1	See Chapter 6 – the Classics.
Gloster	GLOSTER	1925	Seaplane	RACER	Maker	Miscellaneous	RAF	LION	PL1	County Town. Based on the MARS which was a land based Racer, converted into a seaplane Schneider Trophy Trainer and served until 1927. One only. As an RAF seaplane, why not a marine name?
Gloster	GLOSTER II	1924	Seaplane		Maker	Miscellaneous	(RAF)	LION	PL1	A racing seaplane for the Schneider Trophy races but came to grief. The second was a landplane of high performance, which also crashed.
Gloster	GLOSTER III	1924	Seaplane		Maker	Miscellaneous	RAF	LION	PL1	The most successful of the racing seaplanes and 2nd in the Schneider Trophy in 1925. 2 built.
Gloster	GLOSTER IV	1927	Seaplane		Maker	Miscellaneous	RAF	LION	PL1	Org monoplane and then biplane. Schneider Tropy at Venice, when one retired with propellor trouble, but record for the fastest speed for a biplane. 2 built. Also IV A & IV B.
Gloster	GLOSTER VI	1929	Seaplane	GOLDEN ARROW	Maker	Miscellaneous	RAF	LION	PL1	Schneider Trophy monoplane. Whilst having an excellent performance, there was persistent eng trouble. Withdrawn from the 1929 contest but held the Absolute World Speed record for just one hour! 2 built.
A B C	GNAT	1916	Engine		Maker	Insect	RFC		PR	Family of small flying, biting insects.
Folland	GNAT	1954	Trainer	ORPHEUS UNDERSHOOT.	1949	Insect	RAF	ORPHEUS	JT1	Prototype=MIDGE. Also GNAT TRAINER, as used by RAF Red Arrows Team. Also used as a Fighter by Finland, and manf by Yugoslavia and India (AJEET= gnat). 114 to the RAF, retired 1979. (Also civil Miles, 1925) Also nickname of ROLLER.
Gloster	GNATSNAPPER	1928	Fighter	GNAT	1921	Bird	(FAA)	MERCURY	PR1	Continental (Bee Eater) but rare UK. 1st prototype lost, and 2nd after various modifications became a Rolls-Royce 'hack' and engine testbed. Innovations included variable camber wings.
de Havilland	GNOME	1959	Engine		Maker	Occult	RAF		JT	Dwarflike creature. Later manf by Rolls-Royce. No connection with WW I Gnome, or later Gnome et le Rhone engs . . .
De Havilland	GOBLIN	1942	Engine	SUPER CRAB	Maker	Occult	RAF		JT	Mischevious Elfin. SPIDER CRAB = S/C as code for Supercharged version. (Also 1931 Grumman Biplane Fighter for Canada, USA and Spain, later Canadian Car Foundary 1938 Fighter for RCAF, and US McDonnell fighter, 1948) RCAF, US McDonnell fighter, 1948)
Caudron	GOELAND	1938	Transport		Maker	Geography-Land	RAF	RENAULT	PL2	Town in Quebec, Canada. Two aircraft escaped from France in 1940.

Maker	Name	Year	Type	Nickname	System	Classification	Service	Engine	Type	Notes
Gloster	GOLDFINCH	1927	Fighter		x x x	Bird	(RAF)	JUPITER	PR1	Fits 1921, but not 1927 System. All metal version of the GAMECOCK. Lost out to the Bristol BULLDOG. Only one built but of experimental value. Good handling, but lack of range led to just one prototype.
Gloster	GOODWOOD	1924	Transport		1921	Geography-Land	(RAF)	JUPITER	PR1	Town and Airfield, near Chichester. No further record, presumed not completed or submitted for trials?
Grumman	GOOSE	1937	Flying Boat	DUCK	Maker	Bird	RAF	WASP JUNIOR	PR2	Variety of worldwide species. USA. Org USA civil, then ordered by US Navy. 55 delivered RAF for air/sea rescue. 345 built for USA, UK, Canada and Portugal. It is still in demand, particularly in N America.
Gloster	GORAL	1927	Bomber		1926	Animal	(RAF)	JUPITER	PR	Asian goat antelope. Used DH 9a wings, and was an unlovely a/c. Lost out in competition to the WAPITI, but Gloster were rewarded by making the wings. One GORAL only.
Gloster	GORCOCK	1925	Fighter		1921	Bird	RAF	LION	PL1	Game Bird, properly Gorsecock, or Red Grouse. Based on GLOSTER I or BAMEL and modified as GUAN. Only 3 built, but well used as research tools and furthered the use of liquid cooled engs in Fighters.
Fairey	GORDON	1930	Gen. Purpose		1927	People	RAF	PANTHER	PR1	Gen. 'Chinese'GORDON, killed at Khartoum, 1895. Converted Fairey III F. 160 built. 14 serving in 1939 in the Middle East, 1 flying in 1941. 20 to Brazil and 1 to China – obviously CHINESE GORDON . . .
Gloster	GORING	1927	Gen. Purpose		1927	Geography-Land	(RAF)	JUPITER	PR1	Thames town, south of RAF Benson. 1925 requirement for a day/torpedo bomber, but order for one only. Exp float plane, and then bought by Air Ministry as Bristol eng test bed. Trials as both land and seaplane.
Rolls-Royce	GOSHAWK	1931	Engine		1918	Bird	(RAF)		PL	Bird of Prey. Steamcooled KESTREL. but not successful. Eng of the 1st SPITFIRE and other F7/30 "Interceptor"a/c. 24 built. (Also Nieuport 1920s, and US Navy Curtiss. 1932)
Grumman	GOSLING	1938	Flying Boat		Maker	Bird	FAA	RANGER	PL2	Young GOOSE. See WIDGEON. One used by the RAF at Miama.
Avro	GOSPORT	1926	Trainer		x x x	Education	(RAF)	MONOSOUPAPE	PR1	RAF GOSPORT School of Flying, where originated RAF standard training systems. Name an exception-RAF training Schools excluded by systems! No RAF order, but delivered to Peru, Estonia and Argentina.
Slingsby	GRASSHOPPER	1952	Glider		RAF	Insect	AIR CADETS	CADETS		Family of Locustidae. German fuselage + wings of the CADET. (Also Piper. 1940, and Rotorcraft, 1962)
Gloster	GREBE	1923	Fighter		1921	Bird	RAF	JAGUAR	PR1	Diving Fishers. RAF, RNZAF, + Finns fighting the Russians in 1940! Mod of MARS to dev into GAMECOCK. Also experimental for terminal velocity dives, dropped from the R 33 Airship. 133 built. Served to 1931.
Sopwith	GREEK SEAPLANE	1913	Seaplane		1913	Miscellaneous	RNAS	ANZANI	PR1	Built for Greece, but commandeered by the Admiralty in 1914.
Austin	GREYHOUND	1918	Fighter		1918	Animal	(RFC)	DRAGONFLY	PR1	Hunting and racing dog. A/c with others, victim of an unsuccesful eng – one of the blunders of WW I. But for this it might well have replaced the Bristol FIGHTER. 3 built. (Also US Grumman GREYHOUND)
R N Expr. Constr. Dept.	GRIFFIN	1918	Torp. Bomber	GRAIN or VICTORIA G.	R N	Mythological	(RNAS)	BENTLEY	PR1	Greek-winged Lion with head of an Eagle. A/c mod from CUCKOO, and made at Port VICTORIA & Isle of GRAIN.
Rolls-Royce	GRIFFON	1944	Engine		1918	Bird	RAF		PL	Bird of Prey-type of Vulture. Origins in Schneider Trophy 'R' eng. Based on BUZZARD cylinders. Powered later marks of SPITFIRE. GRIFFON is also a breed of dog. (Also French Nord GRIFFON Fighter, and US helicopter) 8108 built.
Gloster	GROUSE	1925	Fighter		1921	Bird	(RAF)	JAGUAR	PR1	Game Bird. Org a civil a/c with high efficiency wings. 3 ordered by Air Ministry for tests. 4 built, but although good reports, there were no production orders. Similar to GREBE.
Schneider	GRUNAU BABY	1932	Glider		Maker	Allegorical	AIR CADETS			Org prewar(German) built by Slingsby under licence. Postwar = EON BABY (EON = Elliots of Newbury). (Grunau is a German Town) Also GRUNAU BABY of 1953.
Gloster	GUAN	1926	Fighter		1921	Bird	(RAF)	LION	PL1	S American bird. like a Curassow. A/c=GORCOCK with LION Eng. Designed for trials of the LION with a turbo supercharger. Problems not solved, and only 2 prototypes.

Maker	Name	Year	Type	Nickname	System	Classification	Service	Engine	Type	Notes
Percival	GULL	1932	Transport		Maker	Bird	(RAF)	GIPSY MAJOR	PL1	Family name for a variety of sea birds. The mount of several long distance record seekers, and that of Jean Batten impressed into the RAF. (Also Pilcher glider, 1896, Short (Gnospelius), 1923, Canadian TRIGULL)
Slingsby	GULL	1942	Glider		Maker	Bird	AIR CADETS			Org for Prince "Bira" of Siam, then to the Air Training Corps, and thus in RAF colours. Individual name of KITTYWAKE. Rebuilt by Hawkridge A/c and also known as the HAWKRIDGE KITTYWAKE. One still flying 1986.
Vickers	GUN CARRIER	1914	Fighter	GUNBUS VICKERS PUSHER	Maker	Miscellaneous	RFC/RNAS	MONOSOUPAPE	PR1	Series FB3-6, 1st British a/c design as a fighting m/c. Downed many enemy a/c. Also STREAMLINE GUNBUS. Prototype, DESTROYER, crashed on 1st take-off, but then a successful a/c. About 210 built, inc Seaplanes.
Burgess	GUNBUS	1913	Fighter		Maker	Miscellaneous	(RNAS)	STURTEVANT	PL1	USA. Possible 1st use of the name,
Sopwith	GUNBUS	1913	Fighter		Maker	Miscellaneous	RNAS	MONOSOUPAPE	PR1	A Greek order foiled by WW 1, and taken over by the Admiralty. 23 built as trainers, but one said to have served in France.
Short	GURNARD	1929	Gen. Purpose		1927	Fish	(FAA)	KESTREL	PR1	A 'grunting' species of Fish. 2 Built, org with JUPITER eng. RAF chose the Hawker OSPREY, the two GURNARDS being used for various experiments, inc as Floatplanes. Dev from the STURGEON.
Fairey	GYRODYNE	1947	Helicopter		Maker	Miscellaneous	(RAF)	LEONIDES	PR1	Gyratory aerodyne. A hybrid helicopter with wings. Also JET GYRODYNE. Org FB1 = Fairey Bennett.
De Havilland	GYRON	1953	Engine		Maker	Miscellaneous	RAF		JT	Heraldic term, but here a made up word indicating rotation. Helicopter eng. Also GYRON JUNIOR.
Parnall	GYROPLANE	1928	Autogyro		Maker	Miscellaneous	(RAF)	GENET	PR1	Cierva C. 10 built under licence. Name open to doubt.
Curtiss	H1	1914	Flying Boat	AMERICA	Maker	Miscellaneous	(RNAS)	CURTISS	PL2	Designed for the first Atlantic flight (funded by WANAMAKER) but WW I intervened. 2 purchased (+ 1?) for evaluation by the RNAS under Cdr Porte. Prototype for the H4 – SMALL AMERICA. Beginning of a very convulated story.
Mann Egerton	H 1 & 2	1917	(RNAS)	SEABOAT SCOUT	Maker	Miscellaneous	(RNAS)	CLERGET	PR1	Designed as shipboard Fighter. Also known as SHIPBOARD SCOUT.
Curtiss	H 12	1915	Flying Boat	LARGE AMERICA	Maker	Miscellaneous	RNAS	EAGLE	PL2	Dev from SMALL AMERICA via H 4 & 12. 48 to RNAS and also used by US Navy. Anti-submarine and Zepellin patrols and shot down Zep L-22. The CONVERTED AMERICAs were a hybrid with a different hull. Also known as PORTES or FELIXSTOWE BOATS.
Curtiss	H 4	1915	Flying Boat	SMALL AMERICA	Maker	Miscellaneous	RNAS	ANZANI	PR2	Modified by Cdr PORTE. 50 for the RNAS. 1 experimental a/c as the INCIDENCE BOAT, but generally also known as the FELIXSTOWE BOATS – plenty of names to choose from! Played a great part in naval patrols, with many mods and developments to follow.
Howard Wright	H W BIPLANE	1910	Trainer	HOWARD WRIGHT	Maker	People	ARMY	E N V	PR1	English Designer & Manufacturer. A/c for Air Battalion, Royal Engrs.
Waco	HADRIAN	1941	Glider		1939	People	RAF			Roman Emperor (HADRIAN's Wall). 1st Glider towed across the Atlantic. American. Built in larger numbers than any other WW II Glider – total of 13,909! Major part in N W Europe, and also served in Burma.
Handley Page	HALIFAX	1939	Bomber	HALIBAG HALI	1939	Geography-Land	RAF	MERLIN	PL4	See the CLASSICS – Chapter 6.
Fairey	HAMBLE BABY	1916	Seaplane		Maker	Miscellaneous	RAF/RNAS	CLERGET	PR1	The 1st a/c to have wing flaps, and here differentially as ailerons. Based on the Sopwith BABY. Anti-sub patrols, and bombing in the Middle East. 180 built + 74 by Parnall and known as BABY CONVERTS.
Luke & Co	HAMBLE RIVER	1914	Seaplane		Maker	Geography-Water	(RNAS)	NAG*	PR1	River off Southampton Water. Exhibited at Olympia, and already ordered by the Admiralty. Failed to take off and sold for £30. Pemberton-Billing paid 5 Shillings for the wings. * = Neue Automobile Gelleschaft.
General Aircraft	HAMILCAR	1942	Glider	JUMBO *	1939	People	RAF			Carthaginian General, Hannibal's son Large, towed by HALIFAX with RATO-rocket assisted take off. Later with two MERCURY engs*1st Glider to carry a tank. Played a great part in the D-Day landings. 412 built.

Maker	Name	Year	Type	Nickname	System	Classification	Service	Engine	Type	Notes
Handley Page	HAMLET	1926	Transport		Maker	People	(RAF)	LUCIFER	PR3	Prince of Denmark. HAMLET is also a small village. Designed as an executive transport with an enclosed cockpit with wing slats. Later with 2 LYNX engs. Bought by Air Ministry but never flown, for reasons unknown.
Handley Page	HAMPDEN	1936	Torp. Bomber	FLYING PANHANDLE	x x x	Miscellaneous	RAF	PEGASUS	PR2	Only fits 1932 system as a 'Night Bomber', and HAMPDEN a Town in New Zealand and Canada. Or John HAMPDEN, a cousin of Oliver Cromwell? Also FLYING SUITCASE, FLYING FRYING PAN and German TADPOLE. 1432 built. Valuable in the early days of the war.
Handley Page	HANDCROSS	1924	Bomber		1921	Geography-Land	(RAF)	CONDOR	PL1	HANDCROSS, highest point on London-Brighton Road, but hardly a 'Town 3 built and tested by RAE. but the contract was won by the Hawker HORSLEY. Said that "7 furniture vans = 1 HANDCROSS".
Handley Page	HANLEY	1922	Experimental		1921	Geography-Land	(RAF)	LION	PL1	Staffordshire Pottery Town. Designed to test the HP wing slats invented by HP (and others) to offset the stall. The invention proved if not entirely approved. 3 built and 2 to Russia. See HENDON.
Hawker	HARDY	1936	Gen. Purpose		1932	People	RAF	KESTREL	PL1	Admiral HARDY, Flag-Captain to Lord Nelson at the Battle of Trafalgar. Dev from HART and built by Gloster. 50 built. In 1939 all HARDYs and AUDAXs in Middle East formed a Rhodesian Sqdn to fight the Italians.
Handley Page	HARE	1927	Torp. Bomber	RABBIT	1921	Animal	(RAF)	JUPITER	PR1	Large Rabbit. Org designed as a high altitude day Bomber, but after tests was considered as a Torpedo Bomber, and was so tested by RAE. But the VILDEBEEST was chosen, so only one HARE. (Nato code for the USSR Mi-1)
Hawker	HARRIER	1927	Torp. Bomber		x x x	Bird	(RAF)	JUPITER	PR1	Bird of Prey, reserved for Rolls-Royce Engs under 1918 system! Possibly a civil name. but a/c evaluated by the RAF. (Only 1 built, and after 1927 only production orders given RAF names)
Hawker-Siddeley	HARRIER	1966	Fighter	HAWKER HOOVER BONAJET	1949	Bird	RAF	PEGASUS	JT1	See the CLASSICS – Chapter 6 Also nickname of HUNTER JET.
Handley Page	HARROW (1ST)	1926	Torp. Bomber		1921	Geography-Land	(RAF)	LION	PL1	Greater London Town. (Also EON ETON, as also an OXFORD & CAMBRIDGE!) 3 prototypes as sea/landplanes for experimental work with slats/flaps. Recurring problems, but much useful experience and data gained.
Handley Page	HARROW (2ND)	1936	Bomber	SPARROW *	1932	Geography-Land	RAF	PEGASUS	PR2	100 built. A stop-gap heavy transport-bomber. One of the first bombers with powered gun turrets. In action against the 1940 German advances, and some lost. About 12. without turrets, as transports *
Hawker	HART	1928	Bomber	HEAVENLY HARP	1921	Animal	RAF	KESTREL	PL1	Male Deer. A/c exported to 16 Countries. Also HART TRAINER and SCOUT. More a/c of HART origin built between WW I & II than any other basic UK design. Sold to many Air Forces. 1031 built in 56 versions. RAF service to 1941. SAAF to 1943.
Hawker	HARTBEEST	1935	Bomber		1932	Animal	(RAF) SAAF	KESTREL	PL1	African Antelope. two species. Dev from the AUDAX, and 67 built for S Africa, and in service until 1946. Served in Kenya and Iraq. Was also known as HARTBEES/TE and HARTBEE. Served in E African campaign.
North American	HARVARD	1935	Trainer	J – BIRD (USA)	1939	Education	RAF/FAA	WASP	PR1	USA University. very noisy a/c, and 5135 used in RAF Flying Schools. US TEXAN. also AWFUL TERRIBLE. and MOSQUITO in the Korean War. Still (1993) used by the S A A F. Sold to 6 countries. 15,000 + built.
Handley Page	HASTINGS	1946	Transport		x x x	Geography-Land	RAF	HERCULES	PR4	Sussex Town. but should have been a 'County or District'. Based on the HALIFAX Bomber. 149 built, inc 4 for the RNZAF. Mainstay of RAF Transport Command 1949-58 – well over one million passengers, 180,000 tons cargo.
Douglas	HAVOC	1937	Bomber	MOON FIGHTER	Maker	Allegorical	RAF	TWIN WASP	PR2	Night Fighter version of BOSTON. (NATO Code for the USSR Mi-28) 5,330 built, and saw considerable service in Europe and the Pacific. Also supplied USSR.
Miles	HAWCON	1935	Transport		Maker	Miscellaneous	(RAF)	GIPSY SIX	PL1	Made up name. and not a bird. Used for drag research at Royal A/c Establishment.

Maker	Name	Year	Type	Nickname	System	Classification	Service	Engine	Type	Notes
Hawker	HAWFINCH	1927	Fighter		1921	Bird	(RAF)	JUPITER	PR1	The Common Grosbeak. HAW=fruit of the Hawthorn Tree. The one prototype used for extensive research, including sea trials, and as a seaplane. Dev into the HOOPOE.
Rolls-Royce	HAWK	1916	Engine		Maker	Bird	RFC/RAF		PL	R-R name before 1918 eng system. (Also Pilcher Glider, 1897. Hawker "Mailplane", 1927, Curtiss, 1931, Sikorsky/Westland Helicopter, 1989, US DKS GOLDEN HAWK, and abandoned Avro Fighter, 1932) 201 built.
Hawker Siddeley (BAe)	HAWK	1974	Trainer		R A F	Bird	RAF	ADOUR	JT1	Bird of Prey. Org suggested TERCEL (male Hawk). Red Arrows mount. US Navy=GOSHAWK. Sold to 10 countries. Later models have combat status. 208 for RAF(1992) (USA HAWK missile = Homing All The Way Killer)
Curtiss	HAWK	1923	Fighter		Maker	Bird	RAF	CHIEFTAN	PR1	Long line of development, from P1 of 1923 to P23 of 1935. Last US Biplane Fighter and one taken on charge in India
Avro	HAWK	1929	Recon		x x x	Bird	(RAF)	PANTHER	PR1	Bird of Prey. x x x as trespass on the Rolls-Royce 1918 naming allocation! Variant of the ANTELOPE. The 1932 Avro HAWK Fighter was not completed. (Also civil Miles, 1932)
Miles	HAWK MAJOR	1936	Transport		Maker	Bird	RAF	GIPSY MAJOR	PL1	Bird of Prey. HAWK with a Gipsy MAJOR.
Miles	HAWK TRAINER	1934	Trainer		Maker	Bird	RAF	GIPSY MAJOR	PL1	Civil a/c and 9 impressed into the RAF 1940. Dev from HAWK MAJOR, and final dev as MAGISTER. Early tests on flying a/c into Balloon cables! 26 built.
Parnall	HECK	1934	Transport	OWL	Maker	Miscellaneous	(RAF)	GIPSY SIX	PL1	Euphemism for Hell! eg; goes like Hell. Also known as HENDY HECK-Basil HENDERSON, Designer. Built by Westland. Also 1938 HECK(Mk III) but a Trainer. 3 impressed into the RAF in 1940. Record UK-Cape Town 1935.
Hawker	HECTOR	1936	Army Co-op.		RAF	Mythology	RAF	DAGGER	PL1	Greek-son of Priam, King of Troy. Replaced AUDAX, and prototype as DAGGER HART. 179 built. 6 HECTORs saw war service as dive bombers during the German advance on Calais in 1940. Later glider/target towers.
Hawker	HEDGEHOG	1924	Recon		1921	Animal	(RAF)	JUPITER	PR1	HEDGE (habitat) + HOG (Piglike face) Good RAF test reports, but not good enough to beat the opposition. One built, converted to an amphibian but wrecked.
Isacco	HELIOGYRE	1929	Autogyro		1929	Miscallaneous	(RAF)	CHERUB	PR2	Made up word. Helicopter & Autogyro not then used names. One engine on the end of each rotor blade.
Grumman	HELLCAT	1942	Fighter		Maker	Allegorical	FAA	DOUBLE WASP	PR1	Furious and evil Woman. USA. Widely used a/c. and 12,275 built. Had the highest 'kill' ratio of WW II, with 4,947 victories. CAT was a generic name for all Grumman Fighters. About 1180 for FAA. org 252 as GANNET.
Curtiss	HELLDIVER	1940	Dive Bomber		Maker	Miscellaneous	FAA	DOUBLE WASP	PR1	Made up name, and previously used by Curtiss. 7200 built, and mostly used in the Pacific campaigns. Purchased by 8 countries, and in use until 1949. 2 previous HELLDIVERs. Marine Corps version of 3rd = SHRIKE (bird)
Fairey	HENDON	1930	Bomber		1918	Geography-Land	RAF	KESTREL	PL2	Org known as the FAIREY NIGHT BOMBER, and the RAF's 1st 'modern' monoplane. Became the HENDON in 1934 serving from 1936 to 1938. 15 built. HENDON = Town, and not Airfield but was "bending" the rules.
Handley Page	HENDON (1ST)	1924	Torp Bomber		1921	Geography-Land	(RAF)	LION	P1	Dev from the HANLEY, and also with wing slats to experiment in carrier operations on Argus and Furious. Landed with torpedo without arrestor wires. 1927 saw the final and simple solution in automatic slats.
Handley Page	HENDON (2ND)	1930	Bomber		1921	Geography-Land	RAF	KESTREL	PL2	Greater London Town(not the Airfield, but could be confusing). The 1st British cantilever monoplane Bomber and Fairey's 1st heavy Bomber, and served until 1939. 14 built. And even had an enclosed cockpit!
Slingsby	HENGIST	1942	Glider		1939	People	RAF			Germanic Chieftan, with brother HORSA invaded Britain, AD 449. 16 built, but never saw service owing to changed requirement.
Hawker	HENLEY	1937	Bomber	HEN	1932	Geography-Land	RAF	MERLIN	PL1	Town on the Thames-HENLEY Regatta. Adapted from HURRICANE, but used as a Target Tower. 202 built by Gloster as sub-contractors.

Maker	Name	Year	Type	Nickname	System	Classification	Service	Engine	Type	Notes
Aircraft Manf. Co.	HENRI FARMAN	1913	Seaplane		Maker	People	RFC/RNAS	GNOME	POR	HENRI FARMAN design. Also Landplane.
Bristol	HERCULES	1935	Engine	HERC	1918	Mythological	RAF		PR	See the CLASSICS, Chapter 12. (Also the US Hughes Flying Boat of 1947, or SPRUCE GOOSE)
Lockheed	HERCULES	1954	Transport	HERK FAT ALBERT	Maker	Mythology	RAF	ALLISON	TP4	Greek-Son of Zeus. '12 Tasks of HERCULES'. USA. sold to 54 Air Forces American HERKY BIRD. with skis is the HOG. Valiant service in the 1991 Gulf War. SNOOPY as weather sampler. Used as many specialised variants. RAF now updating (1994).
Handley Page	HEREFORD	1938	Bomber		1932	Geography-Land	(RAF)	DAGGER	PL2	County Town of Herefordshire. DAGGER engined HAMPDEN. Built by Shorts. and continuing eng problems. Flown to RAE but mostly unserviceable and scrapped in 1939.
Handley Page	HERMES	1945	Transport		Maker	Mythology	(RAF)	HERCULES	PR4	Greek-Messenger of the Gods (Roman Mercurius, MERCURY). Dev from the HALIFAX, with two civil prototypes for RAE evaluation for the prototype RAF HASTINGS. 29 civil HERMES airliners flown over 14 years.
Hawker	HERON	1925	Fighter	TINCOCK	1921	Bird	(RAF)	JUPITER	PR1	Wading, fishing Bird. A/c was Sir Sydney Camm's first Fighter design. Based on the WOODCOCK, and also Hawker's 1st metal a/c. 160mph was phenomenal, but only 1 built. (Also Italian Cant AIRONE=Heron seaplane)
Royal Engineers	HERON	1882	Balloon		Maker	Bird	ARMY			One only, and probably named by Captain. The Army's fist use of gold beater's skin for the envelope.
R C S	HERON	1987	Drone		Maker	Bird	ARMY		PL1	Also HERON HS = High Speed.
De Havilland	HERON	1950	Transport	TAM'S TRAM	Maker	Bird	FAA	GIPSY QUEEN	PL4	As Above. Nickname from the Designer W A Tamblin. Basically an enlarged DOVE. Org civil a/c and 148 built. Used by many Operators at home and overseas. 5 as the SEA HERON to the FAA. Very successful. (Also Grob 115, operated by Shorts for FAA pilot evaluation, 1994)
De Havilland	HERTFORDSHIRE	1938	Transport		x x x	Geography-Land	(RAF)	PERSEUS	PR2	County, but should be Town. Military version of DH FLAMINGO. One only, and two cancelled.
Handley Page	HEYFORD	1930	Bomber	FLYING DUSTBIN	x x x	Geography-Land	RAF	KESTREL	PL2	No 'H' in 1927 system, so presumed named after obsolete 1921 system? No Heyford, but Upper (as distinct from Lower) HEYFORD, an RAF Station – not allowed! With 11 RAF Squadrons, 124 built. Also JOLLY GREEN GIANT.
Hiller	HILLER HT 1	1946	Helicopter		Maker	Miscellaneous	(RAF)	FRANKLIN	PL1	USA. Trainer.
Hiller	HILLER HT2	1954	Helicopter		Maker	Miscellaneous	RAF	FRANKLIN	PL1	USA. Training, and saw service in Borneo 1964/5.
Handley Page	HINAIDI	1922	Bomber		1921	Geography-Land	RAF	JUPITER	PR2	RAF Airfield near Baghdad in Mesopotamia (now Iraq) when this was a British Protectorate. Flew 586 passengers in 82 flight in 1929 during the relief of Kabul. 40 built, and served until 1935. Dev from HYDERABAD and into the CLIVE.
Hawker	HIND	1934	Bomber		1932	Animal	RAF	KESTREL	PL1	Female red Deer. Dev of HART. Also HIND TRAINER. 582 built, 528 for the RAF and 54 to overseas Air Forces. The RAF's last biplane Bomber. One of the classics of its day, serving to 1937. (Also USSR Helicopter, 1985)
Sopwith	HIPPO	1917	Fighter		1918	Animal	(RFC)	CLERGET	PR1	HIPPOpotamus. Greek-River Horse. Hippos + Potamus. Similar to the DOLPHIN. More powerful engines were not available, and with inadequate performance the HIPPO was cancelled. 2 prototypes only.
Admiralty	HMA NO 1.	1911	Airship	MAYFLY	Maker	Miscellaneous	(RN)	WOLSELEY	PL1	His Majesty's Airship No 1. Destroyed before 1st flight. Also NAVAL AIRSHIP No. 1 (Also Seddon MAYFLY of 1910)
Armstrong Whitworth	HMA R 33	1919	Airship	WIGGY'S ZEPP	RAF	Miscellaneous	RAF	MAORI	PL5	HMA = His Majesty's Airship. WIGGY was a bald groundsman at Bedford School, near Cardington, who spoke of my ZEPP. R33 had a good military & civil record. 1st double crossing of the Atlantic. Scrapped 1931.
Miles	HOBBY	1937	Transport		Maker	Bird	(RAF)	GIPSY MAJOR	PL1	A bird of prey of the Falcan family and a remarkable aerobat. Dev from the Miles HAWK. One evaluated by RAE, Farnborough.

Maker	Name	Year	Type	Nickname	System	Classification	Service	Engine	Type	Notes
Weltensegler	HOLS-DER-TEUFEL	1937	Glider		Maker	Geography-Land	(AIR CADETS)			Crag or lookout at the German Gliding centre at Wasserkuppe. TEUFEL = Devil or Demon, and HOLS DER TEUFEL = 'the Devil take it'. Also known as DJAVELAR ANAMMA, a Swedish curse used by two Swedish workmen.
Hawker	HOOPOE	1928	Fighter		1928	Bird	(FAA)	MERCURY	PR1	Upupa Epops, mentioned in the Bible. Dev from HAWFINCH, and 1 built. Trials on board HMS Courageous, and whilst a promising a/c, there was no production order. Flown by RAE and Armstrong Siddeley until 1932.
Hawker	HORNBILL	1926	Fighter		1921	Bird	(RAF)	CONDOR	PL1	Forest Bird of Africa, India and Malaysia. Designed for higher speeds and altitude, the a/c was better suited for research than for Squadron flying. The fastest fighter of its day, with tests up to 1933.
A B C	HORNET	1916	Engine		Maker	Insect	RFC		PR	Large, vicious Wasp. The insect was better than the eng. (Also German Glasfugel glider, US Hiller helicopter and McDonnell-Douglas 1979 jet fighter. See Me 410 HORNISSE)
Hawker	HORNET	1929	Fighter		x x x	Insect	(RAF)	KESTREL	PL1	See Hawker FURY. Under the previous naming systems the name should have been a bird. HORNET is not one, but H alliterated with H! There was much Hawker "Fury" at the name change, but Air Ministry were adamant on the new system.
De Havilland	HORNET	1943	Fighter		1939	Insect	RAF	MERLIN	PL2	Small DH MOSQUITO. Beautiful, possibly the fastest ever UK production propellor a/c. 208 Built. Operational use in the Malayan Emergency. There was also a SEA HORNET. (Also McDonnell Douglas fighter, 1974)
De Havilland	HORNET MOTH	1934	Transport		Maker	Insect	RAF	GIPSY MAJOR	PL1	Trochilium apiformis. Colouring very like a Hornet. Org civil a/c, and 165 built. 25 impressed into the RAF in 1939 for coastal patrols. Also used as a seaplane.
Airspeed	HORSA	1942	Glider		1939	People	RAF		PL1	German Chieftan. See HENGIST. Widely used – 3655 built, many by coach & furniture builders. Memorable war operations were Norway, North Africa Italy, and in the invasion of Europe after D-Day.
Hawker	HORSLEY	1925	Torp. Bomber		x x x	Miscellaneous	RAF	CONDOR	PL1	Org suggested KINGSTON, but named after HORSLEY Towers, home of Sir Tom Sopwith. World's distance record 1927. In service until 1935. DANTORP for Denmark, and also sold to Greece. 116 built.
Hawker	HOTSPUR	1937	Fighter	4-gun Turret	1932	People	(RAF)	MERLIN	PL1	Sir Henry Percy (1364-1403), known as HOTSPUR. HENLEY with 4-gun Turret. 1 built. (Name also given to the FURY Monoplane, never built, but became the HURRICANE) 1 built. Some jigs and components used for HURRICANE.
General Aircraft	HOTSPUR	1941	Glider		1939	People	RAF			Basically a pilot trainer for the larger HORSA. Carried 7 troops and could glide 83 miles from 20,000 ft. About 1000 built by furniture factories. 5 months from design to flight. Also TWIN HOTSPUR.
De Havilland	HOUND	1926	Fighter		1921	Animal	(RAF)	LION	PL1	General name or a Hunting Dog. Said to have been partly designed during drinking hours at the HOUND in Edgware. 2 Built for RAF trials, but no orders. (NATO code for USSR Mi-4)
Westland	HOUSTON-WESTLAND	1931	Transport		Maker	Person	RAF	JUPITER	PR1	Lady HOUSTON sponsored the previously named PV 3 for the 1st attempt to fly over Mount Everest. Successful, and then bought by the RAF for research at RAE and with 501 Sqdn. One only – but more thanm enough.
Hover-Air	HOVER HAWK	1970	Hovercraft		Maker	Allegorical	(RAF)	VICEROY	PR3	No bird as such. Dev from HOVERBAT & HOVERTWIN. 3 Velocette engs. 2 for propulsion and 1 for lift. To RAE Farnborough for evaluation.
Sikorsky	HOVERFLY I & II	1942	Helicopter	FLYING EGGBEATER	Maker	Insect	RAF/FAA	FRANKLIN	PL1	USA. 1st RAF and FAA Helicopter. USA as the FRUSTRATED PALM TREE. The world's 1st production helicopter. About 100 built. Org RAF name of GADFLY, reverting to above in 1945.
Handley-Page	HP 115	1961	Experimental	DELTA	Maker	Miscellaneous	(RAF)	VIPER	JT1	A trials model as a narrow delta wing for supersonic flight. Success with this "mode" led to the supersonic CONCORDE. One HP 115, and flew until 1947.

Maker	Name	Year	Type	Nickname	System	Classification	Service	Engine	Type	Notes
Handley Page	HP 21	1923	Fighter	SHIP FIGHTER	Maker	Miscellaneous	(RAF)	BENTLEY	PR1	H P pioneered the slatted wing or slot to delay the stall, and this small monoplane fighter was ordered by the US Navy for trials. 3 ordered but only one built, being tested by the RAF before despatch to the USA.
Handley Page	HP 39	1928	Experimental	GUGNUNC	Maker	Miscellaneous	(RAF)	MONGOOSE	PR1	Word from 'Pip, Squeak & Wilfrid' cartoon strip. Built for the Light Aeroplane – Guggenheim – Competition and the one prototype later bought and tested by RAE. In 1934 returned to HP, and given to Science Museum.
Handley Page	HP 42	1930	Transport	FLYING BANANA/ HAYSTACK.	Maker	Miscellaneous	RAF	JUPITER	PR4	Org Imperial Airways Airliners, and Heracles, Hano, Horsa, and Helena impressed into RAF service, 1940. 8 built for the 'Empire' routes.. "The first real British Airliner" Large and slow, but very useful.
Handley Page	HP 93	1948	Experimental	DUFAYLITE	Maker	Miscellaneous	(RAF)	GIPSY MAJOR	PL1	A/c was the Miles MESSENGER with an experimental composite wing made of DUFAYLITE (a plastic honeycomb core with an aluminium covering).
Handley Page	HP R2	1950	Trainer	BANDIT	Maker	Miscellaneous	(RAF)	CHEETAH	PR1	Robber, or outlaw belonging to a group. Origin of nickname obscure, but perhaps as 2 prototypes did not meet the 1948 official spec?
Lockheed	HUDSON	1938	Bomber	WHALE*	Maker	Geography-Water	RAF	WRIGHT	PR2	HUDSON River/Bay, after 17th C English Explorer. A/c same lineage as ELECTRA. Early, welcome and successful aid to the UK. 1st RAF victory over a U-Boat. 1946 built, and app 1500 to RAF and RAAF. Mostly coastal service. * = German
De Havilland	HUMMINGBIRD	1922	Transport		Maker	Bird	RAF	TOMTIT	PR1	Trochilidae, numerous chiefly Tropical family of New World, feeding on nectar, with very rapid wing beat. Very small a/c & eng. Launched from Airship R 33. 15 built. (Also USA Lockheed jet lift trials, 1950)
Hawker	HUNTER	1951	Fighter	MEATHOOK	1949	Allegorical	RAF/FAA	AVON	JT1	See the CLASSICS – Chapter 6.
Hawker	HURRICANE	1935	Fighter	HURRIBIRD HURRIBACK	1932	Meteorology	RAF	MERLIN	PL1	See the CLASSICS – Chapter 6.
Beagle	HUSKY	1963	Trainer		Maker	Animal	AIR CADETS	LYCOMING	PL1	Siberian 'Husky', descended from the Wolf, and trained to pull sledges over snow. One presented by Sir Billy Butlin to the Air Training Corps and named 'Spirit of Butlins'. 13 built. (Also US Fairchild. & Kama)
Handley Page	HYDERABAD	1923	Bomber		1921	Geography-Land	RAF	LION	PL2	Capital city of Sind. HP's first bomber design after WW I, and the RAF's last wooden bomber. Yeoman service in the UK, India and Iraq and served until 1934. 45 built. Dev into HINAIDI.
Bristol	HYDRA	1931	Engine		1918	Mythology	(RAF)		PR	Greek-many headed Monster. A Constellation, also known as the Snake. Eng had many piston heads.
Lakes Flying Co.	HYDRO MONOPLANE	1913	Seaplane		Maker	Miscellaneous	(RNAS)	GNOME	PR1	Civil a/c. but trained RNAS Pilots at Lake Windermere.
Peter Brotherhood Ltd	HYDROGEN	1931	Engine		Maker	Miscellaneous	(RAF)		PL	Gas. Engine used Kerosene!
De Havilland	HYENA	1925	Army Co-Op.		1921	Animal	(RAF)	JAGUAR	PR1	Carnivorous scavenger, Africa & Asia. Dev of DINGO, wild dog of Australia. 2 Built for service trials, but no orders.
Heinkel	He 111	1935	Bomber	PEDRO, ZWILLING*	Maker	Miscellaneous	(RAF)	DAIMLER-BENZ	PL2	PEDRO from the Spanish Civil War. Org civil, but bomber throughout WW II-Poland, France, Holland, Norway, UK, Russia, and torpedo bomber in the Atlantic, training to 1970. Twin fuselage=*. Jap BESS. App 7300 built. Also German SPADE.
Heinkel	He 162	1944	Fighter	SALAMANDAR	Maker	Miscellaneous	(RAF)	BMW	JT1	The VOLKSJAGER or People's Fighter was a diminutive aircraft which saw no recorded service in combat. A remarkable design, but too little and too late. 11 captured by the RAF (Also Sopwith SALAMANDER, 1917)
Heinkel	He 177	1939	Bomber	GREIF	Maker	Bird	(RAF)	DAIMLER-BENZ	PR4	German=GRIFFON. Captured 1945 and evaluated at Farnborough. Intended as replacement for the HE-111 but although about 1446 built, was never satisfactory. Planned for Germany's atomic bomb. Also LUFTWAFFENFEURZEUG. = German Airforce FIRE LIGHTER.
Heinkel	He 219	1942	Fighter	UHU MAIKAFEERFUHLER*	Maker	Bird	(RAF)		PR4	German=OWL. Captured 1945, and was evaluated at Farnborough. A fast and manoeuvreable night fighter, but production was stopped in 1944 when 219 had been built. * = Cockroach Feelers=radar aerials.

Maker	Name	Year	Type	Nickname	System	Classification	Service	Engine	Type	Notes
Morane-Saulnier	I, N & V	1914	Fighter	BULLET LE VENGUER *	Maker	Miscellaneous	RFC/RNAS	LE RHONE	PR1	BULLET was an unofficial term used by the RFC for a 'Fighter'. In limited Squadron service – said to fly like a Pig, and have the flying qualities of a Brick. Also * French = Avenger. Type N was a racer and NM = N Militaire.
Fairey	III	1918	Bomber		Maker	Miscellaneous	RAF	EAGLE	PL1	IIIA – F, 1918 – 1935. No name or nickname is a mystery, for which see the Great Un-named. Chapter 5 Part 17.
Target Technology Ltd IMP		1985	Drone		Maker	Mythology	ARMY/RN/RAF		PL1	Mischevious elf, small or young demon. Hand launched, and used by 5 other Air Forces.
Beardmore	INFLEXIBLE	1927	Experimental	IMPOSSIBLE	Maker	Allegorical	(RAF)	CONDOR	PL3	Rigid. Based on German Rohrbach design. Large, but unsuccessful. Also known as INCREDIBLE, BRITTLE and BLOODY IMPOSSIBLE, nevertheless flew well but was undepowered with little military load. One to RAE.
De Havilland	INTERCEPTOR	1929	Fighter		x x x	Allegorical	(RAF)	RAPIER	PL1	A small monoplane, built by Gloster with a Halford eng built by Napier. In RAF trials it was found to be as fast as the Hawker FURY with only 60% of the power. Only 1, as there were new speed and gun requirements.
Douglas	INVADER	1942	Bomber	L'IL RACER/HUMMER(USA)	Maker	Allegorical	FAA	PRATT & WHITNEY	PR2	A-26 Two only delivered. Probably best US attack Bomber of WWII, and also served in Korea as B-26. 2451 built, and used by many AFs
Beardmore	INVERNESS	1923	Flying Boat		1921	Geography-Water	(RAF)	LION	PL2	Scottish Royal Burgh & Port. A/c of Rohrbach design, built in Berlin and assembled in Copenhagen. 2 bought, but found to have poor performance. 1st tested to destruction and 2nd broken up.
Blackburn	IRIS	1926	Flying Boat		Maker	Miscellaneous	RAF	CONDOR	PL3	Flower, but named after a Yacht of that name. 9 built, one with a wood and 8 with metal hulls. The 1st 1918 naming system had a 'flower' code, but it was never used! Flew 11,360 mile tour to India in 1927.
Brittan-Norman	ISLANDER	1965	Transport		Maker	Allegorical	RAF/ARMY	LYCOMING	PR2	Org civil, widely used, and designed in the Isle of Wight. B-N now owned by Swiss Pilatus. RAF purchase 1990. See also maritime DEFENDER. Sold to 30 countries.
Curtiss	J & N = JENNY	1911	Trainer	JENNY THE TIN FORD	Maker	Miscellaneous	RAF/RNAS	CURTISS	PL1	Legend of early US aviation, and in service until 1927. Canadian built = CANUCK. With Hispano eng=HISSO JENNY About 10,000 built, 200 to UK. Post war the great US "barnstormer". Trained app 95% US/Canadian WWI pilots.
Jacobs A/c Eng Co	JACOBS	1936	Engine		Maker	People	RAF		PR	Series of piston radial engs, mostly for training a/c and produced in quantity for the US Forces in WW II. Of RAF note-engined the Canadian Avro ANSON.
Armstrong Siddeley	JAGUAR	1919	Engine	JAG	1918	Animal	RAF		PR	Central America large Cat. Felidae Org Royal A/c Factory RAF 8. Possibly the best aero eng until 1922, and powered 14 RAF() & FAA () a/c. JAGUAR MAJOR=2nd TIGER. (Also Grumman exp Fighter, 1949)
Sepecat	JAGUAR	1968	Fighter	WHEELBARROW BOMBER	Maker	Animal	RAF	ADOUR	JT2	NATO Fighter. Consortium of BAeS, Dessault and Breguet. JAGUAR the same word in English & French. Served 1991 Gulf War as the BOMB TRUCK. 208 for RAF(1992) Overseas as J INTERNATIONAL. Also known as PUSSY CAT.
Schempp-Hirth	JANUS	1974	Glider		Maker	Mythology	AIR CADETS		JT2	Roman God of gates & doorways, depicted with faces looking in opposite directions. German manf. and all Company names ended in 'us', as NIMBUS, DISCUS, CIRRUS and VENTUS.
Gloster	JAVELIN	1951	Fighter	HARMONIOUS DRAGMASTER	1949	Weapon	RAF	SAPPHIRE	JT2	Throwing Spear. Delta wing, and nickname from sound with open cannon ports. Also FLYING FLAT IRON and ACE OF SPADES. Also THIN WING JAVELIN variant. Served for 11 years. and 412 built. See Gloster ACE. (Also Fairey eng, 1932)
Hunting-Percival	JET PROVOST	1954	Trainer		1949	Education	RAF	VIPER	JT1	Head of some Cambridge & Oxford Colleges. Org piston eng PROVOST. RAF's 1st all-through jet Trainer. 331 built for the RAF, and export orders to 6 countries.
Handley Page	JETSTREAM	1967	Transport	ASTAZOU DOVE *	Maker	Meteorology	RAF/FAA	GARRETT	TP2	High speed, narrow airflow in the Troposphere. * as org DH design. Had a chequered career with HP. Scottish Av. and very successful with BAe. Many sold in the USA. Earlier a/c with ASTAZOU engs. 26 to FAA.

Maker	Name	Year	Type	Nickname	System	Classification	Service	Engine	Type	Notes
Government A/c Factory	JINDIVIK	1952	Drone		Maker	Miscellaneous		VIPER	JT	Australian. JINDIVIK is an Aboriginal religious term. The Hunted One. Long production run over several Marks, and still in service (1992) Currently the responsibility of Aerospace Technologies of Autralia.
Vickers	JOCKEY	1930	Fighter		Maker	People	(RAF)	MERCURY	PR1	Rider of a Race Horse. Built to F20/27 INTERCEPTOR Specn. but name given to attract potential French orders. An early monoplane design, but only one built – destroyed in a spin.
General Aircraft	JUBILEE	1935	Transport		Maker	Miscellaneous	RAF	NIAGARA	PR2	Civil a/c ordered, and 2 impressed by the RAF. See UNIVERSAL. 1935 was the year of King George's 25th Jubilee, and hence the name.
Bristol	JUPITER	1918	Engine		1918	Mythology	RAF		PR	See the CLASSICS – Chapter 6.
Junkers	Ju 352	1943	Transport	HERKULES	Maker	Miscellaneous	RAF	BMW	PR3	German = HERCULES. Designed as a successor to the famous Ju 52. 43 built. 5 captured, and 3 ferried released POWs back to the UK.
Junkers	Ju 52	1934	Transport	TANTE JU BOX	Maker	Miscellaneous	RAF	BMW	PR3	German=AUNT JU. Also IRON ANNIE and CORRUGATED COFFIN. Org civil, adapted for many military duties, inc parachute drops, for which it was first used in the Spanish Civil War. Some as RAF transports after 1945. Also German BOX
Junkers	Ju 88	1938	Bomber	WUNDER/SCHNELL BOMBER	Maker	Miscellaneous	(RAF)	JUMO	PL2	German=Fast Bomber. In 1939 had the same speed as the then HURRICANE! A mainstay of the Luftwaffe, 15000+ built, but many problems in some operational roles. Also known as the FLYING BARN DOOR. Jap Code=TRIXIE. German= THE 3 FINGERED 88.
Junkers & Focke-Wulf Ju 88 + Me 109	MISTEL	1943	Composite	MISTEL	Maker	Miscellaneous	(RAF)		PR	German = MISTLETOE. A composite with a top mounted Focke-Wulf 190, whose pilot released the Ju 88 as a flying bomb. 15,000+Ju 88 were built and the Fw 190 was the Luftwaffe's best piston eng Fighter.
Blackburn	KANGAROO	1917	Bomber	HOPPER	1918	Animal	RAF	FALCON	PL2	Australian marsupial, native name. Dev from 'General Purpose' Seaplane (ordered by the RNAS), and much used on N Sea anti-submarine patrol. 20 built. (Also Italian Savoia-Marchetti CANGURU Bomber, 1938)
Boeing-Stearman	KAYDET	1942	Trainer	YELLOW PERIL	Maker	Allegorical	(RAF) RCAF	CONTINENTAL	PR1	Made up name suggesting 'cadet' American. and ex US Air Corps. All Trainers generally painted yellow.. so a common nickname. (Also US Naval Aircraft Factory N3N Trainer as YELLOW PERIL, 1934)
Miles	KESTREL	1937	Trainer		Maker	Bird	(RAF)	KESTREL	PL1	Bird of Prey. Civil prototype, to become MASTER. A private venture in advance of official thinking, and backed by Rolls-Royce. The first RAF a/c to exceed 300mph. a great advance from the biplane trainers.
Rolls-Royce	KESTREL	1927	Engine		1918	Bird	RAF		PL	Also known as WINDHOVER. Originally the F eng. and named as KESTREL in 1930. One of the mainstay engs for many a/c in the RAF at this period. Steamcooled = GOSHAWK, and enlarged = BUZZARD. 4750 built. (Also civil Austin, 1920)
Hawker-Siddeley	KESTREL	1960	Fighter		RAF	Bird	(RAF)	PEGASUS	JT1	P1127, VTOL, org of the classic HARRIER. (See CLASSICS) 9 built. Evaluated by a mixed British, American and German Squadron, but the RAF had already placed an order for HARRIER. PEGASUS = 2nd Bristol eng name.
Power Chute Systems	KESTREL	1988	Parachute		Maker	Bird	(RAF/ ARMY)	ROTAX	PL1	Dev from the 1-seater RAIDER. Military evaluation as at 1991, and the parachute made by Harley Parachutes
Schempp-Hirth	KESTREL	1969	Glider		Maker	Bird	(AIR CADETS)			KESTREL is not a German word, so the name was presumably British. Built by Slingsby from 1970. (Also German Glasfugel glider)
Mitsubishi	KI-46	1939	Recon	DINAH*	Maker	Miscellaneous	(RAF)			*strictly not a nickname but an Allied code. Successful, long range and "Blenheim" of its time, being faster than the Fighters. Used through the Pacific war. 1742 built. One RAF evaluated, now at RAF Museum, Cosford.
Bell	KING COBRA	1938	Fighter		Maker	Reptile	(RAF)	ALLISON	PL1	American. Dev from AIRACOBRA. Ex USAF for RAF evaluation, but not ordered. Most delivered to the USSR with a smaller number (330) to the Free French Air Force.
Vought-Sikorsky	KINGFISHER	1938	Seaplane		Maker	Bird	FAA	WASP JUNIOR	PR1	Family of river Fishers. US Navy's 1st catapult launched monoplane. 1519 built, of which the FAA had 100. Used throughout WW II on Fleet duties, and used by 8 Countries. (Also US Anderson amphibian)

Maker	Name	Year	Type	Nickname	System	Classification	Service	Engine	Type	Notes
English Electric	KINGSTON	1924	Flying Boat		1921	Geography-Water	(RAF)	LION	PL2	Kingston-on-Thames, where Phoenix CORK (org of KINGSTON) was built. 5 built, with various mishaps and did not meet service requirements, and EE stopped a/c work. But Mks II & III retained for experiments.
Hawker	KINGSTON	1925	Torp Bomber		1921	Geography-Water	(RAF)	CONDOR	PF	Kingston-on-Thames. Dev as HORSLEY
Slingsby	KIRBY KADET	1936	Glider		Maker	Miscellaneous	AIR CADETS			See CADET. 1937 KIRBY TUTOR also known as CADET, but not used by ATC.
Slingsby	KITE	1935	Glider		Maker	Bird	AIR CADETS			Bird of Prey, family of Hawks. Org known as the KIRBY (Yorkshire name prefix) KITE. Based on the Gruneau BABY. Also RAF Maintenance Command for early radar trials. (Also Comper, 1934)
RN Experimental Constr	KITTEN	1917	Fighter	KITTY	Maker	Animal	(RNAS)	GNAT	PR1	Young Cat. KITTEN as (Isle of) GRAIN, EASTCHURCH and PORT VICTORIA, all basically the same m/c with different Designers. One prototype of each. (Also Dart, 1937 and Curtiss racer, 1920, Browbach (Tiger) KITTEN eng)
Curtiss	KITTYHAWK	1939	Fighter	KITTY	MAKER	Geography-Land	RAF	ALLISON	PL1	N Carolina. USA. Location of 1st recognised power flight, Wright Bros, 1903. Dev of TOMOHAWK. RAF in Med and N Africa, and also with RAAF & RNZAF 3000 + to Commonwealth Forces. (Also USSR SWDNIK KANIA Helicopter, 1979)
Saunders-Roe	KITTYWAKE	1920	Flying Boat		Maker	Bird	(RAF)	WASP (ABC)	PR2	Gull. The KITTYWAKE is named after its cry. Designed as a civil boat, but only the one proptotype. (Also Shapley, 1937)
Mitchell-Proctor	KITTYWAKE	1973	Glider Tug		Maker	Bird	(FAA)	CONTINENTAL ROLLS-ROYCE	PR1	Built by RN apprentices, later with a civil registration.
Dornier	KOMET	1923	Transport		Maker	Astronomy	(RAF)	LION	PL1	German = Comet, a meteor with a tail. Dev of the 1920 KOMET. Operated by Germany, Ukraine, Switzerland as a a civil airliner, and also built in Japan. One purchased for RAE trials. A/c reassembled by Handley Page.
Mitsubishi	Ki-46	1939	Recon	DINAH *	Maker	Miscellaneous	(RAF)			* strictly not a name, but an Allied code. Long range, successful, a Japanese ''Blenheim'' and similarly faster than the Fighters. Used through the Pacific war. 1742 built and after RAE evaluation one is now at the RAF Museum, Cosford.
Morane-Saulnier	L & LA	1913	Fighter	PARASOL MORANE	Maker	Miscellaneous	RFC	LE RHONE	PR1	9 Monoplane types, & 1 Biplane. Types N, I & V known as BULLETs. Type L was the mount of Flt. Sub-Lt Warneford, winning the VC in being the first to shoot down a German Zeppelin, 1914. 171 built. French AF PARAPLUIE = Umbrella.
Short	L17	1934	Transport	SCYLLA	Maker	Miscellaneous	RAF	JUPITER	PR4	SCYLLA was a mythological monster. The sister ship was SYRINX. These 2 a/c ordered by Imperial Airways as land versions (LAND SCIPIO) of the KENT Flying Boat. SCYLLA was impressed into the RAF in 1940.
Sopwith	L R T T	1916	Fighter	EGG BOX	Maker	Miscellaneous	(RFC)	EAGLE	PL1	Long Range Tractor Triplane! To meet an impossible specn as escort fighter and airship interceptor. A gun nacelle on the top wing, but the whole concept quickly outdated with others for the specn-a strange a/c.
Voisin	LA & LA. S	1915	Fighter	GUN MACHINE CANNON	Maker	Miscellaneous	RFC/ RNAS	CANTON-UNNE	PR1	With 3 French Squadrons in 1914, and shot down 1st German a/c. 28 to the RFC, the last in 1915. 50 built in UK by Dudbridge Iron Works. RFC/RNAS service in France, Mesoptomia and for UK training.
Voisin	LA F	1914	Recon	VOISON	Maker	People	(RFC)	CANTON-UNNE	PR1	French Designer & Manufacturer.
Avro	LAKES WATER BIRD	1911	Seaplane		Maker	Miscellaneous	(RNAS)	GNOME	PR1	Designed by Capt F W Wakefield. Org landplane, but flown as a Seaplane from Lake Windermere and hence name
Gnome	LAMBDA	1916	Engine		Maker	Miscellaneous	RFC/ RNAS		PR	Greek L. This 80 hp eng was an alternative to 8 a/c of the time, and recorded as 'Gnome'. French. LAMDA-LAMDA, 1916, was 160 hp!
Avro	LANCASTER	1941	Bomber	LANC	1939	Geography-Land	RAF	MERLIN	PL4	See the CLASSICS – Chapter 6.
Avro	LANCASTRIAN	1946	Test Bed		Maker	Miscellaneous	RAF	MERLIN	PL4	Pertaining to Lancaster. Civil mod of LANCASTER. 82 Built. Used by BOAC and British South American Airways to open the post war routes. RAF transport, and test bed for NENE JT, and GRIFFON PL for the SHACKLETON.

Maker	Name	Year	Type	Nickname	System	Classification	Service	Engine	Type	Notes
Lebaudy Bros.	LEBAUDY	1910	Airship	MORNING POST	Maker	People	(ARMY)	PANHARD	PL1	French Designers & Manufacturers. A gift from readers of the 'Morning Post, but too big for its Shed and wrecked on its first flight.
Alvis	LEONIDES	1936	Engine		Maker	Astronomy	RAF		PR	Meteor showers, generally from the Constellation LEO, the Lion.
Armstrong Siddeley	LEOPARD	1928	Engine		1918	Animal	RAF		PR	Large Cat, the black variety being known as PANTHER. (Also Chichester-Miles LEOPARD, small jet a/c, 1988)
De Havilland	LEOPARD MOTH	1933	Transport		Maker	Insect	(RAF)	GIPSY MAJOR	PL1	Zeuzera pyrina. Successor to the similar PUSS MOTH. 132 built, and half sold abroad to Korea. Japan and the USA. 47 impressed into the RAF in 1939.
Saunders-Roe	LERWICK	1938	Flying Boat	FLYING PIG *	1939	Geography-Water	RAF	HERCULES	PR2	Mostly Northerly Town and Port in the UK. THE FLYING BULLDOG (German) Beset with many problems, it was an unpopular craft. A short RAF career and only 8 built. (* also the Vickers VULCAN)
Miles	LIBELLULA	1943	Experimental	TANDEM WING	1943	Insect	(RAF) (RNAS)	GIPSY MAJOR	PL1	Generic term for Dragonflys. Tandem Wing, based on Westland DELANNE. An early canard, org with 1 eng as design for FAA Fighter. 2nd with 2 engs as projected Bomber. Suggested BOAC transport with 3 jet engs.
Consolidated-Vultee	LIBERATOR	1939	Bomber	ELECTRONIC SALMON CAN.	Maker	Allegorical	RAF	TWIN WASP	PR4	See the CLASSICS – Chapter 6.
Packard	LIBERTY	1916	Engine	LIB	Maker	Allegorical	RFC		PL	Based on Daimler Mercedes eng of 1914. Used in UK and USA a/c, and made by several US Manfs. Largest US engine of its time, but heavy by European standards. DH4 in USA with this eng known as the LIBERTY PLANE.
Lockheed	LIGHTNING	1938	Fighter	FORKED TAIL DEVIL(Ger)	Maker	Meteorology	(RAF)	ALLISON	PL2	Atmospheric electrical discharge. UK order cancelled, but 3 delivered. 2872 built, and very successful with the USA in N Africa and the Pacific "Forked" = twin booms. 2 seater = CHAIN LIGHTNING.
English Electric	LIGHTNING	1958	Fighter	PIB. TUB. FRIGHTENING	1949	Meteorology	RAF	AVON	JT2	See the CLASSICS – Chapter 6.
Blackburn	LINCOCK	1927	Fighter		Maker	Miscellaneous	(RAF)	LYNX	PR1	No such bird. LYNX eng in a "BLACKCOCK", built only as the TURCOCK. the LINCOCK established a great aerobatic reputation both here and in the USA. 11 built, 5 to Japan and 2 to China. 1 built in Italy.
Avro	LINCOLN	1944	Bomber	LINC	1939	Geography-Land	RAF	MERLIN	PL4	County City of Lincolnshire. Scaled up LANCASTER for Pacific War. Also Test Bed for R-R TRENT and TYNE. Last RAF piston eng Bomber. Also to RAAF and Argentine. 624 built, some in Australia.
Napier	LION	1917	Engine		1918	Animal	RAF		PL	Large Cat of Africa & Asia. Eng name before 1914 system. Cats to A-S. Eng. Widely used, inc Seaplane Racers
Napier	LIONESS	1927	Engine		x x x	Animal	(RAF)		PL	Exception. Although pre-1918 LION, after 1918 Felidae (Cats) for A-S.
Lockheed	LODESTAR	1939	Transport		Maker	Astronomy	RAF	CYCLONE	PR2	Steering, or reference Star. USA, and dev from the civil SUPER ELECTRA. 625 military a/c built. 5 to the RAF as transports, ex BOAC. Sold to 5 countries. Similar to HUDSON, and later variants as LEARSTAR.
British Nieuport	LONDON	1920	Bomber	FIGHTING TRIPLANE	1918	Geography-Land	(RAF)	DRAGONFLY	PR2	City of, and Greater LONDON. Triplane Night Bomber. Another a/c foiled by the unfortunate eng. The nickname more appropriate to a Fighter, such as the Sopwith TRIPE.
Saunders-Roe	LONDON	1934	Flying Boat		1934	Geography-Water	RAF	PEGASUS	PR2	LONDON as a Port. 48 built. With STRANRAERs and SINGAPOREs, the last of the RAF biplane boats. An epic flight of 5 a/c to Australia 37/38 proved their efficiency. Operational to 1941, some retained as trainers.
Fairey	LONG RANGE	1928	Experimental	POSTAL	x x x	Miscellaneous	RAF	LION	PL1	1933. Distance record of 5309 miles from Cranwell to Walvis Bay. South Africa. 2 built, and very successful
Royal A/c Establishment	LRG	1927	Experimental	LARYNX	x x x	Miscellaneous	(RAF)	LYNX	PR1	Small pilotless Long Range biplane "Gun". LR + LYNX = LARYNX, an organ of the mouth. Various trials but later DEMON RAM project cancelled.
Bristol	LUCIFER	1919	Engine		1918	Mythology	(RAF)		PR	Planet Venus as the morning star. Also Archangel cast from Heaven, the Devil.

Maker	Name	Year	Type	Nickname	System	Classification	Service	Engine	Type	Notes
Westland/Aerospatiale	LYNX	1971	Helicopter	LARRY THE LYNX	Maker	Animal	FAA/ARMY	GEM	TP2	Family of wild, short tailed Cats. Also SUPER LYNX. App 380 built. Very successful RN operations in the 1991 Gulf War. (35 civil for Bristow Helicopters = TIGER). Sold to 14 countries. Also BATTLEFIELD LYNX. Later LYNX = "RELIANT ROBIN".
Armstrong Siddeley	LYNX	1923	Engine		1918	Animal	RAF		PR	One half of a JAGUAR engine, becoming the mainstay of the Company for many years. 6000+ built by 1939. The LYNX MAJOR followed in 1929, to become the CHEETAH. (Also Italian Breda LINCE = LYNX, 1937, and Gulfstream)
Westland	LYSANDER	1936	Army Co-op.	LIZZIE	1932	People	RAF	MERCURY	PR1	See the CLASSICS – Chapter 6
Bristol	M 1 C	1916	Fighter	MONOPLANE MICK	Maker	Miscellaneous	RFC	CLERGET	PR1	Monoplanes viewed with disfavour, & M1C not used on the Western Front 'one of the major blunders' . . Performance superior to biplanes, and served with distinction in the Middle East. 125 built.
Miles	M 18	1938	Trainer	TRAINER	Maker	Miscellaneous	(RAF)	GIPSY MAJOR	PL1	Improved MAGISTER as a replacement. OK'd by RAF, but decision twice rescinded in favour of the TIGER MOTH. Landing experiments with "stop" nets – only minor damage! 4 built. Miles Aircraft ceased in 1947.
Miles	M 20	1940	Fighter	MUNICH FIGHTER	Maker	Allegorical	(RAF)	MERLIN	PL1	Wooden, standby Fighter. With fixed u/c, faster than the HURRICANE. One built in two versions, but the requirement ceased with the end of the Battle of Britain. From first design to ready to fly in 65 days.
Macchi	M. C. 200	1938	Bomber	SAETTA	Maker	Miscellaneous	(RAF)	DAIMLER BENZ	PR3	Italian = LIGHTNING, the finest Italian Bomber of the war, and continued with the Co- Belligerent Air Force against the Germans in Italy in 1943. Service in Malta, Russia, Greece & N Africa. App 1000 built.
General Electric Co	MACHAN	1981	Drone		Maker	Miscellaneous	(RAF)	WAM	PL1	Hindu word for a tree top surveillance platform. Dev project with RAE Farnborough.
Miles	MAGISTER	1937	Trainer	MAGGIE YELLOW PERIL	1932	Education	RAF/FAA	GIPSY MAJOR	PL1	Latin = School Master. Monoplane basic RAF Trainer, dev from HAWK TRAINER. 1383 built. MAGGIE MATELOT (sailor in French) in the FAA. WW II RAF UK training UK mostly on the MAGGIE and TIGER MOTH. Also MAGGIBOMBER!
Boulton Paul	MAIL PLANE	1932	Transport		Maker	Miscellaneous	(RAF)	PEGASUS	PR2	Tested at Martlesham Heath 1933. Appeared to be a promising a/c, but the one crashed and the project was abandoned.
Armstrong Siddeley	MAMBA	1946	Engine		Maker	Reptile	RAF/FAA		JT	Deadly snake (1918 system allocated 'Snakes' to Wolseley engines, but Co shortly after ceased production) Also DOUBLE MAMBA. (Also Australian light a/c MAMBA, 1989)
Cody	MAN LIFTING KITE	1901	Kite	CODY	Maker	Miscellaneous	ARMY			Kites received much attention at this time, and trials also took place at sea.
Avro	MANCHESTER (1st)	1918	Bomber		1918	Geography-Land	(RAF)	DRAGONFLY	PR2	Lancashire Metropolis. Variant of the PIKE. Excellent performance and could be looped! 3 built, but too late for the war.
Avro	MANCHESTER (2nd)	1939	Bomber		1932	Geography-Land	RAF	VULTURE	PL2	Unsuccessful engs (double KESTRELs) 209 built. The LANCASTER is sometimes said to be dev from the MANCHESTER but whilst similar they were different designs. Also produced for Canada.
Sunbeam-Coatalan	MANITOU	1918	Engine		Maker	Mythology			PL	'Tribal' class, but word = spirit, used by Algonquin (American) Indians.
Handley Page	MANX	1942	Experimental		Maker	Dog	(RAF)	GIPSY MAJOR	PL2	Tailess Dog (for a tailess a/c) from the Isle of Man. The tailess concept was to reduce drag, but whilst a bold concept, it was not a success and only the prototype was built. Designed by the Austrain Lachmann.
Sunbeam	MAORI	1916	Engine		Maker	People	(RAF)		PL	'Tribal' class – New Zealand.
Miles	MARATHON	1946	Trainer		Maker	Geography-Land	RAF	GIPSY QUEEN	PL4	Scene of Greek victory over the Persians, 490BC. Messenger ran to Athens, hence a MARATHON, now a race. 25 built for the RAF as navigation trainers. Produced by Handley Page who took over Miles. 40 built.
Martin	MARAUDER	1940	Bomber	MARTIAN*	Maker	Allegorical	RAF	DOUBLE WASP	PR2	*USA + WIDOW MAKER, STUMP JUMPER, FLYING PROSTITUTE, BALTIMORE WHORE. Operated in nearly every theatre of WW II with a fine reputation. But unforgiving to the inexperienced. 4708 built.

Maker	Name	Year	Type	Nickname	System	Classification	Service	Engine	Type	Notes
Martin	MARINER	1939	Flying Boat	ANCIENT MARINER	Maker	Allegorical	RAF	DOUBLE CYCLONE	PR2	USA. Any one employed on a Ship. Mostly operated in the Pacific, and used in 6 Air Forces. 1366 built. Of which 20 to the RAF.
Gloster	MARS	1923	Seaplane	BAMEL (Mars I) *	Maker	Mythology	RAF	LION	PL1	Roman God of War (Greek Ares). See GLOSTER. NIGHTHAWK, NIGHTJAR, SPARROWHAWK and GREBE. A complicated story. MARS I sole entrant Schneider 1924/25 Races, Trainer 1925/27. * = Half Bear, half Camel. (Also German DFW, 1912, & US Martin f/boat, 1942)
Auster	MARSHALL	1948	Experimental		Maker	Miscellaneous	(RAF)	GIPSY MAJOR	PL1	Mod by MARSHALL of Cambridge, for University trials on suction lift. First flight in 1961. Successful tests with high angles of attack and low stalling speed. A fatal crash ended the experiment.
Miles	MARTINET	1942	Target Tug		x x x	People	RAF/FAA	MERCURY	PL1	Strict disciplinarian. from French General Jean MARTINET, 17th Century. Also Radio controlled = QUEEN MARTINET. 1st British purpose-built tug. 1789 built, and dev from the MASTER.
Grumman	MARTLET	1937	Fighter	PEANUT SPECIAL	Maker	Bird	FAA	CYCLONE	PR1	USA. Archaic name for a Martin. Org US WILDCAT, and FAA reverted to this name in 1944. An outstanding carrier fighter, and helped turn the Pacific tide against the Japanese. 81 French +340 for FAA. About 17, 000 built)
Martin	MARYLAND	1938	Bomber		1939	Geography-Land	RAF/FAA	TWIN WASP	PR2	US Atlantic State. Spotted 'Bismark' & 'Prince Eugen' leaving Norway, 41. About 365 built, for UK. France and S. Africa. Dev into BALTIMORE.
Miles	MASTER	1938	Trainer		1932	Education	RAF/FAA	KESTREL	PL1	From Latin 'Magister'. Dev from civil KESTREL. Also MASTER FIGHTER. Org Phillips & Powis. A very successful Trainer, and over several Marks totalled 3,302 built. Sold to 5 Air Forces. Also MASTER FIGHTER.
Sunbeam	MATABELE	1917	Engine		Maker	People	RFC		PL	Sunbeam Tribal Class. S. African. the 'disappearing ones', crouched behind their shields. Virtually a double AMAZON, giving 240 hp. Experimental use with the DH 4.
Short	MATS	1975	Drone		Maker	Miscellaneous	ARMY	NGL	PR1	MOD Military Aircraft Target System. Parachute recovery system and 50 built.
Martin-Baker Aircraft	MB 2	1939	Fighter	MARTIN-BAKER	Maker	Miscellaneous	(RAF)	DAGGER	PL1	Sir James MARTIN and Capt V BAKER. This fixed u/c monoplane was to meet an RAF spec for an 8-gun fighter. An excellent a/c but outdated by new specs which led to the SPITFIRE and HURRICANE.
Martin-Baker Aircraft	MB 3	1942	Fighter	MARTIN-BAKER	Maker	Miscellaneous	(RAF)	SABRE	PL1	A beautiful a/c with potential as a great fighter. designed for world-wide operation, high speed and to carry 8 m/c guns or 3 cannon. So it carried 6 cannon! Eng failure killed Capt Baker, and the project ended.
Martin-Baker Aircraft	MB 5	1944	Fighter	MARTIN-BAKER	Maker	Miscellaneous	(RAF	GRIFFON	PL1	The third MB fighter of WWII, but whilst of innovative design and of great promise, none succeeded. The MB 5 was at the peak of piston eng fighter design. recording 484mph. But the age of the jet eng had arrived.
Saunders-Roe	MEDINA	1926	Flying Boat		Maker	Geography-Water	(FAA)	JUPITER	PR2	River MEDINA. Isle of Wight. Attempt to break into the civil market in competition to the Vickers SWAN and with Imperial Airways in mind. Short life and no orders.
Miles	MENTOR	1937	Trainer		1932	Education	RAF	GIPSY QUEEN	PL1	Wise and trusted counsellor. Org Phillips & Powis./dev of the NIGHTHAWK. 45 built, and 5 to the RAF. Also used as a transport. (Also Beech, 1948 USAF trainer)
Miles	MERCURY	1941	Trainer		Maker	Mythology	(RAF)	CIRRUS MAJOR	PL1	Org used by Miles for communications, and rebuilt 1943 as a possible Trainer. Name then dropped as same as Bristol M. This was the M28, and later M38 = MESSENGER. (Also 1962 US space capsule)
Bristol	MERCURY	1926	Engine	MERC	1918	Mythology	RAF		PR	Roman Mercurius, Greek Hermes, Messenger of the Gods, and Planet of the Sun. Org Cosmos eng name. A famous eng and widely used. (Also Blackburn 1911, and 1923 as renamed SWIFTS to Japan. French Boisavia. 1948)
Short	MERCURY	1937	Seaplane		Maker	Mythological	RAF	RAPIER	PL4	MERCURY was flown off on the back of MAIA (EMPIRE Flying Boat) for max payload. In 1937 Capt D C Bennett flew MERCURY to S Africa to gain a world distance record. Impressed by the RAF in 1939 to 230 Sqdn.

Maker	Name	Year	Type	Nickname	System	Classification	Service	Engine	Type	Notes
Percival	MERGANSER	1947	Transport		Maker	Bird	(RAF)	GIPSY QUEEN	PL2	Fish eating Duck, also Sawbill. Dev into PRINCE.
Rolls-Royce	MERLIN	1933	Engine		1918	Bird	RAF/FAA		PL	See the CLASSICS – Chapter 6.
E H I (Westland)	MERLIN	1987	Helicopter		Maker	Bird	FAA	TURBOMECA (R-R)	TP3	Britain's smallest Bird of Prey. Not yet in service (1993). E H I = European Helicopter Industries. Replacement for SEA KING. Also ordered by Canada. (Also civil MERLIN light a/c, 1935)
Miles	MESSENGER	1942	Transport		Maker	Allegorical	RAF	GIPSY MAJOR	PL1	Designed at the request of a group of Army Officers for observation duties. Endorsed by AOP pilots, but Air Ministry angered and so no order. Later a 250 order, but only 21 built. Favourite of F M Montgomery.
Beardmore	METEOR	1928	Engine		Maker	Astronomy	RAF		PL	'Shooting Star'. luminous trail of an object entering the Earth's atmosphere. (also Sara/Seagrave M of 1931)
Gloster	METEOR	1943	Fighter	MEAT BOX THE REAPER	1939	Astronomy	RAF/FAA	WELLAND	JT2	See the CLASSICS – Chapter 6
Percival	MEW GULL	1934	Transport		Maker	Bird	(RAF)	GIPSY SIX	PL1	Achieved 236 mph in racing, and with Alex Henshaw in 1939 flew UK-Cape Town-UK in record time. This record still stands. Now with the Shuttleworth Collection. Many race and long distance successes.
Cody	MILITARY	1912	Trainer		Maker	Allegorical	ARMY	AUSTRO-DAIMLER	PL1	Full name=MILITARY TRIALS BIPLANE. See CODY (V).
D F W	MILITARY ARROW	1912	Reconn		Maker	Miscellaneous	RN	MERCEDES	PL1	German. Purchased by the Admiralty in 1914. Various UK flights up to 1915.
Bristol	MILITARY BOXKITE	1910	Trainer		Maker	Miscellaneous	ARMY	GNOME	PR1	1st Military a/c ordered by British Government. Copy of the Henri Farman but much better built, and 1st a/c to fly in India. Also early flights in Australia, Russia, Malaya, & Africa App 140 built, inc exports.
Martin-Handasyde	MILITARY MONOPLANE	1911	Trainer	TINSIDE?	Maker	Miscellaneous	(ARMY)	ANTIONETTE	PL1	2 delivered but never flown . . .? TINSIDE possibly not used until after 1914. The name Martinsyde coined about this time.
Miles	MINOR	1942	Experimental		Maker	Allegorical	(RAF)	GIPSY MAJOR	PL2	Experimental model for a proposed postwar large airliner with wing blended to the fuselage. RAF colours and serial number, but no official trials? Returned to Miles Apprentice School.
Air Navigation & Eng Co	MISTLE THRUSH	1923	Transport		Maker	Bird	(RAF)	TOMTIT	PR1	One of 1153 species of Muscicapidae ANEC were previously UK Bleriot and Spad. Made as small as possible, and the smallest a/c in RAF colours. 4 built, and 1 flying until 1937. 1 purchased for RAF trials.
North American	MITCHELL	1939	Bomber	BILLY'S BOMBER (USA)	Maker	People	RAF	DOUBLE CYCLONE	PR2	General, US Army Air Corps, advocate of air power, courtmartialled for bombing (and sinking) a target ship. Widely used. 9816 built. (NATO Code of BANK for MITCHELL used by USSR) Used by 7 Air Forces.
ML Aviation	ML-120D	1953	Drone	MIDGET	Maker	Miscellaneous	(RAF) ARMY	PICADOR	PL1	As radio controlled, why not the MIDGET QUEEN? 23 to the Army.
Curtiss	MODEL T	1916	Flying Boat	FORD	Maker	Miscellaneous	(RNAS)	CURTISS	PL4	FORD Model T Motorcar! Mystery – 230 ordered by RNAS but only 1 delivered. At the time the largest and heaviest a/c in the world, with a crew of 5. Evaluated by RNAS at Felixstowe.
Curtiss	MOHAWK	1938	Fighter		Maker	People	RAF	CYCLONE	PL1	US WARHAWK and was org delivered to France as HAWK, some diverted to RAF About 236 direct deliveries 1940. Service in E. Africa (SAAF), India and Burma – 12 Jap kills in one day. The BUMBLEBEE to the Luftwaffe. App 870 built.
Sunbeam	MOHAWK	1914	Engine		Maker	People	RFC/ RNAS		PR	North American Indian Tribe-one of the Sunbeam Tribal class engs. Alternative power plant for 6 a/c types. Used in the Russian Sikorsky Il'ya Muromets, then the biggest a/c to date.
Miles	MOHAWK (1st)	1937	Transport		Maker	People	(RAF)	BUCANEER (MENASCO)	PL1	Tribe of N. American Indians. A/c org built for Lindbergh (pilot of the first solo Atlantic flight in the 'Spirit of St. Louis'). Many fast flights in Europe, and the one to the RAF in 1940 (Also Grumann, 1961) German = BUMBLE BEE
Miles	MOHAWK (2nd)	1951	Transport		Maker	People	(RAF)	GIPSY SIX	PL1	Tribe of N American Indians. (Also French Nord airliner, 1976)

Maker	Name	Year	Type	Nickname	System	Classification	Service	Engine	Type	Notes
Miles	MONARCH	1938	Transport		Maker	Allegorical	RAF	GIPSY MAJOR	PL1	King, or Sovereign. Larger 3-seat version of the WHITNEY STRAIGHT. Some MAGISTER parts used, and 11 built. 5 impressed into the RAF in 1940.
Armstrong Siddeley	MONGOOSE	1926	Engine		x x x	Animal	RAF		PR	Snake slayer, common in India. An ichneamon, but not a 'Cat'. The DOUBLE MONGOOSE became the SERVAL.
Miles	MONITOR	1944	Target Tug		Maker	Maker	FAA	DOUBLE CYCLONE	PR2	Supervisor, as School Monitor. Org. intended as a Trainer (education)? 20 built, out of org order for 600.
Etrich	MONOPLANE	1910	Trainer	ETRICH	Maker	Miscellaneous	(RN)	AUSTO-DAIMLER	PL1	Austrian. Ordered by the Admiralty for evaluation and delivered from Vienna. Not highly regarded and dismantled in 1913.
Deperdussin	MONOPLANE	1912	Trainer	DEPERDUSSIN	Maker	People	RFC	ANZANI	PR1	French Designer & Manufacturer. An early a/c, B5 was purchased by the War Office for Aeroplane Section of the Air Battalion. A 2nd, privately owned, also purchased. Well used, but scrapped with "no monoplane" rule.
Bristol	MONOPLANE	1938	Fighter		Maker	Miscellaneous	(RAF)	MERCURY	PR1	A very promising a/c, and thought to be a "winner". The prototype was crashed in a spin. An improved type was to be designed, but the RAF call for 8-gun fighters led to the end of the project.
Arpin	MONOPLANE	1938	Trainer	ARPIN	Maker	Miscellaneous	(RAF)	CIRRUS MINOR	PL1	2-seat, early tricycle undercarriage
Handasyde	MONOPLANE	1923	Transport		Maker	Miscellaneous	(RAF)	DOUGLAS	PR2	Purchased by RAF from private Owner for evaluation. Has been recorded as the RAYNHAM Monoplane but he was the Test Pilot.
Crawford	MONOPLANE	1925	Transport	CRAWFORD	Maker	Miscellaneous	(RAF)	ABC	PL1	Designed and flown by Flt. Lt Crawford, at RAF Hinaidi. Strictly, not (RAF). RAF colours but no registration number. An off-duty hobby! Single-seat light monoplane.
Sassoon Universal Av Co	MONOPLANE	1911	Trainer	BIRDLING	Maker	Miscellaneous	(RN)	GNOME	PR1	Not strictly (RN), but used by the Naval Flying School, on loan from Frank McClean. An almost exact copy of the org Bleriot. Damaged, and the remains given to the Science Museum Short Bros copy = RN M2, 1912.
Gnome	MONOSOUPAPE	1912	Engine	MONO REGULAR	Maker	Miscellaneous	RFC/ RNAS/ RAF	REGULAR	PR	See the CLASSICS – Chapter 6.
General Aircraft	MONOSPAR UNIVERSAL	1932	Transport	UNIVERSAL	Maker	Miscellaneous	RAF	POBJOY	PR2	Org civil twin of 1932. In 1937 a tricycle undercarriage model was tested at Martlesham Heath as an RAF "tricycle" trainer. Good results but only one built. See also CYGNET. Also named JUBILEE and CROYDON. (Also Embraer trainer, 1966)
De Havilland	MOSQUITO	1940	Bomber	MOSSY MOSQUE SKEETER	1939	Miscellaneous	RAF	MERLIN	PL2	See the CLASSICS – Chapter 6
De Havilland	MOTH	1925	Transport		Maker	Insect	RAF (FAA)	CIRRUS	PL1	Org of the MOTH series, and impetus to the UK light a/c movement. Air Ministry subsidised 5 Flying Clubs to encourage flying. 1209 built, of which 146 were RAF impressed. Also sold S Africa, Australia and Iraq.
De Havilland	MOTH MAJOR	1933	Trainer		Maker	Insect	(RAF)	GIPSY MAJOR	PL1	MOTH with the MAJOR Eng. 135 Built. 10 to the RAF for conversion to the QUEEN BEE. 133 built.
De Havilland	MOTH MINOR	1937	Trainer		Maker	Insect	RAF	GIPSY MINOR	PL1	Monoplane. Smaller a/c, smaller eng. 115 built, of which 42 in Australia. 26 impressed into RAF service as Sqadron "hacks". One as an RAAF Trainer in Australia. Monoplane MOTH
Bristol	MR 1	1917	Fighter	METAL FIGHTER	Maker	Miscellaneous	(RFC)	VIPER	PL1	War Office order for a metal copy of the wooden F 2b, the BRISFIT. Two built. Whilst no production order, much was learned of metal work for the future. Also known as METAL BIPLANE.
North American	MUSTANG	1940	Fighter	FLYING UNDERTAKER	1939	Animal	RAF	MERLIN	PL1	See Chapter 6 – the CLASSICS.
Messerschmitt	Me 108	1934	Transport	TAIFUN	Maker	Meteorological	(RAF)	HIRTH	PL1	German=TYPHOON. Captured 1945, but 3 civil a/c impressed by the RAF in 1940 with the name of ALDON. About 1000 built with Luftwaffe service on all fronts except UK. Also Hawker TYPHOON, and German TAIFUN, 1988)

Maker	Name	Year	Type	Nickname	System	Classification	Service	Engine	Type	Notes
Messerschmitt	Me 109	1938	Fighter	GUSTAV EMIL	Maker	Miscellaneous	(RAF)	DAIMLER-BENZ	PL1	The standard Luftwaffe Fighter at the beginning of WWII and served on all fronts. The early rival of the SPITFIRE, which was eventually the superior. Several Me 109s in RAF hands. Also produced in Spain. German = the SQUARE 109.
Messerschmidt	Me 110	1936	Fighter	ZERSTRORER	Maker	Miscellaneous	(RAF)	DAIMLER-BENZ	PL2	German=Destroyer. Name taken from the ZESTRORER Wader and Gruppen Fighter formations. A very successful twin-eng fighter which downed many RAF Bombers, but no match for RAF Fighters. Quantity production. Captured German a/c = RAFWAFFE!
Messerschmitt	Me 163	1942	Fighter	KOMET	Maker	Astronomical	(RAF)	WALTER	RKT	German=COMET. Captured 1945 and was evaluated at Farnborough. Produced in haste from 1944, this "rocket" fighter downed many US bombers, but killed many of its own pilots, with whom it was not popular. 350 built.
Messerschmitt	Me 262	1942	Fighter	SCHWALBE STURMVOGEL*	Maker	Bird	(RAF)	JUMO	JT2	German=SWALLOW. Captured 1945 and evaluated at Farnborough. This 540 mph jet fighter could have won the war for Germany, but was hampered by High Command disinterest. 1300 built * = Stormy Petrel.
Messerschmitt	Me 323	1941	Transport	GIGANT	Maker	Miscellaneous	(RAF)	GNOME-RHONE	PR6	German = GIANT. A large glider, then with 6 engines. An easy target for cany Fighter, and not an overall success. About 100 built. One captured example at RAE Farnborough. Also German name – GROSSRAUMLASTENEGLER.
Messerschmitt	Me 410	1943	Fighter	HORNISSE	Maker	Miscellaneous	(RAF)	DAIMLER-BENZ	PL2	German = HORNET. Luftwaffe's attempt at the MOSQUITO role, but not so successful. 1160 built, and 6 flown to the UK in 1945 for evaluation. One also captured at Monte Corvino.
Mitsubishi	Mi A6M	1939	Fighter	ZERO ZEKE	Maker	Miscellaneous	(RAF)	SAKAE*	PR1	ZERO=Japanese Navy Type "0". ZEKE=Allied code. boy=fighter, girl=bomber. Also HAMP. * = Prosperity. Built for sheer performance and supreme in the earlier part of the Pacific war, with a spectacular debut at Pearl Harbour. Later built by Nakajima * One (RAF) now in Imperial War Museum.
Norman-Thompson	N 1B	1917	Flying Boat	TANDEM T N T	R N	Miscellaneous	(RNAS)	HISPANO-SUIZA	PL1	Norman Thompson Tandem! Only one.
Supermarine	N 1B	1918	Flying Boat	BABY	R N	Allegorical	(RNAS)	HISPANO-SUIZA	PL1	Designed for the requirement of an escort for the larger Flying Boats, as were the Short and Blackburn N 1Bs. The requirement was cancelled but the BABY was developed as the SEA KING and SEA LION. one built.
Westland	N 1B	1917	Seaplane	SEA SCOUT NIB	R N	Miscellaneous	(RNAS)	BENTLEY	PR1	Built to an Admiralty Spec. Also SCOUT BIPLANE. As the PUP and CAMEL could operate from ships, the small seaplane was no longer needed. As for Blackburn and Supermarine, the Westland Ni B(1) was cancelled.
Northrop	N3P-B	1937	Seaplane	NORTHROP	Maker	Miscellaneous	RAF	WASP	PR1	16 of this reconnaissance seaplane was ordered by Norway for coastal patrols, but were too late for the Nazi invasion. Transferred for Artic patrols in Iceland as a Norwegian Sqdn in the RAF.
Zander & Scott	NACELLED PRIMARY	1937	Glider		Maker	Miscellaneous	(AIR CADETS)			Comfort for the Crew . . . impressed for the RAF.
Blackburn	NAUTILUS	1929	Fighter		1921	Fish	FAA	KESTREL	PL1	'Sailing' mollusc. Greek 'nautilos', a Ship. One prototype only, but used by the FAA for communications until 1932.
Piper	NAVAJO CHIEFTAN	1970	Transport		Maker	People	RAF	LYCOMING	PL2	NAVAJO=N American Red Indian Tribe. Based on NAVAJO of 1964, and later dev as Cheyenne/Mojave TPs. Used by 15 countries.
Beech	NAVIGATOR	1937	Transport		Maker	Person	RAF/FAA			USA. 5 impressed. 2 to Prince Bernhardt of the Netherlands, 1 RAF to India and 2 FAA. See EXPEDITOR and NAVIGATOR. Also used by the RCAF.
Vickers	NAVAL AIRSHIP No 4	1913	Airship	PARSEVAL	RN	Miscellaneous	RNAS	Maybach	PL1	The designer was the German Major August PARSEVAL who in 1905 formed the "Company to Study Airships". Later built by Vickers for RNAS airship training.
Supermarine	NAVYPLANE	1916	Flying Boat		Maker	Miscellaneous	(RNAS)	BENTLEY	PR1	Designed by Air Dept. Admiralty, but handed over to Supermarine to complete design and construction. 2 prototypes ordered but only 1 built. 4 ordered from Shorts, but none built.

Maker	Name	Year	Type	Nickname	System	Classification	Service	Engine	Type	Notes
Samuel White	NAVYPLANE	1914	Seaplane	WIGHT	Maker	Miscellaneous	RNAS	CANTON UNNE	PL1	Known as DOUBLE CAMBER NAVYPLANE. WIGHT as Isle of Wight. "Vast and ponderous pusher with mediocre performance". The Sunbeam MOHAWK eng and the IMPROVED NAVYPLANE with a torpedo could not even taxi!
Royal Aircraft Factory	NE 1	1917	Fighter	NIGHTER	1911	Miscellaneous	(RFC)	HISPANO-SUIZA	PL1	NE = Night Experimental=NIGHTER Farnborough nickname=NIGHT FIGHTER 6 built, but only 4 flown.
Rolls-Royce	NENE	1944	Engine		Maker	Geography-Water	RAF		JT	3 River NENEs in the UK. Prototype built in 6 weeks. First started with an acetylene welding torch. Then probably the most powerful engine in the World.
Lockheed	NEPTUNE	1945	Recon		1939	Mythology	RAF	TURBO CYCLONE	PR2	Roman God of the Sea. Greek Poseidon. 1946 World Distance Record of 11,236 miles. One US a/c known as the TRUCULENT TURTLE. 83 built, and used by 11 countries. In the US Navy for over 20 years.
Pobjoy	NIAGARA	1934	Engine		Maker	Geography-Water	RAF		PR	NIAGARA River & Falls, between Lakes Eyrie and Ontario, USA and Canada.
Supermarine	NIGHTHAWK	1916	Fighter		Maker	Bird	(RNAS)	ANZANI	PR2	Strictly, American NIGHTJAR (jarring note), occ seen in UK. Anti-Zeppelin Quadruplane, similar to Pemberton-Billing QUADRUPLANE. Enclosed cockpit, and project abandoned.
Nieuport	NIGHTHAWK	1918	Fighter		1918	Bird	RAF	DRAGONFLY	PR1	The engine was a total disaster, and thus leading to many problems. 70 built with 54 spare airframes, but a few only used for eng testing. 13 taken by Gloster, and rebuilt as MARS VI-NIGHTHAWK and MARS X – NIGHTJAR.
Gloster	NIGHTHAWK	1920	Fighter		1918	Bird	RAF	JAGUAR	PR1	Modified Nieuport N, now known as MARS VI – NIGHTHAWK. 100 + conversions, but only 6 to the RAF. 25 to the Greek Airforce and some in service until 1938!
Miles	NIGHTHAWK	1935	Trainer		Maker	Bird	(RAF)	GIPSY SIX	PL1	Dev of the FALCON and built as a private venture, but supported by an Air Ministry contract. Variant as MENTOR 6 built, 1 impressed by RAF, and 2 to the Rumanian Air Force.
Gloster	NIGHTJAR	1921	Fighter		1918	Bird	FAA	BENTLEY	PR1	Adaption of surplus Nieuport airframes of that name but now MARS X-NIGHTJAR. 19 built, 8 RAF and then FAA as carrier fighters. In Chanak (Turkey) crisis of 1923 and served until 1924.
Bristol-Siddeley	NIMBUS	1958	Engine		Maker	Meteorology	RAF/FAA		TP	Latin 'nimbus'-heavy rain, rain cloud. Helicopter Eng.
A/c Disposal Company	NIMBUS	1919	Engine		Maker	Meteorology			PL	Another word for the halo surrounding the head in religious art. This NIMBUS had no such halo.
Schempp-Hirth	NIMBUS	1969	Glider		Maker	Meteorology	RAF/ARMY			Also MINI-NIMBUS. Won 1970 World Gliding Championship.
Hawker	NIMROD	1930	Fighter		1921	People	FAA	KESTREL	PL1	Assyrian King & Mighty Hunter. Org HN 1 = HORNET NAVAL, then NORN, from Norse mythology. FAA version of the HORNET, renamed FURY! A famous naval fighter that served until 1939. 88 built. Sold Denmark & Japan.
Hawker-Siddeley	NIMROD	1967	Recon	NIMJOB HAPPY HUNTER	1967	People	RAF	SPEY	JT4	Military (de Havilland) COMET. The name was suggested by the Author. Entered service 1969 to replace the SHACKLETON (which remained in the RAF until 1992). 46 built, and 31 updated as Mk II. A great a/c, to continue with updates. Also MIGHTY BUNTER.
Northrop	NOMAD	1938	Bomber		Maker	People	RAF/SAAF	TWIN WASP	PR1	Wanderer, of no fixed abode. 60 from the US Army Air Corps in 1940 but not used operationally and most assigned to the SAAF (Also US PareAero Trainer)
Napier	NOMAD	1950	Engine	GO MAD *	Maker	People	(RAF)		PL	High power, liquid cooled diesel. * Very noisy!
Noorduyn	NORSEMAN	1934	Transport		Maker	People	(RAF) (RCAF)	WASP	PR1	Ancient Scandinavian, Viking. Canadian. Primarily used by USA and RCAF, and exported to 9 countries. 903 built, and org civil 'bush' transport. 17 still in commercial use (1994)
Short	NORTH SEA	1916	Seaplane		Maker	Geography-Water	(RNAS)	COSSACK	PL1	Uncertain history.

Maker	Name	Year	Type	Nickname	System	Classification	Service	Engine	Type	Notes
Royal Navy	NORTH SEA	1917	Airship		Maker	Geography-Water	RNAS	FIAT	PL2	NS Type. Nos 1-16, most of these Blimps had individual names.
Short	NORTH SEA SCOUT(B)	1917	Airship		R N	Geography-Water	(RNAS)	COSSACK	PL1	NS not North Sea, but 'Non-rigid', Airship endurance ecord, 1919, 101 hours and 4000 miles.
Admiralty	NORTH STAR	1916	Airship	POLARIS	Maker	Miscellaneous	RNAS	Rolls Royce	PL2	NORTH STAR = NS = Non-rigid type. In 1919 one airship achieved an endurance record of 101 hours over 4000 miles.
Norman-Thompson	NT 4	1916	Flying Boat	SMALL AMERICA	Maker	Miscellaneous	RNAS	HISPANO-SUIZA	PL2	The nickname had no linear connection with the Curtiss Boats, and arose as 'AMERICA' represented a category and not a type. 32 ordered but only 28 delivered(?) and a further 20 cancelled. Used for coastal patrols. Experiments with Davis 2 pdr gun – but never fired!
Handley-Page	O/100	1915	Bomber	BLOODY PARALYSER	Maker	Miscellaneous	RNAS	EAGLE	PL2	With Cossack engines known as the H P COSSACK. Built to bomb Berlin, the concept backed by Churchill and 32 built. Action in France (1 Sub sunk) and in the Dardanelles. Led to the 0/400 and the HP tradition.
Handley Page	O/400	1917	Bomber	HANDLEY PAGE	Maker	Miscellaneous	RAF	EAGLE	PL2	Dev of RNAS 0/100 for RFC. Formed 1st RAF Heavy Bomber Squadrons. 507 built, UK and USA. 400 built and some flown with great success in France and the Middle East. Some postwar service, replaced by VIMY.
Rolls-Royce	ODIN	1963	Engine		Maker	Mythology	RN	ROCKET	PR	Norse deity, creator of the cosmos and of humanity. Used in SEA DART.
Airco(de Havilland)	OKAPI	1919	Bomber		1918	Animal	(RAF)	CONDOR	PL1	Rare, from the Congo forests, smaller than and related to the Giraffe. 3 Built. One for trials with RAE at Farnborough.
Elliot	OLYMPIA	1947	Glider		Maker	Geography-Land	(AIR CADETS)			City of ancient Greece, and scene of the Olympic Games. Improved version of the German DFS MEISE, and produced in conjunction with Chiltern A/c
Bristol	OLYMPUS	1950	Engine		1918	Geography-Land.	RAF		JT	Mount OLYMPUS. highest Greek mountain and home of the classic Gods – but not a star or constellation as required by the RAF naming system.
Gnome	OMEGA	1914	Engine		Maker	Miscellaneous	RFC/ RNAS		PR	Third letter of the Greek alphabet. This 50 hp eng was used in 19 a/c types and noted as 'Gnome'. GAMMA-GAMMA was the 140 hp eng! Cooling was a problem and both G and G-G could quickly seize.
Bristol	ORION (1st)	1941	Engine		1918	Mythology	(RAF)		PR	Dev into THESEUS.
Bristol	ORION (2nd)	1955	Engine		1921	Mythology	(RAF)		TP	Greek–a giant, and mighty Hunter. Constellation of ORION. (Also 1960 Lockheed transport, RAAF & RNZAF, and TP4 USN reccn 1969)
Bristol	ORPHEUS	1954	Engine		1918	Mythology	RAF		JT	Greek Poet, who ventured into Hades. Not a Star or Constellation. Several thousand built by Fiat and Hindustan Aeronautics.
Hawker	OSPREY	1928	Fighter		1927	Bird	FAA	KESTREL	PL1	(Sea) Bird of Prey. A/c an adaption of RAF HART. OSPREY to 4 Countries and 134 built. Rolls-Royce name but allowed as a sea bird of prey! R N service until 1942. One to Spain in 1936, and fought in the civil war.
Austin	OSPREY	1918	Fighter		1918	Bird	(RFC)	BENTLEY	PR1	Also known as SEA or FISH EAGLE. Triplane Fighter. One prototype only. As a private venture, Rolls-Royce did not apparently object to the bird of prey name! (Also Bell/Boeing V-22 "Tiltwing" VTOL transport, 1989)
Armstrong Siddeley	OUNCE	1920	Engine		1918	Animal	(RAF)		PR	Snow leopard. 2 opposing cylinders from the PUMA gave good results, with a small production order for light a/c.
Boulton-Paul	OVERSTRAND	1933	Bomber		1932	Geography-Land	RAF	PEGASUS	PR2	Small Norfolk seaside Town. 24 built. Followed SIDESTRAND, and SUPERSTRAND not built. Ceased 1st line service 1937. but some remained as gunnery trainers up to 1941. 1st nose turret in the RAF.
General Aircraft	OWLET	1940	Trainer		Maker	Bird	RAF	GIPSY MAJOR	PL1	Baby Owl. 1st Tricycle u/c in RAF. Dev from the CYGNET.
Airco(de Havilland)	OXFORD	1920	Bomber		1918	Geography-Land	(RAF)	DRAGONFLY	PR2	Town of OXFORD. Only 1 Built. 3 on order, but cancelled as the eng was unreliable.
Airspeed	OXFORD	1937	Trainer	OXBOX OXO	1932	Education	RAF/FAA	CHEETAH	PR2	University. Standard RAF twin trainer. Wooden structure and dev from the civil ENVOY. 8. 586 built and widely used in various roles by the RAF and the Commonwealth Air Training Schemes. Sold to 5 countries.

Maker	Name	Year	Type	Nickname	System	Classification	Service	Engine	Type	Notes
Morane-Saulnier	P	1915	Fighter	MORANE PARASOL	Makere	Miscellaneous	RAF	LE RHONE	PR1	French. High wing monoplane. 595 built and mostly used by France. Some known in France as PILOU-PILOU. Served with 2 RFC Squadrons. All a/c then sent to the UK(as trainers?)
Boulton Paul	P 111 P & A	1950	Experimental	YELLOW PERIL	Maker	Miscellaneous	(RAF)	NENE	JT1	For research into the aerodynamics of delta-wing a/c this was the 1st of only two jets designed and built by B P. Small and clean and very sensitive it was not unpleasant to fly and almost reached the speed of sound. Donated to Cranfield. and then to the Coventry Air Museum
Youngman-Baynes	P 46	1948	Experimental	HIGH LIFT	Maker	Miscellaneous	(RAF)	GIPSY QUEEN	PL6	P = Percival, and built by Heston A/c Co. Fuselage used some PROCTOR parts, with wing high lift devices.
Pitcairn	PA 39	1940	Autogiro	PINWHEEL	Maker	Miscellaneous	RAF	SUPER SCARAB	PR1	Shipped from America, some lost at sea by submarine attack. Ironic, as intended for shipboard anti-sub patrol. Two arrived in UK and used for training and radar calibration.
Bellanca	PACEMAKER	1939	Transport		Maker	Allegorical	FAA	WASP JUNIOR	PR1	USA. Impressed for RN Communications 6-seat cabin monoplane, in land or sea versions. In 1931 made a world record for non-stop endurance without refuelling. The time was 84 hrs and 33 mins!
Siddeley	PACIFIC	1918	Engine		Maker	Geography-Water	RAF		PL	Based on the Galloway ATLANTIC and, but for the Armistice would, have been produced in quantity. (Also US Wassmer, 1973).
Blackburn	PALOUSTE	1953	Engine			Miscellaneous	RAF		APU	French, licence from Turbomeca. Auxiliary Power Unit.
Parnall	PANTHER	1917	Recon		1918	Animal	RNAS	BENTLEY	PR1	Black Leopard, similar to Puma and Jaguar. Also built by Bristol. Designed as a 'Ship Plane' with folding fuselage, watertight fuselage, and flotation airbags. 150 built, service with Home Fleet Carriers.
Armstrong Siddeley	PANTHER	1929	Engine		1918	Animal	RAF		PR	Org known as JAGUAR MAJOR. (Also Grumman 1947, Vought/ Aerospatiale 1992 helicopter. later Eurocopter, and US McClatchie eng)
Parnall	PARASOL	1929	Experimental	PISS POT	Maker	Miscellaneous	(RAF)	LYNX	PR1	Parasol high wing Monplane. Moveable wing in flight with 3 incidence positions. Good performance, and to photograph wool tufts, the one prototype had a camera mounted on a pylon near the tail. Camera = pot!
Bleriot	PARASOL	1913	Transport	BLERIOT-GOUIN	Maker	Miscellaneous	RFC	MONOSOUPAPE	PR1	Mod from the standard Bleriot by Lt. GOUIN, French Army(Air), giving improved visibility. Used as a bomber and artillery spotter in France, and about 15 built. Later as trainers in the UK until 1915.
Boulton-Paul	PARTRIDGE	1928	Fighter		1921	Bird	RAF	JUPITER	PR1	Game Bird. Whilst Air Ministry had specified new and more powerful engs, these were not available when required. The one prototype used for experimental work at Farnborough.
Supermarine	PB 23 E SCOUT	1915	Fighter	SPARKLET	Maker	Miscellaneous	RNAS	LE RHONE	PR1	'Pusher Projectile', with pusher eng, claimed to be the fastest Bi-plane of its time. The project was started by Pemberton-Billing, hence PB. One prototype.
Pemberton-Billing	PB 25	1914	Trainer	PUSH PROJ. FLYING PENIS	Maker	People	RNAS	GNOME	PR1	Dev of PB 23-PUSH PROJ (Also known as SPARKLET) 20 said to have been have been ordered, but probably not all built. Not known to have seen service, and was difficult to handle
Pemberton-Billing	PB 29	1916	Fighter	QUADRUPLANE.	Maker	Miscellaneous	(RNAS)	AUSTRO-DAIMLER	PL2	Also known as NIGHT FIGHTER. Anti-Zeppelin. with long range tanks for extended patrols at height. Flown by several RNAS pilots, but the one prototype destroyed in a crash and no further interest taken.
Pemberton-Billing	PB 9	1914	Trainer	SEVEN DAY BUS	Maker	Miscellaneous	RNAS	GNOME	PR1	Said to have been designed and built in 7 days. The 1st successful 'Supermarine', which was the Co's telegraphic address. One only, used by the RNAS until 1915.
Harlow Aircraft Co	PC-5A	1938	Transport	HARLOW	Maker	Miscellaneous	RAF	GIPSY	PL1	US design, and nickname of HARLOW from the Company. 4-seat monoplane manf by the Hindustan Aircraft Co and 5 impressed by RAF India.
Centrair	PEGASE	1926	Glider			Mythology	RN			German for Pegasus, the Greek Winged Horse. Dev from the HOLS DER TEUFEL. Front spar known as the Schadelsplat = Skull Splitter.
Bristol	PEGASUS (1st)	1931	Engine	PEGGY	1918	Mythology	RAF		PR	Greek-Winged Horse, carried the Thunderbolt of Zeus. Constellation. 4 World altitude records. 20,000 + built, more under licence in 6 other countries. (Also Lockheed Tri-Star, as missile launcher, org 1970)

Maker	Name	Year	Type	Nickname	System	Classification	Service	Engine	Type	Notes
Bristol	PEGASUS (2nd)	1959	Engine		1918	Mythological	RAF/FAA		JT	VTOL engine with 4 swivelling nozzles, powering the HARRIER. Later manufacture by Bristol-Siddeley and Rolls-Royce. Proven in the Falklands campaign and with the US Marine Corps.
Hunting-Percival	PEMBROKE	1952	Transport		1949	Geography-Land	RAF/FAA	LEONIDES	PR2	County of PEMBROKEshire. Dev from civil PRINCE. RN version=SEA PRINCE and dev into civil PRESIDENT. Sold to 8 Countries, and 135 + built. H-P later as Hunting A/c.
Parnall	PERCH	1926	Seaplane		1921	Fish	(FAA)	FALCON	PL1	Freshwater Fish. Land/sea plane, with side-by-side cockpit. Only one, and was a sound a/c with a good pilot view. No orders-no Air Ministry £.
Miles	PEREGRINE	1936	Experimental		Maker	Bird	(RAF)	GIPSY SIX	PL2	Bird of Prey. A/c used for boundary layer experiments at RAE Farnborough. Pneumatic u/c reservoir topped up with a bicycle pump! One only, too busy for more.
Rolls-Royce	PEREGRINE	1937	Engine		1918	Bird	RAF		PL	Bird of Prey, PEREGRINE Falcon. Eng a modernised KESTREL. (Also USA Gulfstream. 198. American Jet Industries, 1978, and Grumman 1981) 301 built.
Bristol	PERSEUS	1932	Engine		1918	Mythology	RAF		PR	Greek-Son of Zeus, and slew the Gorgon Medusa.
Blackburn	PERTH	1933	Flying Boat		1932	Geography-Land	RAF	BUZZARD	PL3	Port & Capital of W. Australia. Larger version of the IRIS. 4 built, 3 for Squadron service, and 1 for the Marine Experimental Unit at Felixstowe. Replaced by Short SINGAPORE.
Parnall	PETO	1929	Experimental		1921	Fish	FAA	MONGOOSE	PR1	Australian 'Wahoo'. Small seaplane used in the Submarine M2, which sank, owing to open 'hangar' doors. Name fits the RAF 1921 system – but PETO = Latin 'I seek' and any connection with Sir Morton PETO?
Percival	PETREL	1938	Transport	STORMY PETREL	1932	Bird	RAF	GIPSY SIX	PL1	Family of sea birds, name said to come from St. Peter, walking on water 'Mother Carey's Chicken'/Storm P PETREL = RAF name for Percival Q6. 8 for RAF. (Also Nash light a/c, 1980 Slingsby glider, 1938, Proctor, 1972)
McDonnell-Douglas	PHANTOM	1958	Fighter	OLD SMOKEY, TOMB	Maker	Mythology	RAF/FAA	SPEY	JT2	USA. Also GHOST, SPOOK, DOUBLE UGLY and RHINO. 170 delivered RAF/FAA. Org US service in Vietnam in 1967. Total 1969 built, and sold to 11 countries. In Japan as the KAI. USA WILD WEASEL in radar attack role.
Bristol	PHOENIX	1932	Engine		1918	Mythology	(RAF)		PR	Greek-guardian of Achilles, Constellation, and Egypt mythical bird that arose from the flames) (Also 1929 Boulton Paul, and GEC-Marconi drone for the Br Army)
Heston	PHOENIX	1935	Transport		Maker	Mythology	RAF	GIPSY SIX	PL1	Civil 6-seat monoplane, and 3 impressed into the RAF in 1940.
General Electric Co	PHOENIX	1987	Drone		Maker	Mythology	ARMY	WAEL	PR1	"Battlefield Target Acquisition Surveillance System". Dev from a SUPERVISOR programme and Westland WIDEYE.
Phoenix-Dynamo	PHOENIX	1917	Seaplane		Maker	Mythology	(RNAS)	Hispano-Suiza	PI1	Long lived legendary bird which dies on its funeral pyre and is reborn from the ashes. Also a constellation.
Avro	PIKE	1916	Bomber		Maker	Weapon	(RNAS)	SUNBEAM	PL2	Most likely a Weapon(spear) but later Co. Adverts shew a Fish.? A/c dev into 1918 MANCHESTER.
Parnall	PIKE	1927	Recon		1921	Fish	(FAA)	LION	PL1	Voracious freshwater Fish. Tested at MAEE, Felixstowe. but report un-favourable (as for the STURGEON). 1st crashed, and 2nd cancelled. Designed as land/sea plane.
Fairey	PINTAIL	1921	Fighter		1918	Bird	(RAF)	LION	PL1	Species of Duck. Designed as an amphibious reconnaisance fighter for land, sea and carrier. A handsome a/c, but only 3 prototypes for the RAF. 3 orders for the Imperial Japanese Navy.
Woolwich	PIONEER	1878	Balloon	GASBAG	Maker	Allegorical	(ARMY)			Individual name, one only and so a 'type'. 1st UK mil a/c, designed by Capt. J L B Templer, costing the War Office £150! The Balloon Section of the Royal Engineers then formed.
Scottish Aviation	PIONEER	1947	Transport		Maker	Allegorical	RAF	LEONIDES	PR1	Very different from the balloon of 1878, but not the last PIONEER, the TWIN PIONEER of 1955 to follow. 53 built – RAF, Ceylon, Iran & Malaya (Also USA Northrop airliner)

Maker	Name	Year	Type	Nickname	System	Classification	Service	Engine	Type	Notes
Parnall	PIPIT	1928	Fighter		1921	Bird	(FAA)	KESTREL	PL1	Family of song birds-Meadow PIPIT. An elegant biplane, with a low speed for deck landings. Both prototypes suffered from aileron flutter, and crashed – as did Parnall's high hopes for this promising design.
Parnall	PIXIE I & II	1923	Experimental		1922	Mythology	(RAF)	DOUGLAS	PR2	Fairylike, or Elfin creature. I & II as wings & engs could be changed for required performance. Seriously considered as an RAF trainer. 2 military a/c. but ? if in RAF colours.
Parnall	PLOVER	1922	Fighter		1921	Bird	FAA	JAGUAR	PR1	Family of migrating(sea shore and moorland) birds. Lost competition to the FLYCATCHER. 14 built, and 7 for service trials on RN carriers.
Parnall	POSSUM	1923	Transport	POSTAL	1921	Animal	RAF	LION	PL1	OPOSSUM-marsupial of Aust. & N. Zeal. A 'Postal' a/c Triplane. 2 propellors on centre wing with the eng in the fuselage. No postal application, but military with 2 gun positions, and extensive tests. Flown until 1926.
Parnall	PRAWN	1930	Flying Boat		1927	Fish	(RAF)	RICARDO-BURT	PL1	Small edible crustacian. Used spare auxiliary eng from R 101 Airship. Experimental, to test pivoting eng in the nose. Built by Short Bros. One at MAEE, Felixtowe.
Avro	PREFECT	1934	Trainer		1932	Education	RAF	LYNX	PR1	Monitor, senior School pupil. Similar to the TUTOR, but a 3-seater and used as a specialist navigation trainer. 7 for RAF and 4 for RNZAF. In service to 1939. 12 exported.
Slingsby	PREFECT	1948	Glider		Maker	Education	AIR CADETS			Civil version known as the KIRBY PREFECT.
Percival	PRENTICE	1946	Trainer	CLOCKWORK MOUSE	1939	Education	RAF	GIPSY QUEEN	PL1	APPRENTICE, one learning his trade. 475 built. 1st RAF side-by-side Trainer, and from 1948-53 most RAF pilots ganied their 'wings' on this type. Supplied to Argentina, and 65 built by India.
Percival	PRESIDENT	1951	Transport		1949	Miscellaneous	RAF	LEONIDES	PR2	Elected to preside or govern. Mk V version of PRINCE. With Central Flying School, 1956.
Bristol	PRIER MONOPLANE	1911	Trainer		Maker	People	(ARMY)	GNOME	PR1	Pierre PRIER, French designer with the Bristol Co. Two for the Air Battalion, Royal Engineers, of which one passed to the RFC. Little flying due to the monoplane ban of 1913. 1st British a/c at war-in the Balkans.
Slingsby	PRIMARY	1941	Glider		Maker	Miscllaneous	AIR CADETS			Basic, first choice. Aircraft impressed by the RAF.
Fairey	PRINCE	1933	Engine		Maker	People	(RAF)		PL	Son of a King. Private venture.
Percival	PROCTOR	1939	Trainer		1939	Education	RAF/FAA	GIPSY QUEEN	PL1	University servant, resp for discipline. Dev from civil VEGA GULL, org suggested as PRECEPTOR. 1000+ built. Mostly used as a radio trainer, but later also for communications.
Percival	PROSPECTOR	1955	Transport		Maker	Allegorical	(ARMY)	CHEETAH	PR1	Designed as an agricultural transport and crop sprayer. The South African Air Force Historic Flight has one grounded PROSPECTOR.
Bristol	PROTEUS	1949	Engine		1918	Mythology	RAF		TP	Greek Sea God, who could change his appearance. Powered the BRITANNIA, and also for Industrial and Marine applications.
Percival	PROVOST	1950	Trainer	PROVO	1949	Education	RAF	LEONIDES	PR1	University Official. Dev as JET P. 18 years in the RAF and served with many Air Forces. Probably most of today's(1993) RAF pilots trained on PROVOST. 461 built, and the last RAF a/c 1969. Overseas= STRIKEMASTER.
Max Kegel	PRUFLING	1931	Glider	STUDENT	Maker	Allegorical	(AIR CADETS)			German. Examinee or Candidate. Impressed for Air Training Corps. Known as 'Kassel' PRUFLING, but this was where it was built, and there was indeed a Kegel KASSEL. Kegel later absorbed by Fiesler.
Westland	PTERODACTYL	1934	Experimental	FLYING FINGERS	x x x	Reptile	(RAF)	GOSHAWK	PL1	Prehistoric flying Reptile. One of a series of WESTLAND-HILL designs, the last being the Mk V. Org a monoplane glider of 1924. Org known as the HILL PTERODACTYL TAILLESS. Mk V was a Fighter with the GOSHAWK eng.
F M A	PUCARA	1969	Recon/ Bomber		Maker	Miscellaneous	(RAF)	ASTAZOU	TP2	Argentina – dialect word for a 'Hill Fort'. Outclassed in the Falklands War, and captured a/c for RAF evaluation. Still used by Argentina for counter-insurgency. 114 built. Org name of DELFIN.

Maker	Name	Year	Type	Nickname	System	Classification	Service	Engine	Type	Notes
Parnall	PUFFIN	1920	Fighter	PARROT	1918	Bird	(FAA)	LION	PL1	Also SEA PARROT. Family of sea birds with large, highly coloured beaks. Amphibian, with central float when a seaplane. Tail heavy and too much spray, and problems not solved. 3 prototypes.
Westland/Aerospatiale	PUMA	1965	Helicopter		Maker	Animal	RAF	TURMO	TP2	Large Am wild Cat. (Cougar, Mountain Lion). Replaced WHIRLWIND. 48 for RAF and served in N. Ireland, Germany, Cyprus, Norway (NATO), Belize and Rhodesia (now Zimbabwe). Sold to 34 countries. Also SUPER PUMA, 1977.
Siddeley-Deasey	PUMA	1916	Engine		Maker	Animal	RFC		PL	Dev from the Royal Aircraft Factory RAF 8 eng. With this established so names of the Felidae-Cats were reserved for A-S. The PUMA was built in larger quantities than any other British eng of the day.
Beagle	PUP	1967	Trainer		Maker	Dog	(RAF)	CONTINENTAL R-R	PL1	In the 'Beagle' tradition. 128 civil built by end of 1969, with 267 on order when the Company closed. Dev for RAF as the BULLDOG by Scottish Aviation. (Also US Keystone, 1929)
Voisin	PUSHER BIPLANE	1915	Bomber	VOISON	Maker	Miscellaneous	RFC/RNAS	CANTON-UNNE	PR1	French.
Robey-Peters	PUSHER SCOUT	1911	Fighter		Maker	Miscellaneous	(RFC)	GNOME	PR1	Also R P Scout. Said to have had an accident on first flight. Mystery.
Samuel White	PUSHER SEAPLANE	1913	Seaplane	WIGHT	Maker	Miscellaneous	RNAS	Salmson	PR1	WIGHT = Isle of Wight, factory at Cowes. Followed by several later variants.
De Havilland	PUSS MOTH	1929	Transport	DESERT CLOUD	Maker	Insect	RAF	GIPSY	PL1	Dicranura vinula, worldwide except America. Org civil a/c. 286 built. 47 impressed into RAF service, 1941.
Wolseley	PYTHON	1918	Engine		1918	Reptile	RAF		PL	Large, crushing snake. From Greek mythology. a female Serpent.
Armstrong Siddeley	PYTHON	1945	Engine		Maker	Reptile	FAA		TP	Org named the ASP.
Samuel White	QUADRUPLANE	1915	Fighter	WIGHT QUAD	Maker	Miscellaneous	(RNAS)	CLERGET	PR2	WIGHT. Isle of, built at Cowes. Also known as WIGHT Type 4. One prototype only,
De Havilland	QUEEN BEE	1935	Drone	BUZZBOX	x x x	Insect	RAF/FAA	GIPSY MAJOR	PL1	Radio controlled TIGER MOTH. Also Seaplane. (all radio controlled 'targets' as QUEEN + name) 380 Built. Some with floats, and catapault launched.
Miles	QUEEN MARTINET	1942	Drone		Maker	Miscellaneous	RAF	MERCURY	PR1	For name see MARTINET. Radio controlled. 65 built.
Curtiss	QUEEN SEAMEW	1940	Drone		x x x	Miscellaneous	FAA	RANGER	PL1	Radio Controlled. See Curtiss SEAMEW
Airspeed	QUEEN WASP	1937	Drone	CLAY PIGEON	x x x	Insect	FAA	CHEETAH	PR1	Radio controlled. The nickname was the original designated name. An efficient a/c, but only 5 built out of an order for 90. The Luftwaffe now provided better targets than a small cabin biplane.
Power Chute Systems	RAIDER	1987	Parachute		Maker	Allegorical	(RAF/ARMY)	ROTAX	PL1	Single-seat powered parachute (made by Harley Parachutes). Dev into the 2-seat KESTREL. Military evaluation as at 1991.
Royal Aircraft Factory	RAM	1917	Fighter		Maker	Animal	(RFC)	ARAB	PL1	Male Sheep. (Also Constellation) AE = Armoured Experimental. A Trench Strafer, the crew cockpit was built of quarter inch plate! 2 forward and 1 aft Lewis guns. 3 built. The only official Farnborough name, but also known as AE 3.
Short	RANGOON	1932	Flying Boat		1927	Geography-Water	RAF	JUPITER	PR3	Port & Capital of Burma. Dev from CALCUTTA-1st commercial Flying Boat with a metal hull. RANGOON served with 2 RAF Squadrons, in Iraq and Gibraltar. 6 Built, and replaced by SINGAPOREs, 1936. 4 built in France.
Napier	RAPIER	1930	Engine		1918	Weapon	RAF		PL	2 edged sword, used in duelling. An H-type eng. A small market but led to the JAVELIN and DAGGER. (Also Lockheed Fighter, 1992, and BAC missile. 1971)
Hiller	RAVEN	1948	Helicopter		Maker	Bird	(ARMY)	LYCOMING	PL1	About 2000 built. Saw military service in the Korean War. Exported to 14 countries. Characteristic 'gold fish' bowl cockpit.
Bristol	RAVEN	1957	Engine		Maker	Bird	RAF		RKT	Largest of the 'crows'. Rocket Motor (Also US Curtiss, 1931, Hiller, Grumann, 1987 & Polish KRUK=RAVEN, 1981)
Flight Refuelling	RAVEN	1983	Drone		Maker	Bird	ARMY	WEBRA	PL1	'Carrion' RAVEN, similar to the Crow RAE concept, purchased and dev by Flight Refuelling.

Maker	Name	Year	Type	Nickname	System	Classification	Service	Engine	Type	Notes
Royal Aircraft Factory	RE 8	1915	Recon	HARRY TATE	1911	Miscellaneous	RFC.	RAF 4A	PL1	RE=Recon Experimental. 'RAF' design and made by several Companies. Replacement for BE2c. 4077 built. Not very manoeuvreable, pilots were to suffer heavy losses, but fought on with RE 8 to the end of the war.
Slingsby	REGAL.	1966	Glider		Maker	Allegorical	(AIR CADETS)			Royal presentation or behaviour. 40 ordered only one built. A conversion of the EAGLE.
Stinson	RELIANT	1933	Transport		Maker	Transport	RAF/FAA	LYCOMING	PR1	Dependent or relying on. USA. Org civil. 53 impressed in the USA, and 500 built for the British, mostly to the FAA. Used for communications and navigation training. 11 civil a/c impressed by RAF in 1940.
Sopwith	RHINO	1918	Bomber		1918	Bomber	(RFC)	BHP-SIDDELEY	PR1	RHINOceros, Africa & Asia. 5 species. Triplane. 'Neither a/c nor animal is a thing of beauty' Also said to be inelegant and ungainly. 4 prototypes and official test report – awful! But it had the first bomb box.
Schleicher	RHONBUSSARD	1933	Glider		Maker	Bird	(RAF)			German. BUZZARD. Evaluated by Royal A/c Establishment, Farnborough.
Schleicher	RHONSEGLER	1934	Glider		Maker	Miscellaneous	RAF			RHON = Rhine. SEGLER = Sailer/Glider. One purchased for the Empire Test Pilots School.
Blackburn	RIPON	1926	Torp. Bomber		1921	Geography-Land	RAF/FAA	LION	PL1	Market Town. N Yorkshire. Replaced DART. A very creditable service career, and 21 Finnish RIPONs fought the Russians in 1939. The last served until 1944. 96 built, the last 4 in the RAF with PEGASUS eng = BAFFIN.
Blackburn	ROC	1938	Fighter		1932	Mythology	FAA	PERSEUS	PR1	Oriental mythical bird ('Arabian Nights'), large and powerful. Similar to the SKUA. Weight and drag of the turret made for a poor fighter, and most used for RN airfield defence, later as Target Towers. 136 built.
Avro	ROTA	1932	Autogiro		x x x	Miscellaneous	RAF/RN	GENET MAJOR	PR1	Made up word. Cierva C-30 (Spanish) built under licence. 100 built. but only 12 known as ROTA. ROTA 2, 1938, mod from C-30, 7 built. The name did not fit the RAF naming system. One later bought by Fairey.
Hafner	ROTABUGGY FLYING JEEP ROTAPLANE	1942	Autogiro	FLYING JEEP ROTAPLANE	Maker	Miscellaneous	(RAF)			Rotor structure attached to a USA 'Jeep', and towed behind a Bentley car, and WHITLEY Bomber, and made 60 flights. "Successful" as an idea, but HORSA & HAMICAR gliders were a better idea. Also a ROTATANK project.
Hafner	ROTACHUTE	1941	Autogiro		Maker	Miscellaneous	(RAF)			Designed for accurate landings as an alternative to the parachute. 20 built, and post War some sent to the USA, leading to the BENSEN gyroplane (later autogiro). Sometimes referred to as the Malcolm ROTAPLANE.
Reid & Sigrist	RS 1	1941	Trainer	SNARGASHER	Maker	Mythology	(RAF)	GIPSY MAJOR	PL2	From the works of Lewis Carrol. Good looking twin, but not accepted after RAE trials. One only, and used for Company transport.
Reid & Sigrist	RS 3	1945	Trainer	DESFORD	Maker	Geography-Land	RAF	GIPSY MAJOR	PL2	Town in Leicestershire. Dev from the SNARGASHER, and purchased for prone pilot trials and thus known as the BOBSLEIGH. One only.
Reid & Sigrist	RS 4	1946	Trainer	DESFORD TRAINER	Maker	Miscellaneous	(RAF)	GIPSY MAJOR	PR2	Dev as a possible RAF trainer but not accepted and used for civil photography. One only.
Short	S 18	1933	Flying Boat	KNUCKLEDUSTER	Maker	Miscellaneous	(RAF)	GOSHAWK	PL2	Weapon fitting over the knuckles. Nickname from the single gull wing, looking like the weapon. Whilst very promising as a design, the steam cooled engs were unreliable, and and only 1 prototype.
Short	S 2	1925	Flying Boat	TIN FIVE	Maker	Miscellaneous	(RAF)	EAGLE	PL2	TIN referred to the experimental duralumin hull. No payment if it leaked! Found successful, and led to the SINGAPORE.
Short	S 27 & 28	1910	Trainer	BIPLANE	Maker	Miscellaneous	RN	GNOME	PR1	S 26, 27 and 28, and 27 property of the senior pilot! Later 28 was the generic "name". Used for training and several adventures. Of military note, some in WW 1. See Short Type S. 38 as later dev.
Bristol	S2A	1916	Trainer	TUBBY PREGNANT BRISTOL	Maker	Miscellaneous	(RNAS)	MONOSOUPAPE	PR1	Shape of fuselage-2 seater side by side.

Maker	Name	Year	Type	Nickname	System	Classification	Service	Engine	Type	Notes
Short	S 31	1938	Experimental	LITTLE BOMBER	Maker	Miscellaneous	(RAF)	NIAGARA	PR4	Half scale design as as 'model' for the STIRLING heavy Bomber. To reduce take off run. more wing incidence was needed, achieved by a longer undercarriage. Hence the stalky u/c of the STIRLING.
Short	S 32	1911	Trainer	SCHOOL BIPLANE	Maker	Miscellaneous	RFC	GNOME	PR1	Very similar to the Wright FLYER. 4 built, 2 for the Central Flying School (RFC). In service to the end of 1913, and trained many RFC pilots some of whom were later RAF.
Short	S 46	1912	Trainer	DOUBLE DIRTY	Maker	Miscellaneous	(RFC/ (RNAS)	(RN)	PR2	One Gnome was 'dirty', so two were thought doubly so, and particularly when sitting between 2 Gnomes spewing castor oil. (same eng layout as in the TANDEM TWIN). Not accepted – too dirty.
Admiralty	S S EXPERIMENTAL	1914	Airship	MULLION TWIN (SSE 2)	RN	Miscellaneous	RNAS	HAWK	PL1	SSE 1-3. MULLION in Cornwall.
Short	S. 38(SEE BIPLANE)	1912	Seaplane	ADMIRALTY	Maker	Miscellaneous	RNAS	GNOME	PR1	First a seaplane, then a land plane, and after various rebuilds. S. 38 can claim 2 records – flown off a gun turret of HMS Africa and carried Winston Churchill, 1st Lord of the Admiralty, for 1 hour's tuition!
Short	S. 41	1912	Seaplane	HYDRO-BIPLANE	Maker	Miscellaneous	(RNAS)	GNOME	PR1	Both wheels & floats. HYDRO-BIPLANE an early name for 'Seaplane'. Not strictly (RNAS) but significant in naval history as meeting the Fleet at sea, escorting the Flagship into Weymouth. This made an impression!
Short	S. 81	1914	Seaplane	GUN CARRIER	Maker	Miscellaneous	RNAS	GNOME	PR1	An early Seaplane 'Gunbus', used for gun trails. When the Vickers gun was fired, the a/c was said to stall! Further trials with the Davis recoiless gun, but abandoned. One only.
Short	S. C. 1	1957	Experimental	FLAT RISER	Maker	Miscellaneous	(RAF)	Rolls-Royce	JT1	Next dev from the Rolls-Royce FLYING BEDSTEAD. Conventional take-off and landing, but also vertical lift with deflected eng exhaust. 2 built. Org flown at Belfast, and 1 to RAE Bedford for further research.
Supermarine	S6 & S6B	1929	Seaplane	SCHNEIDER	Maker	Miscellaneous	RAF	'RF (ROLLS-ROYCE)	PL1	Race won outright, 1931 and led to first SPITFIRE, F7/30 Specn. Higher Octane Fuel & A/c performance a great influence on future RAF & WW II. Ironically, funded privately by £100, 000 from Lady Houston.
Napier	SABRE	1937	Engine		1918	Weapon	RAF		PL	Heavy, curved cavalry sword. Sleeve-valved flat H engine, reaching 2,540 hp.
North American	SABRE	1947	Fighter	SABRE DOG (USA)	Maker	Weapon	RAF	GENERAL ELECTRIC	JT1	Flown to UK, and the 'Operation' known as 'Beecher's Brook'. Built in Canada, USA, Australia, Italy & Japan. Korean war service 1950-53. 2540+ built.
Sopwith	SALAMANDER	1917	Fighter	TIN OF SALMON	Maker	Reptile	RAF	BENTLEY	PR1	Small, amphibious lizard. Armoured Trench fighter, & name from mythical lizard which survived fire. 1300 ordered, but with the end of the war only 216 built. (Also Heinkel SALAMANDAR, 1944)
Short	SANDRINGHAM	1942	Flying Boat		Maker	Geography-Land	(RAF)	PEGASUS	PR4	Not a Port, but a Royal country residence. Dev of the SUNDERLAND on loan to the RAF by BOAC. Some sold to Argentina and New Zealand. HYTHES(ex Sunderlands) also converted to SANDRINGHAMs.
School of Military Eng	SAPPER	1882	Balloon		Maker	People	ARMY			A member of the Royal Engineers. One only.
Armstrong Siddeley	SAPPHIRE	1948	Engine		Maker	Jewel	RAF		JT	Precious blue Gem. Later A-S jewels. Eng taken over from Metropolitan-Vickers.
Short	SARAFAND	1932	Flying Boat		1927	Geography-Land	(RAF)	BUZZARD	PL6	RAF Airfield near Tel Aviv, a British Protectorate. 2nd largest a/c of its time. Very successful, but mono= plane boats in the offing, and used for extensive RAF trials. 1 only, and plans sold to Japan.
Supermarine	SCAPA	1932	Flying Boat		1927	Geography-Water	RAF	KESTREL	PL2	British Home Fleet base, SCAPA Flow Scotland. Developed from SOUTHAMPTON 14 built, serving in the UK and the Mediterrannean. All withdrawn by 1938 with the end of the biplane Flying Boat.
De Schelde	SCHELDEMUSCH	1935	Transport		Maker	Bird	(RAF)	GIPSY MAJOR	PL1	Dutch. MUSCH = SPARROW. A small tri-cycle, pusher, trainer. A flying boat version was the ScheldeMEEUW=GULL. Strictly, not (RAF), but flown in RAF colours+ Dutch registration at a Glider Training School. 6 built.

Maker	Name	Year	Type	Nickname	System	Classification	Service	Engine	Type	Notes
Sopwith	SCHNEIDER	1914	Fighter		Maker	People	RNAS	MONOSOUPAPE	PR1	Mon. SCHNEIDER, French, donated the S Trophy. A/c dev from TABLOID (1911 Winner). Civil landplane version was the RAINBOW. 160 built. Zep patrols over N Sea and found 2. Fine service E Med. Red Sea and Dardanelles.
Grahame-White	SCHOOL BIPLANE	1911	Trainer		Maker	Education	(RFC)	GNOME	PR1	Taken over by the Military Wing of the RFC in 1912 after much service as a trainer. The RFC found it then difficult to service, and it flew with them for just 10 minutes!
Sopwith	SCHOOL BIPLANE	1912	Trainer	HYBRID	x x x	Allegorical	R N	GNOME	PR1	'Hybrid' as the engine from a BLERIOT and the wings of a Burgess-Wright Biplane. Slow but great weight lifter. One sold to Admiralty for £900. Based at RN Training Base at Whitstable. 11 built.
D F S	SCHULGLEITER	1946	Glider		Maker	Miscellaneous	(AIR CADETS)			German. School Glider.
Armstrong Whitworth	SCIMITAR	1934	Fighter		Maker	Weapon	FAA (RAF)	PANTHER	PR1	Curved, oriental Sword. Not RAF name as Weapons reserved to A-Siddeley. 2 prototypes but no RAF orders due to unreliable eng. 4 to Norway as Fighter trainers up to 1939, and 2 sold to China. A W's last Fighter.
Supermarine	SCIMITAR	1956	Fighter		1949	Weapon	FAA	AVON	JT2	A-S name system reservation no longer applicable. 1st FAA a/c with nuclear capability. Blown flaps to reduce take off/landing speed. 79 built, and served until 1969. Kuwait crisis. Followed by Blackburn BUCCANEER.
Short	SCION SENIOR	1935	Seaplane		Maker	Miscellaneous	RAF	NIAGARA	PR2	SCION = descendent, heir, or young member of a family. Also (1934) SCION JUNIOR. Both with wheels or floats. Series build = 28. As SCION, 11 were impressed into the RAF in 1939.
Napier	SCORPION	1956	Engine		Maker	Insect	RAF		RKT	Desert Insect with poisonous sting
Martinsyde	SCOUT	1914	Fighter	TINSIDE	Maker	Allegorical	RFC	FALCON	PL1	'Scouts' and 'Bullets' v confusing! Small and fairly fast, and served with some success until 1915, when it was superseded by the PUP. 65 built.
Sopwith	SCOUT	1914	Recon	SPINNING JENNY	Maker	Allegorical	RNAS	MONOSOUPAPE	PR1	Landplane, from S. 108 Seaplane. Also known as TWO SEATER SCOUT. 24 built.
Saunders-Roe	SCOUT	1958	Helicopter		Maker	Allegorical	FAA/ ARMY	NIMBUS	JP1	Dev from SKEETER. 1959 take over by Westland. Served in many countries, including Falklands. App 300 built.
Westland	SCOUT	1959	Helicopter		Maker	Allegorical	FAA/ ARMY	NIMBUS	TP1	Revival of an oft-used WW I name. Org Saunders-Roe, with org name of SPRITE. Taken over by Westlands. Sales to 4 o/seas countries and 151 built. Saw service in the Falkland war and 4 other countries.
Parnall	SCOUT	1916	Fighter	ZEP STRAFFER	Maker	Miscellaneous	(RFC)	MAORI	PL1	Upward firing gun. Also NIGHT FLYER but in spite of its many names, it never flew, and was destroyed with all technical records. (A lost a/c 'found' by the author).
Admiralty	SCOUT	1915	Fighter	SPARROW	R N	Allegorical	(RNAS)	MONOSOUPAPE	PR1	Anti-Zeppelin. Biplane pusher with the fuselage at top wing level and designed as anti-Zeppelin. 4 built under contract, but found to be difficult to fly, and abandoned.
Bristol	SCOUT C & D	1913	Fighter	BULLET	Maker	Allegorical	RFC/ RNAS	GNOME	PR1	1914 Pilot praise in France led to production orders. Succesful, but lacked a synchronized gun to be used to full effect. Series C & D. 642 built, with RFC and RNAS competing for priority. Widely used.
Bristol	SCOUT E & F	1918	Fighter		Maker	Allegorical	(RFC)	ARAB	PL1	SCOUT E was to have a watercooled CRUCIFORM eng, but used the Cosmos (later to be Bristol) MERCURY. With an ARAB engine, it became F1, but a large order was cancelled with the Armistice. 1 prototype.
Brooklands/Asta	SCOUTMASTER	1988	Drone		Maker	People	(ARMY)	VOLKSWAGEN	PL1	Developed from the OPTICA SCOUT, civil transport designed for low level surveillance.
Supermarine	SCYLLA	192	Seaplane		Maker	Mythology	(RAF)	CONDOR	PL2	Female monster who devoured sailors in the Straits of Messina. SCYLLA is a mystery story. Ordered, hull built and photographed, RAF colours+ serial, many drawings missing, and no subsequent history??? (Also Short, 1934)

Maker	Name	Nickname	Year	Type	System	Classification	Service	Engine	Type	Notes
Short	SCYLLA & SYRINX		1934	Transport	Maker	Mythological	RAF	JUPITER	PR4	Sea Monster, and the Pipes of Pan. Short KENT flying boat on wheels, an urgent Imperial Airway's order for more passenger capacity. Both a/c impressed by the RAF in 1940, the last of the Short Biplanes.
Royal Aircraft Factory SE 1		MANKILLER CANARD	1911	Experimental	1911	Miscellaneous	(ARMY)	WOLSELEY	PL1	'Rebuilt' Bleriot. SE=Santos Dumont Experimental, later Scout Exp. This a/c was a subterfuge to enable the 'Factory' to build its own a/c, this having been forbidden by the War Office. Crashed and thus the name.
Royal Aircraft Factory SE 2		BULLET	1913	Fighter	1911	Miscellaneous	RFC	GNOME	PR1	Org BS 1, rebuilt SE2, rebuilt SE2a(?) and sent to France. Only one. The fate of this SCOUT is unknown. (Also Northrop BLACK BULLET Fighter, 1940 and Bristol Racer BULLET, 1920)
Royal Aircraft Factory SE 5A		SEPHA	1916	Fighter	1911	Miscellaneous	RFC	VIPER	PL1	See the GREAT UN-NAMED – Chapter 5 Part 17
Supermarine	SEA ATTACKER		1946	Fighter Bomb	1932	Allegorical	FAA	NENE	JT1	To bombard, assail, storm, assault, beset. Designed as a land fighter with SPITEFUL wings, but switched to FAA as 1st standard jet carrier Fighter. 148 for FAA and served 1951-57. Also 36 to Pakistan.
Boulton-Paul	SEA BALLIOL		1948	Trainer	R N	Education	FAA	MERLIN	PL1	Adaption of RAF BALLIOL with deck landing capability. 30 built.
De Havilland	SEA DEVON		1946	Transport	R N	Miscellaneous	FAA	GIPSY QUEEN	PL2	See DEVON. RAF (org civil DOVE) 13 to FAA, winning Boyd Trophy for efficiency in 1959. Replaced by SEA HERONS in 1961, and some to the civil market.
Fairey	SEA FOX	TROUT	1936	Seaplane	x x x	Animal	FAA	RAPIER	PL1	Adaption of RAF FOX, so exception of name which should be a sea bird. Spotted 'Adml Graf Spee' at 1939 Battle of the River Plate, and 1st gunnery direction at sea in WW II. 66 built.
Hawker	SEA FURY		1944	Fighter	1939	Allegorical	FAA	CENTAURUS	PR1	Adaption of RAF FURY. 200 FURY order for the RAF cancelled by end of WW II. Then 668 SEA FURIES for the FAA with a final build of 829 for 10 Air Forces. Fought with distinction in the Korean War. Some still flying.
Gloster	SEA GLADIATOR	GLAD	1934	Fighter	1932	Allegorical	FAA	MERCURY	PR1	Adaptation of RAF GLADIATOR. 'Faith', 'Hope' and 'Charity' borrowed by RAF to fight alongside Hurricanes in the Battle of Malta. 60 built, and fought in the North Sea, Malta and the Mediterranean.
Hawker-Siddeley	SEA HARRIER		1966	Fighter	R N	Bird	FAA	PEGASUS	JT1	Adaption of RAF HARRIER. See the Classics – Chapter 6.
Hawker	SEA HAWK		1948	Fighter	R N	Bird	FAA	NENE	JT1	No SEA HAWK as such, other than the Galapagos Hawk. With the advent of the jet eng. Rolls-Royce no longer claimed Bird of Prey names. Superseded ATTACKER & SEA FURY, and saw action at Suez. Sold to 6 AFs. 534 built.
De Havilland	SEA HERON		1950	Transport	Maker	Bird	FAA	GIPSY QUEEN	PL4	Scaled up DOVE with 4 engs. Org civil a/c, with extensive home and overseas sales. 150 built, with 5 to the FAA for communications.
De Havilland	SEA HORNET		1943	Fighter	R N	Insect	FAA	MERLIN	PL2	Small RAF MOSQUITO. Possibly the fastest UK propeller a/c. Adapted from the RAF HORNET. 157 Built. The 1st British carrierborne single seater with twin engines. Most use in the Pacific area. Also 2-seater.
Hawker	SEA HURRICANE		1935	Fighter	R N	Meteorology	RAF/FAA	MERLIN	PL1	Served with 40 escort carriers, and 35 merchantmen by catapult launch. Tamed the CONDOR, Russian Convoys, and in a Malta Convoy shot down 39 German and Italian fighters for the loss of 8. About 800 built.
Supermarine	SEA KING		1921	Flying Boat	Maker	Miscellaneous	(RAF)	HISPANO-SUIZA	PL1	An amphibious fighter, developed from SEA LION I and into SEA LION II. I was entered for the 1919 Schneider Trophy race, and as II won the race in 1922. But no further RAF interest. 1 prototype.
Westland	SEA KING		1967	Helicopter	R N	Miscellaneous	FAA	GNOME	TP2	Org. Sikorsky S-61B, 1959. Rescued 1500 in Turkish invasion of Cyprus. 321 built, and served in many operations, inc 1991 Gulf War and the Falklands. Dev from WESSEX. Used by 9 AFs.
Supermarine	SEA LION	BABY BOAT	1919	Flying Boat	Maker	Mammal	RAF	LION	PL1	Dev from the BABY, and LION from the eng. Schneider Trophy entrant 1919, 1920 and 1923, 1920 was a great triumph and the first a/c to clock 200 mph. SEA LION I, II & III, and the hull was built in 1916!
De Havilland	SEA MOSQUITO	SMOSSY	1945	Fighter	R N	Insect	FAA	MERLIN	PL2	Adaptation of RAF MOSQUITO (1940) Carrier borne torpedo and recon Fighter with folding wings. 1st twin eng FAA a/c to land on a carrier. As popular and effective as the 'LAND' MOSQUITO. 92 built.

Maker	Name	Year	Type	Nickname	System	Classification	Service	Engine	Type	Notes
Supermarine	SEA OTTER	1938	Flying Boat		x x x	Animal	RAF/FAA	MERCURY	PR1	Aquatic Mammal. A/c dev from WALRUS 290 built. Supermarine's and FAA's last Biplane. Built by Saunders-Roe. Replaced the WALRUS for air-sea rescue, and org known as the STINGRAY. Also active service in Korea.
Percival	SEA PRINCE	1950	Transport		R N	Miscellaneous	FAA	LEONIDES	PR2	FAA version of RAF PEMBROKE (org civil PRINCE) Used as transports and for anti-submarine and observor training. 49 built. As a flying classroom was replaced by the JETSTREAM.
Admiralty	SEA SCOUT	1914	Airship		R N	Miscellaneous	RNAS	GREEN	PL1	SS(SEA SCOUT)-Blimp. SSZ=ZERO Type. Also TWIN AIRSHIP, 2 Engs.
Avro	SEA TUTOR	1929	Seaplane		1927	Education	RAF	LYNX	PR1	See TUTOR. 15 built.
De Havilland	SEA VAMPIRE	1943	Fighter		1939	Animal	FAA	GOBLIN	JT1	Adaption of RAF VAMPIRE. 1st UK Carrierborne jet a/c in 1945. 96 built. In action during the Suez Canal campign.
De Havilland	SEA VENOM	1949	Fighter		1949	Allegorical	FAA	GHOST	JT1	Adaption of RAF VENOM. Succeeded SEA HORNET. Total build VENOM + SEA VENOM =887. Also built in France. 1st jet all-weather FAA fighter. Saw action in the Suez Canal campaign. 256 to the FAA.
De Havilland	SEA VIXEN	1960	Fighter		1949	Animal	FAA	AVON	JT2	Female Fox. No RAF VIXEN. 151 Built. Org RAF requirement as all-weather Fighter as 'brother' to VAMPIRE. FAA interested as strike fighter, and served until 1972. The FAA now fought with guided weapons!
Supermarine	SEAFANG	1944	Fighter		R N	Allegorical	FAA	GRIFFON	PL1	FANG=long tooth. FAA version of SPITEFUL. 150 ordered but only 9 built. The last variant of the SPITFIRE line and too late to meet the needs of WW II. The NENE powered ATTACKER was soon to come.
Supermarine	SEAFIRE	1942	Fighter		R N	Allegorical	FAA	MERLIN	PL1	FAA version of SPITFIRE. Action inc attacks on 'Tirpitz' in Norway. Also HOOKED SEAFIRE – ie: hook for deck landing. 2649 built. Apart from distinguished RN service in WW II, also served in Malaya anfd Korea.
Short	SEAFORD	1944	Flying Boat		x x x	Geography-Water	(RAF)	HERCULES	PR4	Sussex Port. Improved SUNDERLAND for the Pacific war, but then for civil use with BOAC. 2 prototypes + 6 converted into SOLENTS, + 12 already delivered direct from Shorts. Swords into ploughshares. . . .
Supermarine	SEAGULL (1st)	1920	Flying Boat	DUCK	1921	Bird	FAA	LION	PL1	Should be a 'Fish'. Org named SEAL. from SEAL. Later (1935). About 18 for the FAA and 6 for RAAF, the latter being the more successful. (Other SEAGULLs -Deperdussin 1912. Polish lightplane 1973, Curtiss 1918 & 1939)
Supermarine	SEAGULL (2nd)	1933	Fling Boat		1932	Bird	FAA	PEGASUS	PR1	Update of the 1st SEAGULL, with one prototype (reluctantly) ordered for FAA. Again. Australian AF keener and surveyed the Great Barrier Reef with great success. However, the UK SEAGULL was to become the WALRUS.
Supermarine	SEAGULL (3rd)	1948	Flying Boat		1932	Bird	(RAF)	GRIFFON	PL1	Last of the Supermarine boats. An innovative design, STOL and with a variable-incidence wing. As further development required, and with the advent of the helicopter, only two prototypes built.
Fairey	SEAL	1930	Seaplane		1927	Fish	FAA	PANTHER	PR1	Aquatic, fish eating Mammal. Land & Seaplane. FAA version of RAF GORDON. Served in 3 RN Carriers 1933-36. 91 to the FAA(RAF) with sales to Peru, Argentine, Chile and Latvia.
Supermarine	SEAL	1920	Flying Boat		1918	Fish	(RAF)	LION	PL1	Dev from civil COMMERCIAL AMPHIBIAN and renamed SEAGULL in 1922. See SEAGULL. One SEAL went to JAPAN in 1922.
Supermarine	SEAMEW	1928	Flying Boaf		1928	Bird	(FAA)	LYNX	PR2	The common Gull. Designed as a small flying boat amphibian, orders were given for two prototypes. Both were scrapped after a short life, due to corrosion and metal fatigue-this being Supermarine's 1st metal a/c.
Curtiss	SEAMEW	1940	Seaplane		1939	Bird	FAA	RANGER	PL1	Originally 1935 USN SEAGULL. Land & Seaplane (Biplane). Total = 800. Central float or wheels. Deemed to be unsuccesful, but 250 diverted to the FAA. Another 30 were converted for radio control = QUEEN SEAMEW.
Short	SEAMEW	1953		Recon	1949	Bird	FAA	MAMBA	TP1	Anti-Submarine. 19 Built. Designed to meet the growing USSR submarine threat, but handling problems led to cancellation of orders, including those for the RAF.

Maker	Name	Year	Type	Nickname	System	Classification	Service	Engine	Type	Notes
Slingsby	SEDBERGH	1944	Glider	THE BARGE	Maker	Geography-Land	AIR CADETS			Town in Cumberland (also SEDBERGH) Presented to 123 Gliding School.
Bristol	SEELEY	1920	Experimental		Maker	People	(RAF)	JUPITER	PR1	SEELEY was Secretary of State for War. Also known as the SEELEY PUMA with that engine. A civil adaption of the Bristol FIGHTER bought by Air Ministry for trials. Reached 23,000 ft. 1 only.
Martinsyde	SEMIQUAVER	1920	Experimental		Maker	Miscellaneous	(FAA)	LION	PL1	Musical interval of time, but reason for the name not known. Aluva High Lift Wing. Believed tested by at the Isle of Grain. Scrapped after RAE tests.
Vultee-Stinson	SENTINEL	1941	Transport	FLYING JEEP	Maker	Allegorical	RAF	LYCOMING	PL1	Sentry. USA, and dev from VOYAGER. Org civil, and militarised by the USA and UK. Widely used, especially by the US Army. 5258 built. 100 to the RAF. Yeoman service in the evacuation of wounded in Burma.
Boeing	SENTRY	1977	Transport		RAF	Allegorical	RAF	GENERAL ELECTRIC	JT4	Soldier on guard, sentinel. AWACS for a/c = Airborne Warning & Control System. 1991. Dev of civil Boeing 707. About 50 built, and 7 to the RAF.
Farman (Maurice)	SERIES 7	1911	Trainer	LONGHORN	Maker	Miscellaneous	RFC/RNAS	RENAULT	PR1	LONGHORN =+ front elevator, SHORTHORN = minus same. Also RUMPETY, BIRD CAGE and MECHANICAL COW. Trainer for many early, and RFC Pilots. Very forgiving and served until 1918. 438 built. (Also US Gates Learjet, 1977)
Armstrong Siddeley	SERVAL	1928	Engine		1918	Animal	(RAF)		PR	Wildcat. Org known as DOUBLE MOONGOOSE.
Saunders-Roe	SEVERN	1929	Flying Boat		1927	Geography-Water	(RAF)	JUPITER	PR3	UK's longest River, 211m. from Wales to the Bristol Channel. Metal hull and dev from the wooden SOUTHAMPTON, which was already in production One long proving flight. 1 only, but led to the dev of the LONDON.
Avro	SHACKLETON	1949	Recon	SHACK BEAR HUNTER	1949	People	RAF	GRIFFON	PL4	British Artic Explorer(1874-1922). One of the longest serving RAF a/c. '100,000 Rivets in loose formation' Mk 1 RAF service 1951, and Mk 3 flying until 1992 – 41 years! Also FLYING NISSEN HUT and WHITE FUNNEL LINE. 181 Built.
CFM Metal-Fax	SHADOW	1983	Microlight		Maker	Miscellaneous	(RAF)	ROTAX	PL1	Named after the Grand Prix Motor racing team. V successful, and sold to 24 countries. Over 200 built (1991). Also STREAK SHADOW. Used by Turkey for night surveillance at 14,000 ft.
Blackburn	SHARK	1934	Torp. Bomber		1927	Fish	FAA	PEGASUS	PR1	Family of Ocean predators. 246 built with 17 by Boeing Canada. Some 149 with TIGER eng – why not TIGER SHARK? Later relegated as a Trainer when replaced by SWORDFISH. Also sold to China, Canada and Portugal.
Supermarine	SHELDRAKE	1926	Flying Boat		1921	Bird	(RAF)(FAA)	LION	PL1	Female Shelduck. UK's largest Duck. In 1924 Spain ordered 12 SCARABs (not RAF) for their Navy. A dev of this and the SEAGULL was the SHELDRAKE, and one prototype was ordered by the RAF.
Northrop	SHELDUCK	1945	Drone		Maker	Bird	RN	NORTHROP	PL1	Male of the species. Dev from the RADIOPLANE. With 65, 000+, probably built in larger numbers than any other Drone. USA.
Short	SHETLAND	1944	Flying Boat		1939	Geography-Water	(RAF)	CENTAURUS	PR4	UK's northermost Islands. 1st Prototype destroyed by fire, and 2nd used as a test bed for the Napier NOMAD eng. The a/c was virtually an enlarged SUNDERLAND, but a new design. See Saunders-Roe A 31, the SHRIMP.
Short	SHIRL	1918	Torp. Bomber		1918	Bird	(RAF)	EAGLE	PL1	UK's largest Thrush. An RAF need to carry larger torpedoes led, amongst others, to the SHIRL and 4 built. The Sopwith CUCKOO was the better, and 1 SHIRL dev as the TRANSATLANTIC or SHAMROCK. But too late – see VIMY.
Boulton-Paul	SIDESTRAND	1926	Bomber		1921	Geography-Land	RAF	JUPITER	PR2	Village on the Norfolk Coast. 18 built. Experimental work with B-P power gun turrets led to the development of the OVERSTRAND. The further development of the turret led to the DEFIANT Fighter.
Sunbeam	SIKH	1923	Engine		Maker	People	(RAF)		PL	One of the Indian SIKH religion. Tribal series of Engs.

Maker	Name	Year	Type	Nickname	System	Classification	Service	Engine	Type	Notes
Short	SILVER STREAK	1919	Fighter		Maker	Allegorical	(RAF)	PUMA	PR1	All metal. Org known as SWALLOW. The official mind was totally opposed the use of duralumin, but bought the a/c after noting its performance. Good RAE reports, but then grounded for no published reason.
Beardmore	SIMOON	1923	Engine		Maker	Meteorology	(RAF)		PL	Strong, hot and sand laden wind of the Sahara and Arabian Deserts.
Siddeley-Deasey	SINAIA	1921	Bomber		x x x	Geography-Land	(RAF)	TIGER	PL2	Part of Egypt, E of the Gulf of Suez and in 1921 Egypt was a British Protectorate. 2 Gunner positions in the 2 eng nacelles. One prototype and problems with eng and a/c.
Short	SINGAPORE	1926	Flying Boat		1927	Geography-Water	RAF	CONDOR	PL4	Island in the Br. Empire. Now an ind Republic. A/c org suggested as 'Saturn'. Later 4 KESTREL engs. Prototype of 1926 famous with Alan Cobham's flight round Africa. Mk III was RAF version. 37 built-I, II & III.
Westland	SIOUX	1945	Helicopter	CLOCKWORK MOUSE	Maker	People	RAF/ ARMY	LYCOMING	TP1	US name. N Am Indian Tribe. Built under licence from Augusta/Bell. 1st flight 1965. 253 built, and served in Belize, Borneo, Cyprus and N. Ireland. In total, used by 26 countries. Also the IRON BUDGIE.
Armstrong Whitworth	SISKIN	1919	Fighter	FORESKIN	1918	Bird	RAF	JAGUAR	PR1	Small, yellow-green Finch. Siddeley-Deasey org designers-6 Prototypes. RAF's 1st all-metal Fighter, 437 built. Also served with the RCAF, and Estonia. RAF until 1932, and RCAF until 1939. Also civil a/c.
Armstrong Whitworth	SISKIN DUAL	1920	Trainer		1918	Bird	(RAF)	JAGUAR	PR1	See SISKIN.
Short	SKEET	1979	Drone		Maker	Miscellaneous	ARMY	WESLAKE	PR1	Clay Pigeon Shoot, from the Old Norse 'skjota'-to shoot. On command, a parachute is released for landing.
Saunders-Roe	SKEETER	1952	Helicopter		Maker	Insect	FAA/RAF/ ARMY	GIPSY MAJOR	PL1	Slang for 'Mosquito'. Dev from 1948 Cierva design, and taken over 1951. 88 built. Served until 1968, and also sold to West Germany. Westland took over Saro in 1959, who continued production (Also Curtiss light a/c, 1930)
Blackburn	SKUA	1937	Dive Bomber		1932	Bird	FAA	PERSEUS	PR1	Large, predatory Gull. Dev into ROC. 1st British Dive Bomber and 1st Fleet a/c with retractable u/c, flaps and VP propellor. SKUAs sank the Cruiser Koningsberg. Later used for training and towing. 192 built.
Slingsby	SKY	1957	Glider		Maker	Meteorological	RAF			Excellent name, and surprising that not earlier or later used. One for the Empire Flight Test School.
Slingsby	SKYLARK	1953	Glider		Maker	Bird	AIR CADETS			Noted for singing whilst in flight. Also to frolic or have fun. Many national & international records. SKYlark from Slingsby, Kirbymoorside Yorks.
Douglas	SKYMASTER	1938	Transport		Maker	Allegorical	RAF	PRATT & WHITNEY	PR4	USA. Military version of civil DC 4 1,122 built. A great work horse. 24 C-54s-RAF, total military = 1163. 79, 642 ocean crossings up to D-Day. World wide use. inc Korea. Presidents Roosevelt/Truman a/c = SACRED COW.
Douglas	SKYRAIDER	1945	Recon	GUPPY (USA) *	Maker	Allegorical	FAA	CYCLONE	PR1	USA. WW II, first with USN, later Korean War, and finished with the French at Djibouti. 3180 built, and 50 to FAA. *Large radome with 1 ton of radar. FAA's last piston eng a/c, and saw action in the Suez campaign.
Savoia-Marchetti	SM 83	1937	Transport	PORCO	Maker	Miscellaneous	RAF	ALFA ROMEO	PR3	Italian. PORCO=Pig. Several of these civil airliners captured, and 2 made serviceable. Flown extensively over Europe in 1946. 23 built, and used by Italy and Belgium(Sabena).
Sopwith	SNAIL	1918	Fighter		Maker	Miscellaneous	(RFC)	WASP	PR1	Gastropoda mollusc. One a/c had a monocoque or 'snail' fuselage. Not RAF 1918 naming system! Smaller than the CAMEL, but even more difficult to handle. But the WASP was its undoing. 2 built.
Sopwith	SNAPPER	1919	Fighter		x x x	Fish	(RAF)	DRAGONFLY	PR1	A type of Sea Bream. By its name the a/c should have been a Seaplane. When the eng worked, this was a very speedy Fighter, but there was no production order. 3 prototypes only.
Sopwith	SNARK	1919	Fighter	BOOJUM	Maker	Mythology	(RAF)	DRAGONFLY	PR1	Lewis Carrol – Hunting of the SNARK' mixture of snail and shark, and was a BOOJUM. This Triplane was one of the best performers of this type at the time, but doomed by the dreaded DRAGONFLY engs.

Maker	Name	Nickname	Year	Type		System	Classification	Service	Engine	Type	Notes
Aero Research	SNARK		1934	Experimental		Maker	Mythlogy	(RAF)	GIPSY MAJOR	PL1	Designed by De Bruyne who later to found Aero Research. An innovative one-off and successful monoplane, later bought by Air Ministry for RAE trials. Then sold to (Sir) Peter Masefield but lost in a 1940 air raid on Croydon.
Aero Electronics Ltd	SNIPE		1978	Drone		Maker	Bird	(ARMY)	PIPER	PL1	Sold to 20 Countries, and about 400 built.
Sopwith	SNIPE		1918	Fighter		1918	Bird	RFC/RAF	BENTLEY	PR1	'Heather bleater' – worldwide long-billed shore bird. 2122 built. Successor to the CAMEL. A short career in WW I, but with a great reputation in five RFC Squadrons. 1st line fighter to 1926, then a trainer.
Scicon	SOARFLY		1986	Drone		Maker	Miscellaneous	(ARMY)			Made up name. Battlefield recon.
Sopwith	SOCIABLE	TWEENY CHURCHILL	1912	Trainer		Maker	Allegorical	RNAS	GNOME	PR1	2 seat Trainer, specified and used by Winston Churchill, hence also the CHURCHILL. The TWEENIE may have seen action on the Western Front. (Also Vickers monoplane No 6, 1912)
Short	SOLENT		1946	Flying Boat		Maker	Geography-Water	(RAF)	HERCULES	PR4	Channel between Isle of Wight and the English S coast. Dev from SUNDERLAND via SANDRINGHAM for BOAC. 12 built and 1 'on loan' to the RAF. All had 'S' individual names, and SOUTHAMPTON was doubly suitable.
Supermarine	SOUTHAMPTON		1925	Flying Boat		1921	Geography-Water	RAF	LION	PL2	See the CLASSICS – Chapter 6.
S P A D	SPAD 7, 12 &13	SCOUT	1916	Fighter		Maker	Allegorical	RFC/ RNAS	HISPANO-SUIZA	PL1	French. Great demand, so produced in France and the UK. A classic of WW I and amongst others, the mount of Guynemer and Rickenbacker. Type 12 (one only)=CANNON SPAD. 387 built for the RFC.
Sopwith	SPARROW		1915	Experimental		x x x	Bird	(RFC)	GNOME	PR1	Dev from PUP and Hawker's ROUNDABOUT of 1914. Some doubt as to which were ROUNDABOUTs and which SPARROWs Proposed for RFC 'wireless' trials. 4 ordered but no record of delivery although serial numbers given.
Supermarine	SPARROW		1924	Transport		Maker	Bird	(RAF)	THRUSH	PL1	Common SPARROW, but unusual with a (Blackburn) THRUSH Eng. Designed for 1924 Air Ministry 2-seater Light Aeroplane Competition, and used for RAE wing trials. The SPARROW contributed much to future light a/c.
Miles	SPARROWHAWK		1935	Experimental		Maker	Bird	(RAF)	GIPSY MAJOR	PL1	As Above. Based on HAWK. Used by RAE Farnborough for high lift flap research. 8 built, 2 for RAE. Later SPARROW JET, which won the King's Cup Air Race in 1951.
Gloster	SPARROWHAWK		1920	Fighter		1918	Bird	(RAF)	BENTLEY	PR1	Family of small Hawks. Mod of Nieuport NIGHTHAWK. FAA Fighter as MARS. (Also USA Curtiss S, 1930) MARS III as SAPRROWHAWK for Japaneese Navy.
Fairey	SPEARFISH		1945	Experimental		1939	Fish	(RAF)/ FAA	CENTAURUS	PR1	Family name-eg: Marlin. A/c replacement for BARRACUDA. Whilst of much potential with many new features, it was outdated by the advent of the jet engine. Only 5 built from an order for 100.
Sopwith	SPECIAL		1914	Torp Bomber		Maker	Allegorical	(RNAS)	SALMSON	PL1	1st British a/c specifically designed to carry a torpedo. Also adapted as a bomber, but intended weapons never carried. Abandoned 1915.
Short	SPERRIN		1951	Bomber		1949	Geography-Land	(RAF)	AVON	JT4	N Ireland Mountains. (Shorts moved from Rochester, Kent, to Belfast). Two prototypes, used for research and as eng test beds. Valuable for British civil and military a/c.
Rolls-Royce	SPEY		1960	Engine		Maker	Geography-Water	RAF		JT	Scottish River. Powered RAF PHANTOM, and also built by China.
Avro	SPIDER		1918	Fighter		x x x	Insect.	(RAF)	CLERGET	PR1	Family of Arimandae, the web spinners. More likely a nickname from interplane struts!One of the 1st a/c without bracing wires. 2 built. (Also Fokker SPINNE = Spider series from 1912)
Supermarine	SPITEFUL		1944	Fighter		1939	Allegorical	(RAF)	GRIFFON	PL1	Dev of SPITFIRE. FAA=SEAFANG. New wings and undercarriage. 20 built and used for experimental work and made obsolete by the advent of the jet fighter.
Supermarine	SPITFIRE (1st)		1934	Fighter		1932	Allegorical	(RAF)	GOSHAWK	PL1	See Type 224.
Supermarine	SPITFIRE (2nd)	SPIT SPITTY	1936	Fighter		1932	Allegorical	RAF	MERLIN	PL1	See the CLASSICS – Chapter 6.

Maker	Name	Nickname	Year	Type	System	Classification	Service	Engine	Type	Notes
Blackburn	SPRAT		1926	Trainer	1921	Fish	(FAA)	FALCON	PL1	Small fish, alias the 'Brisling'. Designed as a 'simple' trainer with wheels for carriers, and also with floats. The Vickers VENDACE was chosen. but both cancelled. One SPRAT prototype only.
Short	SPRINGBOK		1923	Fighter	1921	Animal	(RAF)	JUPITER	PR1	Small South African antelope or buck. Based on the all metal Short SILVER STREAK, the SPRINGBOK was well ahead of its time as a metal fighter. But RAF fitters were not thus trained, so only 5 prototypes.
De Havilland	SPRITE		1948	Engine	Maker	Mythology	(RAF)	ROCKET	RKT	Elf or Pixie. Assisted Take Off Eng. Also SUPER SPRITE. (Also Aero Engine SPRITE, 1934)
Saunders-Roe	SR 53 & 177	MANNED MISSILE	1957	Fighter	Maker	Miscellaneous	(RAF)	VIPER + SPRITE ROCKET.	JT1	1st flight recorded 1. 33 Mach and a very high rate of climb. A fatal crash, never explained, led to cancellation of SR 53. SR 177, ready to fly, cancelled by the Sandys edict, but many AFs interested.
Saunders-Roe	SR A/1	SQUIRT SEA JET	1947	Flying Boat	Maker	Miscellaneous	(RAF)	BERYL	JT1	Flying Boat Fighter. Whilst a good idea, it could not compete with a land based equivalent, and was cancelled. But the RN showed some interest in its use in the Pacific war. 3 built.
British Aerospace	STABILEYE		1974	Drone	Maker	Miscellaneous	(RAF)	WAEL	PL1	Name chosen to indicate stability. MOD evaluation.
De Havilland	STAG		1926	Gen. Purpose	1921	Animal	RAF	JUPITER	PR1	Adult male of various Deer, and Stag Lane was DH's Company address. The final derivative from WW I DH 9a assemblies. The one crashed. The West land WAPITI was grateful for the eng. But new type u/c oleos manf'd, so some recompense.
Armstrong Whitworth	STARLING		1927	Fighter	1921	Bird	(RAF) (FAA)	JAGUAR	PR1	Many local names, such as Plover, Storn and Chimney Pot. STARLING II of 1929 had a PANTHER engine. The FAA version known as the FLEET FIGHTER. 6 STARLINGs built. leading to SCIMITAR (Also Swedish S, 1988)
Armstrong Siddeley	STENTOR		1962	Engine	Maker	Allegorical	RAF		RKT	Loud voiced Herald in the Greek 'Iliad'. Powered the BLUE STEEL missile which was cancelled.
Short	STIRLING		1939	Bomber	1932	Geography-Land	RAF	HERCULES	PR4	Burgh(town) in Central Scotland. One of the Big Bombers of WW II. Piloted flying scale model was the Short S. 31, the 'Mini Stirling' 1938. 2,383 STIRLINGs built. The first of the RAF's big 4-eng Bombers. See S 31.
Supermarine	STRANRAER	STRANY STRAINER	1934	Flying Boat	1932	Geography-Water	RAF	PEGASUS	PR2	Port, W Scotland. Org. SOUTHAMPTON Mk V. Also WHISTLING BIRD CAGE. Also RCAF. Demilitarised S=THARK, lacked two of everything . . .17 built, and the last of the Supermarine boats. 14 Canadian built for the RCAF.
Airships Ltd	STREAMLINE		1912	Balloon	Maker	Miscellaneous	ARMY			Observation Balloon.
Miles	STUDENT		1957	Trainer	Maker	Education	(RAF)	MABORE	JT	One following a course of study. After evaluation by, but with no order from the RAF, orders were received from South Africa, but were cancelled by the arms embargo. CENTURION was a projected dev.
Wolf Hirth	STUMMEL-HABICHT		1943	Glider	Maker	Miscellaneous	(RAF)			German = KITE. High wing loading glider for pilot jet training.
Short	STURGEON (1st)		1927	Seaplane	1921	Fish	(FAA)	JUPITER	PR1	Family of large Fish, source of caviare(roe). Based on the CHAMOIS, required to replace the Fairey III Flew well, good water handling and two prototypes, which led to the GURNARD.
Short	STURGEON (2nd)		1946	Recon	RN	Fish	FAA	MERLIN	PL2	Torpedo/Recc role no longer required with the end of WW II, and phasing out of the big Carriers. 23 built and used as high speed Target Towers. One modified with the MAMBA turboprop.
Admiralty	SUBMARINE SCOUT	FLYING BEDSTEAD(SS. 31)	1914	Airship	RN	Miscellaneous	RNAS	HAWK	PL1	SS Class 1914-1918. SS1-49. Various Manufacturers. See COASTAL & ZERO.
Admiralty	SUBMARINE SCOUT PATROL		1915	Airship	RN	Miscellaneous	RNAS	GREEN	PL1	SSP 1-6.
Admiralty	SUBMARINE SCOUT TWIN		1915	Airship	RN	Miscellaneous	RNAS	HAWK	PL2	SST 1-115
Admiralty	SUBMARINE SCOUT ZERO	ZERO	1916	Airship	RN	Miscellaneous	RNAS	HAWK	PL2	Standard Patrol Blimp. SSZ 21-93. Excellent work in anti-submarine petrols.

Maker	Name	Year	Type	Nickname	System	Classification	Service	Engine	Type	Notes
Short	SUNDERLAND	1937	Flying Boat	WONDERLAND, TYNE BOAT	1932	Geography-Water	RAF	PEGASUS	PR4	See the CLASSICS – Chapter 6
Piper	SUPER CRUISER	1941	Transport		Maker	Allegorical	RAF	LYCOMING	PL1	Dev from the CRUISER of 1940, and 10 built. 1 RAF impressed in India.
Warner	SUPER SCARAB	1933	Engine		Maker	Insect	RAF		PR	Various large Beetles, sacred to the Egyptians. Dev from SCARAB & JUNIOR SCARAB, and widely used in the USA. Known to the RAF and ATA with the Fairchild ARGUS transport (Also 1924 Supermarine Flying Boat for Spain)
Stampe et Vertongen	SV 4	1933	Trainer	STAMPE	Maker	Miscelleneous	(RAF)	GIPSY MAJOR	PL1	Belgian. Very similar to the DH TIGER MOTH, but a new design for enhanced aerobatic capability. 600+ built pre 1939, and 500+ post war. Used by Belgian, German and French AFs. 11 impressed by RAF 1940.
Short	SWALLOW	1920	Fighter		1918	Bird	(RAF)	PUMA	PR1	Migrating, graceful flier eating on the wing. SWALLOW was the org name of what became known as the SILVER STREAK, an early all-metal design. (Also 1926 Blackburn eng, and series of US Swallow Co SWALLOWS from 1923)
Sopwith	SWALLOW	1918	Fighter	SCOOTER	Maker	Bird	(RAF)	CLERGET	PR1	Org MONOPLANE No 1, a CAMEL fuselage with a parasol wing. Org the unarmed SCOOTER. Hawker's own runabout. Modified as a Fighter. No advantage and one built. (Also British Klemm, and DH SWALLOW MOTH, both 1930)
Slingsby	SWALLOW	1955	Glider		Maker	Bird	AIR CADETS			See above. 1 presented to the Air Training Corps.
De Havilland	SWALLOW	1946	Experimental		Maker	Miscellaneous	RAF	GOBLIN	JT1	Based on the VAMPIRE fuselage, and tailess to explore swept wings for the first design of projected COMET 1st British supersonic a/c. Broke up whilst attempting height record, and Geoffrey de Havilland lost. 3 built.
Supermarine	SWAN	1924	Flying Boat		1921	Bird	(RAF)	EAGLE	PL2	Heavy water bird, best known MUTE SWAN. Amphibian. Name org intended for the SEA EAGLE. The experimental SWAN was tested at RAE, succesful, (precursor of the SOUTHAMPON). Then civil Imperial Airways until 1927.
Blackburn	SWIFT	1923	Torp. Bomber.		1921	Bird	(RAF)	LION	PL1	Similar to Swallow & Martin, but living almost entirely on the wing 8 built, civil and military, and also supplied to USA, Japan and Spain. Dev into the DART and BLACKBURN. (Also US SWIFTFIRE ex SWIFT, 1988)
Supermarine	SWIFT	1948	Fighter		1950	Allegorical	RAF	AVON	JT1	Fast, speedy. Speed Record 1953. Dev from ATTACKER. Fighter role spoiled by pitch up at speed and load, but a useful Recon Fighter. About 100 built. Scrapped just as the problems were solved!
Comper	SWIFT	1929	Transport		Maker	Bird	(RAF)	POBJOY	PR1	Bird, as above. Well known and was succesful on the race circuits. One at least still flying (1993) 2 impressed into the RAF in 1939. (Also Curtiss, 1933, and US Globe, 1941)
Fairey	SWORDFISH	1933	Torp. Bomber	STRINGBAG FISH	1932	Fish	FAA	PEGASUS	PR1	See the CLASSICS – Chapter 6.
Bristol	SYCAMORE	1948	Helicopter		Maker	Miscellaneous	RAF	LEONIDES	PR1	Tree, whose seed are winged & rotate (See Feb, 1918 system. 5-seater(!) Fighters to be Trees). Served Kenya, Cyprus and Borneo. Also W German Air Force. 178 built. Designed by Raoul Hafner, used by 4 countries.
Blackburn	SYDNEY	1930	Flying Boat	SID	1921	Geography-Water	(RAF)	Rolls-Royce	PL3	Based on projected civil NILE. The SYDNEY was the first British heavyweight military flying boat, having the one wing topmounted on a single central pylon (similar to the later CATALINA). 1 only.
Blackburn	TB	1915	Torp. Bomber TWIN		Maker	Miscellaneous	(RNAS)	MONOSOUPAPE	PR2	Twin fuselage, with pilot in one and observor in the other, with communication only by hand signals – not suitable for an anti-Zeppelin fighter! Also a poor performance. but 9 built.
Bristol	TT A / F3A	1916	Fighter	TWIN FIGHTER	Maker	Miscellaneous	(RFC)	Beardmore	PL2	TT = TWIN TACTOR. The planned RAF 4a engs were not available and the Beardmores had insufficient power. With Rolls Royce engs (and now as the F 3A) this was a more promising fighter, but abandoned with the advent of reliable gun interrupter gear.

Maker	Name	Year	Type	Nickname	System	Classification	Service	Engine	Type	Notes
Sopwith	TABLOID	1913	Fighter	GORDON BENNETT	Maker	Miscellaneous	RFC/ RNAS	GNOME	PR1	Small a/c, and 'nicknamed' after a small medicinal pill. As a Seaplane won 1914 Schneider Trophy Contest. Valuable early WW I record, two attacking German Zeppelin Sheds and causing severe damage. 36 built.
Tarrant	TABOR	1919	Bomber	TABOO	Maker	Miscellaneous	(RAF)	LION	PL6	Small drum to accompany the fife. Vast Triplane, designed by Tarrant and assembled by the Royal A/c Est. Fatal crash on take-off. Note 6 Engs Designed to fly non-stop from UK to bomb Berlin.
Armstrong Whitworth	TADPOLE	1920	Recon		1918	Fish	(FAA)	FALCON	PL1	Young of the Frog. A converted Westland WALRUS (based on the DH 9a), which was nicknamed TADPOLE.
Slingsby	TANDEM TUTOR	1950	Glider		Maker	Miscellaneous	AIR CADETS			T31 standard Trainer with the T21 SEDBERGH. Based on the KIRBY TUTOR, and ordered in quantity for the Air Training Corps, where known as the CADET (Mk 3)
Short	TANDEM TWIN	1910	Trainer	VACUUM CLEANER	Maker	Miscellaneous	(RNAS)	GNOME	PR2	Also GNOME SANDWICH. Later TRIPLE T See Short BIPLANE. The 'S types' were somewhat confusing, and the nicknames refer to two engs (as DOUBLE DIRTY). Not strictly (RNAS) but lent to the Naval Flying School.
Bristol	TAURUS	1936	Engine		1918	Astronomy	RAF		PR	Latin for Bull, Constellation, and 2nd Sign of the Zodiac.
Rolls-Royce	TAY	1974	Engine		Maker	Geography-Water	RAF		JT	Scottish River. One prototype eng only but in 1984 licensed to several Companies. Used in the Ministry of Defence BAC 111.
Bristol	TB 8	1913	Transport	COANDA	Maker	Miscellaneous	RFC/ RNAS	GNOME	PR1	TB = Tractor Biplane. Coanda was the designer – see COANDA MILITARY. The TB 8 was a biplane version. 52 built for the RNAS, some in service as a Bomber in France in 1914. Also a seaplane.
Tellier	TELLIER	1917	Flying Boat		Maker	People	(RNAS)	HISPANO-SUIZA	PR1	French Designer. Weird design. 2 supplied for 'big gun' (cannon) experiments.
Hawker	TEMPEST	1942	Fighter	TEMP TAMPAX	1939	Miscellaneous	RAF	SABRE	PL1	Fierce wind, poetical. Org known as TYPHOON II, and dev from TYPHOON. 2,793 built. Devastating close support Fighter, and credited with 638 of the 1771 V1 DOODLE BUGs destroyed by the RAF. Also POONA TEMPEST – India.
Avro	TEN	1927	Transport		Maker	Miscellaneous	(RAF)	GENET MAJOR	PR3	8 Passengers and 2 Crew. Similar to and based on Fokker tri-motor civil transport. 24 built, 1 for RAF.
Bristol	TEN SEATER	1921	Transport		Maker	Miscellaneous	(RAF)	LION	PL1	Civil a/c based on the projected GRAMPUS and after service on the London-Cologne route was bought by Air Ministry for RAF trials. Then loaned to Handley Page Trans port. 2 built.
Beagle	TERRIER	1945	Reccon		Maker	Animal	RAF	GYPSY MAJOR	PL1	Org a hunting dog. Dev from the AUSTER series, and served with the AOP. Air Observation Post. Squadrons. 312 built for the RAF.
Bristol	THESEUS	1945	Engine		1918	Mythology	RAF		PR	Hero of Athens, who slew the Minotaur, but not a Constellation or Star Dev from 1941 ORION.
Robey-Peters	THREE SEATER	1915	Trainer		Maker	Miscellaneous	(RNAS)	EAGLE	PL1	Designed for the USA Davis non-recoil gun, which was not adopted. 3 seater, as 2 gunners and 1 pilot who was seated near the tail. No pilot commendation – 1 prototype.
Rolls-Royce	THRUST MEASURING RIG	1953	VTOL	FLYING BEDSTEAD	x x x	Miscellaneous	(RAF)	NENE	JT2	2 engs mounted back-to-back, with deflectors to give vertical lift. Experimental, but leading to the later HARRIER success.
Republic (USA)	THUNDERBOLT	1941	Fighter	JUGGERNAUT, and so JUG	Maker	Meteorology	RAF	DOUBLE WASP	PR1	Discharge of lightning. 830 to the RAF, mostly used in the Far East. 15,683 built, more than any other US Fighter – a prestigious fighter and performer. Also SUPERBOLT. (Also Fairchild Republic A10, 1972 and Japanese RAIDEN 1940).
Air Vehicles Ltd	TIGER	1985	Hovercraft		Maker	Animal	ARMY	DEUTZ	PL1	Various models. Also built in Singapore. (Also Brownbach TIGER KITTEN eng. Northrop, 1973, US Grumann and Gulfstream)
Armstrong Siddeley	TIGER (1st)	1920	Engine		1918	Animal	(RAF)		PLF	Panthera Tigris. V-12 eng with PUMA cylinder blocks. Small production and powered the SINAIA Bomber.
Armstrong Siddeley	TIGER (2nd)	1931	Engine		1918	Animal	RAF		PR	Large Asian Cat. Org as JAGUAR MAJOR. Small production. Powered the ENSIGN (Also Eurocopter helicopter, 1991)

Maker	Name	Year	Type	Nickname	System	Classification	Service	Engine	Type	Notes
De Havilland	TIGER MOTH	1931	Trainer	TIGER TIGGY	Maker	Insect	RAF/FAA	GIPSY MAJOR	PR1	See Chapter 6 – the Classics.
Grumman	TIGERCAT	1943	Fighter		Maker	Allegorical	(RN)	PRATT & WHITNEY	PR2	Any small cat resembling a Tiger. Excellent tricycle u/c Fighter used by the US Marine Corps, but too late for WW II. 102 built, and 2 to the FAA for evaluation.
Fairey	TITANIA	1923	Flying Boat		1921	Mythology	(RAF)	CONDOR	PL4	Wife of Oberon, and Queen of the Fairies. Satellite of Planet Uranus. See ATALANTA.
Curtiss	TOMAHAWK	1938	Fighter	TOMMY, GYPSY ROSE LEE*	Maker	Miscellaneous	RAF	ALLISON	PL1	N Am Indian axe/weapon. Dev from the MOHAWK and earlier WARHAWK. later with MERLIN eng* Stripped down a/c! US Sqdn in China v Japanese before WW II, then in almost all fronts. 87 to RAF, total 13, 738. Also SHARK.
Burney & Blackburn	TOMTIT	1922	Engine		Maker	Bird	(RAF)		PR	Small bird, esp the Blue Tit. (Also Heath Parasol, 1949, known as TOMTIT with this eng)
Hawker	TOMTIT	1928	Trainer		1921	Bird	RAF	MONGOOSE	PR1	Bearded, Blue, Coal, Great, Marsh, and Willow, but officially no TOMTIT. Replacement for the Avro 504. 25 of 36 built were for the RAF. Some sold as civil a/c, UK, Canada and New Zealand.
Beardmore	TORNADO	1929	Engine		Maker	Meteorology	RAF		PL	Deep, localised depression. Water or Dust Spout. (Also N. American Tornado jet Bomber, 1947)
Hawker	TORNADO	1939	Fighter		1932	Meteorology	RAF	VULTURE	PL1	TORNADO with VULTURE, and the contemporary TYPHOON with SABRE were designed and built in parallel as an engine insurance. VULTURE was a failure and so TYPHOON was abandoned. 4 built. Basis for later radial eng Fighters.
Panavia	TORNADO	1979	Fighter	FLYING FLICKNIFE*	Maker	Meteorology	RAF/ NATO	TURBO UNION	JT2	See the CLASSICS – Chapter 6. * Also FIN and ELECTRIC JET.
Dart	TOTTERNHOE	1936	Glider		Maker	Geography-Land	(AIR CADETS)			Small Town in Bedfordshire. Dart A/c based at Dunstable, Beds.
Zlin	TOURIST	1937	Transport		Maker	Allegorical	RAF	MIKRON	PL1	1st named Zlin a/c. 1 impressed by RAF in India, belonging to the Bata Shoe Co of Czechoslovakia. Zlin was a subsiduary of Bata.
Perry-Beadle	TRACTOR	1914	Trainer	PERRY TRACTOR/ BEADLE	Maker	People	(RNAS)	ANZANI	PR1	Designer & Manufacturer. One off, and no order. Perry was killed in France in the same year.
Sloane	TRACTOR	1916	Trainer		Maker	Miscellaneous	(RNAS)	Sloane-Daniel	PL1	Not the Farm Tractor, but a pulling as distinct from a pushing propellor.
Robey-Peters	TRACTOR SCOUT	1915	Fighter		Maker	Miscellaneous	(RFC)	GNOME	PL1	Delivered to Hendon, but no record that it ever flew. Somewhat of a mystery.
Sopwith	TRAINER	1913	Trainer		Maker	Educational	RFC/ RNAS	GNOME	PR1	One who trains
Tipsy	TRAINER	1937	Trainer		Maker	Allegorical	RAF	MIKRON	PL1	Org Belgian, but also made in the UK 17 built, 8 to the Civil Air Guard, and 1 RAF impressed in India.
Avro	TRAINER	1929	Trainer		Maker	Education	(RAF)	LYNX	PR1	One who trains, a teacher. With the TUTOR. 561 built.
Robert Esnault-Peltrie	TRAINER	1914	Trainer	PARASOL	Maker	Miscellaneous	RNAS	GNOME	PR1	R E P. French Design & Manufacture. Small batch ordered, but ungainly and unsuccesful.
White & Thompson	TRAINER	1915	Reconn	BOGNOR BLOATER	Maker	Education	RNAS	RENAULT	PL1	Origin of Nickname unclear, but the wooden monocoque fuselages were built at Littlehampton, near Bognor. Bloater ?12 built, underpowered and limited use, to RNAS and 2 unassembled as spares.
Bristol	TRAMP	1921	Transport		Maker	People	(RAF)	PUMA	PR4	Vagrant, as TRAMP Steamer. Dev from civil PULLMAN & military BRAEMAR. 2 built, but never flown. A large Triplane, but the project abandoned. See BRAEMAR
Beech	TRAVELLER	1932	Transport	STAGGERWING	Maker	Alegorical	RAF/FAA	WASP JUNIOR	PR1	USA. 740 built. 93 to FAA, 12 to RAF One allocated to Prince Bernard of Netherlands, and given the letters PB1.

Maker	Name	Year	Type	Nickname	System	Classification	Service	Engine	Type	Notes
Rolls-Royce	TRENT	1944	Engine		Maker	Geography-Water	RAF		TP	River, joining the Ouse, to form the Humber Estuary. The first prop-jet eng in the world. Basically a DERWENT with a gear box. Evaluated in 2 METEORs. TRENT(2) was a cancelled civil project. TRENT(3) is also civil (1992)and the world's first eng to exceed 1000, 000 thrust.
Gloster	TRENT METEOR	1943	Experimental		Maker	Miscellaneous	(RAF)	TRENT	TP2	Exp Turbo-prop. See METEOR.
Ford	TRIMOTOR	1926	Transport	TIN LIZZIE	Maker	Miscellaneous	RAF	WASP	PR3	USA civil 'airliner', metal and successful. One impressed into RAF in 1940, and with 217 Squadron. Also known as the TIN GOOSE. The oldest a/c to serve in the RAF in WW II!
Blackburn	TRIPLANE	1916	Fighter		Maker	Miscellaneous	(RNAS)	CLERGET	PR1	Anti-Zeppelin. Similar to AD (Air. Dept Admiralty) SCOUT. A very odd machine – 1 as a biplane and 3 as a triplane, the latter with the fuselage at the top wing. Overweight and very difficult to fly.
Sopwith	TRIPLANE	1916	Fighter	TRIPEHOUND	Maker	Miscellaneous	RFC/ RNAS	CLERGET	PR1	Successful, with high rate of climb. Based on the fuselage and tail of the PUP, and most of the 149 built were RNAS. Regained air superiority on the Western front, and inspired the German Triplane Fighters.
Austin	TRIPLANE	1917	Fighter	TRIPE	Maker	Miscellaneous	(RFC)	Bentley	PR1	Too late as the Sopwith TRIPLANE was in full production and later biplane designs presaged the end of the triplane.
Blackburn	TRIPLANE	1916	Fighter	TRIPE	Maker	Miscellaneous	(RNAS)	Clerget	PR1	An attempt to improve on the AD SCOUT (SPARROW), but no more successful. The advent of the gun interruptor gear now marked the end of the 'Pusher' types.
Short	TRIPLE TRACTOR	1912	Trainer	FIELD KITCHEN	Maker	Miscellaneous	(RN)	GNOME	PR1	2 seperate engs drove wing mounted propellors as in the early Wright machines. Very hot in the fuselage, and thus the nickname. S 47 used for radio trials, picking up signals at 30 miles.
Lockheed	TRISTAR	1970	Transport	FLYING PIGS*	Maker	Miscellaneous	RAF	Rolls-Royce	JT3	3 Engs. USA. From British Airways and Pan Am. mod as Tankers. * In the Gulf War camouflaged in pink. One named as PINKY and another PERKY. 250 built.
British Aircraft Corp.	TSR 2	1964	Fighter	T S R	RAF	Miscellaneous	(RAF)	OLYMPUS	JT2	TSR = Tactical Strike & Reconnaissance. Designed as a super CANBERRA, but dogged by over-specification and cancelled by political spite. Of great potential and one of UK's great aviation manf tragedies.
Short	TUCANO	1980	Trainer	TUC	Maker	Bird	RAF	GARRETT	TP1	'Hornbill' of the S. Am tropical forests. Designed and made by Embraer of Brazil for its Air Force and dev by Shorts for the RAF. Also used by 13 AFs, the Short version going to Kenya and Kuwait. 130 to RAF.
Avro	TUDOR	1948	Test Bed		Maker	Miscellaneous	RAF	NENE	JT4	House of TUDOR. English period Henry VII, 1485, to Elizabeth I, 1603. Org civil Airliner with MERLIN PL4. 24 Built. Useful freighter for the Berlin Air lift. 20 converted to civilian use.
Blackburn	TURMO	1954	Engine		Maker	Miscellaneous	RAF		JT	Lake in the Pyrenees Mountains. Later Rolls-Royce. Eng under licence from Turbomeca. France.
Avro	TUTOR	1930	Trainer		1927	Education	RAF/FAA	LYNX	PR1	Standard RAF Trainer 1930-38. 795 built. 380 for RAF. Others to 7 o/seas Countries. Also SEA TUTOR. TUTOR for the Irish Army as TRITON. (Also Canadian CAE Aviation trainer and US Timm Trainer).
Fokker (Holland)	TW 8	1936	Seaplane	FOKKER	Maker	People	RAF	WHIRLWIND	PR2	Escaped from Holland in 1940 after the German invasion, and used for navigation training. 5 impressed by RAF for Coastal Command.
Avro	TWIN BOMBER	1916	Bomber		Maker	Miscellaneous	(RFC)	EAGLE	PL2	Name from 2 engs.
Curtiss	TWIN CANADA	1913	Bomber		Maker	Misvellaneous	(RNAS)	Curtiss	PL2	Designed in America but built in Canada.
Piper	TWIN COMANCHE	1962	Transport		Maker	People	(RAF)	LYCOMING	PL2	COMANCHE = N American Red Indian Tribe. A/c used by Cranfield College of Aeronautics.
General Aircraft	TWIN HOTSPUR	1942	Glider		1939	People	(RAF)		PR2	See HOTSPUR. 2 fuselages with a new centre section wing. One built.
Scottish Aviation	TWIN PIONEER	1955	Transport	TWIN PIN DOUBLE SCOTCH	Maker	Miscellaneous	RAF	LEONIDES	PR2	Dev of single-engine PIONEER. 91 built, of which the RAF took 39. Service in Bahrain, Far East and Kenya, 1958-68 in various roles. Sold to 20 countries.
Samuel White	TWIN SEAPLANE	1914	Torp Bomber		Maker	Miscellaneous	(RNAS)	Salmson	PR2	Twin fuselage and dev from the TWIN AEROPLANE.

Maker	Name	Year	Type	Nickname	System	Classification	Service	Engine	Type	Notes
Bristol	TWIN TRACTOR	1916	Fighter		Maker	Miscellaneous	(RFC)	BEARDMORE	PL2	Also known as TTA, or TWIN FIGHTER, but looked more like a Bomber.
Pratt & Whitney	TWIN WASP	1932	Engine		Maker	Insect	RAF		PR	USA. See WASP.
Nieuport	TWO SEATER	1917	Fighter		Maker	Miscellaneous	RFC/RNAS	Clerget	PR1	French and built in the UK by Beardmore.
Sopwith	TWO-SEAT SCOUT	1914	Fighter	SPINNING JENNY	Maker	Miscellaneous	RNAS	MONOSOUPAPE	PR1	Armed with rifles, grenades, shotgun and a signal pistol to attack Zeppelins. but none engaged. Frequent eng failures, and tendency to spin hence the nickname. 24 built.
Rolls-Royce	TYNE	1955	Engine		Maker	Geography-Water	RAF		TP	River NE Enland. N & S Tyne join at Hexham, and thence to the N Sea. The 1st 2-spool turbo-prop, an excellent eng but jets more prominent. Later, of more power on the BELFAST, and foriegn a/c. About 3000 built.
Nieuport	TYPE 11	1914	Fighter	BEBE BABY SCOUT	Maker	Allegorical	RFC/RNAS	LE RHONE	PR1	In full, BB 11, so French BEBE and English BABY, name by RAF & RNAS for all Nieuports. Challenged supremacy of the Germans at Verdun, and exact copies made. A sesquiplane, and also '18 METRE'. (Also Jodel BEBE, 1948)
Farman (Maurice)	TYPE 11	1911	Trainer	SHORTHORN RUMPETY	Maker	Animal	RAF/RNAS	RENAULT	PL1	LONGHORN Cattle(also 'Durham'). A/c had no front elevators, thus the SHORTHORN. Whilst a trainer, was used in anger in the Middle East. Also used by France, Italy and Russia. 860 built for the RFC.
British Aerospace	TYPE 111	1963	Transport	ONE ELEVEN	Maker	Miscellaneous	(RAF)	SPEY	JT2	Org H. 107 of Hunting A/c which was absorbed into BAeS. This airliner was a great success and sold to 63 countries. One purchased for the Ministry of Technology.
Nieuport	TYPE 12 & 20	1915	Fighter	BEARDMORE NIEUPORT	Maker	Allegorical	RFC/RNAS	LE RHONE	PR1	Type 12 was built in France for the RNAS, and Type 20 in the UK for the RFC by Beardmore, and hence the nick name. In 1916 the RFC 'borrowed' some from the RNAS. Also SCOUT and BABY. A poor Fighter. 61 to the RFC.
Vickers	TYPE 123/141	1926	Fighter	SCOUT	Maker	Miscellaneous	(FAA)	Rolls-Royce	PL1	Org the HISPANO SCOUT with that eng, awaiting the new R-R F. XI eng. Type 123 was rebuilt as 141 with the new eng. Tested at RAE and at sea, but not popular with pilots. 1929 Kings Cup Race in civil guise.
Grahame-White	TYPE 13	1914	Seaplane	SEAPLANE SCOUT	Maker	Miscellaneous	(RNAS)	MONOSOUPAPE	PR1	Seaplane Trainer, but flew as a landplane in the Circuit of Britain Rave. No official interest, but sold to Japan.
Bristol	TYPE 138A	1936	Experimental	HIGH ALTITUDE	Maker	Miscellaneous	(RAF)	PEGASUS	PR1	The 30's was a time for records – Capt Cyril Uwins (Bristol) 43976 fit in a VESPA. S/Ldr Swain in 138a – 49,967 ft. F/Lt Adam – nearly 54,000ft – good publicity for Bristol engs. 2nd 138a with R-R eng uncompleted.
Vickers	TYPE 141	1928	Fighter	SCOUT	Maker	Miscellaneous	(FAA)	KESTREL	PL1	Dev from Type 123 (whose projected names were Valour, Vassal, Vandal, Villian and Virago!). Type 141 was evaluated om HMS Furious, but not ordered. But Bolivia ordered 6 with the JUPITER eng.
Nieuport	TYPE 16	1916	Fighter	V-STRUTTER BABY	Maker	Miscellaneous	RFC	LE RHONE	PR1	Single V wing struts. Dev of Type 11 Should be RNAS/RAF, as all 17 were ordered by RNAS and 'lent' to RFC by urgent request for Battle of the Somme. Mount of Ball, Bishop, Navarre and Nungesser-men & plane of note.
Vickers	TYPE 161	1931	Fighter	COW	Maker	Miscellaneous	(RAF)	JUPITER	PR1	See Westland F29/27 for explanation of COW. The Vickers cannon fighter goes back in concept to the GUNBUS of WW I, the gun being fitted in the nose. But a slow firing gun, and more speed was now required. 1 built.
Vickers	TYPE 163	1931	Transport	BATTLEPLANE	Maker	Miscellaneous	(RAF)	Rolls-Royce	PL4	Scaled up version of Type 150, to also serve as a heavy bomber and in various other roles. Sole prototype had several deficiencies and only flew for 40 hours.
Nieuport	TYPE 17 & 23	1916	Fighter	BABY	Maker	Miscellaneous	RFC	LE RHONE	PR1	Whilst Type 16 was the mount of the 'Aces', Type 17 was much improved and the RFC was indebted to the French for priority deliveries. Squadron service France and Palestine. 300 + to the RFC.
Short	TYPE 184 (SEAPLANE)	1915	Seaplane	HOME FROM HOME	Maker	Miscellaneous	RFC/RNAS	MAORI	PL1	ADMIRALTY SEAPLANE, TWO-TWO-FIVE (eng hp) & DOVER. First a/c to sink a ship (Turkish) by torpedo. Service in UK waters, Dardanelles, Bulgaria, Red Sea, Indian Ocean, Arctic. Fleet spotter Battle of Jutland. 938 built.

Maker	Name	Year	Type	Nickname	System	Classification	Service	Engine	Type	Notes
Bristol	TYPE 188	1962	Experimental	BRISTEEL * MAYFLY	Maker	Miscellaneous	RAF	GYRON JUNIOR	JT2	Stainless steel research a/c to investigate kinetic heating at Mach 2. 2 prototypes, but with short range and thirsty engs it was found unsuitable for sustained research. * or may not . . .
Sage	TYPE 2	1916	Fighter	GREENHOUSE	Maker	Miscellaneous	(RFC)	MONOSOUPAPE	PR1	Enclosed cockpit (with 10 windows) for Pilot & Gunner, the latter able to fire over the top wing. Excellent performance but outdated by the new synchronised gun system. One only, destroyed in a crash.
Slingsby	TYPE 20	1943	Glider	SPROULE	Maker	Miscellaneous	FAA			Flown by Lt. Cdr John Sproule RN in the first glider experiments from aircraft carriers – HMS Pretoria Castle and HMS Illustrious in 1949. Glider sunk, and attention now given to helicopters.
Supermarine	TYPE 224	1934	Fighter	SPITFIRE	Maker	Allegorical	(RAF)	GOSHAWK	PL1	1st but unofficial SPITFIRE, a name opposed by Mitchell. Chief Designer. Cranked wing with fixed u/c, it was a sensation but the GOSHAWK eng was a failure. by which time thoughts were on the 2nd SPITFIRE.
Short	TYPE 310/320	1914	Torpedo. Bomb	COSSACK	Maker	Miscellaneous	RFC/RNAS	COSSACK	PL1	Type 310/320 was actually the hp of the engine! COSSACK after the eng. The 310 was virtually the 184 with this new eng. Other nicknames as for Type 184. 127 built, and 50 taken on charge by the new RAF in 1918.
Supermarine	TYPE 322	1943	Experimental	DUMBO	Maker	Miscellaneous	(RAF)	MERLIN	PL1	Nickname from the shape of the fuselage. Designed to examine the feasibility of a variable incidence wing. Successful, but difficult. 2 built, and the chosen variable incidence a/c was the BARRACUDA.
Folland	TYPE 34/37	1939	Eng Test	FOLLAND FRIGHTFUL	x x x	Miscellaneous	RAF	MERLIN	PR1	Specifically designed as an eng test bed. 12 were built, but were unpopular with the early test pilots. But they did yeoman work with several Companies with various engs. The last, at DH, was flying in 1946.
Vickers	TYPE 432	1942	Experimental	TIN MOSSIE	Maker	Miscellaneous	(RAF)	MERLIN	PL2	Type 432. High altitude experimental Fighter similar to the MOSQUITO. TIN as of metal construction, and was designed for 6 Hispano cannon. Two built, but only one flew.
Sage	TYPE 4A	1917	Seaplane	SAGE	Maker	Miscellaneous	RNAS	HISPANO-SUIZA	PL1	Dev from Sage 3 landplane. Fully aerobatic and used for advanced training for seaplane pilots. Later 4b also.
Avro	TYPE 504	1913	Trainer	MONO AVRO	Maker	Miscellaneous	RFC/RAF	MONOSOUPAPE	PR1	See the GREAT UN-NAMED, Chapter 5 Part 17.
Avro	TYPE 519	1916	Fighter	BIG AVRO	x x x	Miscellaneous	(RNAS/RFC)	NUBIAN	PL1	Name given by RAF Farnborough. Developed from Type 510 seaplane. 4 built but little official interest. Their ultimate fate is unknown.
Avro	TYPE 528	1916	Bomber	SILVER KING	Maker	Miscellaneous	(RNAS)	SUNBEAM	PL1	Ordered by the Admiralty as a 'bomb dropper', but one prototype only.
Avro	TYPE 605	1926	Autogyro	CIERVA	Maker	Miscellaneous	(RAF)	GENET	PR1	Built by Avro to a CIERVA design. One of the first RAF autogyro evaluations.
Avro	TYPE 707	1949	Experimental	DELTA	Maker	Miscellaneous	RAF	DERWENT	JT1	Experimental use for 14 years, and also a scale model for the later VULCAN. 5 built.
Sopwith	TYPE 807	1915	Seaplane	FOLDER	Maker	Miscellaneous	RNAS	MONOSOUPAPE	PR1	Developed from Sopwith (Daily Mail) Circuit Of Britain Contest. Nickname from Folding wings and also known as ADMIRALTY SEAPLANE.
Sopwith	TYPE 9700	1915	Fighter	1 & ½ STRUTTER. COMIC	Maker	Fighter	RNAS/RAF	CLERGET	PR1	Named from arrangement of interplane struts. Famous fighting a/c, and 'father' of the CAMEL. Also SHIP STRUTTER when aboard RN Ships. UK built 1513, and the French about 3 times as many. Also known as '1.5'. 1st Br. a/c with a synchronised gun.
Sopwith	TYPE 9901	1915	Fighter	PUP SHIP'S PUP	Maker	Animal	RFC/RNAS	LE RHONE	PR1	Nickname from small size. Most succesful Fighter, giving the RFC air superiority in 1916-17. 1st a/c to land on a moving ship. Anti Zeppelin rockets fitted in 1917, and also flew from RN Cruisers. 1776 built.
S. P. A. D.	TYPE S7	1916	Fighter	SPAD	Maker	Miscellaneous	RFC	HISPANO-SUIZA	PL1	French. Types 7, 12 & 13. Manf in UK by Bleriot (Aeronautique). Also used by US Army Air Corps. and most of Rickenbacker, top US air ace. S P A D = Societe pour Aviation et Derives. 8,472 built for 15 countries.
Beardmore	TYPHOON	1920	Engine		Maker	Meteorology	(RAF)		PL	Small, intense Tropical cyclone in W Pacific & China Sea. (Also French Caudron)

Maker	Name	Year	Type	Nickname	System	Classification	Service	Engine	Type	Notes
Hawker	TYPHOON	1940	Fighter	TIFFY BOMB/ ROCKPHOON	1939	Meteorology	RAF	SABRE	PL1	See the CLASSICS – Chapter 6
D F S	Type 108-70	1937	Glider	FEISE	Maker	Miscellaneous	(RAF)			German = Titmouse (Paridae) family, of which there are 65 species. Small bird and small glider.
Sopwith	Type 807	1915	Seaplane	FOLDER	Maker	Miscellaneous	RNAS	MONOSOUPAPE	PR1	Dev from Sopwith (Daily Mail) Circuit of Britain Contest. Nickname – folding wings. Also known as ADMIRALTY (Type 80) SEAPLANE.
Fairey	ULTRA LIGHT	1955	Helicopter		Maker	Miscellaneous	(RAF)/ (RN)	PALOUSTE	TP1	Rotor blade tip jets. 6 built. This small helicopter was an innovative design and deserved to fare better. An org Army/RAF requirement, the War Office withdrew. Successful trials at sea with the R N but no orders.
General Aircraft	UNIVERSAL	1937	Transport	TRIKE	Maker	Miscellaneous	RAF	NIAGARA	PR2	Early tricycle undercarriage. Dev from the JUBILEE. Both designed as civil aircraft, and 60 built. RAF ordered 2 JUBILEEs and 3 UNIVERSALs and 12 impressed in 1939 as transports. (Also Fokker Transport, 1926)
ML Aviation	UTILITY	1953	Experimental	FLYING MATTRESS	Maker	Miscellaneous	(RAF)	MCCOLLOUGH	PL1	Portable a/c with inflatable wings. Also the CARDINGTON KITE. Various experimental wings had individual names.
Handley Page	V/1500	1917	Bomber	SUPER HANDLEY	Maker	Miscellaneous	RFC/RAF	ATLANTIC	PL4	Dev of smaller O/400 to be twice the weight and have twice the pay load. 60 built, with some historic flights, but the only action was the bombing of Kabul by one a/c. V/1500 was replaced by Vickers VIMY. Org designed to bomb Berlin.
Vickers	VALENTIA (1st)	1918	Flying Boat		x x x	Geography-Land	(RAF)	CONDOR	PL2	Proposed as Valencia(error?) and changed to VALENTIA. Does not fit 1918 system, but was a British province established by Rome in 368 AD. Saunders Hull, but otherwise Vickers. Dev from VICTORIA. 82 built.
Vickers	VALENTIA (2nd)	1934	Transport	VAL	x x x	Geography-Water	RAF	PEGASUS	PR2	Following VALENTIA (1st), VALENCIA is in Trinidad & Tobago, of Spanish origin. 81 built, inc 54 converted VICTORIAs. 60 in 1939, and two in Iraq until 1944. Suggested names as Victory, Vinhya and Vancouver.
Short	VALETTA	1930	Seaplane		x x x	Geography-Water	RAF	JUPITER	PR3	Capital/Port of Malta. Designed as a large civil seaplane. Used by Sir Alan Cobham for pioneering routes in Africa. Then converted to a land plane for RAF research. The largest seaplane of its time.
Vickers	VALETTA	1946	Transport	PIG	1939	Geography-Land	RAF	HERCULES	PR2	Dev from civil VIKING. Nav Trainer with multiple astro domes known as the INVERTED SOW. 250 + built. With 5 different RAF roles, also known as FIVE AEROPLANES IN ONE.
Schleicher	VALIANT	1966	Glider		RAF	Allegorical	AIR CADETS			German manufacture. RAF system of 'v' names for Gliders.
Vickers	VALIANT (1st)	1927	Fighter		Maker	Allegorical	(RAF)	JUPITER	PR1	Brave, bold, valourous. A dev of the VIXEN. Vickers first all-metal a/c. RAF evaluated, but preference given to the Westland WAPITI. One prototype, and one to Chile. (Also 1939 US Vultee Fighter)
Vickers	VALIANT (2nd)	1951	Bomber		1950	Allegorical	RAF	AVON	JT4	First of 3 types of V-Bombers and dropped 1st British H-Bomb. Org suggested as VIMY and LONDON. Name decided by Vickers straw poll, and agreed by the Ministry. 107 built. One low level a/c as BLACK BOMBER.
Aeronautical Syndicate	VALKYRIE	1910	Trainer		Maker	Mytghology	(ARMY) (RN)	GNOME	PR1	Norse-Odin's handmaidens. 2 given to each Service, but not known if flown. But grateful for the Engs . . . (Also US North American, Concorde type bomber, 1964)
Saunders-Roe	VALKYRIE	1926	Flying Boat		1921	Mythology	(RAF)	CONDOR	PL3	(Also Horatio Barber 1911) Hull of Saunders copper wire sewn plywood, but prototype only as Air Ministry now decided on all metal Large and impressive, but 1 only.
Vickers	VAMPIRE	1917	Fighter		Maker	Animal	(RFC)	BENTLEY	PR1	A tropical Bat, feeding on animal blood. Armoured ground Attacker, or Trench Fighter. Similar design to the Vickers GUNBUS, but with guns in the nose. 4 prototypes built.
De Havilland	VAMPIRE	1943	Fighter	KIDDY CAR VAMPI(Swiss)	1939	Animal	RAF	GOBLIN	JT1	The second British Jet Fighter. Ministry code name of SPIDER CRAB which was not popular with DH. Also SEA VAMPIRE. 2928 built. 250 built by France as the MISTRAL. VAMPIRE also used by 5 other countries.

Maker	Name	Year	Type	Nickname	System	Classification	Service	Engine	Type	Notes
Vickers	VANELLUS	1924	Flying Boat		Maker	Miscellaneous	(RAF)	EAGLE	PL1	Name meaning not known. Alias VIDGEON. Alias VIKING Mk VII, and the last Vickers Amphibian. One only for sea trails on the carrier Argus.
Vickers	VANGUARD	1923	Transport		Maker	Allegorical	(RAF)	LION	PL2	Foremost, position or van of an army or fleet. Based on the VIRGINIA and built to the order of Instone Air Line. Both an RAF, and civil career with Imperial Airways. Highly regarded, but crashed 1928. 1 only.
Schleicher	VANGUARD	1980	Glider		RAF	Allegorical	AIR CADETS			German manufacture. (Also civil Vickers, 1923 & 1959, and Vultee fighter of 1939)
Vultee	VANGUARD	1939	Fighter		Maker	Allegorical	(RAF)	TWIN WASP	PR1	Vultee's first Fighter and which was considered one of the fastest at that time. 100 to RAF (who previously rejected the type) and some to Canada as advanced trainers. All released to China, some in RAF colours.
Vickers	VANOX (VANNOCK)	1929	Bomber		Maker	Miscellaneous	RAF	KESTREL	PL4	Sometimes known as VANNOCK, but not correct. This was a Vickers, and not an RAF name. The meaning of VANOX is unknown. The prototype used for armament tests until 1937 with RAE.
Holle	VARIOPLANE	1917	Experimental		Maker	Miscellaneous	(RFC)	ANZANI	PR1	Made up name. Exp variable camber wing. Tested at Farnborough.
Vickers	VARSITY	1949	Trainer		1949	Education	RAF	HERCULES	PR2	Slang for University. Replacement for WELLINGTON and VALETTA Trainers 163 built, and were in RAF service for 25 years. The last was delivered to Sweden. A very successful type.
Vickers	VC 10	1962	Transport	VICKY TEN IRON DUCK	Maker	Miscellaneous	RAF	CONWAY	JT4	See the GREAT UN-NAMED, Chapter 5 Part 17.
Percival	VEGA GULL	1935	Transport		Maker	Miscellaneous	(RAF)	GIPSY QUEEN	PL1	Made up name-dev from GULL+ VEGA, star in the Constellation Lyra-the falling Vulture. 20 impressed into RAF service in 1939. 90 built, and dev into military PROCTOR.
Vickers	VELLORE	1928	Transport		1921	Geography-Land	RAF	JUPITER	PR2	Indian Town. Dev into civil VELLOX. 2 to the RAF, one being loaned to Vickers for a long distance flight to Australia – force landed and never came back. The other on general duties for 3 years.
Blackburn	VELOS	1926	Seaplane		Maker	Miscellaneous	(RAF)	LION	PL1	Italian=speed. from Latin velox. See DART. VELOS ordered for the Greek Navy.
Vickers	VELOX	1931	Transport		x x x	Allegorical	(RAF)	PEGASUS	PR2	VELOX = Latin for swift(from which the word Velocity). Org civil a/c.
Vickers	VENDACE	1926	Transport		1921	Fish	(FAA)	FALCON	PL1	Small white fish, in some European Lakes. Also of Brazil & Venezuela. Chosen against the SPRAT, but both cancelled. 1st prototype retained by RAF for experiments. II & III were civil, mapping in Brazil.
Vultee	VENGEANCE	1938	Dive Bomber	TOGO'S REVENGE*	1938	Allegorical	RAF/FAA	DOUBLE CYCLONE	PR1	USA. Revenge. retribution. avenge. * difficult to pull out of a steep dive. 1345 built. 564 to the UK and used operationally in Burma and India. Then mostly as target tugs.
De Havilland	VENOM	1949	Fighter		1949	Allegorical	RAF	GHOST	JT1	Successor to the VAMPIRE. 887 built. 23 Squadron RAF a/c with names of different venemous snakes. Excellent performance with 50,000 ft ceiling. 62 to Swedish AF. (Also UE COBRA VENOM helicopter)
Vickers	VENOM	1936	Fighter		1932	Allegorical	(RAF)	AQUILA	PR1	Reptile poison. Venom was a dev of the JOCKEY. Very manoevrable and with a full battery of guns, but emphasis was now on the SPITFIRE and HURRICANE. However, radial eng Fighters of WW II were formidable.
Lockheed	VENTURA	1938	Bomber	PIG	1939	Geography-Land	RAF	TWIN WASP	PR2	USA. Californian Coastal Town, and probably named after an Italian Jesuit Priest. Mil dev of LODESTAR, and later US name LEXINGTON. 875 shared RAO(mostly Coastal)and RAAF. Portugese version as HARPOON.
Vickers	VENTURE	1924	Army Co-op.		Maker	Allegorical	RAF	LION	PL1	Daring, or dangerous undertaking. Org suggested as VULPES (Fox) and VORTEX. Variant of VIXEN. 6 built. RAF reported that 'too large' but all 6 used for experimental work until about 1926.
Slingsby	VENTURE	1977	Glider		RAF	Allegorical	AIR CADETS	VOLKSWAGEN	PL1	Name from Air Training Corps motto-VENTURE Adventure. Licence, German Scheibe FALKE Motor Glider. 15 built in the UK by Slingsby.
Schempp-Hirth	VENTUS	1980	Glider		Maker	Glider	(AIR CADETS)			German. Latin for Wind.

Maker	Name	Year	Type	Nickname	System	Classification	Service	Engine	Type	Notes
Vickers	VERNON	1921	Transport		1921	Geography-Land	RAF	LION	PL2	Town in British Columbia, Canada. (Also Australia) Dev of VIMY. RAF 1922-26, evacuation of sick British troops from Iraq in 1922. Main transport Cairo-Bagdhad mail. 60 built. Dev from VIMY.
Vickers	VESPA	1925	Test Bed		Maker	Insect	RAF	JUPITER	PR1	Italian for wasp. 1932 altitude record of 43, 976 ft, piloted by Capt Cyril Uwins. Bristol Chief Test Pilot. Used by the RAF for high altitude research. Similar to Parnall ZEP STRAFFER, 1916.
Vickers	VIASTRA	1929	Transport		Maker	Miscellaneous	RAF	JUPITER	PR2	Probably a made up word. Used for RAF radio experiments. A civil a/c, with 2 and 3 engs it was used in Australia. One was built for the Prince of Wales. It was this a/c that was handed over to the RAF.
Handley Page	VICTOR	1952	Bomber	VICKS TOURS	RAF	Allegorical	RAF	SAPPHIRE	JT4	V-Bomber, and later Tanker, and played a conspicuous role in Falklands and GULF wars. 84 built. Suggested names were HADES, HOSTILE, LONDON, and by HP as HARPOON. The last of the long line of HP Bombers.
Vickers	VICTORIA	1921	Transport	VIC	1921	Geography-Land	RAF	LION	PL2	Capital of British Columbia, of Hong Kong, and Australian State. Replacement of VERNON. Also Roman God of Victory (Greek NIKE). The service in Iraq (1920s) with VICTORIAs known as CARTER PATTERSONs, a UK freight Co. 48 built – a mainstay of Empire.
Vultee-Stinson	VIGILANT	1938	Transport	VIGGY	Maker	Allegorical	(RAF)	LYCOMING	PL1	On the alert, watchful, aware. Small high wing monoplane, with good short field performance 17 to RAF, and 6 taken from the SAAF. Service in the PACIFIC, and Europe. Followed by the smaller 'Grasshoppers'.
Grob	VIGILANT	1982	Glider		RAF	Allegorical	AIR CADETS	VOLKSWAGEN	PL1	German Motor Glider.
Grahame-White	VII	1912	Trainer	POPULAR	Maker	Miscellaneous	(RFC)	ANZANI	PR1	5 of these small biplanes were purchased by the War Office in 1918. 4 were in Squadron service, but no record is known of the fifth. Org a 'sporting biplane'. The VIIc was the POPULAR PASSENGER BIPLANE.
Grob	VIKING	1979	Glider		RAF	People	AIR CADETS			German manufacture. RAF name for the TWIN ACRO.
Scott	VIKING	1939	Glider		Maker	People	RAF			Impressed for Special Duty Flight, for radar trials. 4 for ATC in 1942.
Vickers	VIKING (1st)	1920	Flying Boat		Maker	People	(RAF)	EAGLE	PL1	Scandinavian pirate, pillaging N & W Europe. 8-II Centuries. Dev from civil V. Later variants= VULTURE and VIDGEON not allowed, so VANELLUS. VIKING widely used. (Also US VIKING, 1976, and Blohm & Voss VIKING, 1940)
Vickers	VIKING (2nd)	1945	Transport		Maker	People	RAF	HERCULES	PR2	Developed from the classic WELLINGTON. Org civil a/c. 12 built for the RAF The NENE-VIKING was a test bed for the NENE(JT2). Also sold to Pakistan and Indonesia. (Also Lockheed jet for electronic warfare, 1947)
Vickers	VILDEBEEST	1928	Torp. Bomber	BEAST	1921	Animal	RAF	PEGASUS	PR1	S African antelope. Served to 1942. Suggested as VICUNA & VULPES(Fox) 169 built, 27 for RNZAF. 25 built in Spain. Last RAF a/c used with disastrous results in the Far East against Japan. Dev as VINCENT.
Vickers	VIMY	1917	Bomber		1918	Geography-Town	RFC/RAF	EAGLE	PL2	See the CLASSICS – Chapter 6
Vickers	VINCENT	1926	Gen. Purpose	VINNEY	1932	People	RAF	PEGASUS	PR1	Admiral Earl St VINCENT, Victor of the Battle of St. Vincent, 1797. Dev from VILDEBEEST, and suggested as VERTIGIUM and VERULAM. 197 built. Officially scrapped', but fought in the N African fronts, 1940/41.
Wolseley	VIPER	1916	Engine		Maker	Reptile	RFC		PL	Family of various venomous Snakes. Famous with the SE 5a of WWI. (Also German Bachem NATTER = VIPER, VTO interceptor, WW II)
Armstrong Siddeley	VIPER	1951	Engine		Maker	Reptile	RAF		JT	Originally designed as a short life eng for the JINDIVIK, but dev into a successful long life eng, later manufactured by Bristol-Siddeley and Rolls-Royce.
Vickers	VIREO	1928	Fighter	VISCIOUS	1918	Bird	(FAA)	LYNX	PR1	S. Am. Greenfinch (Latin 'vireo'). A monoplane, but the RAF/FAA favoured biplanes. The first British aircraft to carry wing guns firing outside the propeller arc. With a viscious stall, only 1 prototype.

Maker	Name	Year	Type	Nickname	System	Classification	Service	Engine	Type	Notes
Vickers	VIRGINIA	1922	Bomber	GINNY	1921	Geography-Land	RAF	LION	PL2	Town in N Zealand, S Africa (& Ireland) Suggested as VULCAN, and based on VIMY. 126 built. Some still flying as late as 1941 as engine test beds. Pioneered cross Africa routs. Widely used Africa and India.
Vickers	VISCOUNT	1948	Transport		Maker	Miscellaneous	(RAF)	DART	TP4	Used by Empire Test Pilot School. No military application as such, but used by several Air Forces as high speed VIP Transports. Basically the civil airliner, of which 444 built. VISCOUNT=Peer ranking below an Earl.
Vickers	VIVID	1927	Fighter		Maker	Allegorical	(RAF)	LION	PL1	Bright & distinct. Org VIXEN III, rebuilt as VII with metal wings. One as sea/land plane, but no RAF order.
Vickers	VIXEN	1923	Fighter		Maker	Animal	(RAF)	LION	PL1	Female Fox. Mil VALPARAISO fighter for the Portuguese A F. 6 to the RAF for reconnaisance role. This was now known as VENTURE, but used for experimental work. See also variants as VALIANT and VIVID.
Stinson	VOYAGER	1940	Transport		Maker	Allegorical	(RAF)	LYCOMING	PR1	USA. Dev as SENTINEL. One impressed by the RAF, and sent to France in 1940. Fate unknown.
Avro	VULCAN	1952	Bomber	ALUMINIUM OVERCAST	RAF	Mythology	RAF	OLYMPUS	JT4	See the CLASSICS – Chapter 6.
Vickers	VULTURE	1923	Flying Boat		Maker	Bird	(RAF)	EAGLE	PL1	Bird of Prey, reserved to R-R! Does not fit RAF 1921 system. VIKING with a redesigned and thicker wing. Org suggested as WIDGEON or VIDGEON (as was the VANELLUS) (Also 1920 Breguet Bomber, and 1951 French Fighter)
Rolls-Royce	VULTURE	1939	Engine		1918	Bird	RAF		PL2	A 4-bank PEREGRINE, but not a success. 97 Squadron was known as '97th Foot' as their MANCHESTERs were so often u/s and grounded. Failure of the VULTURE led to urgent dev of the similar LANCASTER with 4 MERLIN engs. 538 built.
Cierva	W 9	1945	Helicopter	NOTAR	Maker	Miscellaneous	(RAF)	GIPSY	PL1	NOTAR = No Tail Rotor, but this nick name seems to have been used later than 1945. (Also McDonnell Douglas NOTAR helicopter, 1981)
Beardmore	W B III	1916	Fighter	FOLDER	Maker	Miscellaneous	(RNAS)	Le Rhone	PR1	Basically a Sopwith PUP but with folding wings and a retractable u/c for shipboad use. Probably the 1st retractable u/c but not for use in the air!
Commonwealth	WACKETT	1938	Trainer		Maker	People	RAAF	SUPER SCARAB	PR1	Australian. Designed by W/Cdr L J WACKETT, RAAF. Some RAF training.
Westland	WAGTAIL	1918	Fighter	WASP	Maker	Bird	(RFC)	WASP	PR1	Grey, Pied & Yellow-tail waggers. 3 built with WASP engines which were unreliable. and 2 with LYNX engines. May well have been successful but for the WASP eng. Last flown about 1922.
Westland	WALLACE	1931	Gen. Purpose	NELLIE, HOUSTON-WALLACE	x x x	???	RAF	PEGASUS	PR1	'W' is not a Class letter in 1927 system. A Town in Ontario? WALLACE the Bruce, Scots patriot? 'Nellie W' was a comedienne. Org sponsored by Lady Houston for the Everest Expedition. 175 to RAF.
Westland	WALRUS	1920	Recon		1918	Animal	RAF/FAA	LION	PL1	Large aquatic Mammal., the 'whale fish'. Made from DH9a spare parts. 'TADPOLE' has been associated with the WALRUS, but this was an individual name. 'Unlovely' a/c. (See Armstrong Whitworth TADPOLE) 36 built.
Supermarine	WALRUS	1933	Flying Boat	SHAGBAT PUSSER'S DUCK	1932	Animal	RAF/FAA	PEGASUS	PR1	See the CLASSICS – Chapter 6
Westland	WAPITI	1927	Gen. Purpose	WOP	1921	Animal	RAF	JUPITER	PR1	Large N Am Deer. Shawnee name = white rump. Dev from DH9a. 60 converted to WALLACE. 558 built, and 80 still in RAF service in India in 1939. 'Held the Empire together', and sold to 6 countries.
Westland	WARDEN	1969	Hovercraft		Maker	Allegorical	(RAF) (FAA)	GNOME	JT1	WARDEN=Keeper, principal, governor. 2nd converted to WINCHESTER. 1st UK hovercraft in quantity production. Served also in Canada, USA and S E Asia.
Wicko	WARFERRY	1936	Transport		Maker	Miscellaneous	(RAF)	GIPSY MAJOR	PL1	Made up military name. Company name was Foster WICKNER. 3 of this 3-seat civil monoplane were impressed into the RAF in 1940.

Maker	Name	Year	Type	Nickname	System	Classification	Service	Engine	Type	Notes
Vickers	WARWICK	1939	Bomber		1939	Geography-Land	RAF	CENTAURUS	PR2	County Town of WARWICKshire. Name chosen from 119 'W' Towns. Stretched WELLINGTON, and dev into WINDSOR. 839 built. 14. Many dev problems, but in the air-sea rescue role saved many 'ditched' pilots.
Boeing	WASHINGTON	1942	Bomber	EDDIE ALLEN (USA)	1939	Geography-Land	RAF	DOUBLE CYCLONE	PR4	Federal capital of USA. US name of SUPERFORTRESS, dropped 1st atomic bomb on JAPAN. 14 to the RAF 1950. Suggested name as LINCOLN, UK city and Abraham. A monumental a/c with similar achievements. 3627 built.
A B C	WASP	1916	Engine		Maker	Insect	RFC		PR	Family of stinging insects, from Latin 'Vespa'. (Also Stinson WASP with Pratt & Whitney WASP eng, 1923)
Pratt & Whitney	WASP	1926	Engine			Insect	RAF		PR	Widely used and a classic US engine.
Westland	WASP	1962	Helicopter		1958	Insect	FAA	NIMBUS	TP1	Dev from Saro SCOUT (org SPRITE). Good service in S Africa, Holland, Indonesia, Brazil & New Zealand. RN 'shipworthy' and carried 2 torpedoes. 98 for FAA, 4 to Indonesia, and 12 to New Zealand.
Lakes Flying Company	WATERHEN	1912	Seaplane		Maker	Bird	–	GNOME	PR1	Ralline Birds, especially the MOORHEN. Not a military a/c, but one as a (contract) Trainer for RN Pilots on Lake Windermere.
Beardmore	WB V	1917	Fighter	FIGHTER	Maker	Allegorical	(RNAS)	HISPANO-SUIZA	PL1	Requirement for a 37mm cannon to fire through a hollow propellor boss. Pilots found it dangerous to reload in the cockpit, and the project cancelled. 2 built.
Westland	WEASEL	1918	Fighter		1918	Animal	RAF	DRAGONFLY	PR1	Small, vindictive hunter. Dev of WAGTAIL. Designed as a succesor to the Bristol FIGHTER, it was doomed by its engine. 4 built, and 1 used by Farnborough as an eng test bed until 1923.
Westland	WELKIN	1942	Fighter		1939	Miscellaneous	RAF	MERLIN	PL2	Cloud (Anglo-Saxon), later firmament or vault of Heaven. Successor to WHIRLWIND, and designed to combat high altitude German bombers, which threat didn't materialise. 103 built and used for high altitude research.
Rolls-Royce	WELLAND	1943	Engine	WHITTLE	Maker	Geography-Water	RAF		JT	River in Northamptonshire. Org Rover eng, taken over by Rolls-Royce Sir Frank Whittle's early design.
Vickers	WELLESLEY	1935	Gen. Purpose		1932	People	RAF	PEGASUS	PR1	Sir Arthur WELLESLEY, 1st DUKE of WELLINGTON. World Distance record of 7,162 m, in 1938. 176 built. Geodetic construction, first used in the R 100 Airship, and later in the WELLINGTON. In service until 1941.
Vickers	WELLINGTON	1936	Bomber	WIMPEY SHARK(GERMAN)	1932	Geography-Land	RAF	HERCULES	PR2	See the CLASSICS – Chapter 6.
Br Hovercraft	WELLINGTON	1970	Hovercraft		Maker	People	(RAF)	PROTEUS	TP1	For notes on name, see Chap. 12. For RAF trials.
Westland	WENDOVER	1933	Experimental		x x x	Geography-Land	(RAF)	MERCURY	PR1	Town in Buckinghamshire. 'Experimental' a/c had no particular name allocation, but WENDOVER would have been a night bomber in 1932 system
Westland	WESSEX	1958	Helicopter		Maker	Geography-Land	RAF/FAA	GNOME	TP2	SW area of England, now a County (Westland) based at Yeovil). Sikorsky S-58 design. FAA=GAZELLE TP1, RAF = GNOME TP 2. 382 built, sold 5 o/seas Countries. (Also Westland civil, 1930
Westland	WESTBURY	1927	Fighter		1921	Geography-Land	(RAF)	JUPITER	PR2	Town in Wiltshire. Twin eng COWGUN (Coventry Ordnance Works) cannon Fighter to meet the new (French) generation of Bombers. A good a/c, but the heavy armed fighter now of little official interest. 2 built.
Wright	WHIRLWIND	1924	Engine		Maker	Meteorology	RAF		PR	Org Lawrence J 4 engine and backed by US Navy. Purchased by Wright in 1923. Then a long series of engs, and widely used by mil and civil a/c.
Westland	WHIRLWIND (1st)	1938	Fighter	CRIKEY WHIRLY	1932	Meteorology	RAF	PEREGRINE	PL2	Local low pressure system with violent rotation, as TORNADO. 'CRIKEY' from Shell advertisement. 'WHIRLIBOMBER' as also a Bomber. 116 delivered. Very successful as a Fighter-Bomber in Channel sweeps.
Westland	WHIRLWIND (2nd)	1952	Helicopter	WHIRLYBIRD	RN	Meteorology	RAF/FAA/ARMY	LEONIDES	PR1	Originally the Sikorsky S-55. RN name decision, agreed by RAF. 364 built in 13 versions and sold to 16 Countries. Updated with DH GNOME TP1 Unusual quadracycle undercarriage. 2 with the Queen's Flight. 45 built.

Maker	Name	Nickname	Year	Type	System	Classification	Service	Engine	Type	Notes
Blackburn	WHITE FALCON	DINGBAT	1916	Trainer	Maker	Miscellaneous	(RFC)	ANZANI	PR1	Very doubtful military connections, but appeared in RFC colours without a serial number. Built for the Test Pilot, Rowland Ding to visit RFC and RNAS stations. No record of it going like a 'Dingbat' . . .
Armstrong Whitworth WHITLEY	WHITLEY	FLYING COFFIN WOMBAT	1936	Bomber	1932	Geography-Land	RAF	MERLIN	PL2	Town in N Yorkshire. Site of A W Factory, near Whitely Abbey Airfield RAF's 1st Heavy Bomber. German nickname of BARN DOOR. 1476 built and many converted as transports. Retired as a Bomber in 1942. Also nickname of SOD.
Miles	WHITNEY STRAIGHT		1935	Transport	Maker	People	RAF	GIPSY MAJOR	PL1	Built to the order of W S, a BOAC executive and pilot, and later an RAF Wing Commander. 21 of this civil type was impressed into the RAF in 1940. The only RAF a/c with the same name as a serving RAF Officer!
British Thomson Houston	WHITTLE		1937	Engine	Maker	People	(RAF)		JT	Air Cdr Sir Frank Whittle, ex RAF Halton cadet, pioneer of UK jet propulsion. 1st UK JT. Dev as the WELLAND.
Wibault	WIBAULT SCOUT	WIBAULT	1928	Fighter	Maker	People	(RAF)	LION	PL1	French Designer. Designed and built in France and Vickers installed the eng. The design was of experimental interest but there was no RAF order.
Foster Wickner	WICKO		1937	Transport	Maker	Miscellaneous	(RAF)	GIPSY MAJOR	PL1	Also known as the GIPSY WICKO.
Westland	WIDEYE		1978	Drone	Maker	Miscellaneous	(ARMY)	WESLAKE	PL2	MOD MRUASTAS programme= Medium Range Unmanned Aircraft Surveillance & Target Acquisition System. Helicopter Drone, 'Supervisor' Programme.
Grumman	WIDGEON		1938	Flying Boat	Maker	Bird	FAA	RANGER	PL2	Strictly WIGEON, European and USA, but in UK only in Scotland. Org RAF name of GOSLING for 1st 15 a/c, reverting to WIDGEON in 1944. Communication, mostly in the West Indies 317 built (Also Westland Hel, 1955)
Vickers	WILD GOOSE		1949	Experimental	Maker	Bird	(RAF)		RKT	This was a Barnes-Wallace variable-geometry model to a MOD contract, with Code name of GREEN LIZARD. Also later SWALLOW of 1955, this research leading to the US Gen Dynamics F111 and the Panavia TORNADO.
Grumman	WILDCAT	PETULANT PORPOISE(USA)	1937	Fighter	Maker	Allegorical	FAA	TWIN WASP	PR2	Eurasian cat, but not American. USA, with RN name of MARTLET, reverting to WILDCAT in 1944. US name probably allegorical. See MARTLET.
Willows	WILLOWS		1912	Airship	Maker	People	RNAS	ANZANI	PR1	Welsh Designer from Cardiff. Naval Airship No 2, and envelope later used for RN SUBMARINE SCOUT (SS). Series of 4 WILLOWS Airships.
Westland	WINCHESTER		1964	Hovercraft	Maker	Geography-Land	R C T *	GNOME	JT1	County Town of Hampshire and once Capital of Wessex. Converted from WARDEN. * = Royal Corps of Transport.
Vickers	WINDSOR		1943	Bomber	1939	Geography-Land	RAF	MERLIN	PL4	Berkshire Town (WINDSOR Castle) Dev from WARWICK, and suggested as WORCESTER and WENTWORTH. Rear of the inboard eng nacelles with cannons fired by the pilot. 4 prototypes.
Australian Commonwealth	WIRRAWAY	WIRRAWON'T	1939	Gen Purpose	Maker	Meteorology	RAAF	Wasp	PR1	Australian for "Whirlwind" and to the Aboriginee a "Challenger". RAAF but also used for RAF training. 775 built and also used by the Dutch East Indies. Dev into the BOOMERANG.
Westland	WISP		1976	Drone	Maker	Miscellaneous	(ARMY)	KOLBO	PL2	Bunch or bundle of hair, grass or straw. Co-axial, contra-rotating small helicopter.
Westland	WITCH		1928	Bomber	Maker	Miscellaneous	(RAF)	JUPITER	PR1	Woman who practices black magic. A/c org suggested as WHELP. Designed for the Bristol ORION, which did not materialise. An innovative design. but Air Ministry decided to cancel. 1 prototype.
Westland	WIZARD		1926	Fighter	Maker	Miscellaneous	(RAF)	Rolls-Royce	PL1	Male Witch. 'Wizard' was a WWII RAF term for excellent or outstanding. A/c based on WIDGEON, and inspired by the HERON. 1 prototypes, wood and then metal. Good performance in trials until 1931. No orders, but basis of 1927 Interceptor specification.
Armstrong Whitworth WOLF	WOLF		1923	Recon	1921	Animal	RAF	JAGUAR	PR1	Wild dog of N Regions. Said to be one of the ugliest of aircraft, but had a useful life. Used by RAE for research, inc automatic controls. 6 for RAF. inc 3 at Reserve Schools. (Also US Consolidated SEA WOLF)

Maker	Name	Year	Type	Nickname	System	Classification	Service	Engine	Type	Notes
Hawker	WOODCOCK	1923	Fighter		1921	Bird	RAF	JUPITER	PR1	Hawker's (previously Sopwith) first aircraft, and 63 built, including some in Denmark. Supplied from the UK as the DANECOCK, and a Museum Museum exhibit remains. Popular with pilots and served until 1928.
English Electric	WREN	1923	Experimental		Maker	Bird	(RAF)	A B C	PR1	UK's smallest bird, and one of the smallest a/c ever on RAF charge. 4 built and one remains with the Shuttleworth Trust.
Westland	WYVERN	1947	Fighter		Maker	Mythological	FAA	CLYDE	TP1	2-legged Dragon, with wings and a barbed and knotted tail. Westland's last fixed wing a/c. 1953-58, and saw action in the Suez crisis 1956. Early versions had the EAGLE eng. Contra-props, and 124 built.
Grahame-White	XV	1913	Trainer	GRAHAME WHITE	Maker	Miscellaneous	RFC/RNAS	GNOME	PR1	Also NACELLE. Pusher biplane with twin boom tailplane. Primary Trainer throughout WW I. 50 to the RFC but total numbers not known. Also used at the Grahame-White Flying School.
North American	YALE	1938	Trainer		Maker	Education	(RAF)	WHIRLWIND	PR1	US University in Connecticut. A TEXAN – UK HARVARD – with fixed, spatted u/c. 290 ordered by France, but 119 diverted to the RCAF. Evaluated by the RAF. See HARVARD.
North American	YALE	1938	Trainer		1939	Education	RAF	WHIRLWIND	PR1	USA. YALE University in Connecticut.
Westland	YEOVIL	1925	Bomber		1921	Geography-Land	(RAF)	CONDOR	PL1	Town in Somerset, home of Westland Aircraft. Designed for long range, as was the BERKELEY, HANDCROSS and HORSLEY, the last being preferred. 3 prototypes, the last in metal.
Avro	YORK	1942	Transport	YORKY	Maker	Geography-Land	RAF	MERLIN	PL4	Cathedral City, Yorkshire. 'Camouflage' name of ASCALON, also for Churchill's a/c. Dev from LANCASTER. Stalwart of the Berlin Air Lift, and 212 built for the RAF. 25 civil a/c for BOAC. In service for 20 years.
Brunswick Tech College	ZAUNKONIG	1936	Trainer		Maker	Bird	(AIR CADETS)	ZUNDAPP	PL1	German for Wren. Based on Fiesler STORCH (Stork) of the Luftwaffe, evaluated at Farnborough post war. Designed as easy to fly, the min speed was 27 k!
Parnall	ZEPELLIN CHASER	1916	Fighter	ZEP STRAFFER	Maker	Allegorical	(RFC)	SUNBEAM	PL1	Upward firing gun. Also NIGHT FLYER, but in spite of these names, never flew and destroyed with all technical records. "Re-discovered" by the author.
Royal A/c Establishment	ZEPHYR	1923	Transport		Maker	Meteorology	(RAF)	DOUGLAS	PL1	Greek – the west wind, or gentle breeze. Produced by the RAE Flying Club. Strictly not (RAF) but flew in RAF colours. Similar, but smaller than the Vickers GUNBUS and based on RAE FE 8 (Harry Tate).
Kassel	ZOGLING	1935	Glider		Maker	Miscellaneous	AIR CADETS			LING = German diminituve. ZOG? Probably a nickname.

CHAPTER 8 — BIBLIOGRAPHY

TITLE	AUTHOR	PUBLISHER
Aircraft of the RAF	Thetford	Putnam
Supermarine Aircraft	Morgan	Putnam
Vickers	Morgan	Putnam
Handley Page	Barnes	Putnam
Short Bros	Barnes	Putnam
Miles	Brown	Putnam
Royal A/c Factory	Hare	Putnam
Avro	Jackson	Putnam
Blackburn	Jackson	Putnam
De Havilland	Jackson	Putnam
Gloster	James	Putnam
Schneider Trophy	James	Putnam
Saunders & Saro	London	Putnam
Royal Flying Corps	Bruce	Putnam
Armstrong Whitworth	Tapper	Putnam
English Electric	Ransom & Fairclough	Putnam
Hawker	Mason	Putnam
Fairey	Taylor	Putnam
Westland	James	Putnam
Bristol	Barnes	Putnam
The British Fighter	Mason	Putnam
American Navy	Swanborough & Bowers	Putnam
Captive Luftwaffe	West	Putnam
American Military	Swanborough & Bowers	Putnam
Shuttleworth — The Historical Aircraft	Ogilvie	Airlife
A Span of Wings	Russell	Airlife
RAF Squadrons	Jefford	Airlife
Chronicle of Aviation	Gunston	Int Publishing

TITLE	AUTHOR	PUBLISHER
Reaching for the Sky	Rendall	BBC
Directory of Aviation	Robinson	Orbis
Aeroplane Magazine		IPC
Flight Magazine		IPC
Aeroplane Spotter	(WW II)	IPC
Air BP	Taylor	British Petroleum
Eagles of the Third Reich	Mitcham	Guild Publishing & Airlife
British Military Aircraft Serials	Robertson	Ian Allen
Birth of a Legend — The Spitfire	Quill	Quiller Press
Pure Luck	Bramson	Patrick Stephens
World Encyclopedia of Aero Engines	Gunston	Patrick Stephens
Aviation Enthusiast's Reference Book	Robinson	Patrick Stephens
British Aerospace — A Proud Heritage	Green	Green
By Jupiter! Sir Roy Fedden	Gunston	Royal Aeronautical Society
Test Pilots	Middleton	Collins Willow
Flight — five Ages of Aviation	Blake	Haynes
Fighting Aircraft of World War One & Two		Jane's All the World's Aircraft
Military Aircraft Markings	March	a b c
Jane's Encyclopaedia of Aviation	Taylor	Bracken Books
The Great War in the Air	Morrow	Smithsonian (USA) Airlife (UK)
British Piston Aero-Engines	Lumsden	Airlife